4TH Edition

Seattle SURVIVAL Guide

The Essential Handbook for Seattle and Eastside Living

ERIC LUCAS

SASQUATCH BOOKS
SEATTLE

**TO BALLARD'S TWO LOVELY DAIRY GIRLS,
LESLIE AND KIRSTEN,
WHO TAUGHT ME THAT MILK AND BUTTER
ARE STILL PRICELESS STAPLES OF MODERN LIFE.**

Copyright ©2005 by Sasquatch Books
All rights reserved. No portion of this book may be reproduced or utilized in any form,
or by any electronic, mechanical, or other means without the prior written permission
of the publisher.

Printed in the United States of America
Published by Sasquatch Books
Distributed by Publishers Group West
10 09 08 07 06 05   10 9 8 7 6 5 4 3 2 1

Book design: William Quinby
Maps: Greeneye Design

Library of Congress Cataloging-in-Publication Data

Lucas, Eric, 1951-
  Seattle survival guide #4 : the essential handbook for Seattle and Eastside living /
Eric Lucas.
   p. cm.
  Rev. ed. of: Seattle survival guide / Theresa Morrow. 3rd ed. c1996
  Includes index
  ISBN 1-57061-339-7

  1. Seattle (Wash.)—Handbooks, manuals, etc. 2. Seattle (Wash.)—Guidebooks. I.
Title: Seattle survival guide number 4. II. Morrow, Theresa. Seattle survival guide.
III. Title.

F899.S43L83 2005
979.7´772—dc22   2005042560

SASQUATCH BOOKS
119 South Main Street, Suite 400, Seattle, WA 98104
(206) 467-4300

www.sasquatchbooks.com / custserv@sasquatchbooks.com

CONTENTS

PREFACE v
INTRODUCTION: An Emerald with Many Facets **viii**

1: SEATTLE NEIGHBORHOODS 1

Ballard • Beacon Hill • Capitol Hill • Central District • Downtown • Eastlake • Fremont • Greenlake/Greenwood/Phinney Ridge • Laurelhurst • Madison Park • Magnolia • Montlake • Mount Baker/Leschi • Pioneer Square/International District • Queen Anne • Rainier Beach/Rainier Valley • Ravenna • Seward Park/Columbia City • U District • Wallingford • West Seattle

2: EASTSIDE NEIGHBORHOODS 87

Bellevue • Bothell • Issaquah • Kirkland • Mercer Island • Redmond • Sammamish • Snoqualmie Valley • Woodinville

3: NEARBY BURGS 111

Auburn • Bainbridge Island • Burien • Enumclaw • Everett • Federal Way • Kent • Lynnwood • Puyallup • Renton • SeaTac • Tacoma • Vashon Island

4: NO PLACE LIKE HOME 133

Buying a Home • Building Permits • Property Titles • Property Taxes • Recycling • Renting a Home • Pets • Pests

5: STREET SMARTS 153

Commuting • Shortcuts • Traffic Report Lingo • Licenses • Speed Traps • Alternative Transportation • Navigating City Streets • Parking • Ferries • Taxis and Limos • Driving and Parking at Sea-Tac Airport

6: A HARD DAY'S WORK 181

Job-Hunting Central • Newspapers • Word of Mouth • Ask the Experts • Job Fairs • Web Searches • Temporary Work • Unemployment • Seattle-based Businesses • Public Company Profiles • Bill Gates & Paul Allen

7: SCHOOL DAZE 201

Seattle Public Schools • The ABCs of Public School • Major School Districts • Private Schools • Alternative Schools • Colleges and Universities • Community Colleges and Vocational Schools • Child Care

8: THAT'S ENTERTAINMENT 223

Classical Music • Musical Theater • Pop/Rock • Clubs • World/Jazz • Dance • Theater • Museums and Attractions • Art Walks • Animal Viewing • Festivals • Readings & Lectures • Libraries & Bookstores • Movies • Newspapers • Magazines • Television • Radio

9: GET OUT & PLAY 251

Spectator Sports • College Sports • Biking • Hiking • Golf • Fishing • Kayaking • Running • Sailing • Skiing • Soccer • Swimming • Parks • Fitness • Skating

10: BY THE PEOPLE, FOR THE PEOPLE 275

Seattle Politics • The Mayor • City Council • King County Politics • County Executive • Port of Seattle • Governor • State Legislature • Federal Government • Building & Zoning Issues • Courts • Politics by Initiative

11: A PICTURE OF HEALTH 287

Health Care In Seattle • Hospitals & Medical Research • Alternative Medicine • HIV/AIDS and STD Resources • Insurance • Substance Abuse • Mental Health Services • Social & Community Services • Counseling • Charitable Giving • Cultural Diversity

12: WEATHER WISE 305

Weather Statistics • Puget Sound's Convergence Zone • Rain City • Winter Blues • Stormy Weather • Resources

13: MOTHER NATURE 317

Puget Sound • The Cascades & Olympics • Air Quality • Old-Growth Forests • P-Patches • Gardening • Farmers Markets & Subscription Farming • Essential Gardening Resources • Whale-Watching • Urban Wildlife • Fishing for Knowledge

INDEX 335

Preface

The universe has changed since the last edition of the *Seattle Survival Guide*. That edition, the third, came out in 1996 and has spent almost a decade as the most popular, respected, and useful reference for life in the Seattle area. Reading it now is an entertaining exercise in modern history—we chuckle over the things that are utterly different and nod in appreciation of those immutable Seattle characteristics that are as enduring as rain.

One simple example will serve to illustrate: 1996 was the dawn of the Internet era, and the third edition's introduction took note of "Web sites taking over" (but included URLs for very few of them). Since then, of course, the Internet boom has come and gone, and come again. (Maybe it will go again—who knows?) Today Amazon.com, which opened for business in 1996, is a global Internet power, and its founder, Jeff Bezos, is one of Seattle's most nationally prominent figures. You will find Amazon's URL—along with every other one we could find—in the text of this fourth edition.

Besides including Internet addresses, we have made other changes to this guide so it is more practical, lasting, and descriptive. For example, we concentrate more on describing and cataloging organizations, institutions, and companies than the individuals associated with them, as the latter change constantly. You won't find long lists of corporate boards of directors; instead, we've expanded the number of descriptions of Seattle-area companies.

Other things have changed, too. In 1996 Seattle had not known a recession since the mild one that accompanied a Boeing slowdown in the early '80s. In the first years of the 21st century, riven by downturns in the aviation, high-tech, and travel industries, the city has sometimes led the nation in unemployment.

It's the nature of human affairs to be cyclical. The purpose of this book is not to track changes so much as to freeze-frame life in Seattle today—and to do so in a fashion that makes it useful far beyond the day it appears on bookshelves. In 1999, for instance, the most essential employment question was how business owners could find good workers: Back then, jobs went begging. Today the opposite is true: How can good workers find jobs? Thus we include comprehensive information on both sides of the employment equation.

In some cases we simply explain how you can acquire information. Academic test scores for individual schools offer useful information to parents trying to decide where to buy a home, but printing all such data for every school in the Seattle metro area would consume more than half the book and would be out of date less than a year from now. Instead, we include details on how parents can easily find academic data.

We have also given more space to descriptions of the Seattle environs, from Tacoma to Everett. This is truly one interconnected metropolitan area, a fact ably illustrated by the struggles over and the desperate need for regional light rail.

This edition also contains a fair amount of cultural grounding—explanations of the traditions and histories that comprise the Seattle character. Anyone who lives here ought to know what "acres of clams" refers to, who Junior was, why the Dash 80 barrel roll is a historic event, and what "opening day" means. You'll find many of these tidbits in sidebars we call "GBNF" (Gone But Not Forgotten). Other tips are sprinkled throughout the text to entertain and inform you.

Seattle Survival Guide is meant to be, then, an urban encyclopedia. You'll find the best shortcut to the Mariners game when there's an accident on I-5 beneath the convention center. You'll learn where savvy Ballard residents go for sunset beach walks, how to get from Redmond to Fremont by bike, where you can find durian (an exotic Asian fruit), what to do if a cougar wanders into your yard, and thousands of other needs and wants of modern life.

As you use this book, a couple things to consider. First, all phone numbers have an area code of 206 unless otherwise noted. Second, given the limitations of space, we naturally had to be selective in what we included. We've also included as many Web sites to help direct you to sources of additional information, however they can—and do—change frequently.

The first three editions of this book (published in 1990, 1993, and 1996) were the voice of Theresa Morrow, who thereby became surely the most knowledgeable of all Seattle-area residents. Aside from such vision and knowledge that carries through today, substantial contributions were made by Alison Peacock, Eastside expert Ericka Chickowski, David Volk, and Manny Frishberg. Additional research was provided by Sean Axmaker, Christine Benedetti, Mary Bradley, Phil Campbell, Nathan Carter, Deb Cronheim, Melody Datz-Barr, Christopher DeLaurenti, Jennifer Elam, Bret Fetzer, Brian Goedde, Maria

Gregorio, Emily Hall, Joseph Hoch, Pat Kearney, Brandon Kinports, James Larrabee, Scott McGeath, Amanda Ovena, and Claire Wagenseil. Melody Moss contributed early help with Chapters 1–4 and 8–13.

I'm grateful to Sasquatch managing editor Heidi Schuessler for her support, faith, and help in the task of making the fourth edition a reality. The first three editions proved to be indispensable to newcomers, long-term residents, and visitors alike; if we have done our job properly, this one will be, too.

In my time in "Seattle" I have worked in Everett, Kent, Tacoma, and downtown Seattle. I've lived in Kirkland, Federal Way, Tacoma, Puyallup, Vashon Island, and Ballard. There are notable differences between those areas, but they all share some common characteristics that hold true throughout the Seattle area: They have vibrant and distinct identities. Their residents are proud to live where they do and take an active role in maintaining and improving their communities. And they are all—as is Seattle as a whole—wonderful places to live.

This book is meant to help you enjoy that wonder as fully as possible.

INTRODUCTION
An Emerald with Many Facets

When I introduced myself as a resident of Seattle to a fellow diner at a banquet in Budapest, he grinned and nodded to acknowledge his recognition of the name. I could see he was about to add something, so I expected the usual "Ah, Seattle—Boeing, yes?" Or maybe, "Microsoft, yes?" I was wrong. He said, with great delight, "Ah, Seattle. Chihuly, yes?"

Well, yes, Chihuly. And Microsoft, and Boeing, and Nirvana, and Starbucks, and Nordstrom. And traffic and rain; *Sleepless in* and Amazon.com; Mount Rainier and the Space Needle; REI and the Mariners and Pike Place Market; and even big, towering, old-growth trees.

Our city has cut such a wide swath through national and international consciousness over the past half-century that we enjoy iconic status. In the two decades I've been in the Seattle area, I have traveled much of the world and never met anyone who had not heard of the city. That banquet in Budapest was in 1990, and if anything, Seattle looms even larger in the public mind today, at times over the past decade enjoying as much exposure as New York or LA. Outsiders expect everyone in Seattle to revere Jimi Hendrix, wear informal Eddie Bauer slacks and shirts to work, and have a Boeing or Microsoft card key strung around their neck on a lanyard. We all shop at Nordstrom, start every day with a Starbucks double grande, buy our staples at Costco, and send books willy-nilly worldwide using Amazon.

Of course, that's not true.

We don't all do all of those things. We know there are as many Starbucks detractors as there are advocates—one of the most prominent local competitors, Tully's, was founded by a real estate figure who designed it deliberately as the anti-Starbucks. Some of us are oblivious to rain; some have never seen *Sleepless in Seattle;* some wear pinstripe suits to work; some have never bought anything online at Amazon. And, in the heartland of Microsoft, Seattle has as many Macintosh adherents as does Silicon Valley.

We not only have a multifaceted identity, we have multiple nicknames. Sure, this is the "Emerald City." It's also "Jet City," "Latteland," and "Rain City." Our icons sport nicknames, too: "The Lazy B" (Boeing), "Nordy's," "the Market."

You don't have to see every side of a gem to appreciate its value, but the more facets you do see, the greater your appreciation. So how did we get to be who we are? And who are we, anyway?

Like most great cities, Seattle owes much to geography and historical circumstance. Its character and significance have come about as much by accident as by design—no human hand made Puget Sound the deepest, easily accessible port north of San Francisco. No human hand raised the Olympics and the Cascades, which combine with the Pacific to make our weather and our landscape.

Coast Salish people had long lived in relative abundance along Puget Sound, enjoying seemingly limitless salmon runs and turning cedar into everything from housing to headgear, when British explorer George Vancouver sailed into and charted the area in 1792. The region attracted little colonizing interest until a few settlers drifted north from the Oregon Trail in the 1850s and the Denny party arrived at Alki Point in 1851—November 13, to be exact, a quintessentially chilly, gray day.

A month later a brig from California hove to offshore and established three themes that are key to Seattle history: resource extraction, shipping, and gold rushes. The *Leona* was seeking timber to take to San Francisco, which was booming and building at a frenzied pace. Could the settlers supply the wood?

By the Numbers

	Seattle	King County
Population	572,000	1,780,000
Area (square miles)	84	2,126
Employment	320,000	948,000
Median household income	$46,000	$63,000
Households*	259,000	763,000

(*In Seattle, owner-occupied, 48%; renter-occupied, 52%)

They could, and did. Moving across Elliott Bay to find a better harbor, they set up a city they named (sort of) after the local Duwamish leader, Chief Seatlh (usually transliterated today as "Sealth"). For 40 years Seattle underwent the usual growth throes of Western cities: The railroad bypassed it in favor of Tacoma, and when the nearby timber was depleted, the city was forced to mine and ship coal. Hysteria about Chinese immigrants swept the city in 1885, and after a few mob episodes most Asian residents were evicted. A great fire leveled the city in 1889, but it was quickly rebuilt. Problems with tide flows forced residents to raise the whole city an entire story, leaving behind the "underground" so popular today in Pioneer Square.

Then, in 1898, the first of three entirely circumstantial events took place that would determine Seattle's future. A ship from Alaska (ironically named the SS *Portland*) docked here with gold from the Yukon. News about the "ton of gold" flashed around the world, and the dateline was Seattle. The city became the gateway to the last big frontier gold rush, the Klondike, and as in San Francisco, lasting prosperity came not to the gold rushers but to the outfitters and shippers. Seattle entered the 20th century as a major West Coast city.

Then, in 1916, an already wealthy lumberman decided to try his hand at flying. Bill Boeing built his first floatplane along the Duwamish and set in motion an enterprise that remains central to Seattle almost a century later. The company and the city reached their first economic heyday during World War II, building the hundreds of bombers key to the Allied

Top 10 Local Seattle Icons

1. SPACE NEEDLE
2. FREMONT TROLL
3. PIKE PLACE MARKET
4. J. P. PATCHES (TV CLOWN, 1958–1981)
5. SLO-MO-SHUN HYDROPLANE (NOW AT MOHAI)
6. RAINIER BREWERY "R" SIGN (NOW A TULLY'S "T")
7. LINCOLN TOE TRUCK (ALSO AT MOHAI)
8. HAT 'N' BOOTS (OXBOW PARK, GEORGETOWN)
9. ELEPHANT CAR WASH SIGN
10. TWIN TEEPEES RESTAURANT (DEMOLISHED 2001)

(Source: *Seattle Times* reader poll, May 2004)

victory; a second boom came in the 1960s with the dawn of the jet travel age.

Boeing and shipping were the mainstays of the area until a young entrepreneur, born and raised in the city, decided to locate a start-up tech company on the Eastside. Bill Gates had the notion that software would dominate the computer revolution; a decade later he had been proven right, and the term "Microsoft millionaire" entered the American consciousness.

Three University of Washington grads casting about for work opened a coffee shop in Pike Place Market; a decade later an entrepreneurial Brooklynite took over Starbucks and aimed it toward global prominence. Meanwhile, an equally inventive young man named Kurt Cobain seized global attention with a new wrinkle on rock music—grunge. Suddenly, Seattle was popping up on "most desirable city" lists, and the Space Needle was appearing on magazine covers for the first time in three decades. The result was an unprecedented economic and demographic boom. Would Seattle supersede Silicon Valley as the U.S. tech capital?

King County population grew almost a quarter million in one decade. In that same decade, 1992–2001, the county's median household income soared from $42,000 to almost $63,000, and the average home price skyrocketed from $149,000 to $250,000. At one point it seemed like almost everyone in town was working for a tech company or an Internet start-up; I, myself, after a lifetime in newspaper and magazine publishing, spent two years doing nothing but Internet work.

Top 10 National Seattle Icons

1. SPACE NEEDLE
2. BOEING
3. STARBUCKS
4. JIMI HENDRIX
5. DALE CHIHULY
6. PIKE PLACE MARKET
7. MICROSOFT
8. RAIN
9. NORDSTROM
10. AMAZON.COM

It was a boom that made the subsequent slump all the more painful: Just a couple years later King County vied with Portland, Oregon, for worst unemployment in the nation. Internet start-ups vanished overnight. Boeing slumped. Even the Mariners, who had enjoyed a decade of sports prominence, turned woeful.

In the first years of the 21st century Seattle seems quiescent. We haven't been on the cover of a national magazine for a while. Microsoft is evolving from a start-up, world-shaking tech company to a mainstream blue chip. Boeing, which didn't actually have its headquarters in Seattle proper (for tax reasons), moved them halfway across the continent to Chicago in 2000. King County's population is nearing 2 million, and many of the challenges the city faces seem not only unresolved, but unlikely to be.

Seattle area traffic is often, by some measures, as bad as LA's. We are the only West Coast city without light rail. Boeing has lost its preeminence in commercial jet production to a European consortium. Most public improvement programs are beaten back by an antitax demagogue. Puget Sound is so polluted its most conspicuous residents, our native orcas, are dying.

But agitated as I may sometimes become about Seattle's problems, virtually any evening I want I can wander over to Golden Gardens Park; stroll a clean, sandy beach; watch the sun set over the Olympics; and listen to impromptu bands strike up bluegrass or reggae beats. Kayakers paddle into the wake of passing freighters. Glistening new 777s coast into Boeing Field before they start winging their way around the world. I sit down on a patch of grass with a supper of leftover salmon from Pike Place Market, tucked into a baguette from the best bakery in Ballard (Tall Grass).

And I recall the words of Chief Seatlh: "Man did not weave the web of life; he is merely a strand in it. Whatever he does to the web, he does to himself."

Of course, Seatlh may not have actually said that (see sidebar), but in a way, that's the point. We make our own communities by the way we frame them and the way we care for them. Our myths and icons clarify our realities. Whatever Seattle is and will be, it's up to us. I hope this book can help Seattle achieve much more than the "survival" in its title. Please take a walk around your neighborhood soon and treasure everything that's good, and think about what might become better still.

GONE BUT NOT FORGOTTEN
Chief Seatlh

As with so many Native American leaders, what's real and what's not about the Coast Salish leader's life is difficult to determine. He was, indisputably, the tyee (leader) of the Duwamish band that inhabited the Elliott Bay area when white settlers arrived in the 1850s. Here's what else seems sure: He was born in 1786 on Bainbridge Island, a child of the Suquamish people, and apparently saw George Vancouver's boats sail into the Sound six years later. He became a leader of the Duwamish, his mother's people, and offered friendship and assistance when settlers arrived—thus pioneer leader Doc Maynard's idea to name the young city after the old chief. He died in 1866, back on Bainbridge.

Here's what isn't certain: How to spell his name. Sealth? Seatlh (most likely)? Seattle?

Oh, and there's the famous speech. When a brief uprising was quelled and a treaty signed for Western Washington in 1856, the chief declaimed a now-famous, oft-quoted eulogy for the western landscape. Thing is, he spoke in Coast Salish. The one observer who took notes did not speak that tongue, and this worthy (Henry Smith) did not even transcribe his notes until 30 years later. Furthermore, Smith's efforts, printed in a Seattle newspaper, seem to have benefited from further embellishment by later "editors."

Withal, the "speech" is legendary, eloquent, and more than a bit disturbing. "We are part of the earth, and it is part of us. . . . All things are connected like the blood which unites one family. Whatever befalls the earth befalls the sons of earth." Numerous versions of the entire speech, plus debate about its provenance, can be found online.

No matter who actually conjured up the words, it's worth recalling them the next time you're stuck in traffic on I-5, trying not to breathe diesel fumes under the Washington State Convention Center.

There's a statue of Chief Seatlh in a sycamore-shaded pocket park at 5th and Denny in Belltown. He'd doubtless be bemused by the fact the shade is provided by nonnative trees planted for their adaptability to urban street life.

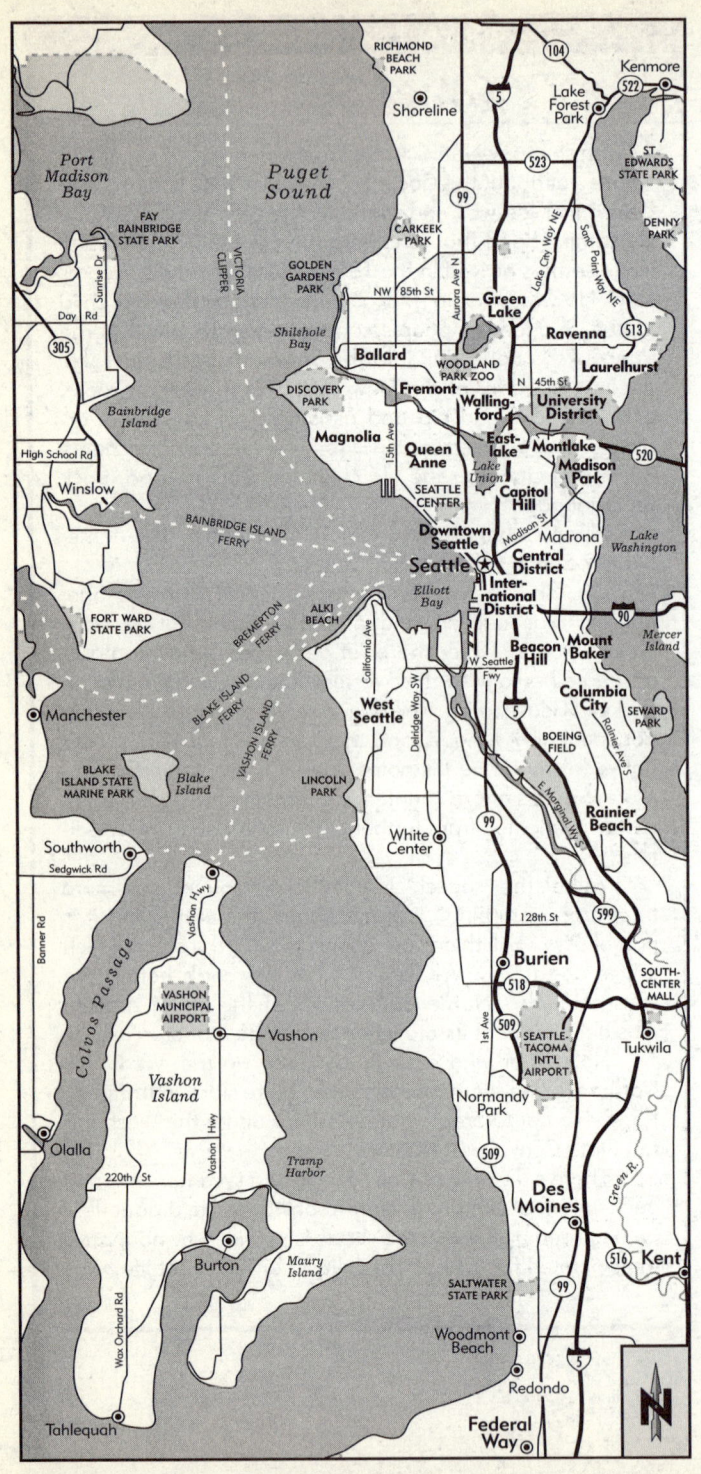

CHAPTER 1

Seattle Neighborhoods

Seattle has close to 600,000 people—and on most maps more than 45 neighborhoods. That's about 13,000 residents per neighborhood, and virtually all of them would tell you that *their* particular corner of the Emerald City is the most distinctive and colorful, the quietest and safest, or any one of a dozen other attributes. And a good many residents of every neighborhood would tell you theirs is, quite simply, the best.

They can't all be right. Can they?

Well, yes. One of the beauties of Seattle's character is that, more than most other modern American cities, its neighborhoods are dynamic and cohesive. Ballardites, Fremontians, Magnolia and Columbia City residents, and all the rest feel great loyalty to their locales, each of which has something special to offer. Is there a better view than from the Discovery Park bluffs in Magnolia? Is there a more exotic international area than the International District? Are there quieter streets than in Laurelhurst?

Of course, we're merely posing the questions—not even a saint would dare try to answer them. What we do attempt in this chapter is a lucid, loving, and useful description of Seattle's major neighborhoods, with twin goals: to guide newcomers to Seattle who are choosing a place to live and (hopefully) to enhance established residents' enjoyment of their neighborhoods.

We haven't covered every single neighborhood (there simply isn't space in this book), and please keep in mind that the facts and figures listed date to the time this book was prepared (summer 2004); in some cases we have consolidated and rounded off. Demographic statistics are from U.S. Census reports; housing prices are from the Seattle–King County Association of Realtors; and crime statistics are from local police departments. "Major crimes" are defined as murder, rape, assault, burglary, robbery, felony theft, and car theft. For more information, the City of Seattle's neighborhoods office is an invaluable resource: 684-0464, www.seattle.gov/neighborhoods. The city's baker's dozen **NEIGHBORHOOD SERVICE CENTERS** (NSC) are places where you can pay your bills, find out what's going on, ask for help, or just visit (see "Neighborhood Service Centers," below).

Once you've perused the description of your neighborhood or a neighborhood you're interested in, we can't urge you too strongly to lace up your walking shoes or hop on your bike and explore. The one constant throughout Seattle's diverse neighborhoods? They are inhabited by friendly people who are glad to tell you about where they live. There's no telling what you'll find—but it's guaranteed to be something new and wonderful.

Neighborhood Service Centers

BALLARD: 2305 NW Market St 98107; 684-4060; Mon–Fri 9am–5pm, Sat 9am–1pm

CAPITOL HILL: 425 Harvard Ave E 98122; 684-4574; Mon–Fri 9am–5pm

CENTRAL: 2301 S Jackson St, #208, 98144; 684-4767; Mon–Fri 8am–7pm; Sat 9am–5pm

DELRIDGE: 5405 Delridge Wy SW 98106; 684-7416; Mon–Fri 10am–6pm

DOWNTOWN: 820 Virginia 98101; 233-8560; Mon–Fri 9am–5pm

GREATER DUWAMISH: 3801 Beacon Ave S 98108; 233-2044; Mon–Fri 9am–5pm

GREENWOOD: 8515 Greenwood Ave N 98103; 684-4096; Mon–Fri 9am–5pm

LAKE CITY: 12707 30th Ave NE 98125; 684-7526; Mon–Fri 9am–5pm

LAKE UNION/FREMONT: 908 N 34th 98103; 684-4054; Mon–Fri 9am–5pm

QUEEN ANNE/MAGNOLIA: 157 Roy St 98109; 684-4812; Mon–Fri 9am–5pm

SOUTHEAST: 4859 Rainier Ave S 98118; 386-1931; Mon–Fri 9am–5pm, Sat 9am–1pm

UNIVERSITY DISTRICT: 4534 University Wy NE 98105; 684-7542; Mon–Fri 10am–6pm

WEST SEATTLE: 4205 SW Alaska St 98116; 684-7495; Mon–Fri 9am–5pm

BALLARD

One of Puget Sound's oldest communities, first settled in 1853 and incorporated by Captain William Ballard in 1888, Ballard has managed to enjoy the heady vitality of gentrification without sacrificing its **NORDIC HERITAGE**, industrial character, and neighborly attitude. It is both hip—antiwar demonstrators perch on the curb at the "town square," Bergen Plaza, every Wednesday evening at NW Market Street and Leary Way—and old-fashioned: Sidewalk corners have tile markers recalling the old names of streets before the town was subsumed by Seattle in 1906, and many seedy taverns cling to life along one of the main drags, defiantly wafting the aromas of cheap bourbon and cigarettes out on the street. (Old Ballard legend posits an ordinance that required one church for every three taverns.) The clatter of ship-fitting, commercial fishing, and other blue-collar enterprises still rings daily in the industrial district south of NW Market Street.

Here, north of the Ship Canal and east of Shilshole Bay, lies one of Seattle's best visitor attractions, the **BALLARD LOCKS**. Here is **BALLARD AVENUE**, a "main street" on which small artisan shops mingle with gourmet restaurants. Ballard's lutefisk store is long closed, but the neighborhood supports a profusion of independent coffee shops and bakeries, and you can still get lutefisk in December at several local Scandinavian specialty stores. (Lutefisk is pickled white fish, a Norwegian holiday "treat." Like Korean kimchee, it is definitely an acquired taste.) The Norwegian flag still flies proudly outside Leif Erikson Hall on NW 57th Street, as well as outside at least one home on every block.

In Ballard you can go "rock climbing" at one of the first indoor climbing walls in the Seattle area; stroll a subtropical garden; experience top-notch live music at a longstanding intimate venue; start a 30-mile bike ride on the **BURKE-GILMAN TRAIL**, which begins in Ballard and stretches all the way to Redmond; and watch what most say is the best sunset view in Seattle, at the aptly named **SUNSET PARK**.

Ballard residential districts are composed mostly of modest, well-kept Craftsman and World War II vintage bungalows, with a few taller Victorian homes. The commercial districts have few chain stores, reflecting the area's still-strong sense of independence and separate identity. A large area of apartments and multifamily units is located between 26th Avenue NW and 15th Avenue NW, north of NW Market Street.

The **BRAND-NEW "MUNICIPAL CENTER,"** containing the new library and neighborhood service center, at 2056 NW 56th Street, convincingly captures Ballard's discrete identity. A popular topic of conversation for the past century in the district's taverns remains current: how to secede from Seattle. Maybe the resulting city could designate lutefisk the official holiday dish.

Ballard by the Numbers

Boundaries: W 85th St; Lake Washington Ship Canal; 8th Ave NW; Shilshole Bay

Included neighborhoods: Sunset Hill, Crown Hill, Loyal Heights, Blue Ridge

NSC: Ballard

Population: 43,300

Median age: 37.3

Median household income: $66,325

Median home sales price: $350,000

Major crimes/1,000: 21.2

Web sites: www.inballard.com, www.ballardchamber.com

Media: Ballard News-Tribune

Main drags: NW Market St, Ballard Ave, 15th Ave NW, 24th Ave NW

Slogan: "Ya Sure Ya Betcha"

Key date: Norwegian Constitution Day, May 17

Farmers market: Sun 10am–4pm at Ballard Ave NW, north of 22nd Ave NW

Ballard Attractions & Institutions

ARCHIE MCPHEE'S: A quirky, zany, and utterly unique collection of novelties, toys, party favors, and other esoterica. 2428 NW Market St, 297-0240, www.mcphee.com.

BALLARD LOCKS: More than 100,000 boats a year pass from Seattle's lakes to Puget Sound through this 1917 facility, formally known as the Hiram M. Chittenden Locks (no one calls them that). Visitors can see boats descend and ascend the locks, and it's the best spot in the Seattle area to watch salmon

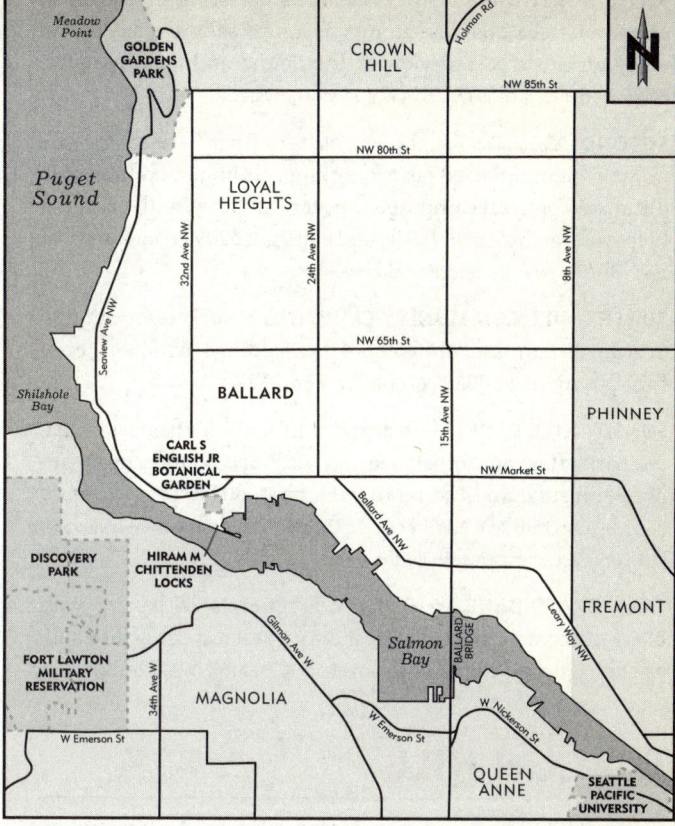

BALLARD

climb a fish ladder. The grounds include a lovely garden/arboretum, with many subtropical plants and flowers. 3015 NW 54th St, 783-7059, www.nws.usace.army.mil/lwsc.cfm.

BALLARD MARKET: Outstanding local market for fresh produce, meats, and fish, with an amazing wine section. 1400 NW 56th St, 783-7922, www.townandcountrymarkets.com/ballard.

GOLDEN GARDENS PARK: One of Seattle's best Puget Sound beaches. In July and August hardier Ballardites test the water on incoming, sun-warmed tides. Bonfires in the beachside fire rings are a summer and fall tradition—bring your own wood. At the north end of Seaview Ave NW, www.cityofseattle.net/parks/parkspaces/Golden.htm.

NORDIC HERITAGE MUSEUM: All five Nordic peoples have their place here: Danish, Finnish, Icelandic, Norwegian, and Swedish. 3014 NW 67th St, 789-5707, www.nordicmuseum.com.

RAY'S BOATHOUSE: One of Seattle's oldest, best, and most glamorous seafood restaurants is universally considered to enjoy an unsurpassed view of the Sound and the Olympics. 6049 Seaview Ave NW, 789-3770, www.rays.com.

SECOND ASCENT: Frugal adventurers turn here for a wide range of new and used gear for hiking, climbing, cycling, paddling, and general camping. The store is folksy, with excellent help; you can buy, sell, trade, and consign. 5209 Ballard Ave NW, 545-8810, www.secondascent.com.

SUNSET HILL COMMUNITY CLUB: Oldest such association in Seattle, its hall is a popular spot for weddings, banquets, even film premieres. 3003 NW 66th St, 784-2927.

SUNSET HILL PARK: High atop a bluff above Shilshole Marina, the park offers an unmatched view of Puget Sound, the Olympic Peninsula, and the mountains beyond. Sunset is best, of course. On 35th Ave NW between 75th & 77th Sts, www.seattle.gov/parks/parkspaces/sunsethill.htm.

TALL GRASS BAKERY: Ballard's European-style bakery, with big, dark, heavy loaves. Stop by about 6:15 each evening for a still-warm baguette just out of the oven. 5907 24th NW, 706-0991.

BEACON HILL

Beacon Hill in many ways represents a little of each neighborhood in the city: It has the cultural diversity of the Central District—almost half of its residents hail from Asia and speak such languages as Chinese, Japanese, Tagalog, and Vietnamese. It has the ridgetop views of Queen Anne and Magnolia, the full sun of Greenwood and Phinney Ridge, and a strong gay community, like Capitol Hill. There's the quirky artistic bent of Fremont, the Craftsman bungalows of Wallingford, and the fighting spirit of such neighborhoods as Ravenna and Montlake.

But while it has similar attributes to many other areas of town, it does not have the same amenities—which residents think stems from discriminatory attitudes toward such an ethnically varied but economically poor part of town. Only 25 percent white, this is the most diverse neighborhood in Seattle, but with a 19 percent poverty rate, it is also the most financially bereft. Residents have battled a slew of inequalities, such as having to choose between keeping one of only two neighborhood banks or losing their library; hosting a "tent city" of homeless people far longer than other neighborhoods would;

and enduring not only emissions from the VA hospital incinerators but also cell phone antennas on top of tall buildings.

Even **EL CENTRO DE LA RAZA**, the esteemed civil rights organization that reaches out mostly to the Hispanic community, was born from strife. When the city ignored requests for an English-as-a-Second-Language program, El Centro's founders occupied the school building where the classes would have been held. After four months of this, the city gave

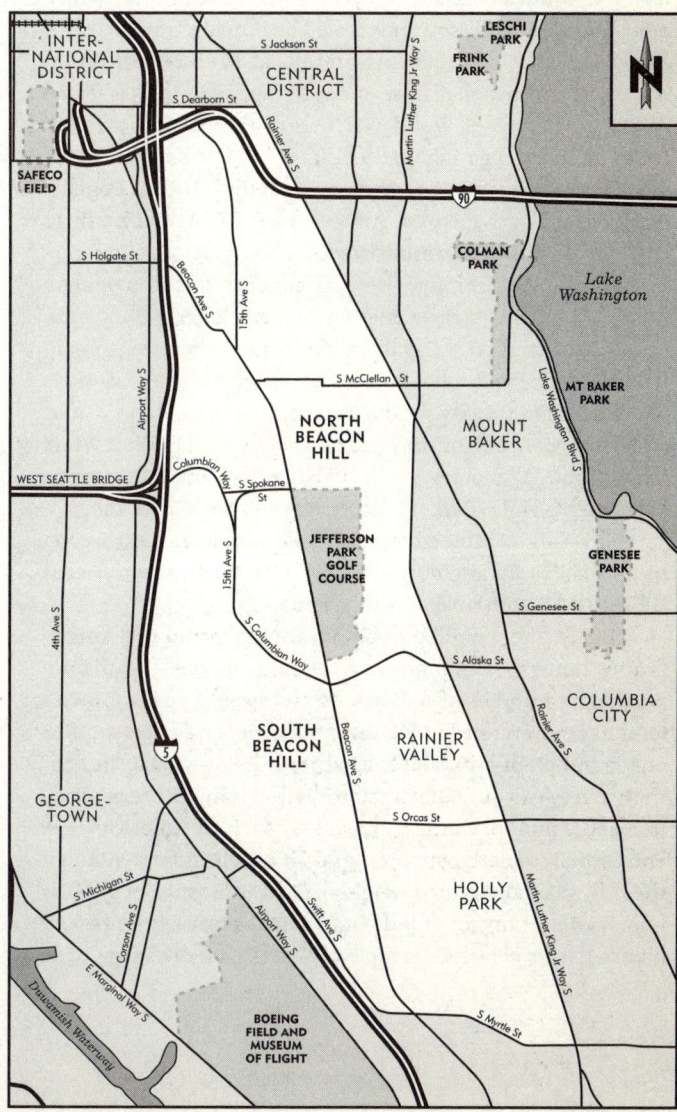

BEACON HILL

in and leased the building to them for $1 a month. Still in that building today, El Centro is a powerful force for Latinos and other minorities in need, funding everything from a bilingual program for infants and tots to a telephone bank for job seekers with no home phone.

Unlike other parts of the city that grew with the railroad and transit lines or the mills, Beacon Hill was rural farmland until World War II, when Boeing needed workers nearby and fast. It did gain a famous municipal golf course in 1915, named after President Jefferson and created by inmates from a nearby stockade; today, lawn bowling prevails at **JEFFERSON PARK**. A U.S. Marine hospital arose on top of the hill in 1933; it served disabled veterans of World War I. Now the 16-story art deco tower lights up the night like a beacon, but it has not served as a hospital since 1981. It earned a spot on the National Register of Historic Places in 1979. Amazon.com has its main offices there, as do hospital administrators.

World War I brought several changes to the neighborhood: When U.S. Army planes visited on a Liberty Bond tour, they had to land on the golf course because there was no airfield; Boeing Field followed 10 years later. Shipyard workers who flocked to the city for the war effort needed places to live, so Liberty Courts Housing was created in 90 days flat. World War II brought another public housing park, but this one was permanent: Holly Park. Housing stayed scarce after the war, so Holly Park continued to offer low-income shelter. A community collaboration in 1996 successfully recast the project as **NEW HOLLY** with mixed-income housing.

Today the neighborhood is almost primarily single-family homes—although one resident decries the disproportionate number of nail salons and beauty parlors. Buses tend to be overcrowded, he says, "as if the city takes an 'it's-only-a-bunch-of-ethnic-people' attitude." But what a "bunch" they are: Mexican, Guatemalan, Salvadoran, Eritrean, Vietnamese, Filipino, Chinese, Japanese, African American, gay and lesbian, elderly, yuppies, and so much more. Although the hill was named for a neighborhood in Boston, that fairly homogeneous one of orderly brownstones bears little resemblance to this colorful example of West Coast diversity.

Beacon Hill by the Numbers

Boundaries: Dearborn St; city limits; Rainier Ave S/Martin Luther King Jr. Wy S; I-5 and Airport Wy S

Included neighborhoods: North and South Beacon Hill

NSC: Greater Duwamish

Population: 22,300

Median age: 36

Median household income: $41,540

Median home sales price: $207,012

Major crimes/1,000: 91

Web sites: www.neighborhoodlink.com/seattle/sbnc, www.elcentrodelaraza.com, beaconhillchamber.com

Media: Beacon Hill News, South Seattle Star

Main drags: Beacon Ave S, Rainier Ave S

Key date: Juneteenth (African American Emancipation Day), June 19

Beacon Hill Attractions & Institutions

BEACON HILL OLD INDIAN CEMETERY: Abandoned and overgrown until a few years ago when a relative of the deceased convinced the city to do something, this cemetery contains the graves of pioneers, circa 1900, such as the first woman doctor in Seattle. Rumor says this was once an Indian burial ground as well. On Graham St between 19th & 22nd Aves S.

JOSE RIZAL PARK: These 9.6 acres are named for Dr. Jose Rizal, a Filipino patriot who made significant contributions to medicine, social and political reform, and engineering, among other disciplines. Views of south downtown and Elliott Bay are stunning, and dogs can explore here without leashes. 1008 12th Ave S, www.ci.seattle.wa.us/parks.

BELLTOWN

See "Downtown," page 17

CAPITOL HILL

Capitol Hill is all about height—high society, high education, natural (and unnatural) highs, and very tall trees. The hill itself rises 444 feet—walkable, but hard on automatic transmissions. Energy crackles here: The combustion of old-world utopian ideals and new-world young idealists makes it a heady place to visit.

Before the nose rings, the piercings, the hair dye, and the attitudes, Capitol Hill was a peaceful, fashionable society of wealthy bankers, lumber barons, and shipping executives. That was in 1908. By 1912 the Hill had more than 40 "additions," or residential sections with similar styles of architecture. The famous mansions of **MILLIONAIRES' ROW** still stand in grand silence from 11th to 15th Avenues E. Near St. Mark's Cathedral, the Harvard-Belmont area has been designated a landmark district for its many architectural styles, from brick and half-timbered elegance to classical symmetries and the Spanish styles of the 1920s. Architect Richard Norman Shaw's influence is alive and well throughout the district.

At the other end of the ridge in **FIRST HILL** (a smaller neighborhood often lumped in with Capitol Hill because of uncertain boundaries), life was similarly posh—although the high life started sooner and was already starting to unravel by 1907. Before Henry Yesler's sawmill began disposing of the forests, residents feared what lurked between the branches. Some said pumas lived in there, and the Yakama Indians made their presence known with occasional unfriendly fire. The military responded with exploding cannon balls—remains of which appeared when the city dug out the I-5 highway. By 1883 the upper crust escaped Seattle's increasing rabble by fleeing to First Hill, ushering in a golden era of wealth and leisure. During that time the wives of the wealthy started causes that still continue today: Emily Carkeek founded the Seattle Historical Society, and splendid mansions became the homes of the Woman's Century Club, the University Men's Club, and the Rainier chapter of the Daughters of the American Revolution. (Today Capitol Hill is better known for its other kind of clubs, the ones with a beat, glamorous drag queens, and plenty of same-sex couples.)

Some of the grandest homes on First Hill have since been demolished to make way for the many hospitals that now decorate what is called "Pill Hill." But the remaining mansions aren't the only majesties scraping the sky. Rare trees—some as tall as 70 feet—trim the neighborhood with green and give it texture.

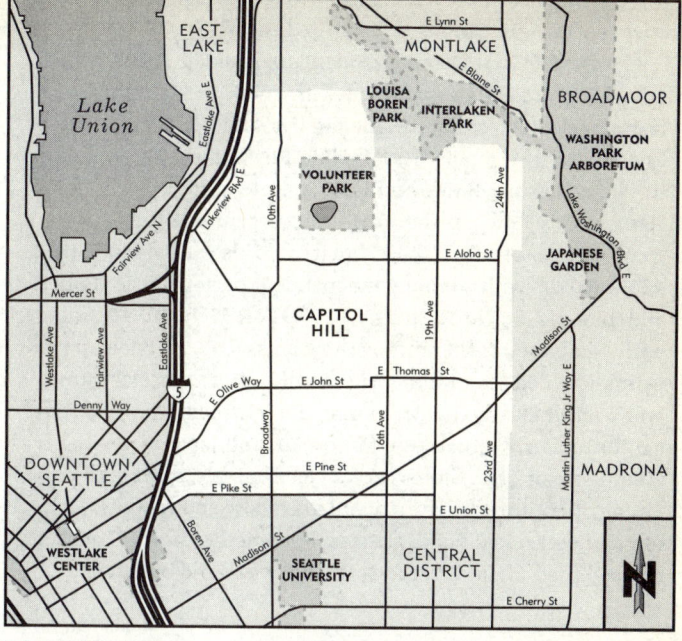

CAPITOL HILL

Capitol Hill's early well-to-do were also do-gooders with solid faiths. At one time the Stevens neighborhood of Capitol Hill had the most Catholics north of San Francisco and west of St. Paul, Minnesota. On First Hill the Italian Renaissance–style **ST. JAMES CATHEDRAL** cuts an impressive picture, its two 167-foot towers visible from I-5. (The ceremonial bronze doors at the west entrance, depicting the human journey toward heaven, are only opened on the most solemn occasions of the year.) Nearby is **SEATTLE UNIVERSITY**, a private religious college founded as a Jesuit school for boys in 1891.

One of three campuses on the Hill, Seattle U is the most serene—and the most modern, especially its architecturally acclaimed Chapel of St. Ignatius. Nearby on Broadway at Pine Street sits **SEATTLE CENTRAL COMMUNITY COLLEGE (SCCC)**, with its tiered courtyard of trees, lawns, and abstract sculpture. SCCC is one of the most successfully diverse colleges in the country: 26 percent of students are over 35 years old, 25 percent are immigrants, 52 percent are from minority groups. At the other end of Broadway, back near the Harvard-Belmont District, is the original campus of **CORNISH COLLEGE OF THE ARTS**, a prestigious place to hone skills in visual arts, graphic design, dance, music, and theater. The convergence of these three campuses—one theological, one generalist, and one creative—brings the Hill its free-spirited curiosity.

Nowhere is this more evident than along **BROADWAY**, a backbone street so crammed with shops, restaurants, and fashionable bodies that it's one big live stage. The end closest to downtown began as "Automobile Row" (there are still vestiges, such as the BMW and Honda dealerships), but became "Decorator's Row" in the '60s and "Restaurant Row" in the '70s. Now it is all of the above, but it could also answer to **"THEATER ROW,"** with so many independent performance venues and historic movie theaters. **BOOKSTORES ABOUND**, most with plenty of gay literature. (Don't miss Toys in Babeland, a woman-owned sex-toy emporium with a great sense of humor and a feminist vibe.) Eateries range in ethnicity from American to Indian, Vietnamese, Moroccan, and Japanese, with an abundance of Thai. Stores carry eclectic goods, from high-end vintage furniture and functional art to low-end recycled fashion and occasional bondage gear. But whether new (Panache) or used (Red Light, Le Frock), it's all trendy and oh-so-hip.

Capitol Hill by the Numbers

Boundaries: Fuhrman Ave E; E Pike St; 24th Ave E; I-5

NSC: Capitol Hill

Population: 24,993

Median age: 36

Median household income: $29,697

Median home sales price: $272,616

Major crimes/1,000: 85.7

Web sites: www.capitolhillblockparty.com, www.capitol-hill.com

Media: Capitol Hill Times, The Stranger

Main drags: Broadway, Pike/Pine corridor, 19th Ave, 15th Ave

Key dates: Arts Orbit, first Sat of every month; Seattle International Film Festival, May–June; Gay Pride Parade, June; Capitol Hill Block Party, July

Famous residents: Sam Hill, August Wilson

Farmers market: Tues, May–Oct, 5–7:30pm, Broadway and E Pine St

Capitol Hill Attractions & Institutions

CHAPEL OF ST. IGNATIUS: Conceived by architect Steven Holl as "seven bottles of light in a stone box," this unusual chapel offers several types of reflection. Colored lenses in the ceiling bring shifting light to the interior at various times of day, and the reflecting pool outside catches the colored lights at night. Sculpture inside the chapel offers contemporary depictions of biblical themes and is quite unexpected. Seattle U campus, 1310 E Union, 296-6000, www.seattleu.edu/chapel.

DILETTANTE CHOCOLATES: Founded by a descendant of the Romanovs' chocolatier and focuses on dark, semisweet preparations. Its Capitol Hill café, which serves various chocolate concoctions and other desserts, is a very, very popular place on weekend nights. 416 Broadway, 329-6463, www.dilettante.com.

FRYE ART MUSEUM: Charles and Emma Frye, meat-packing magnates who hailed from Europe, started collecting art at the 1893 Chicago World's Fair. Some 230 works later, their home was practically an art museum. When Charles died, he set aside funds in his will to create a real museum, one that would always offer free admission. The Frye opened in 1952 and has since been remodeled. It specializes in 19th-century painting and sculpture. 704 Terry Ave, 622-9250, www.fryeart.org.

LAKE VIEW CEMETERY: This is the most familiar cemetery in town . . . or so it seems because the names on the gravestones—Denny, Boren, Meydenbauer—are of Seattle pioneers. Most people come here to see the graves of Bruce Lee, the martial arts master who died mysteriously, and his son Brandon Lee, who died on the set of the movie *The Crow*. Others come for the trees: towering specimens, many rare, 66 of which have labels. 1554 15th Ave E.

SORRENTO HOTEL: Built in 1909, this curving masterpiece, inspired by Sorrento, Italy, has been a historic landmark for 90 years. It opened at the time of the Alaska-Yukon-Pacific Exposition and has hosted such luminaries as the Vanderbilts and the Guggenheims. Even if a stay here is too much for most pocketbooks, anyone can experience the hotel's grandeur by dining in the cozy English-style Hunt Club or taking afternoon tea in the Fireside Room. 900 Madison St at Terry Ave, 622-6400, www.hotelsorrento.com.

VOLUNTEER PARK: Named for the volunteers who fought in the Spanish-American War of 1898–1899, Volunteer Park boasts the planet's tallest hawthorn tree of any species. In fact, it has 175 different kinds of trees, many of which are rare. Other attractions include the **SEATTLE ASIAN ART MUSEUM**, which sits on a bluff in the former home of the Seattle Art Museum; a glass Victorian-style conservatory, mail-ordered and constructed on-site to hold 800 plants; and an old water tower with 108 steps to the best free 360-degree view in the city. 1400 E Prospect St.

CENTRAL DISTRICT

If any Seattle neighborhood has stretch marks, it's the Central District. Its rich heritage is marbled with change, all of which has kept it vibrant, even in down-and-out times. Evidence of the ebb and flow shows in the architecture of its historic churches, schools, and firehouses; palatial Victorian, Tudor, and Craftsman homes; as well as in its casual and colorful business district, consisting mostly of family-owned eateries.

Proud of its ethnic diversity, the Central District, commonly known as the CD, has built its population in layers. After the Duwamish Indians departed but before World War I, the neighborhood belonged to German Jews and some Italians. Japanese Americans joined the mix until World War II forced their evacuation. After the war African Americans flocked to the neighborhood, some to work on the railroads, others because of now-illegal redlining by banks, Realtors, and insurance companies. As African Americans became the predominant culture in the CD, the black community saw its share of historical milestones.

In the 1940s there were thriving jazz clubs on Jackson Street, filled with saxophones and the voices of Quincy Jones and Ernestine Anderson. There was Garfield High School in the '50s, unintentionally ethnic and proud of its record number of college-bound graduates. The '60s brought forth the question of desegregation, as well as civil rights struggles and protests of Dr. Martin Luther King's assassination. (An unusual granite memorial honors the leader's "mountaintop" speech in Martin Luther King Jr. Park.) Throughout, there were Sunday mornings rich with gospel at **MOUNT ZION BAPTIST CHURCH** and First African American Episcopal, and Sunday afternoons filled with soul food at **EZELL'S** and **CATFISH CORNER**. There also were gangs, syringes, and gunshots. Now, there is gentrification.

Condos, townhouses, strip malls, and fixed-up fixer uppers have forced many African Americans out, some with small

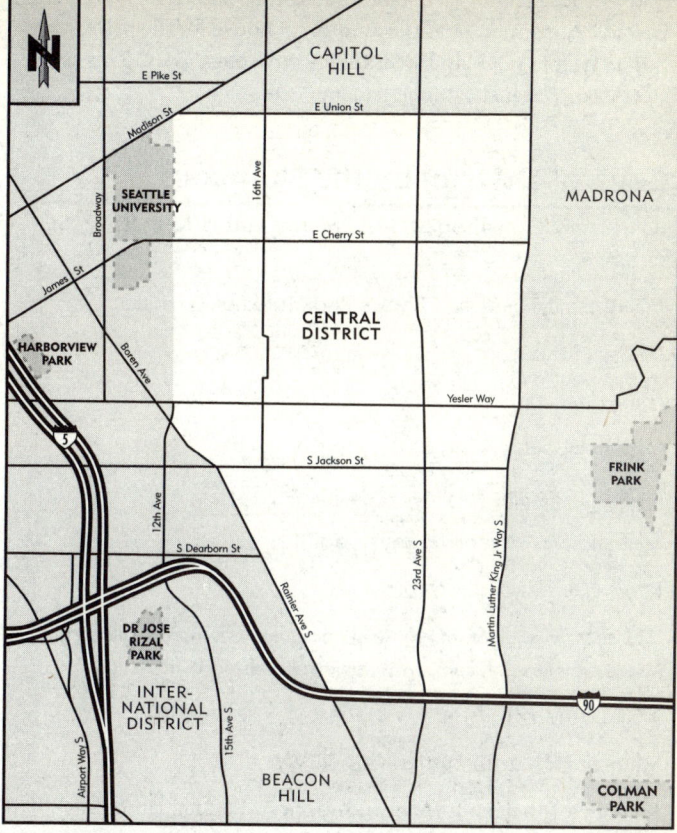

CENTRAL DISTRICT

fortunes from the sales of their in-demand homes, others with the hurt pride of not being able to meet soaring property taxes. Seattle's oldest church, First African American Episcopal, has moved from its historic landmark building, complete with Italian stained glass, to parking-rich Renton, where most of its constituents now live. From 1990 to 2000 the Central District lost nearly 20 percent of its black residents; now only 32 percent of CD residents are black, whereas 43 percent are white. In fact, the black population has dwindled to its lowest in 30 years, causing many to ask for the first time in decades, Where is Seattle's African American community? The answer appears to be: outside the city. Renton and surrounding areas south of Seattle have seen a 125 percent increase in African American residents.

Ironically, the energy and culture of the African American community were part of the attraction for newcomers, also encouraged by decreasing crime, a handy location for Eastside commutes, and the amount of house for the price tag. But as people flock and flee, the culture ebbs away. This is a layer cake that just can't be had and eaten, too.

Central District by the Numbers

Boundaries: E Madison St; I-90; Martin Luther King Jr. Wy S; 12th Ave

Included neighborhoods: Squire Park, Judkins, Garfield

NSC: Central

Population: 28,328

Median age: 32.5

Median household income: $33,449

Median home sales price: $275,000

Major crimes/1,000: 69

Web sites: www.cdforum.org, www.cacf.com, www.rainiervalley.org, www.therainiervalley.com, www.rainiervalleyhistory.com

Media: Diversity News

Main drags: Martin Luther King Jr. Wy

Key dates: Juneteenth (African American Emancipation Day), June 19; Central Area Community Festival in July

Famous residents: Quincy Jones, Ray Charles, Jimi Hendrix, Ernestine Anderson

Central District Attractions & Institutions

EZELL'S FRIED CHICKEN & CATFISH CORNER: These two neighborhood institutions have been cooking award-winning fried chicken and deep-fried catfish for more than 20 years. Go hungry—you won't leave that way. If you want something more exotic, look for the many Ethiopian restaurants in the area and prepare to eat with your fingers! Ezells: 501 23rd Ave, 324-4141; Catfish: MLK Jr. Wy & E Cherry, 323-4330, www.mo-catfish.com.

LANGSTON HUGHES CULTURAL CENTER: This is the city's leading arts and culture facility for the African American community, offering classes and performances in everything from native African languages to hip-hop dancing. It's also a community gathering place and social center. 104 17th Ave S, 684-4757, www.cityofseattle.net/parks/centers/langston.htm.

DOUGLASS-TRUTH BRANCH, SEATTLE PUBLIC LIBRARY: Opened in 1914 as the Yesler branch library, this handsome brick building assumed a new identity and role in 1975 when it was renamed for black freedom activists Frederick Douglass and Sojourner Truth. Today it serves as an educational resource for the Central District community; its collection includes 9,000 items related to African American history and culture, the largest such in the Northwest. The branch will undergo expansion in 2005–06 but remain open. 2300 E Yesler Wy, 684-4704, www.spl.org.

COLUMBIA CITY

See "Seward Park/Columbia City," page 72

DOWNTOWN

Both downtown Seattle and its nouveau riche sibling, Belltown, are rife with facets of the city's past and portents of its future. Along the south Alaskan Way waterfront, some of the land is actually California rocks and dirt used as ballast in clipper ships that sailed north to load timber for San Francisco. The same waterfront now sports cruise ships that by themselves hold more people than were living here when the clipper ships first called.

WESTLAKE PARK was ground zero for the WTO protests that put Seattle on front pages worldwide in 1999; it's also where city voters hewed to Nordstrom's wishes and opened Pine Street to traffic so the retailer would take over the old Frederick & Nelson building as its flagship store. Smith Tower was the tallest building west of the Mississippi in 1914, the pinnacle of Seattle's first burst to prominence; now the Bank of America Tower is tallest and reflects the start of the city's late-20th-century reascendance. In both cases residents complained at first that the modern skyscrapers "ruined" the city skyline.

BELLTOWN, the north end of downtown (between Elliott and Fifth Ave, from Virginia north to Denny Wy), is actually a man-made plateau. Once a towering hill that horse-drawn carts could not climb, it was sluiced into Elliott Bay by city engineers and renamed the Denny Regrade at its finish in 1911. This is where ambitious schemes to turn the downtown commercial core into a thriving residential area have finally borne fruit—a spectacular boom in condominium complexes and gourmet restaurants has yielded a dynamic district that thrums well into the night. And here again, grousing has been heard about the gentrification of the area (and the dearth of parking).

Downtown has both spectacular architectural wonders—for example, the new **SEATTLE PUBLIC LIBRARY** on Fourth Avenue (see page 240)—and "How could they?" dreck such as the Westin Hotel. There are few sidewalk vendors and food carts, but plenty of coffee stands and cafés to make up for it. Transients pursue nickels from passersby; one of the country's best communities of gourmet restaurants draws international attention; and **PIKE PLACE MARKET** (see sidebar, page 24) lends an essential element of down-home soul.

There's no better place to be on a sunny day than on Pike Street, a sack of fresh fruit and bread in hand, listening to the King Jesus Disciples belt out old doo-wop songs. Those who live downtown and enjoy this every day wouldn't trade it for any amount of suburban lawnscape.

The best view of the Seattle skyline, from the Space Needle to the Smith Tower, is from the back of a Washington State Ferry pulling out of Colman Dock. On a summer evening at dusk, with an indigo sky behind and the buildings reflected in Elliott Bay, it's the finest cityscape in the United States.

Downtown by the Numbers

Boundaries: Denny Wy; Cherry St; I-5; Elliott Bay

Included neighborhoods: Belltown, Denny Triangle

NSC: Downtown

Population: 16,600 (10,000 Belltown and Denny Triangle)

Median age: 37

Median household income: $67,000

Median home sales price: $295,000

Major crimes/1,000: 52.6

Web sites: www.belltown.org, www.downtownseattle.com

Media: Seattle Times, Seattle Post-Intelligencer

Main drags: 1st Ave, 4th Ave, Pike St

Farmers market: Naturally, Pike Place Market, every day (except for Thanksgiving, Christmas, and New Year's Day)

Downtown Attractions & Institutions

ACE HOTEL & CYCLOPS: Belltown's quintessential lodging and café are housed in an older brick building that represents the neighborhood's less refined past. The Ace is hip, hip, hip, with high ceilings and brushed metal. The old Cyclops was a Belltown legend as the place arty types went for New Age cafeteria food (falafel burgers, say); the new version has been hoisted upscale considerably. Both hotel and restaurant are the sort of places where cell-phone headsets drape nearly every noggin. Ace: 2422 1st Ave, 448-4721, www.theacehotel.com; Cyclops: 441-1677.

BANK OF AMERICA TOWER: Though Bank of America took over Seafirst in the early '90s and tacked its name on this sky-

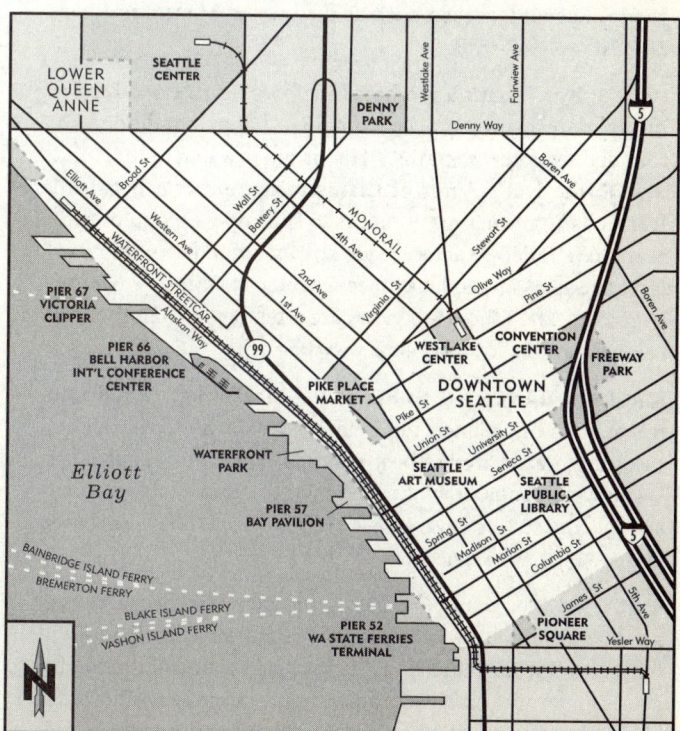

DOWNTOWN

scraper, its old appellation, Columbia Center, remains widely used. Like its forebear the Smith Tower used to be, this is now the tallest building west of the Mississippi, at 937 feet and 76 floors. The legendary women's bathroom at the top offers floor-to-ceiling views of Puget Sound. Sorry, guys. 701 5th Ave.

FARESTART: This unique culinary-jobs program has given more than 1,250 homeless and disadvantaged around Seattle a leg up in the local workforce. Not only does the downtown kitchen/school serve meals—more than 2 million since its inception—to the community, but it offers a unique "Guest Chef" program. On Thursday nights Seattle's top chefs work with students in the FareStart kitchen preparing a three-course meal for 200 guests. Meals are $19.95, and featured chefs have included Tom Black (Barking Frog), Christine Keff (Flying Fish), and Charles Ramseyer (Ray's Boathouse), among many others. One of the best food values in town. 1902 2nd Ave, 443-1233, www.farestart.org.

FEDERAL ARMY & NAVY SURPLUS: OK, so you don't need an old Korean War ammo canister. But what if you did? This is the place grunge pioneers like Kurt Cobain supposedly acquired their boots and flannel wardrobe. Today you can rely on it for good-value outdoor gear such as discounted Thermarest pads. 2112 1st Ave, 443-1818.

IVAR'S: Ivar Haglund promoted seafood, Seattle, and himself in equal measure, proclaiming his "happy condition, surrounded by acres of clams." His original waterfront stand is next to the Ivar's Acres of Clams restaurant that began the Ivar's chain; numerous attempts to spiff up its menu over the years have failed to deter steady streams of tourists who gawk (and shudder) at geoducks (see Chapter 13, "Mother Nature," page 334). The Elliott Bay views are often better than the food. Pier 54, Alaskan Wy, 624-6852, www.ivars.net.

MACRINA BAKERY & CAFE: Leslie Mackie left Grand Central to open this pioneering Belltown icon, whose pastries and morning breads are the best around. Lunchtime sandwiches, salads, and soups draw crowds, though service is sometimes snappish. 2408 1st Ave, 448-4032 (also a satellite location on Queen Anne), www.macrinabakery.com.

MACY'S: Older than Nordstrom, the Bon Marche name was finally subsumed by its corporate parent, but Seattleites will forever call it just "the Bon." Lighting its 3,600-bulb holiday star is an annual early December event; the store windows are given over to lovely displays of Santa legends around the world.

The clothing and housewares are slightly more mainstream and economical than at Nordstrom. 3rd Ave & Pine St, 506-6000, www.macys.com.

NORDSTROM: It's ironic to think that the epitome of modern upscale retailing (sorry, Neiman Marcus) began life in literally pedestrian fashion as a shoe store. The heritage is strong; the flagship store stocks 150,000 pairs. Nordstrom still employs live pianists to serenade shoppers; the annual anniversary sale in late July is an anthropological event. The downtown flagship store is the former Frederick & Nelson building. **NORDSTROM RACK** (1601 2nd Ave, 448-8522) is a place to get sometimes astounding bargains on shoes and other daily apparel. 500 Pine St, 628-2111 (also in Bellevue, Tacoma, Alderwood, Southcenter), www.nordstrom.com.

PACIFIC PLACE SHOPPING CENTER: Big-name glitter downtown. Key stores: Tiffany & Co., Cartier, Coach, Restoration Hardware, to name a few. Its parking garage is popular for its central location and relatively low rates. 600 Pine St, 405-2655, www.pacificplace.com.

PIKE PLACE MARKET: The market advertises itself as "the soul of Seattle," and that's exactly right (see "Pike Place Market," below). Not only is this a fantastic place to buy fresh food, wander amid 300 shops and stalls, watch tourists go ape over flung salmon, and listen to the finest buskers on the West Coast, but the market's history reflects the best of Seattle's character. Founded in 1907 as a place for food vendors to safely sell groceries to Seattleites, it was slated for "urban renewal" (read: demolition) until Seattle voters resoundingly chose to preserve it in 1971. It's easy to grouse about all the tourists, but their dollars help the market thrive. There are fewer tourists but more transients just down the street at Victor Steinbrueck Park (Pike St and Western Ave), which honors the leader of the drive to save the market and affords the best views downtown of Elliott Bay and the Olympics. Even if you weren't around to vote for it in 1971, you can still buy a tile with your name on it; proceeds benefit the Market Foundation. Pike St, west of 1st Ave; 682-7453, www.pikeplacemarket.org.

SEATTLE ART MUSEUM: See "Museums & Attractions," page 236.

SEATTLE PUBLIC LIBRARY: See "Libraries & Bookstores," page 240.

SMITH TOWER: Klondike prosperity brought Seattle's first

So Many Restaurants, So Little Time

Not long after Alice Waters brought Berkeley's Chez Panisse to national prominence with California cuisine using fresh, local ingredients, Seattle-area chefs began to create their own Northwest cookery. The underlying philosophy was similar: use locally available foodstuffs, blend styles from several different cuisines, adapt classic techniques to regional mainstays. Asian, Italian, French provincial, even Latin styles all meld into a distinctive, regional cuisine.

Northwest contemporary cuisine relies heavily on seafood—salmon, crab, oysters, and more exotic items such as sea cucumber—and the produce that innovative chefs find at Pike Place Market. The early outpost of the new cooking, Café Sport (1984–1994), was a sleek bistro just down the street from the market; its chef-owner, Tom Douglas, rose to local fame and national renown. (Douglas now operates four Seattle restaurants.) And Seattle became one of the culinary capitals of the United States.

There are literally hundreds of standout restaurants in the Seattle area; the list below simply catalogs a few of the most prominent.

CAMPAGNE: French provincial cooking was just beginning to rear its head above haute cuisine when Campagne started offering gourmet diners cassoulet in the '80s. 86 Pine St, Pike Pl Market, 728-2800, www.campagnerestaurant.com.

CANLIS: See "Queen Anne Attractions & Institutions," page 62.

CASCADIA: Famed chef Kerry Sear is a fervent advocate of regional ingredients ("Cascadia" is a term for the region from Vancouver to Portland). 2328 1st Ave, 448-8884, www.cascadiarestaurant.com.

DAHLIA LOUNGE: Tom Douglas's longstanding flagship restaurant offers a hearty, full-flavored eclectic menu. 2001 4th Ave, 682-4142, www.tomdouglas.com.

EL GAUCHO: Dark corners, lots of black clothing, steaks and salads and cigars—this is the resurrection of the martini supper club. 2505 1st Ave, 728-1337, www.elgaucho.com.

FLYING FISH: When Christine Keff opened this hip, classy seafood bistro in 1994, no one thought there was much new to do with seafood. Think again—the restaurant's shareable plates and whole roasted fish are signatures. 2234 1st Ave, 728-8595, www.flyingfishseattle.com.

HERBFARM: See "Woodinville Attractions & Institutions," page 109.

KINGFISH CAFÉ: Gumbo, okra, fried chicken, and sweet potato pie—real Southern food done in genuine fashion. No reservations, so be ready to stand in line. 602 19th Ave E, 320-8757.

METROPOLITAN GRILL: Let the tourists patronize the big-name chain steakhouses; Seattle's own is clubby and refined, with expert service and faultless meals (including fish). 820 2nd Ave, 624-3287, www.themetropolitangrill.com.

RAY'S BOATHOUSE: With the sun setting over Shilshole Bay and the Olympics, many a Seattle gent has placed ring in hand and proposed here at Ray's. The seafood is reliably fine, though not inventive. 6049 Seaview Ave NW, 789-3770, www.rays.com.

ROVER'S: Hat-clad raconteur Thierry Rautureau melds Northwest and Continental cuisine better than anyone. The restaurant's restored Madison Park home is a comfortable delight. 2808 E Madison, 325-7442, www.rovers-seattle.com.

SEASTAR: No one executes gourmet seafood better in the Seattle area. The "appetizer tower" astounds newcomers and sates connoisseurs. 205 108th NE, Bellevue, 425-456-0010, www.seastarrestaurant.com.

WILD GINGER: Pacific Rim cuisine had its start at Wild Ginger, perhaps Seattle's best-known restaurant to out-of-towners. Its huge, glittering home opposite Benaroya Hall is a bit intimidating, but the food is ever choice. 1401 3rd Ave, 623-4450.

---

boom, which culminated in construction of the tallest office building (38 floors) west of the Mississippi in 1914. Though longtime Seattleites still remember when it was the tallest building in the city, Smith Tower fell on hard times until late-'90s renovation made it a home for small tech firms. 508 2nd Ave.

WESTLAKE PARK & CENTER: In many ways this is the heart of downtown Seattle, where both protesters and Christmas shoppers congregate, where the city rallied after 9/11, where the **SEATTLE CENTER MONORAIL** starts its short 1.4-mile journey, and where crowds flock for the Nordstrom shoe sale

Pike Place Market

People can, and do, shop at the market; that's one of the sales points for those very-high-priced condos that overlook Pike Place. In addition to the 300-plus permanent shops and food stalls, summer and autumn bring organic growers to the street (Pike Pl, west of 1st; 682-7453, www.pikeplacemarket.org). Selected highlights:

BEECHER'S CHEESE: Handmade cheeses from organic ingredients by a local entrepreneur. 1600 Pike Pl, 956-1964, www.beecherscheese.com.

DELAURENTI: Oh, the imported cheeses. All the shapes, sizes, densities, and aromas you can imagine, and many you can't. You can watch regulars taste a dozen kinds before buying—you can even do that yourself. This is the place for everything deli, from artichoke hearts to $500 a pound truffles, should you need some for your morning omelet. 1435 1st Ave, 622-0141, www.delaurenti.com.

EL MERCADO LATINO: Nopalitos, habaneros, posole, and more, plus a wide selection of hot sauces of American, Mexican, and Caribbean origin. 1514 Pike Pl, 623-3240.

JACK'S FISH SPOT: This market mainstay is the only seafood stall on the east side of Pike Place and so hews its own path—slightly better prices and a smaller selection but higher quality. The lunch counter has prize-winning cioppino and fish & chips. 1514 Pike Pl, 467-0514, www.jacksfishspot.com.

MAGIC SHOP: One of the best-known purveyors of magic supplies, tricks, and games is hidden in a lower-level warren of the market. 1501 Pike Pl #427, 624-4271.

and to peruse the Bon's (oops—Macy's) holiday window displays. The bus tunnel lies beneath; buskers and political orators and skateboarders and thousands of ordinary citizens linger above. In December an old-fashioned carousel is a delight; in summer weekly concerts entertain workers on lunch break. Westlake Center, on the north side of Pine Street, is a tony collection of boutiques; the third-floor food court has every kind of comestible imaginable, from burgers to bok choi. 3rd Ave & Pine St, 467-1600, www.westlakecenter.com. Monorail: 905-2620.

MARKET SPICE: Teas of every flavor and description, including their own blends, which make ever-popular gifts. 85A Pike Pl, 623-3240, www.marketspice.com.

ORIENTAL FOOD MART: Aside from the Seattle Slug toys that entertain so many kids (and adults), this grocery mart/lunch counter has a wide array of Asian cooking ingredients. The Filipino lunchtime meals, especially pork adobo, will ease any drizzle-induced chill. Corner of Pike St and Pike Pl, 622-8488.

PIKE PLACE FISH: Fish fly through the air from this legendary stall, while market regulars mutter imprecations against the crowds of tourists who block the walkway to watch. Flinging fresh fish is hardly the best way to preserve its quality, but this stand does have a wide selection. 86 Pike Pl (at the pig), 682-7181, www.pikeplacefish.com.

PIKE & WESTERN WINE: Just try to name a Northwest wine they haven't heard of—if they don't have it, they'll get it for you. Corner of Pike & Western Ave (naturally), 441-1307, www.pikeandwestern.com.

THE SOUK: Serving tamarind-abalone curry, are you? Better have some garam masala to make it and lime pickle to go with it; this is the place. 1916 Pike Pl, 441-1666.

WORLD SPICE MARKET: The aroma when you enter this multilevel store is intoxicating. Go up and you enter an olfactory kaleidoscope of spices; downstairs, the musty, crisp odor of tea takes over. The premixed stew and rub mixtures are especially redolent. 1509 Western Ave, 682-7274, www.worldspice.com.

MAGIC SHOP: One of the best-known purveyors of magic supplies, tricks, and games is hidden in a lower-level warren of the market. 1501 Pike Pl #427, 624-4271.

EASTLAKE

There are plenty of places to live on the water in Seattle, but Eastlake takes the idea literally. Rows of **FLOATING HOMES** bob offshore, 10 or so in each lineup. From the miniature gardens and evidence of landscaping on the docks to the summerhouse-style interiors, these homes are as permanent as it gets. They float, but they don't really travel.

Pretty posh digs, these listing cabins once served a more practical purpose as housing for migrant workers digging the

LAKE WASHINGTON SHIP CANAL in 1911. Known as "floating shanties" or "Hooverville," they remained long after the migrant workers moved on. Loggers and fishermen used them as seasonal homes, and by the 1920s there were more of them than there are now.

The very same spark for these houseboats' existence, the canal, caused Eastlake to become an industrial neighborhood with a working lake. There, in 1916, William Boeing started testing seaplanes, which he later sold to the government. The first airmail flight to Vancouver occurred from his historic hangar in 1919. World War II brought droves of ship workers to Eastlake—they built 16 minesweepers at Lake Union Dry Dock alone. But as soon as the war ended, industry stalled and a service atmosphere prevailed. Restaurants, marinas, and boating repair shops lined the shore, while offices and apart-

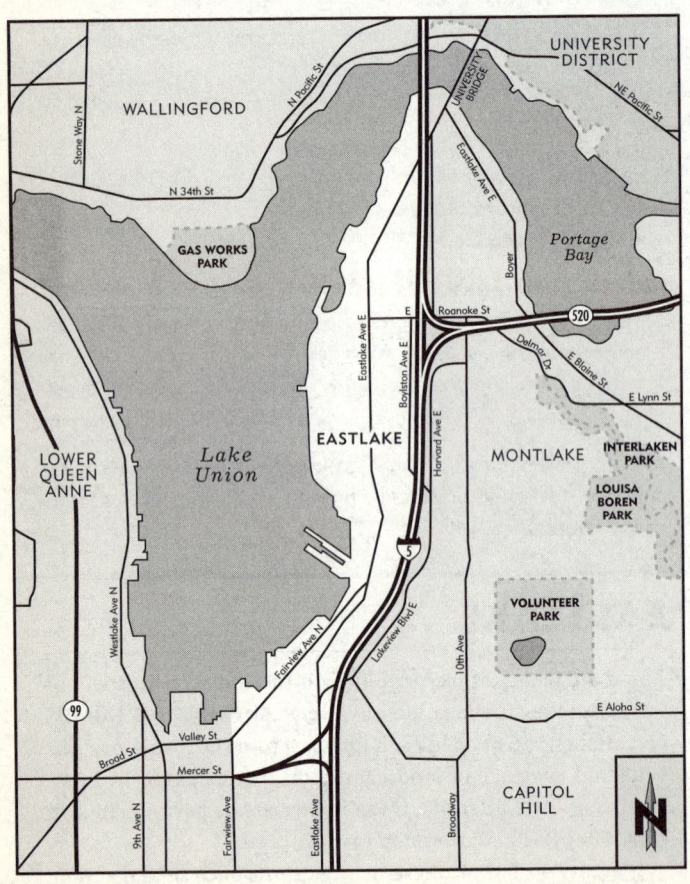

EASTLAKE

ments sprang up across the street. But the National Oceanic and Atmospheric Administration's (NOAA) presence in 1962 meant the loss of 73 moorages from the houseboat community. That same year the World's Fair brought hundreds of visitors to Seattle, and those new apartment complexes came in handy.

Houseboat may steal the limelight with their sheer uniqueness, but a few streets back from shore some pretty interesting **ARCHITECTURE** hides in residential areas, from Victorian farmhouses to Craftsman-, Mission Revival-, and art deco–style homes and apartments. This neighborhood also boasts a hefty collection of commercial buildings designed by such leading Modernists as Paul Kirk, Paul Thiry, and Gena Zema. Sadly, I-5 boxed in the neighborhood, bringing traffic, noise, and mass destruction of homes—but also definite boundaries. Eastlake's flanking bridges feed traffic to I-5 regularly, making Eastlake Avenue the most heavily traveled road east of Chicago and north of San Francisco.

From floating homes and shoreline gardens to laid-back residential areas, this is a down-to-earth neighborhood of low-key liberals who "go with the flow." Just don't say anything bad about its floating jewels.

Eastlake by the Numbers

Boundaries: University Bridge; Eastlake Ave E where it hits Fairview; I-5; Lake Union

NSC: Lake Union/Fremont

Population: 4,178

Median age: 31.8

Median household income: $47,500

Median home sales price: $400,000

Major crimes/1,000: 24

Web sites: eastlake.oo.net, www.seattlefloatinghomes.org

Media: The Eastlake News

Main drag: Eastlake Ave

Key dates: Wooden Boats Festival in July; houseboat tour in Sept

Famous resident: Glass artist Dale Chihuly

Eastlake Attractions & Institutions

CENTER FOR WOODEN BOATS: Occasionally, a glance at Lake Union shows tiny wooden boats with miniature sails—Beetle Cats, Concordia sloops, Blanchard Juniors, and Petrels. These are all rentable from the Center for Wooden Boats, a nonprofit organization dedicated to restoring, protecting, and teaching the craft of wooden-boat sailing. Just walking along the dock of this outdoor museum takes you back in time, but tacking across the lake is even better! 1010 Valley St, 382-2628, www.cwb.org.

14 CARROT CAFÉ: Since 1978, this homey restaurant has served giant cinnamon rolls, unusual healthy fare, and tons of omelet options. Don't miss the Tahitian French toast with tahini spread. 2305 Eastlake Ave E, 324-1442.

FRED HUTCHINSON CANCER RESEARCH CENTER: See Chapter 11, "A Picture of Health," page 289.

PATRICK'S FLY SHOP: Fly-fishing aficionados swear by this Eastlake institution, which carries everything related to fly-fishing, from ties and tackle to instructional videos and fish updates. Technique classes are popular, too. 2237 Eastlake Ave E, 325-8988, www.patricksflyshop.com.

RED ROBIN: In 1962 a burger baron opened a restaurant overlooking Portage Bay; now he owns 222 similar burger palaces across the United States and Canada. The one in Eastlake is the first, and it still retains its original personality. 3272 Fuhrman Ave E, 323-0918.

SERAFINA: Two New Yorkers brought Eastlake this swank, sensuous homage to romance. That might explain the snobbish attitude of the servers—but the sumptuous food by candlelight makes up for it. 2043 Eastlake Ave E, 323-0807, www.serafinaseattle.com.

THE ZOO TAVERN: Old, crusty, and set in its ways, this dive is the only bar in Seattle that operates as a cooperative. 2301 Eastlake Ave E, 329-3277.

FIRST HILL

See "Capitol Hill," page 10

FREMONT

Fremont is proud to call itself a neighborhood where "anything goes." But some of its most cherished aspects have been doing just that—going—in the wake of skyrocketing home prices and an influx of new retailers. The **PUGET CONSUMERS' CO-OP**, once a bohemian store in an intimate spot, has moved into designer digs, complete with underground parking and over-the-top prices. Condos stack up above the market. Other upscale franchises round out the block that once housed an old tavern with a red door and an Irish pub with a green door. (Both bars moved just blocks away, but the magic of proximity has been broken.) Once a great bargain-hunting district, Fremont is now a Shopping Destination with capital letters, and only a few of the antique and consignment stores remain, the most renowned being Deluxe Junk, a purveyor of alternative furnishings since 1978.

This is not the first time Fremont has changed so rapidly. In 1887 it took only two years for the area known as the Outlet to gain a railway, a new name, an electric streetcar, a mill, an iron foundry, and a blue-collar population that bought home sites for $100 each (that amount would buy half a skirt there today). The transformation of its thin stream into a canal took longer—the concept of a connecting waterway first struck in 1851, but the Ballard Locks didn't open until 1917. So did a new bascule bridge to Fremont. With a business district at its end, this counterweighted drawbridge became the most popular of the four installed that year. More than 1,200 streetcars passed through Fremont every 24 hours; by 1931, more than 35,000 Model Ts crossed it daily. The **GUINNESS BOOK OF WORLD RECORDS** deemed it the world's most active drawbridge, but that honor also contributed to the area's decline as traffic was rerouted to Highway 99. Just as the Depression was quelling jobs and livelihoods, a new 1932 span, now known as the Aurora Bridge, siphoned off Fremont's traffic. People had a choice of routes, and they abandoned Fremont to vacant storefronts, dried-up industry, and a struggling populace of bikers and vagrants. Nicknamed "Freeload," the area struggled well into the '70s, when it again underwent rapid change.

Cheap studios in relative solitude had drawn plenty of artists, whose creative energy was transforming the place. Now people called it the "Artists' Republic of Fremont." In 1972 the first Fremont Street Fair showcased the area's now legendary quirkiness. Within five years Fremont had pulled itself up by its biker boots with several new governing bodies:

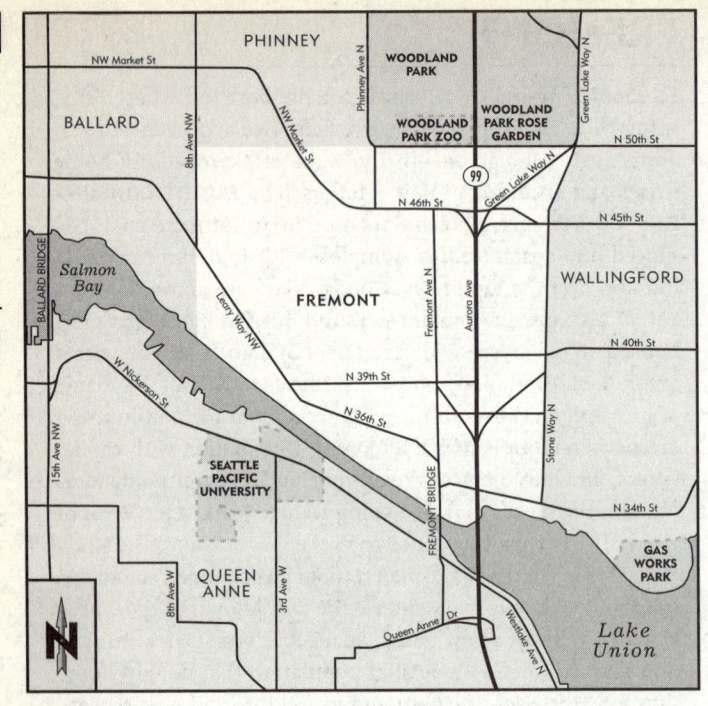

FREMONT

the Fremont Public Association, which helped the needy with food, shelter, and counseling; the Fremont Arts Council; and a progressive curbside recycling program. Soon Fremont earned a new reputation as a funky, hip place where anything could happen. It had become "the community that recycles itself," or, more proudly, "The Center of the Universe." **MICROBREWERIES** such as Redhook and Hale's started in the '80s, and Adobe, the world's second-largest software company, expanded its headquarters there in 1998. From 1990 to 1997 housing prices and rents rose 50 percent, and then kept on going.

Fremont owes its constant reinvention to a pioneering spirit. Things get done in Fremont, usually before anywhere else. Fremont had the first public electric railway on the West Coast (the first private line also ran through Fremont on its way to owner Guy Phinney's estate); honorary mayor Armen Stepanian started the first local curbside recycling program; the **FREMONT PUBLIC ASSOCIATION** opened the first local food bank; and in 1982 Gordon Bowker, already a pioneer for founding Starbucks, paired up with Paul Shipman to start Redhook, the first craft brewery to usher in the microbrew revolution.

The irony of Fremont's defiant identity is that the area shamelessly borrows—and generously shares. For instance, many of its most beloved icons came from elsewhere—the rocket on the side of the Bitters building was rescued from AJ's Surplus in Belltown in 1991, and the **LENIN STATUE** traveled all the way from the Soviet Union. The **SOLSTICE PARADE**, renowned for its creative displays and nude cyclists, was inspired by a similar event in Santa Barbara. Even the name "Fremont" belonged first to the Nebraska hometown of founders Edmond Blewett and Luther Griffith. But for all it has taken, Fremont continues to give back. **HISTORY HOUSE** on 35th Street showcases the history and culture of other neighborhoods; the Fremont Public Association reaches out to anyone in need. Whether through art, inventions, politics, or parades, Fremont enriches the entire city.

Fremont by the Numbers

Boundaries: N 50th St; Lake Washington Ship Canal; Stone Wy N; 8th Ave NW

NSC: Lake Union/Fremont

Population: 12,387

Median age: 32.3

Median household income: $42,671

Median home sales price: $266,487

Main drags: Fremont Ave, N 36th St/Leary Wy, N 39th St

Major crimes/1,000: 39

Web sites: www.fremontseattle.com, www.ilovefremont.com, www.fremontpublic.org, www.fremont.com, www.fremontmarket.com.

Media: The North Seattle Sun, The North Seattle Herald-Outlook, The Forum

Key dates: Fremont Street Fair, weekend of the summer solstice; Oktoberfest, third weekend in Sept; Trolloween on Oct 31

Motto: "De Libertas Quirkas," Freedom to Be Peculiar

Famous resident: Stone Gossard of Pearl Jam

Farmers market: Sun year-round, more than 150 vendors sell fresh-cut flowers, antiques, arts and crafts, clothes, jewelry, and accessories along N 34th St between Phinney Wy and Evanston St

Fremont Attractions & Institutions

BUCKAROO TAVERN: Up a few blocks from the main business core, you'll find this throwback to the neighborhood's Harley days. Pull up a chair and raise a glass to the leather-clad clientele of this biker bar. 3508 Fremont Pl N, 634-3161.

DUSTY STRINGS: Need a hammered dulcimer? Enough people do to keep this staple of the neighborhood—and of the Seattle-area acoustic music scene—in business. The woodwork alone on the harps and other instruments is worth a visit. 3406 Fremont Ave N, 632-5816, www.dustystrings.com.

ESSENTIAL BAKING CO.: Fremont's artisan bakery, with appropriately quirky style. 1604 N 34th St, 545-0444, www.essentialbaking.com.

LENIN SQUARE: Named for the imposing bronze statue of Lenin—that's right, the Soviet leader—this square has a few eateries and places to lounge. Created over 10 years by Emil Venkov, the sculpture had been abandoned during the 1989 revolution in Slovakia, until the late Lewis Carpenter mortgaged his home to transport it here. The piece could be yours for $150,000, a price that would fund Fremont Arts Council projects. In the meantime, the neighborhood enjoys Lenin despite his politics—during the 2004 Fremont Fair he wore a John Lennon mask and held a cardboard guitar. At the intersection of Evanston Ave and N 35th St.

THE ROCKET: This Cold War missile is not much to look at, but its position on the side of the Bitters building is so preposterous, you know there's a story. The nearby plaque has been faded by the elements, but the story goes like this: Rescued from AJ's Surplus in Belltown in 1991, the rocket's first unsuccessful "launch" was in 1993. Then, in 1994, a real rocket scientist, Werner von Hoge, reassembled the rocket piece by piece. With working electronic features, the rocket made a five-minute flight, and then lighted permanently on the side of the Bitters building. Alas, it no longer steams and blinks at the drop of a quarter, since the coin-operated mechanism has disappeared. 602 N 34th St.

SONIC BOOM RECORDS: What makes this thriving independent music store so special is that it caters not only to a specific type of music (rock, mostly), but most of its customers even listen to the same radio station: If something is played on 90.3FM KEXP, this store has it. 3414 Fremont Ave N (with branches in Ballard & Capitol Hill), 547-BOOM, www.sonicboomrecords.com.

GONE BUT NOT FORGOTTEN
Fremont Novelties

GLAMORAMA was a store filled with surprises from glam dresses to fun gag gifts. The best part? Impromptu weddings performed under an upside-down wedding cake—and a "bride" and "groom" made from old-time viewing machines.

THE GARDEN OF EVERYDAY MIRACLES was the name given an ivy-strangled hillside, which also cradled the occasional television set, discarded doll, pinwheel—any sort of trivial part of everyday life, carefully placed to create a refreshing reminder that art can exist in even the most mundane objects. Unfortunately, it was displaced in 2002 by a new mixed-use building.

STILL LIFE IN FREMONT CAFÉ: Only a mural remains of this long-lived and well-loved café, a gathering place to experience wholesome food and intense conversation. Its reincarnation is the sleekly designed 35th Street Bistro.

THE TROLL: If the Chamber of Commerce had gotten its wish, there would be no cement troll underneath the Aurora Bridge. But art won out, and this giant hairy troll with big nostrils and a glinting eye gobbles up a very real Volkswagen (legend has it that vandals once broke into its trunk, seeking treasure). It's become, arguably, the best-known object in Fremont. N 36th St & the Aurora Bridge.

WAITING FOR THE INTERURBAN: This cast-aluminum sculpture by Richard Beyer speaks to Fremont's creativity, history, and politics all in one. The Interurban that serves the five sculpted figures was the old electric railway, and the human face on the dog is that of unofficial mayor Armen Stepanian, who disagreed with the artist and now is immortalized as a canine. Residents regularly decorate the sculpture to celebrate occasions or post political messages; the unwritten rules condemn commercial messages and condone cleaning up afterward. Groups leave the statue respectfully bare between adornments. Corner of N 34th St & Fremont Ave.

GREEN LAKE/GREENWOOD/ PHINNEY RIDGE

This former woods—now three distinct neighborhoods with few trees—began as muddy swampland studded with cedar, fir, and hemlock trunks up to 6 feet thick. Greenwood (which runs from 70th to 105th Sts) was once the boggy Woodland Cemetery, later relocated to Crown Hill to make way for the living. The Seattle-Everett Interurban Railway brought plenty of people, and by the late '20s and early '30s, Greenwood Avenue sported a "Miracle Mile" of brick-and-stone storefronts, still present today.

What did not come with the railway was proper drainage, a serious problem as late as the '70s. Early brick ramblers and Tudors now mix with bungalows and '60s split-levels in this eclectic residential area steeped in history. Whether as a nod to history or a bow to economic necessity, Greenwood is a hub for **ANTIQUES, USED BOOKSTORES, CONSIGNMENT BOUTIQUES, AND THRIFT SHOPS**. And while the area may have lost the trees honored in its name to sawmill blades, the community stays green with plenty of wild gardens and bright window boxes, benefiting from full sun.

Phinney Ridge overlaps Greenwood from 75th to 85th Streets and shares much of its character. Most residents say they feel safe there. Parker's Mill removed the thick stands of trees—a tragedy, until you drive the main drag and gasp at the Cascades on one side and the Olympics on the other. Phinney Avenue, the backbone between Ballard and Green Lake, also edges **WOODLAND PARK**, now a zoo and picnic area, formerly the luxurious estate of Guy Phinney and his wife, Nellie, who lived and died long before Greenwood gained its graves. The Phinneys' private trolley from Fremont brought future residents right to their doorstep from 1890 to 1897. Around the same time, the gold rush crowds pushed families with children outward. Schools began to appear in Phinney Ridge and Green Lake—the 1905 clapboard Allen School at 65th Street and Phinney Avenue still stands today, home of the active and earnest **PHINNEY RIDGE COMMUNITY CENTER** since 1981. (Of note: The nearby metal tower served as an air-raid siren in World War II.)

The Phinney landscape is changing as housing prices rise (from $300,000 to as much as $600,000–$700,000). Once the realm of blue-collar workers, the area started changing in the '80s and '90s. Now tensions rise and fall as plumbers and

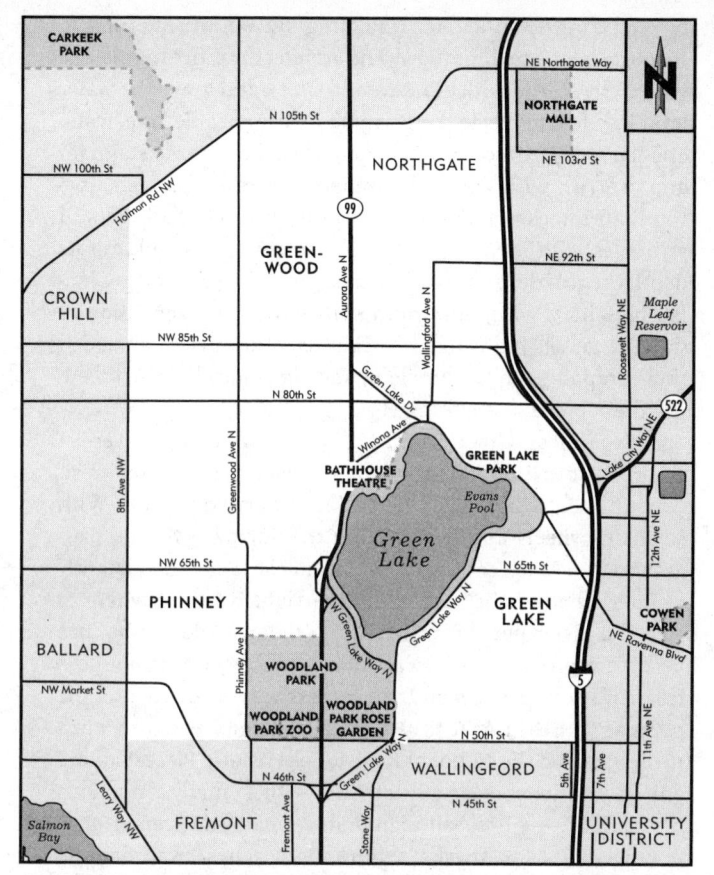

GREEN LAKE/GREENWOOD/ PHINNEY RIDGE

biotech engineers try to live next to each other. Of course, with the zoo at its core, residents must try to sleep despite howling wolves and shrieking monkeys. Dogs and cats join in the racket as well—some say there are three dogs for every hydrant in Phinney Ridge. Overall, the area is fairly laid-back, perhaps because of its central location, with easy access to both the interstate and Highway 99, as well as quick trips to surrounding neighborhoods. As one resident puts it, Phinney Ridge has a nice urban intimacy: Main Street, USA, with metropolitan sophistication.

Down the slope and on the other side of Woodland Park is the Green Lake neighborhood. By 1910 thousands had ridden the scenic trolley around Green Lake and decided to move there. So the city hired the **OLMSTED BROTHERS** (their father designed New York's Central Park) to revive the 50,000-year-old lake, carved from the same Vashon glacial ice sheet that formed Puget Sound. Accumulating silt was threatening to turn the lake into a meadow. The architectural firm's mistake was to cut off the outlet to Ravenna Creek and lower the water level by 7 feet to create the perimeter where people bike, walk, and jog today. Almost immediately, the lake became stagnant and overrun with algae and underwater milfoil forests, giving it an intense green hue. A century later Green Lake still struggles with its designers' folly. Dredging boats plumb its depths regularly, and park officials combat algae and replenish blue hues with aluminum sulfate. A large population of Canada geese, red-winged blackbirds, and ducks has added their droppings to the problem, and signs plead against feeding them bread or anything else.

Regardless, Green Lake's beauty is as alluring as ever—a sunny day can draw as many as 7,200 visitors, including President Clinton, who jogged here, Secret Service and all. With so many wheels and feet sharing the narrow 2.8-mile path around the lake, confusion is inevitable. People constantly wonder whether they are going the right way and where to step if a faster person catches up to them. Parking, too, has become a problem; the local Albertson's grocery announces frequently that any Green Lake parkers will be towed, and the popular **GREEN LAKE LIBRARY** (a Carnegie structure, circa 1910, listed on the National Register of Historic Places) allows only 15-minute parking at best. Still, with so many attractions in one place—a baseball diamond, a small craft center with rowing shells and kayaks, swimming beaches, trout fishing, a nine-hole golf course, a 1929 field house with a pool, pottery studio, gym, plus ping-pong and foosball tables, even a theater in a 1928 bathing pavilion and the occasional eagle sighting near Duck Island—it's no wonder everyone wants to come here.

Green Lake/Greenwood/Phinney Ridge by the Numbers

Boundaries: N 105th St; N 50th St; Stone Wy; 8th Ave NW
Included neighborhoods: Greenwood, Phinney Ridge, Green Lake
NSC: Greenwood
Population: 41,244
Median age: 34
Median household income: $55,608

Median home sales price: $269,905

Major crimes/1,000: 20

Web sites: www.greenwood-phinney.com, www.northseattle.com, www.phinneycenter.org, www.friendsofgreenlake.org

Media: Seattle Sun, Phinney Ridge Review, North Seattle Herald-Outlook

Main drags: 85th and Greenwood all the way to 65th and Phinney, Green Lake Wy

Key dates: Greenwood Garage Sale Day in Apr; Greenwood–Phinney ArtWalk in May; Greenwood Classic Car & Rod Show in June; Milk Carton Derby in July; Pathway of Lights, the first Sat night in Dec

Green Lake/Greenwood/Phinney Ridge Attractions & Institutions

CARKEEK PARK: Technically, this park is in the Broadview neighborhood, but it's big enough for Greenwood residents to share. With trails through the woods, plenty of picnic grounds, and swings in the trees, it makes a nice, sunny place to spend the day. But take the curious chain-link stairway to the beach, and you'll think you escaped to the ocean for the day. Waves lap at the pebbly shore as boats fill the vast horizon, and children build sand castles as trains chug by on the bluff. Breathe in the saltwater scent—just hold off down by the sewage treatment plant. 950 NW Carkeek Park Rd, www.ci.seattle.wa.us/parks.

DUCK ISLAND: You can't actually set foot on this small bird sanctuary 100 feet off the shore of Green Lake, but you can row out to it every week when the adjacent Green Lake Small Craft Center hosts the Duck Island Challenge. Created as part of a Works Progress Administration project in 1936, the manmade island of mud rises 10 feet above the lake surface. Originally called Swan Island, the reserve had to change its name when numerous attempts at breeding swans failed. 5900 W Green Lake Wy N.

GREGG'S GREENLAKE CYCLE: This Seattle institution stocks kids' bikes, all-terrain bikes, Japanese-, Italian-, and American-made racing bikes, and the city's largest collection of touring bikes. They also rent bikes, roller skates, and in-line skates—handy for hopping on the Green Lake paths just across the street. 7007 Woodlawn Ave NE (and branches in Bellevue and on Aurora), 523-1822, www.greggscycles.com.

MAE'S PHINNEY RIDGE CAFÉ: At this funky café overdecorated with cow kitsch, breakfasts are farm-sized and complex—don't miss the scrambles or the blueberry-walnut coffeecake. 6492 Phinney Ave N, 782-1222, www.maescafe.com.

RED MILL BURGERS: This original location for this institution draws crowds with its smoky house-made mayo, awesome onion rings, and real ice-cream shakes. 312 N 67th St, 783-6362. Second location at 1616 W Dravus St, Interbay, 284-6363.

74TH STREET ALEHOUSE: With its neon marquee and a polished-wood interior, this popular watering hole is an excellent place to sample exotic beers and chat in a warmly lit, nonsmoking setting. 7401 Greenwood Ave N, 784-2955. Nearby **PROST TAVERN** offers a wide variety of German beers and plenty of lively conversations—just choose one and join in. 7311 Greenwood Ave N, 706-5430.

SPUD FISH AND CHIPS: Since 1940, this family-owned fish joint has brought a beach atmosphere to Green Lake, offering hand-battered fish and hand-cut chips with all the extras—russet skins, fat, and flavor. 6860 Green Lake Wy, 524-0565.

VIEWLAND-HOFFMAN ELECTRICAL SUBSTATION: Inside a chain-link fence, 27 folk-art windmills put a new spin on discarded items, from a frying pan to spoons to an old boot. The best viewing is from the chain-link tunnel created for that purpose. The first artist-architect collaboration on a public artwork in Seattle, this installation includes comical signs, a chain-link armchair, and a color-coded illustration of the path of electricity through the substation. N 105th St & Fremont Ave.

WOODLAND PARK ZOO: Surrounded by residences, the Woodland Park Zoo feels like a backyard rather than a destination. It houses 1,100 animals from at least 280 species on 92 acres. One of the oldest, most revered zoos in the country, it was a pioneer in re-creating native habitats rather than keeping animals in cages. If the Elephant Forest, animals of the Tropical Rainforest, and the butterfly tent don't interest you, consider the 7,000 trees and 50,000 shrubs throughout the park. Playfields and picnic spots fill the lawns outside of the zoo as well (try your hand at lawn bowling), and the free Woodland Park Rose Garden offers 280 species of roses in a charming 2.5-acre garden. With blooms named Betty Boop, Cherry Parfait, and Playboy, this esteemed garden is one of just 24 All-American

Rose Selections test gardens nationwide. Between Phinney Ave & Aurora Ave N, N 50th & N 59th Sts, 684-4800, www.zoo.org.

INTERNATIONAL DISTRICT

See "Pioneer Square/International District," page 55

LAURELHURST

In the beginning, before the million-dollar homes and neighborhood names coined by real estate companies, the community now known as Laurelhurst was marshland. The Duwamish Indians hunted, fished, and camped there seasonally, carrying their dead to nearby Foster Island, now part of the Washington Park Arboretum.

The Native Americans may be gone, but the native plants have remained. Walk or bike down this section of the **BURKE-GILMAN TRAIL** with its tall leafy trees, ivy, and thick foliage, and you can almost feel the past—almost, but for the mansards of Tudor, colonial, and Craftsman mansions peeking above the leaves on one side and the cars whizzing down Sand Point Way on the other.

Laurelhurst is a neighborhood of subtle details—save the not-so-subtle views of Lake Washington and Mount Rainier. Streets bear names like Princeton Avenue and Ivanhoe Place. Children are the focus—even Paddington Pizza nods to them with its name. Hired landscapers keep gardens in shape and in bloom, the most ordinary-seeming shops carry upscale items, and art lurks in the most unexpected places. The entrance to **WINDERMERE PLACE**, the most prestigious section of Laurelhurst, boasts art deco columns of cement topped with delicately decorated square lampshades. Just off Sand Point Way at 55th Street, a dated-looking apartment complex called Windermere Vista holds a semi-hidden sculpture by the bronze master Daryl Smith, renowned for his statue of Jimi Hendrix on Broadway. Called *At Gram's*, the intricately detailed sculpture depicts a young girl leaning on the partly opened gate with her grandmother nearby.

Along with its understated taste for art, architecture, gardens, and views, this insular community has its causes, from airplane noise and traffic issues to parking troubles and anything related to children's well-being. **CHILDREN'S REGIONAL HOSPITAL AND MEDICAL CENTER**, just off Sand

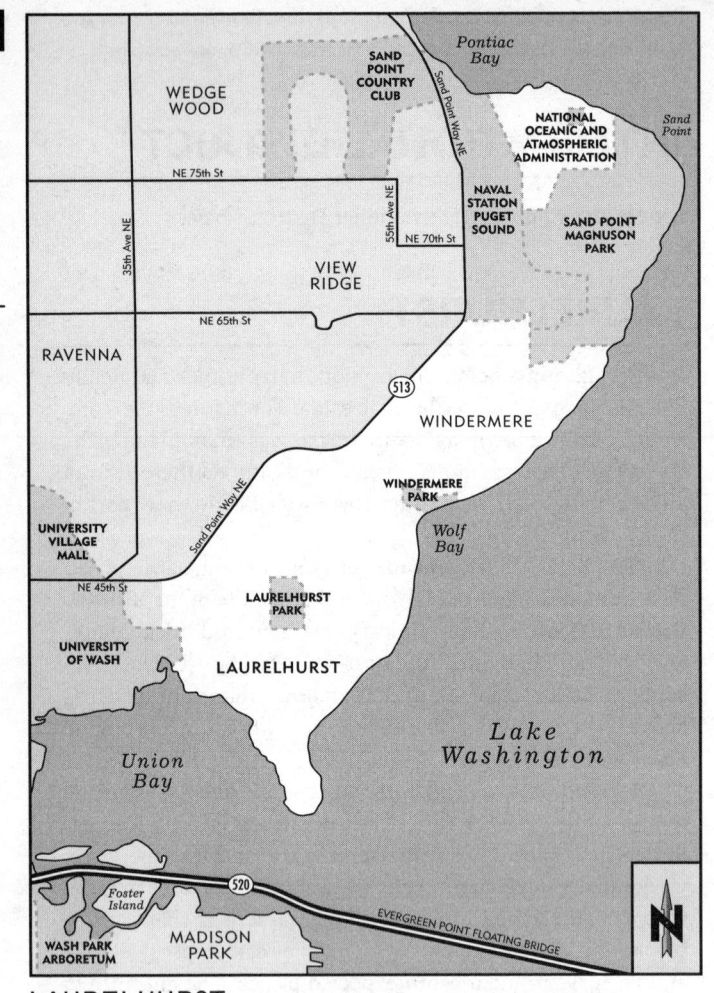

LAURELHURST

Point Way, moved here in 1956 from Queen Anne. Started by Anna Herr Clise in 1907, the hospital has an all-female board, and the grounds and interior are designed as if through children's eyes. But as progressive as Laurelhurst residents can be, they are still fairly homogeneous.

If one symbol sums up Laurelhurst, it would be the sculpture *In Memory of Parents* at Sand Point Village. Moving gears, blimps, and flying frogs—that's right, frogs with umbrellas—rise and fall as if on two Ferris wheels above a merry-go-round of sculpted animals with endearing faces. The plaque for this 1999 piece reads: "In memory of Joie and Lee Jacobi, who were simply great. One was seldom early, and one was seldom late."

Donor Derek Jacobi commissioned the piece from sculptor Ronald Petty, one of only three Washington sculptors accepted by the prestigious National Sculpture Society and known for his whimsical pieces at Wallingford Center and Fishermen's Terminal. The unsaid story here is of means—the means to commemorate parents in steel, the means to recognize artistic talent, and the means to give the community a place to reflect on the fantasies of childhood. Most of all, Petty's piece stands for Laurelhurst's means to do good things.

Laurelhurst by the Numbers

Boundaries: Sand Point Wy N; Union Bay; Lake Washington; 37th Ave NE

Included neighborhoods: Windermere

NSC: University District

Population: 7,500

Median age: 38

Median household income: $81,000

Median home sales price: $540,000

Major crimes/1,000: 10.4

Web site: www.northeastseattle.org

Media: North Seattle Herald-Outlook

Main drag: Sand Point Wy

Key dates: Salmon Bake, first Thurs in Aug; home tour in the fall; Christmas Ships Celebration at Magnuson Park

Famous residents: Cartoonist Gary Larson, Bill Gates as a child

Laurelhurst Attractions & Institutions

CITY PEOPLE'S MERCANTILE: Need a trendy gift for friend, a lightbulb for the porch, and a new garden hose? You've come to the right place! City People's merges practical needs with irresistible wants, all jumbled together in an upscale general store with hints of the old days. 5401 Sand Point Wy, 324-9510.

FIORINI SPORTS: A ski emporium and teaching institution for 57 years, this retailer also specializes in warmer-weather gear for tennis, swimming, jogging, and just being outdoors. 2686 NE 49th St, 523-9610.

KATTERMAN'S SAND POINT PHARMACY: Designer dog dishes, Chanel fragrances, stained glass lamps, canes, and walking sticks . . . this is not your typical place to fill a prescription! Have your bone density checked, but don't miss Beverly's Book Nook, a place where book fanatic Beverly has compiled good reads in a cozy space. 5400 Sand Point Wy, 524-2211.

LAURELHURST BEACH CLUB: Children love this private beachfront in the summer, and doting parents have been known to move to Laurelhurst just to indulge them. Volleyball, sailing, swimming, and picnics are just the beginning. 3638 49th Ave NE, 524-4646.

MAGNUSON PARK: This unusual park is not only giant in size—it's the second largest park in Seattle with 350 acres and a mile of shoreline—but also in scope. In addition to the usual waterfront park amenities, this one has old buildings from the Sand Point Naval Station; beloved permanent sculptures along the NOAA Art Walk, such as Doug Hollis's auditory sculpture Sound Garden; Kite Hill for flying objects; and the largest off-leash area for dogs in Seattle. Performing artists and musicians make use of the Sand Point naval hangar, with its excellent acoustics (John Cage recorded here). 7400 Sand Point Wy, 684-4946, www.ci.seattle.wa.us./parks.

SAIL SAND POINT: This nonprofit organization teaches children to sail—and adults, too. The small-boat center hosts a fleet of Hunter 140s, Optimist dinghies, Lasers, and Bytes. Midweek, the Sand Point Youth Sailing group rocks the boats as children race dinghies around buoys. 7777 62nd Ave NE, Suite 101, 525-8782, www.sailsandpoint.org.

WINDERMERE REAL ESTATE: John Jacobi established Windermere Realty in 1972, placing its headquarters in the Windermere neighborhood of Seattle (look for the gold plaque with the date). In 2001 the company went regional, with a total of 200 affiliates in the Northwest, Arizona, California, Montana, and Nevada. 5424 Sand Point Wy NE, 527-3801, www.windermere.com.

MADISON PARK

Long before there was Mercer Island, Medina, Hunts Point, or anything but trees on the other side of Lake Washington,

Madison Park was the toniest section of Seattle—a beachfront escape connected to Pioneer Square by a cable car. It still can lay claim to that distinction of affluence: Household incomes are well above the rest of the city, and the stately Victorian, Georgian, and Craftsman homes rest serenely in a quiet, leafy-green neighborhood.

The neighborhood's visible highlights are two huge green spaces. **WASHINGTON PARK ARBORETUM** is a 200-acre expanse of grassy fields and peaceful forests. The **BROADMOOR GOLF CLUB** and the **SEATTLE TENNIS CLUB**, lakeward from the arboretum, are allied organizations that are among the most exclusive in the city. You still have to pass social muster to join, and golf club memberships have sold for a price ($125,000) sufficient to buy a starter home in a small town.

The main drag, Madison Street, is lined with clothing and kitchen shops, a well-stocked corner bookstore, the beloved Red Apple Market with its impressive wine selection, a new spa and wine bar, and several hangouts that are local favorites (such as the Attic pub on Friday nights and the Madison Park Bakery on Saturday mornings). People come from around the metro area for sangria and tapas at Cactus (4220 E Madison, 324-4140), which despite an expansion still has a long wait for dinner (but it's worth it). Madison Park itself is a lovely little pocket park with a nice beach and a pleasant prospect across Lake Washington toward Mercer Island, where the mansions of more recent vintage are bigger, but not better. Perhaps best of all, Madison Park provides a handy 10-minute commute to downtown.

Madison Park by the Numbers

Boundaries: Washington Park Arboretum; Lake Washington Blvd; 24th Ave E; E Denny Wy

Included neighborhood: Broadmoor

NSC: Capitol Hill

Population: 5,000

Median age: 45

Median household income: $75,100

Median home sales price: $430,000

Major crimes/1,000: 15.7

Main drags: Madison St NE; Lake Washington Blvd

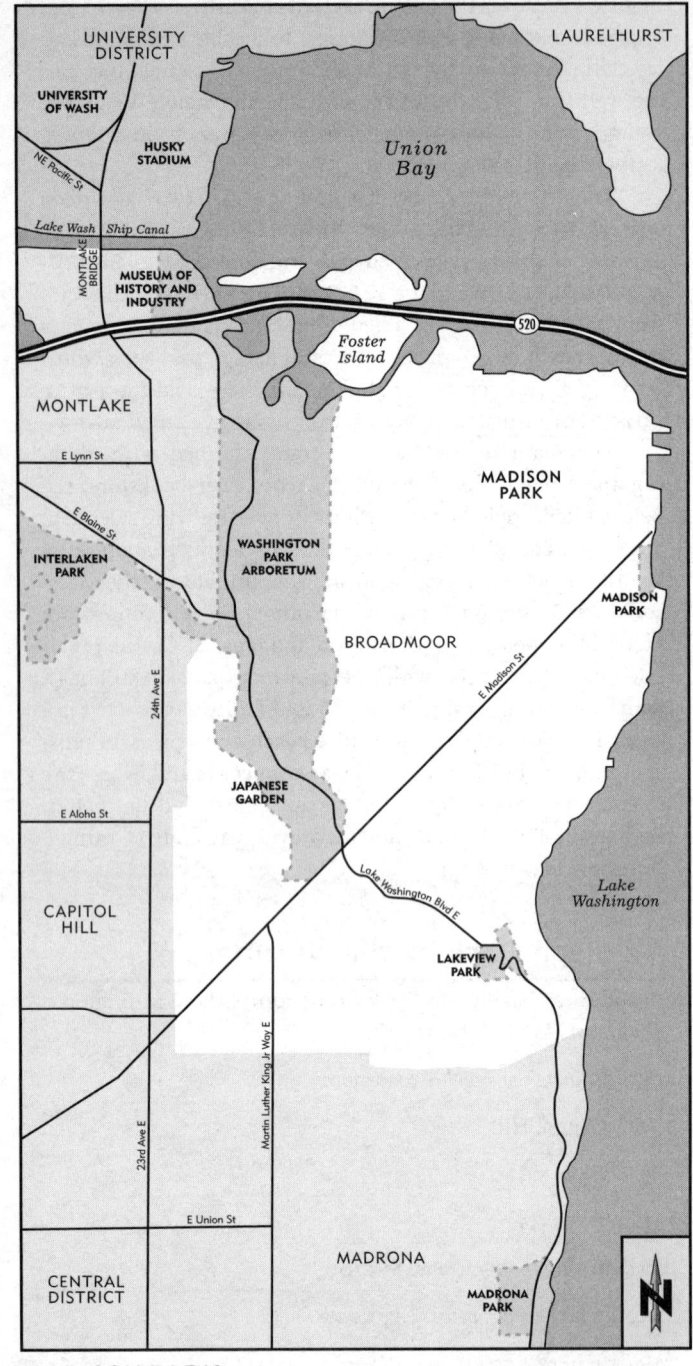

MADISON PARK

Madison Park Attractions & Institutions

CAFÉ FLORA: This isn't the godmother of vegetarian cuisine in Seattle, but it's close. When Café Flora opened in 1991, such present-day staples as its portobello sandwich (now found in brewpubs everywhere) were innovative. The atmosphere is a delightful cross between fern bar and herb garden. 2901 E Madison, 325-9100, www.flora.com.

WASHINGTON PARK ARBORETUM: Created and managed by the University of Washington, this pleasant park space is theoretically devoted to horticulture exposition, featuring most of the trees that can be grown in North America. With modest gardens along strolling paths, it's a great place for a winter walk on a mild day to experience the fragrance of winter-blooming shrubs and vines. The meditative Japanese Garden at the south end is one of the finest in the country. Lake Washington Blvd & Boyer Ave, 543-8800, www.depts.washington.edu/wpa.

MAGNOLIA

Magnolia may be the quietest neighborhood in Seattle—except for the train switches late at night. Perched atop two hills on a bluff overlooking Puget Sound, this remote community works hard to keep to itself. Since the only ways in are by bridge or Dravus Street, most people write the whole place off as hard to reach, like an island. In truth, it's easier to get to than most of traffic-clogged Seattle—unless you want easy interstate access.

As a result traffic is light, the pace is slow, and the neighborhood functions like a small town, complete with a **CENTRAL VILLAGE** of shops next to a playfield, community center, and pool. Dry cleaners, banks, the occasional spa, a wine shop, several gift boutiques, a handful of coffeehouses, and several pet stores fill most resident's needs, and the handful of pizza, pasta, and sub places feeds hungry teens after a hard day on the playfields. (There's even a Gaelic football league.)

The community has traditionally drawn conservative, wealthy professionals; landscaping trucks fill the streets during the day, as day laborers help each home hide behind pruned shrubs, flowers, terraced gardens, even palm trees. (Perfect topiaries have earned Magnolia the nickname "Hooville," after Dr. Seuss.) The namesake tree of the neighborhood was a case of misidentification. From offshore, madrona trees with their peeling bark looked like magnolias to early explorers, and the name stuck.

The axiom used to be that old-timers live in Ballard and their parents live in Magnolia—but both neighborhoods are diversifying. Senior citizens do thrive here, but so do teenagers, and judging by the number of stores that cater to babies, this dyed-in-the-wool community is embracing strollers. Rumor has it that the bluff is slowly turning Democratic as well. That would be a change for the neighborhood Ronald Reagan's son calls home.

Landslides have afflicted the neighborhood more than once, pulling million-dollar homes down the hillside. In fact, the Magnolia Bridge has been damaged twice, despite its 4,000 feet of reinforced concrete—once by a 1997 landslide and again by the 2001 earthquake. Before the bridge arose in 1930, there were eight wooden trestles connecting Magnolia to the mainland. Construction of a new bridge is scheduled for 2007.

Magnolia's **LANDMARK LIBRARY** embodies the laid-back isolationist character of the whole neighborhood: Built like a house with open beams, shake siding, and great landscaping, the library is easy to miss as you drive by. But inside, there's a whole community of intellectuals.

Magnolia by the Numbers

Boundaries:	Lake Washington Ship Canal; Puget Sound; 15th Ave W
NSC:	Queen Anne/Magnolia
Population:	21,579
Median age:	39.48
Median household income:	$58,288
Median home sales price:	$428,000
Major crimes/1,000:	13.7
Web sites:	www.magnoliachamber.org, www.discoveryparkfriends.org
Media:	The Magnolia News
Main drags:	W McGraw St, 34th Ave, Dravus St, 31st, Thorndyke/22nd Ave
Key dates:	Bike the Bluff in July, Summerfest in Aug
Famous resident:	Ron Reagan Jr.
Farmers market:	Sat in summer, 10am–2pm in Magnolia Village

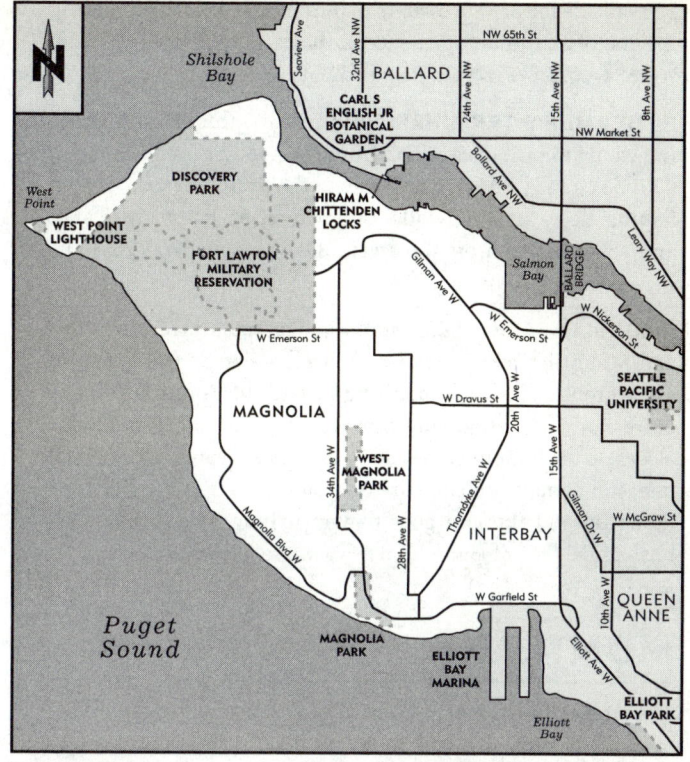

MAGNOLIA

Magnolia Attractions & Institutions

DISCOVERY PARK: Formerly the site of Fort Lawton Army base, Discovery Park is the largest of Seattle's parks—at more than 500 acres—and it is also one of the most popular. Its windswept hills and clifftops offer broad views of Puget Sound, and trails lead down through the trees to a sandy beach. The visitors center schedules walks and nature workshops, as well as birding tours. The Daybreak Star Indian Cultural Center showcases modern art by Indians, and herons, falcons, eagles, foxes, and beavers feel comfortable out in the open here. Named for Captain George Vancouver's boat, the HMS *Discovery*, it seems fitting that this park would edge so much open water. The West Point Lighthouse, built in 1881, is the oldest lighthouse in the Puget Sound area. The park will soon gain another 23 acres as the Capehart Navy housing complex is demolished and the land preserved as open space. In part of the same deal between the city, the navy, and an outside developer, the 100-year-old Georgian revival officers quarters on the bluff, however, will be available for private owners to purchase—officially marking the end of all military presence in the park. 3801 W Government Wy, 684-4075, www.ci.seattle.wa.us/parks.

FISHERMEN'S TERMINAL: Built in 1911, this is an intriguing wharf to visit or overlook from the popular breakfast spot, Chinook's (283-4665). It is home to the Seattle-based Alaskan fishing fleet, and individual skippers often hang out a sign and sell fresh fish off the stern. 3919 18th Ave W, 728-3005, www.portseattle.org/seaport.

MAGNOLIA PARK: There's nothing like watching cruise ships and Mount Rainier in your peripheral vision as you swing in a playground, your feet pointing toward the Sound below the bluff. For a view that isn't moving, stand on the picnic table closest to the bottom of the hill by the fence—you'll know which one; someone is probably there already. Watch as the cityscape lights up and the sun goes down, turning Mount Rainier a hazy pink. 1461 Magnolia Blvd E, www.ci.seattle.wa.us/parks.

MONTLAKE

The small community of Montlake lives in a fairy-tale world—one surrounded by reality on all sides. With cozy streets bordered by the dripping forests of Interlaken Park (alas, second-growth) and several bodies of water, it seems idyllic. The predominant houses look like English cottages straight from Hansel and Gretel, including styles such as colonial Revival, builder's Tudor, Prairie, Mission, Northwest wood, and New England shingle. But outside those cozy doors, there's parking trouble, car prowlers, rowdy Huskies games, and the whoosh of cars on the 520 Bridge. Clogged thoroughfares greet residents who try to leave the nest for supplies: a necessity, since Montlake lacks its own supermarket, post office, shopping district—even its own churches. The only house of worship here is **ST. DEMETRIOS GREEK ORTHODOX CHURCH** (2100 Boyer Ave E, 325-4347, www.saintdemetrios.com), and most of its parishioners commute.

The amenities that do exist serve visitors more than residents, which adds to the area's eclectic charm. The stately 1919 **SEATTLE YACHT CLUB** with its mock lighthouse sprawls along the shore of Portage Bay. On the other side of the Montlake Bridge stands the unusual **MUSEUM OF HISTORY AND INDUSTRY (MOHAI)**, which will unfortunately leave its historic building for a swank downtown site in 2007. And, complete with a marble statue of mother and child in front, the Boyer Children's Clinic specializes in treating children with cerebral palsy.

Montlake used to be an enclave of college professors, until housing prices shot up and software workers moved in. The proximity to 520 paired with delightful historic homes drew so many Eastside workers that Montlake has been called Microsoft West. Professors watched in disbelief as their once-affordable neighborhood surpassed their salaries—in the early 2000s a $785,000 home sold in three days.

Beleaguered by the same 520 span that brought new neighbors, Montlake does have a soft spot for its other bridges. The **MONTLAKE BRIDGE**, circa 1925, is pleasantly Gothic in style, with flanking octagonal towers and pyramid steeples. The small arches in the metal railings allude to the pointed windows of Suzzallo Library. On the tower roof there is a row of stained glass windows, and let's not forget the 33 lights. (In 1983 all the lights were restored to working order for the first time since the '60s.) An even earlier bridge, circa 1912, arches over 26th Avenue as part of Interlaken Boulevard. But the 520 Bridge defines the area most. Expansion plans constantly land in the community's lap, garnering a perpetual battle cry as residents try to protect their yards and homes from any more invaders.

ARCHITECTURE is the neighborhood's crowning glory. When people talk about the housing stock here, they mention specific addresses, styles, and names of designers. The most revered name is Paul Thiry, the Seattle World's Fair architect who built MOHAI and also the Greek Orthodox church.

In addition to its homes and bridges, Montlake has one other claim to fame: Montlake Mousse. Entrepreneur Jack Burg and his wife, folk singer Ginny Reilly, whipped it up in their Montlake kitchen the year the Huskies won the national championship, 1991. Now in five flavors, the mousse graces market shelves all over town. Once again, Montlake gives its best to everyone else.

Montlake by the Numbers

Boundaries: Montlake Cut/520 Bridge over Portage Bay; Interlaken Park; Washington Park Arboretum; Lake Union

NSC: Capitol Hill

Population: 3,800

Median age: 38.7

Median household income: $101,319

Median home sales price: $372,000

Major crimes/1,000: 87

Web site: montlake.net/montlake.asp

Media: Montlake Flyer

Main drag: 24th Ave E between E Lynn and E McGraw Sts

Key dates: Opening Day of boating season, first Sat in May; St. Demetrios Greek Orthodox Church festival in the fall

Montlake Attractions & Institutions

INTERLAKEN PARK: This surprising swath of green at the edge of Montlake is so hilly and forested that it seems remote from the city, damp and dripping like a rain forest. Built in 1905, this 60-acre site also contains a 25-mile system of bicycle paths. 11th Ave to Lake Washington Blvd, www.ci.seattle.wa.us/parks.

MUSEUM OF HISTORY AND INDUSTRY (MOHAI): Open since 1952, this unusual museum attracts more than 60,000 visitors a year. It contains the largest private heritage collection in the state and presents engaging exhibits on everything from the Pacific Northwest Ballet to working conditions in salmon canneries. 2700 24th Ave E (to be relocated in 2007 to 800 Pike St), 324-1126, www.seattlehistory.org.

SEATTLE YACHT CLUB & MONTLAKE PARK: Once slated to be a casino, this handsome colonial Revival–style structure is the impetus for Montlake's biggest celebration: Opening Day of sailing season. The Montlake tradition began on May Day in 1920, as part of the formal dedication of the clubhouse. Now it includes crew and sailboat races and a parade, heralded by a cannon blast and the opening of the Montlake Bridge. Some say the only event like it is the annual parade of commercial vessels in Venice. 1807 E Hamlin St, 325-1000, www.seattleyachtclub.org.

WASHINGTON PARK ARBORETUM WATERFRONT TRAIL: Prepare for a surreal nature experience. Step off the shore onto a pontoon boardwalk and bounce across the water to Marsh Island, where a soggy trail leads you past marsh plants, birds, flowers, and eye-level views of Union Bay and Lake

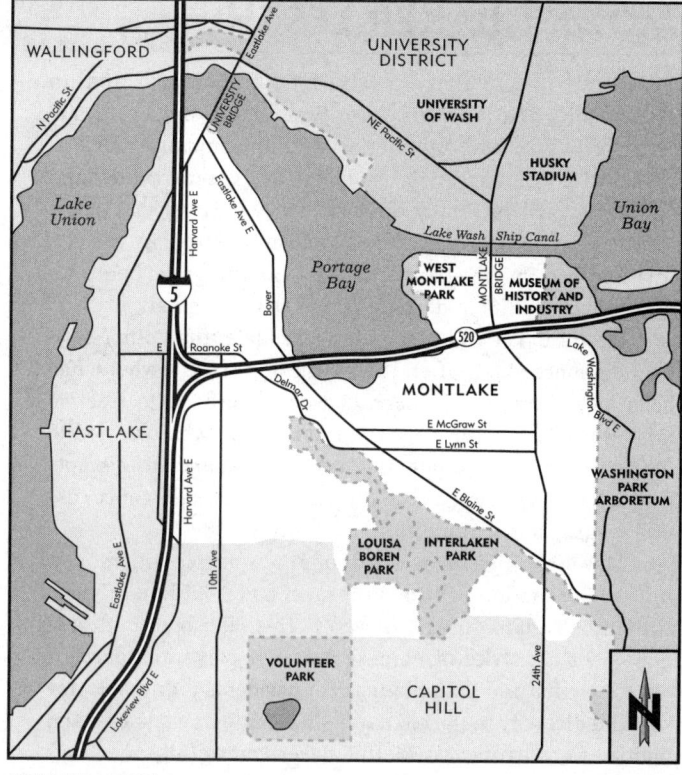

MONTLAKE

Washington. Another floating pathway connects Marsh Island to Foster Island, once an Indian burial ground where coffins hung from the trees. If you keep following it to the right, you'll step across a puny stream into the Washington Park Arboretum. Trail starts behind MOHAI. 543-8800, depts.washington.edu/wpa.

WATERFRONT ACTIVITIES CENTER (WAC): This hub of vessel clubs and water play offers canoes and rowboats for as low as $7.50 an hour—unless you are affiliated with the university, and then it's even less. Plenty of waterways, lily pads, water birds, and arboretum shore await both those who are adept with paddles and those who are not. 3900 Montlake Blvd & Pacific Ave NE, 543-9433, depts.washington.edu/ima/.

MOUNT BAKER/LESCHI

These two neighborhoods, named for a mountain and an Indian chief and linked by Lake Washington Boulevard, are an eclectic mix: well-kept homes and unkempt fixer-uppers, hillside bungalows and lakeside estates, green ravines and sprawling gardens, many with water views. Here, east meets south and west, as blacks, whites, and every ethnicity you can imagine live in the shadow of the I-90 Bridge. (There's an unusual view of its underpinnings at Day Street Park.)

Mount Baker and Leschi developed later than other Seattle neighborhoods—after the prime timber elsewhere had been logged and the Indians had been confined to reservations. (Leschi is named for the Indian chief who objected to the terms of the Nisqually treaty. He was hanged as a scapegoat for the resulting Battle of Seattle. In 2004 a court case was seeking to redeem him.)

Like other hills in town, this one drew people with money. But unlike the top echelons of, say, Capitol Hill and Queen Anne, the well-to-do who moved to this lakeshore built less homogeneous styles of homes, and their parks and gardens were more natural than manicured. Residents didn't welcome cultural diversity in the old days—that came much later—and politics were banned at Mount Baker community meetings until the '60s.

Slightly more refined than Leschi, Mount Baker boasts the oldest continuously active community club in the country. "Active" can be demonstrated by the wellspring of support when the 1924 Romanesque-style Mount Baker Park Presbyterian Church lost its 90-foot bell tower in the Nisqually Quake. "Save the Tower!" was the rallying cry, and donations came forth from some 100 people, some who didn't even belong to the church—or any church. It wasn't enough money for the repairs, but the message of support was as clear as a bell.

Earthquake damage is passé in these parts, where landslides, glaciers, tsunamis, and quakes created the gullies, ravines, and steep banks of its varied terrain. Since these features are hard to build on and around, Leschi and Mount Baker enjoy quite a few **UNUSUAL PARKS**, plenty of terraced gardens, and lots of bridges over ravines. Jacob Umlauff, a Johnny Appleseed of the Pacific Northwest, planted **GIANT SEQUOIAS** that still stand today. The community has inherited his mantle and continues to plant, their most stunning achievement being **BRADNER GARDENS**.

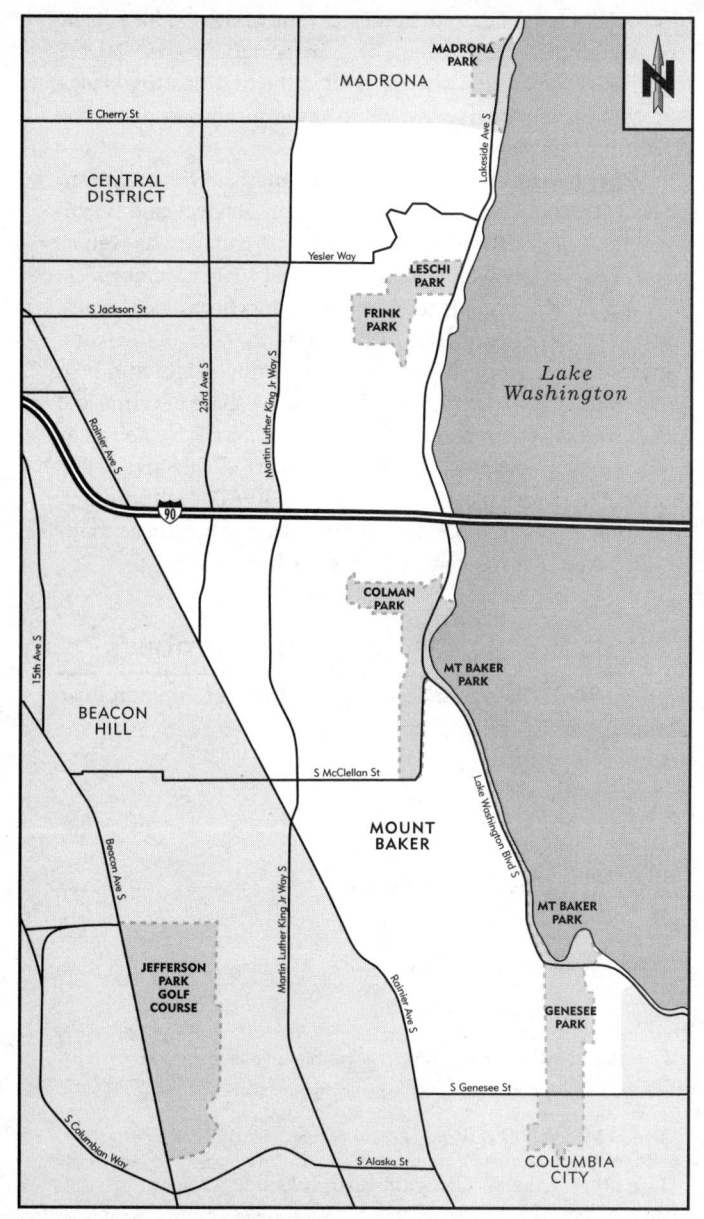

MOUNT BAKER/LESCHI

On a clear day views across the lake show the Cascades and Mount Rainier, but the 10,778-foot Mount Baker—a misshapen lump of snow on the horizon that Indians called "white, shining, steep mountain"—attracts the most attention. Sadly, the namesake views are becoming endangered as people snap up and add on to lakeside homes, recently released for sale by the Washington Department of Transportation. (The WDOT purchased the homes when it created the first floating bridge across the lake.) Even the Grayline bus tours have stopped, due to diminished views.

The houses themselves create another view entirely. **ARCHITECTURE** ranges from Georgian Revival and Victorian to Old English Tudor and California cottages, as well as diverse styles from Ellsworth Storey and Victor Steinbrueck. Wealthy neighborhoods tend to have monochromatic themes, such as stone or brick. Here, it's all about the color of the paint. Homes are purple, teal, red, gold—anything bright and bold with contrasting trim. The area has had its share of crime and destitution over the years, so the bright colors raise spirits as well as housing values. The southern part of this area is the home of the hydro races that conclude **SEAFAIR** each summer. If you like rowdy crowds, this is your place. If not, do as many residents do that weekend—head elsewhere.

Mount Baker/Leschi by the Numbers

Boundaries: E Cherry St; S Genesee St; Lake Washington Blvd; Rainier Ave S

NSC: Central District

Population: 8,100

Median age: 39

Median household income: $53,000

Median home sales price: $328,000

Major crimes/1,000: 7.8

Web sites: www.mountbaker.org, www.rainiervalley.org, www.therainiervalley.com, www.rainiervalleyhistory.com

Media: Mount Baker View, Leschi News

Main drags: Lake Washington Blvd, Lakeside Ave

Mount Baker/Leschi Attractions & Institutions

BRADNER GARDENS: Once slated for 18 market-rate homes, this garden oasis offers a P-patch (see Chapter 13, "Mother Nature," page 326), wrought-iron creations, an Aermotor windmill, seven ornamental theme gardens, a children's A-Z garden, basketball courts, mosaic benches, and 50 varieties of ornamental street trees—all in just 1.6 acres. 29th Ave S & S Grand St, 684-4075, www.ci.seattle.wa.us/parks.

FRINK PARK: This dense ravine offers 1.3 miles of pleasant trails, chock-full of thick foliage, giant maple trees, pools, benches, bridges, and a 7-foot waterfall. 398 Lake Washington Blvd S, www.ci.seattle.wa.us/parks.

LESCHI PARK: Well-manicured and sprawling, this hillside green has Victorian-style grounds and 200-foot sequoia trees and tulip trees. 201 Lakeside Ave S, www.ci.seattle.wa.us./parks.

MOUNT BAKER COMMUNITY CLUBHOUSE: The lodge-style meetinghouse, built in 1915 by renowned architect Ellsworth Storey, began as a dance hall and is on the National Register of Historic Places. 2811 Mount Rainier Dr S, 722-7209, www.mountbaker.org.

MOUNT BAKER PARK & COLMAN PARK: One sits at water's edge, the other slopes gently down to the bathing beach. Both are sweepingly beautiful with their lawns, beaches, and views. Don't miss the stone lantern in Mount Baker Park, a gift from Japan. Mount Baker Park, 2521 Lake Park Dr S; Colman Park, 1800 Lake Washington Blvd S; www.ci.seattle.wa.us./parks.

PHINNEY RIDGE

See "Green Lake/Greenwood/Phinney Ridge," page 34

PIONEER SQUARE/ INTERNATIONAL DISTRICT

Erupting toilets, underground "cities," the home of Skid Row—Pioneer Square's history is colorful. Clangorous street markets, Chinese herbal medicines, the scents of exotic spices, and the music of a dozen languages—the International District's present is equally colorful. Taken together, the two neighborhoods are not only popular visitor attractions (for Seattleites as well as folks from elsewhere), but they comprise a good part of the unique character of Seattle as a whole.

Pioneer Square is the "original" Seattle; this is where the first settlers wound up when they tired of tempest-tossed Alki

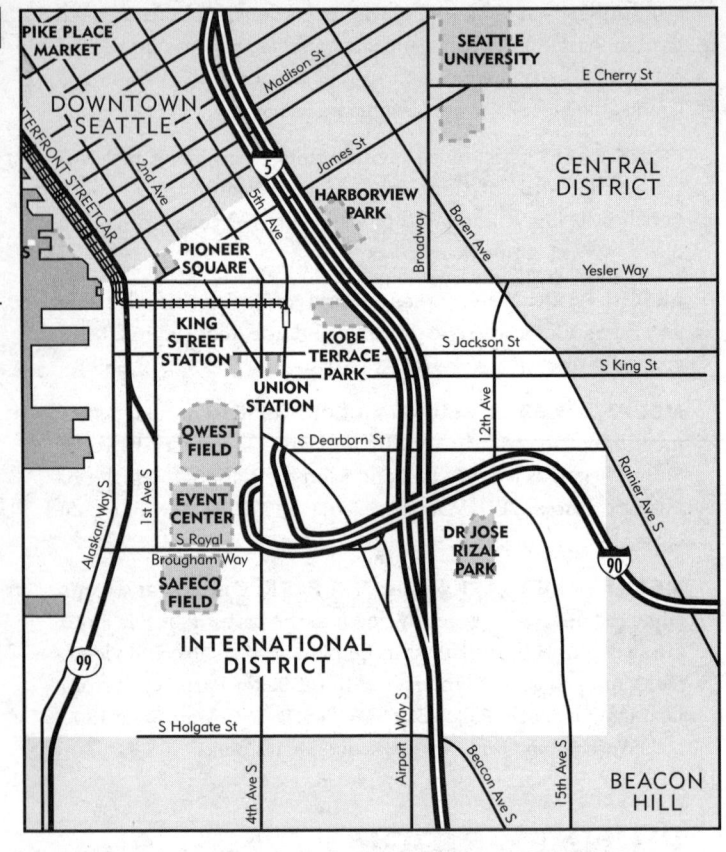

PIONEER SQUARE/INTERNATIONAL DISTRICT

Point. It is **ONE OF THE LARGEST AND BEST HISTORIC DISTRICTS** in the United States, with many buildings that date back before 1900. One of the reasons for such widespread preservation is that after the great fire of 1889, which burned Seattle nearly to the ground, building codes required brick and stone structures that have proved long-lived and sturdy, so much so that virtually all survived the Nisqually Quake of 1997.

Later, problems with sewage backups during storm tides led the city to raise itself an entire story, making the original street level a subterranean home for brothels, opium dens, and other ne'er-do-well enterprises. The **UNDERGROUND TOUR** (see "Attractions & Institutions," below) describes and explains it all.

The International District was "Chinatown" until it dawned on everyone that the refugee migrations of the '70s and '80s had given the area a multicultural Asian flair.

Japanese, Vietnamese, Cambodian, Lao, and other allied peoples all lend their culture to the area, but Mandarin and Cantonese still prevail. The sights, smells, sounds, and aromas that a walk through the district yields are memorable. So is the reminder that our country still draws immigrants for whom this is the "Golden Mountain."

Today Pioneer Square has two distinct identities. Daytimes and early weeknight evenings it is a pleasant **HISTORIC DISTRICT** of small cafés, shops, and art galleries—its First Thursday (of each month) **ART WALKS**, when galleries remain open until 9pm, are popular events. Strolling the neighborhood on a sunny afternoon is a European-style treat, with light dappling the plazas and café patrons sitting outside. On Friday and Saturday nights, and after Mariners and Seahawks games, the area assumes another identity entirely: rowdy **NIGHTCLUB DISTRICT**. Bar-goers crowd the sidewalks (particularly on First Avenue); bouncers try to keep order; and at some times the police presence is necessarily strong. The riots of the Mardi Gras period in the late '90s embarrassed Seattle nationally, and the city vowed to crack down.

Pioneer Square/International District (ID) by the Numbers

Boundaries: Cherry St; Royal Brougham Wy; I-5; Elliott Bay

NSC: Downtown

Population: 5,000

Median age: 42, Pioneer Square; 46, ID

Median household income: $30,000, Pioneer Square; $15,165 International District

Median home sales price: $260,000

Major crimes/1,000: 27.5

Web sites: www.pioneersquare.org, www.seattlechinatown.com

Main drags: Yesler Wy, 1st Ave, S Jackson St, S King St

Key date: Chinese New Year, late Jan/early Feb

Pioneer Square/International District (ID) Attractions & Institutions

BUD'S JAZZ RECORDS: When the new owner took over several years ago, he carried on Bud's name but began incorporating visual art into the repertoire of traditional/Dixieland jazz, blues, Latin, big band, and local jazz. Expect to see work by emerging Seattle artists featured on the walls; the store also hosts a gallery opening on the first Thursday of every month. 102 S Jackson St, 628-0445.

CENTRAL TAVERN: Seattle's self-proclaimed oldest saloon dates to 1892 and is a popular spot for lunch (decent pub food) and weekend-night entertainment. Squeeze yourself in with several hundred other fun-seekers after a Mariners or Seahawks game, and you'll be taking part in a quarter-century of tradition. 207 1st Ave, 622-0209.

ELLIOTT BAY BOOK COMPANY: Seattle's homegrown independent bookseller is not only the best place for Pacific Northwest books and numerous other titles, but the downstairs café/coffee shop is a peaceful refuge for literary and political conversation. The schedule of readings and author appearances is unsurpassed. 101 S Main St, 624-6600, www.elliottbaybook.com.

FILSON: Long before Columbia sportswear was a glint in some grandma's eye, Filson was procuring outdoor gear and clothing for Northwesterners—no-nonsense stuff such as oilcloth coats that stand up to any weather. South of Pioneer Square at 1555 4th Ave S, 622-3147, www.filson.com.

FIRST THURSDAY ART WALK: See Chapter 8, "That's Entertainment," page 237.

GRAND CENTRAL BAKERY: Back when most of the world was still relying on soft white bread, Grand Central rolled out dark, dense whole-grain loaves. That's still their forte. 214 1st, 622-3644, www.grandcentralbaking.com.

OCCIDENTAL PARK: This is the actual Pioneer Square for which the district is named. Its tree-shaded cobblestone expanse draws surprisingly few crowds; a resident population of transients is one deterrent. The modern monument at the south end honors four firefighters who died in a horrible late '90s arson. The plaza continues southward, across S Main, past a fine gathering of art galleries. Between S Main St and S Washington at Occidental.

QWEST FIELD (SEAHAWKS STADIUM): See Chapter 9, "Get Out & Play," page 255

SAFECO FIELD: See Chapter 9, "Get out & Play," page 253

UNDERGROUND TOUR: Local historian/entrepreneur/impresario Bill Speidel not only created this engaging tour, he started an industry—a half-dozen other cities now sport their own such. *They* don't have stories about spouting toilets, though (this tide-caused sanitary problem is what forced the whole young city to hoist itself upward one story). Tours wend their way beneath Pioneer Square, starting at Doc Maynard's Tavern. Reservations are imperative during visitor season. 608 1st Ave, 682-4646, www.undergroundtour.com.

UWAJIMAYA VILLAGE: Even if you don't feel an urgent need for durian, live tilapia, or bitter melon, the Northwest's most complete Asian grocery is a colorful, savory place to visit. More than a grocery store, the village features Asian gifts and a large collection of Asian-language books and periodicals. There's also free validated parking, a blessing in one of the most parking-challenged areas in the whole city. Its success has spawned stores in Bellevue and Beaverton, Oregon; this is the original. 600 5th Ave S, 624-6248, www.uwajimaya.com.

WING LUKE ASIAN MUSEUM: On top of the choice collection of Asian art and artifacts here, representing 10 ethnic groups, is a sobering depiction of Camp Harmony, the prison camp in which Seattle-area Japanese were held during World War II. 407 7th Ave S, 623-5124, www.wingluke.org.

QUEEN ANNE

Queen Anne Hill is like a basketball player in high heels: pretty intimidating. Actually, the hill is 456 feet high—only 12 feet taller than Capitol Hill, but those added inches and an 18 percent grade make it a killer for clutches and knees alike.

That formidable grade saved the area from being milled, like so many other hills and ridges were. It also made Queen Anne a desirable haven for the wealthy, who wanted a place away from the noisy, smelly harbor and all of its burgeoning industry in the 1890s. High-up breezes and the best views in the city inspired Thomas Mercer to name the hill "Eden." (Southern Queen Anne Hill has more views per square inch than anywhere else in Seattle.) Today Queen Anne is still known for its wealthy residents, but the millionaires share the hill with quite a few lower-income workers.

Eden was slow to grow, again because of that grade. Transportation became necessary, and as other areas of the city started building trolley tracks, the solution arose: Build deep tunnels under the hill and set up a series of weights and counterbalances underneath the trolley tracks to make the hill mountable. The idea worked—the tunnels are still under the asphalt today, even though the trolley is long gone. The steepest path up the hill, Queen Anne Avenue N, still answers to the nickname "the Counterbalance," although some say that only applies to the place at the top where the trolley turned around.

With access to those lovely views, residents came running to Eden. They built majestic homes, mostly in the Victorian style, which led the Reverend Daniel Bagley to nickname the area "Queen Anne Town" in jest. The name stuck, although the hill has also been called Galer Hill, after Robert E. Galer, a WWII Marine fighter pilot who earned a Medal of Honor, and Temperance Hill, because so many of its denizens were teetotalers. When broadcasting came into vogue, the hill's height attracted radio towers, a surreal blight of blinking lights at night. Today the towers still blink, but few of those Victorian homes still stand.

Noise is a serious problem for Queen Anne these days; the population skyrocketed in the 1990s (as it did in the 1890s), and both commercial cores—at the top of the hill and at the bottom—changed drastically. The **HILLTOP** became even more upper-scale with plenty of neighborhood restaurants, spas, and home-furnishing boutiques. The **UPTOWN DISTRICT** at the base of the hill, which always lagged behind its loftier counterpart, transformed from a comfortable array of blue-collar bars, barbers, and nightclubs to a thriving district of restaurants catering to the opera and theater crowd. Condo buildings popped up between old brick apartment buildings, and suddenly parking got worse, driving got frantic, and criminal activity appeared. The path to I-5 on Mercer Street has become a teeming mass of frustrated vehicles—some 20,000 clog the street every day. With two museums, three playhouses, one opera house, the old World's Fair site, an eclectic performing arts space, and two sports arenas in the space of a few blocks, noise and traffic from graduations, festivals, performances, and rowdy sports fans have plagued Lower Queen Anne for years.

There are still respites from the human hubbub, however. Queen Anne has plenty of unusual parks, each with their own

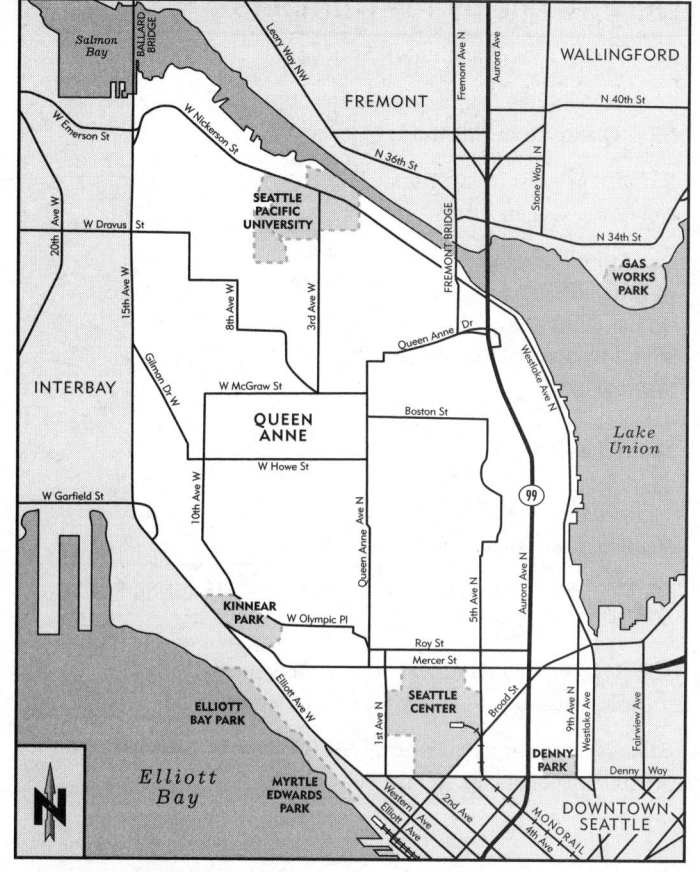

QUEEN ANNE

charms. **KERRY PARK** is the most tourist-friendly, located halfway up the **HILLCLIMB** (Queen Anne Avenue at Highland). It offers a stunningly peaceful overview of Mount Rainier, the skyline, the Space Needle, Puget Sound, and the ferries, all close enough to each other to fill a camera viewfinder. At sunset, tripods line the wall overlooking this view, and no one says a word as dozens of shutters click. Farther along Highland, a string of parks makes a charming promenade between the expansive view of the water and a row of well-tended mansions. Parsons Gardens is the only one with gates and fences, which adds to its feel of a private garden. For those who seek exercise with their views, the hill offers 100 different staircases embedded in its sides, each with different personalities, greenery, graffiti, and architecture.

Queen Anne by the Numbers

Boundaries: Lake Washington Ship Canal; Denny Wy; Lake Union; 15th Ave W

NSC: Queen Anne/Magnolia

Included neighborhoods: Ross, Uptown, the Hillclimb, Upper and Lower Queen Anne

Population: 34,050

Median age: 33.3

Median household income: $50,703

Median home sales price: $413,034

Major crimes/1,000: 29

Web sites: www.qahistory.org, www.qachamber.org

Media: Queen Anne News

Main drags: Queen Anne Ave N, 5th Ave N, Mercer St, Roy St, 10th and Howe Sts

Key dates: Folk Life Festival in May; Bite of Seattle in the summer; Bumbershoot during Labor Day weekend

Famous residents: Former governor Gary Locke, Seattle Symphony conductor Gerard Schwartz

Queen Anne Attractions & Institutions

A&J MEATS: Once, Queen Anne teemed with butchers, tailors, and candlestick makers. Now A&J Meats is the only remnant left of that old-world society. In fact, it's one of the few neighborhood butchers left in Seattle. 2401 Queen Anne Ave N, 284-3885.

CANLIS: One of Seattle's oldest, most renowned, best, and most upscale restaurants, Canlis hides its grandeur within a '70s-style façade perched at the edge of the Aurora Bridge overlooking Lake Union. The food is consistently excellent, and service here is the best in town. 2576 Aurora Ave N, 283-3313, www.canlis.com.

THE INTERNATIONAL FOUNTAIN AT SEATTLE CENTER: Many Queen Anne residents call Seattle Center their backyard park—and why not? There's plenty of people-watching on any given day, with children squealing as they run into and out of the gigantic fountain, synchronized to music and unpredictable in its spurt patterns. Grassy lawns are perfect for Frisbee,

To Market, to Market

Man cannot live by bread alone. Whether it's fresh West Coast seafood you seek, or locally grown produce, or regional wine, or even ethnic comestibles that don't show up anywhere in Betty Crocker, Seattle's coastal location and multicultural character ensure you can find almost anything humanly edible here—even lutefisk and sea cucumbers.

Though some homegrown chains have been absorbed by larger entities elsewhere (QFC was bought by Kroger, as was Oregon-based Fred Meyer), the Seattle area grocery market remains unusually competitive.

LARRY'S MARKETS: Like Metropolitan, Larry's used redevelopment at the foot of Queen Anne to reconfigure its market niche toward the upscale market (100 Mercer St, 213-0778, www.larrysmarkets.com). Also in North Seattle, Tukwila, Bellevue, Kirkland, and Redmond.

METROPOLITAN MARKETS (formerly Thriftway): One of the early pioneers at balancing quality and value; the Queen Anne store is nonpareil, pioneering culinary events such as its annual Peach-O-Rama (1908 Queen Anne Ave N, 284-2530, www.metropolitan-market.com). Also in the Admiral District, Sand Point, and Tacoma's Proctor District.

PUGET CONSUMERS' CO-OP (PCC): Long before the commercial chains paid any attention to fresh, local, natural foods, PCC made it the focus of its stores. They're also great places for herbal medicines and supplements (600 N 34th, Fremont, 632-6811, www.pccnaturalmarkets.com). It's a co-op, go ahead and join. Also in West Seattle, Green Lake, Seward Park, View Ridge, Issaquah, and Kirkland.

TOWN & COUNTRY MARKETS: Both Ballard Market (1400 NW 56th St, 783-7922) and Greenwood Market (8500 3rd Ave NW, 782-1610) offer extensive selections of fresh regional produce, wine, and natural foods. Also on Bainbridge Island; www.townandcountrymarkets.com.

Hacky Sack, and drum circles, and if you get hungry, restaurants are right inside the Seattle Center. 684-7200, www.seattlecenter.com.

KERRY PARK VIEWPOINT: Set amid the grand old-money mansions near the top of the hill, this park offers a smashing

> **GONE BUT NOT FORGOTTEN**
>
> ## The Blob
>
> This landmark was not especially beloved, but it certainly was a fixture in Lower Queen Anne, causing plenty of debate. Shaped like a melting, gaseous marshmallow, the structure was built as an authentic Greek restaurant. After the restaurant had its day, a few nightclubs tried the spot, but complaints about noise and fights in the streets shut most of them down. It sat vacant for years, until the Blob came down in the '90s to make room for a condo complex. It was the most controversial structure Seattle had until Paul Allen built the Experience Music Project—a much more elaborate, expensive, and internationally recognized Blob.

outlook (especially at sunrise) over downtown, Elliott Bay, the Space Needle, and on a clear day, Mount Rainier. Never fails to impress out-of-town visitors. 3rd Ave W & W Highland Dr.

MECCA CAFÉ: Do you smoke? You will if you enter this retro-punk haven with checkerboard floors, a jukebox, myriad shades of black, and attitude galore. Smoking is encouraged, so suck it up; the amusement factor is worth it, if the greasy-spoon fare isn't. What do you expect from Seattle's oldest family-run restaurant, circa 1929? 526 Queen Anne Ave N, 285-9728.

MOUNT PLEASANT CEMETERY: This is the place for unusual graves. Among the pioneers are members of the Chinese Chong Wa society, a Jewish congregation, the Industrial Workers of the World, and victims of the Wellington train disaster. 700 W Raye St, 282-1270.

RAINIER BEACH/ RAINIER VALLEY

Rainier Beach, with its bright sun, terraced hillsides, and manicured lawns overlooking Lake Washington, seems more California than Seattle—until you see Mount Rainier and the Cascades looming on the horizon. That partly explains its former moniker, Atlantic City, still attached to the bathhouse at **PRITCHARD ISLAND BEACH**. The adjacent Rainier Valley, a narrow area between Rainier Avenue S and Martin Luther King Jr. Way S, brims with **CULTURAL AND GEOGRAPHIC DIVERSITY** but is often lumped in with its surrounding neighborhoods, collectively considered to be the Rainier Valley. The many ethnicities that live in Rainier Valley proper have such a strong identity it's ironic that their neighborhood name would be so muddled.

Religion drives this community, whether Catholic, Methodist, Presbyterian, Macedonian Orthodox, or Greater Victorious. Even though Rainier Beach residents speak 60 different languages, they all understand one collective goal: keeping their community together. This has been a hard task in the once-crime-ridden valley, but determination seems to have won out. A program called **BUS WATCH** (in which businesses adopt and care for bus shelters) has decreased idle loitering, and some neighbors have been known to porch-sit for each other. Neighbors Against Drugs work tirelessly, and the ingenious **BIKE WORKS PROGRAM** approached the problem from the inside out, targeting the angst of unskilled youth and teaching them to repair bicycles. Bike Works allows children to earn their own bikes while honing their skills, giving them both upward and outward mobility. **BEAUTIFICATION**, too, has helped deter vandals, from the saplings growing in front of people's yards courtesy of the Seattle Street Trees program to paint-out parties for tackling graffiti.

Once called "garlic gulch," Rainier Valley was the closest Seattle ever came to having a **LITTLE ITALY**. Remo Borracchini's Bakery and Oberto meats remain as testaments to the old days, when Italians thronged to the area as coal miners and sold produce from their large vegetable gardens. Other ethnicities came and went because of the wars. World War II took away the Japanese Americans and drew tens of thousands of workers for the shipyards and Boeing—more workers than there were homes. Even with temporary housing projects, overcrowding continued after the war, and crime came with it. In 1975 the end of the Vietnam War brought Indochinese refugees.

One war-housing project deteriorated so much that it was known as "New Jack City," after the 1991 movie about Harlem. Public and private agencies spent $22 million to recast the units as affordable housing, and crime dramatically decreased from 1993 to 1997.

African Americans who had come during the war found themselves in the Rainier Valley afterward, thanks to discriminatory restrictions on housing and insurance. Affordable housing brought Latinos into the mix later, making Rainier Avenue S a stew pot of Italian bakeries, Vietnamese *pho* kitchens, and authentic taco stands. The Jewish population near Be'er Sheva Park in Rainier Beach, a large population of Southeast Asians, and the occasional Eritrean round out this small world just inside the southern city limits.

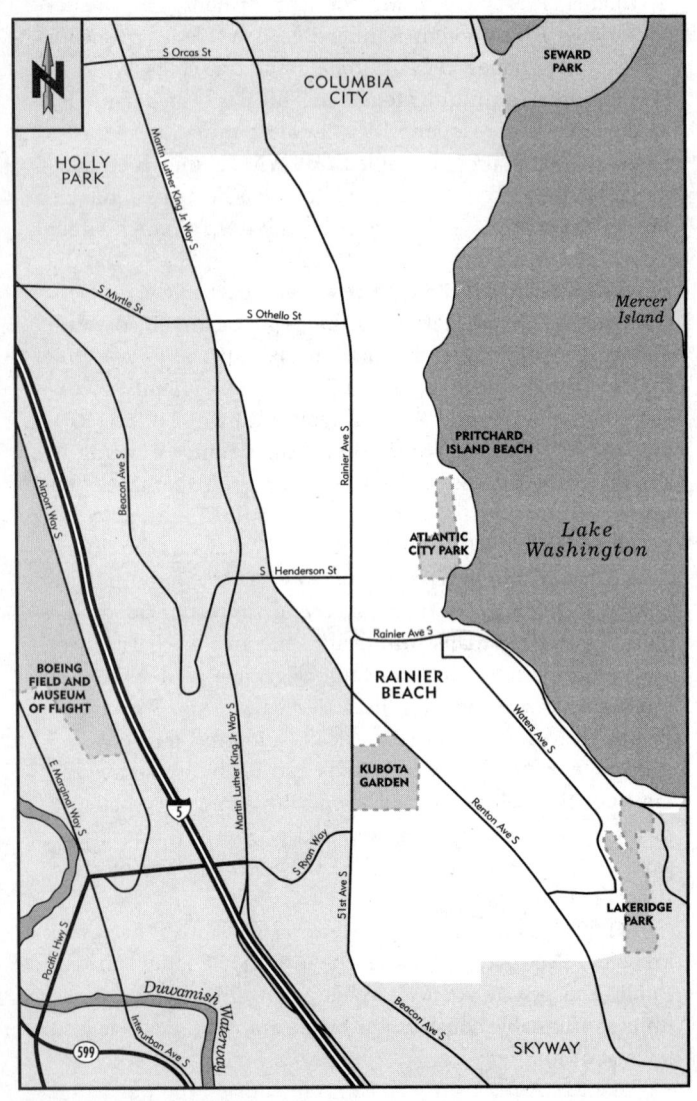

RAINIER BEACH/RAINIER VALLEY

Rainier Beach/Rainier Valley by the Numbers

Boundaries: S Graham St; city limits; Lake Washington; Martin Luther King Jr. Wy S

Included neighborhoods: Rainier Beach, Rainier Valley proper, Rainier View, Dunlap, Brighton

NSC: Southeast

Population: 10,195

Median age: 34

Median household income: $30,789

Median home sales price: $200,000

Major crimes/1,000: 66

Web sites: www.therainiervalley.com, www.rainiervalley.org, www.therainiervalley.com, www.rainiervalleyhistory.com

Media: South Seattle Star

Main drags: Rainier Ave S, Waters Ave

Famous resident: Famed Seattle baseball player Fred Hutchinson

Rainier Beach/Rainier Valley Attractions & Institutions

BE'ER SHEVA PARK: Named for Seattle's sister city in Israel, this park sits across from Rainier Beach High School and offers unparalleled views across the water. 55th Ave S & S Cloverdale St, www.ci.seattle.wa.us/parks.

DEAD HORSE CANYON: Down a side pathway off Rainier Ave S is a curving road over a hilly ravine where a pioneer's horse once died. Look for the port-a-potty on the left, and there is the faded sign for Dead Horse Canyon, a refreshing hike through a canopy of thick, 50-foot trees. You can see Taylor Creek trickling at the bottom of the steep banks, but the trees, shade, and birdsongs are what transport you away from the city. Rainier Ave S/68th St to Cornell.

KUBOTA GARDENS: This landmark created by Fujitaro Kubota has more personality than most Japanese gardens. Perhaps it's the hilly setting or all of the carefully chosen and displayed rocks—or maybe it's the slight scruffiness of a loved park rather than a manicured showpiece. Regardless, the place earned Kubota honor from the Japanese government: the Fifth Class Order of the Sacred Treasure, for building respect for Japanese gardening in his new country. 5500 Renton Ave S, 684-4584, www.kubota.org.

MUTUAL FISH: Huge selection and peerless quality mark this seafood merchant with an Asian bent. 2335 Rainier Ave S, 322-4368, www.mutualfish.com.

PRITCHARD ISLAND BEACH: With no boat ramp, this is a pleasant swimming hole with high and low diving boards bordered by large cottonwood trees. 8400 55th Ave S, 386-1925, www.ci.seattle.wa.us/parks.

REMO BORRACCHINI'S BAKERY: A local institution serving up homemade cookies, biscotti, éclairs, and cakes since Mario and Maria Borracchini arrived in Seattle from Florence in 1922. 2307 Rainier Ave S, 325-1550.

RAVENNA

The Ravenna neighborhood should claim the Lorax as its mascot; Dr. Seuss's impassioned tree-hugger would understand the plight of this still-green neighborhood that long ago lost all of its giant trees—some the size of sequoias! Despite the felling of these giants, the streets and parks are still sprinkled with hundreds of **OLD-GROWTH MAPLES AND OAKS**, making it seem like a Cascades forest rather than residential lawns and driveways. Not many neighborhoods can claim as many leaves, which makes Ravenna the perfect in-city destination in the fall.

No matter what time of year, it's a low-key, upscale community of folks who want to make the world better. The yen for improvement starts at home with yards and bathrooms, which people are constantly renovating. Housing stock varies from red-brick Tudors and bungalows to Cape Cod and Craftsman styles. Some say this is the best part of Seattle for raising children—a point well taken by the many toy stores and child-friendly retailers. Bryant, the most high-end community within Ravenna, boasts one of the largest elementary schools in Seattle. Proud volunteers invest plenty of time in making Bryant Elementary a positive, supportive learning

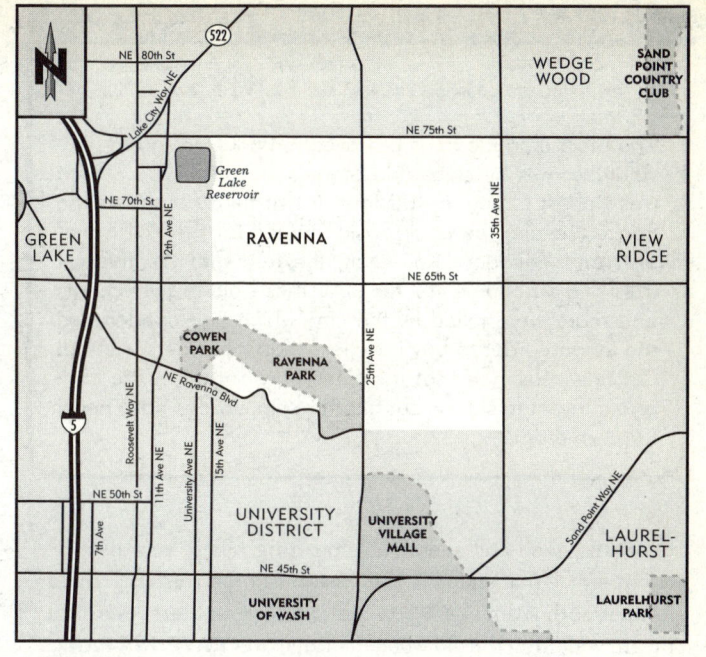

RAVENNA

environment, with a top-notch after-school program heavy on the humanities.

Next to its trees, the community loves its sidewalks best. This is a **WALKER'S REFUGE**—which suits the large Ashkenazi Jewish population fine, since many honor the tradition of walking to synagogue on the Sabbath. The name Ravenna has its own Europe heritage—it honors a seaside town in Italy, not the ravine in Ravenna Park.

With good incomes but no pretense, citizens of Ravenna practice **ECO-ACTIVISM** fervently, often saving themselves and the rest of the city from ill. For instance, in 1948 the City Engineer wanted to turn Ravenna Creek into sewers, but the community fought for their beloved Ravenna Park, still one of Seattle's most pleasant spots. In the '60s residents helped stop a proposed freeway that would have slashed several neighborhoods into fragments. And in 1983 gypsy moths invaded, and in their wake, the pesticide carbaryl. Ravenna residents protested until the State Department of Agriculture used an alternative spray, which was safer but also successful.

Ravenna activists don't always win. In the early '90s vegetarians lost when they protested the new meat department at the Puget Consumers' Co-op, known for its commitment

GONE BUT NOT FORGOTTEN

Toppled Giants

The most gigantic trees of Ravenna Park were given individual names by clubs and organizations in 1908. There was Robert E. Lee, a 400-foot fir two-thirds as tall as the Space Needle; the Paderewski, named for the Polish pianist; and Theodore Roosevelt, the tree with the thickest trunk—a whopping 44 feet! All these old-growth giants and more were felled by the city, which had condemned the land in order to buy it for less than its owners wanted. Officials reasoned that the trees were rotten at the core and a threat to safety, but heartbroken citizens have never forgiven them.

---

to organic food and sustainable farming. There was also the compromise that ended in their favor: In 1970 the city wanted to turn 20th Avenue NE into a major thoroughfare, even if it meant widening the old wooden bridge over **RAVENNA PARK**. When the community complained, the city countered that it would close the bridge to traffic and make 20th a dead end. Surprisingly, the community accepted this solution—and now the footbridge offers a unique view of the uniform tops of maples, evergreens, and redwoods planted in the ravine below. The creek appears in the winter, when the trees thin out, but in the summer the view is a green thatch of leaves.

Today neighborhood causes center on UW students parking en masse in Ravenna and taking the Burke-Gilman Trail to campus, and mounting traffic that could cause an expansion of the Montlake Bridge. Not if Ravenna residents can help it!

Ravenna by the Numbers

Boundaries: NE 75th St; University Village and Calvary Cemetery; 35th Ave NE; 15th Ave NE

Included neighborhoods: Bryant (between NE 65th and 75th Sts)

NSC: University District

Population: 18,747

Median age: 41.5

Median household income: $61,000

Median home sales price: $335,000

Major crimes/1,000: 44.7

Web sites: www.northeastseattle.com, www.seattlepress.com

Media: North Seattle Herald-Outlook

Main drags: Ravenna Blvd, NE 65th

Key date: In Dec, residents display an incredible—and free—array of holiday lights and decorations along "Candy Cane Lane" (officially Park Road NE, just off Ravenna Blvd at 21st Ave NE), a gift to all passersby; www.candycanelane.org.

Ravenna Attractions & Institutions

COOK'S WORLD: This is the comforting world of Nancy Brecher, French-trained chef and character in her own right. Her shop is filled with colorful, sculptural, and practical items for preparing meals, but her classes in the back are the real delight. Students in particular hang on every word—and bite—in her "Basics of Cooking" courses, and no one should miss out on the knife skills. 2900 NE Blakeley St, 528-8192, www.cooksworld.net.

QUEEN MARY TEAROOM: On a cozy side street, this stiff-upper-lip tearoom is a charming place to pause with a friend over scones and a fragrant teapot. A scattering of tea-related gifts adds to the décor. 2912 NE 55th St, 527-2770, queenmarytearoom.com.

RAVENNA PARK: One of Seattle's leafiest parks and the only one with a ravine, this 55-acre passel of woodland and paths was topographically averse to development. William Beck, a Kentucky minister, fenced the ravine, imported exotic plants, and created a park with picnic grounds. He decided the gigantic trees deserved names and offered naming rights to organizations such as the United Daughters of the Confederacy (see sidebar, page 70). Beck also tried to sell the park to the city, but rather than pay his $150,000 price tag, officials condemned the land and paid $144,920. The Seattle Parks Board cited rot and toppled many of the giants, leaving stumps as tall as 20 feet. The park today is a green haven in the middle of the city—and getting greener. A $6 million project is restoring Ravenna Creek and coaxing back the spawning salmon. 5520 Ravenna Ave NE, www.ci.seattle.wa.us/parks.

UNIVERSITY VILLAGE: It started as a small outdoor smattering of stores but has grown gargantuan while managing to keep its village atmosphere—complete with covered passages from store to store, and benches and sculptures arranged as if on a village square. You'll find plenty of upscale franchises, small boutiques, restaurants, and Seattle's first official Apple computer store. Montlake Blvd, north past Husky Stadium, then left on 25th Ave NE, 523-0622, www.uvillage.com.

SEWARD PARK/ COLUMBIA CITY

A peninsula or a village green; old architecture or old-growth forests; drastic changes or the status quo. Besides sharing a few boundaries, Seward Park and Columbia City residents lead fairly different lives. Both, however, garner protected status, albeit for different reasons.

Seward Park is a small neighborhood sprinkled around a gigantic park—one of the most spectacular in Seattle, with its 1,000-year-old cedar forests, fairy-tale structures built by the Works Progress Association in the 1930s, and a peninsular path outlined by the lapping waters of Lake Washington. Asians, African Americans, and Europeans all share the park's swimming beach, picnic tables, and clay pottery studio. The oldest synagogue in the city is nearby, and 90 percent of Seattle's Orthodox Jews live close to it and two others. **SPRAWLING ESTATES** from days gone by tuck themselves into the meandering streets, and all seems fairly quiet in this Shangri-la, where 80 percent own their homes, be they 1950s ramblers or mansions.

Eagles nest in the park, which inspired the Audubon Society to build an **ENVIRONMENTAL CENTER** on site. Poison oak grows there, too—a good thing, actually, because it saved the trees from being milled at the turn of the last century. Once named Bailey Peninsula and Graham Peninsula after previous owners, the city named it Seward after the secretary of state who bought Alaska. The nature of its geography, a peninsula off the southeastern edge of Seattle, gives it a private feel, like a protected cove.

Columbia City, protected as one of Seattle's seven landmark districts, has seen its share of booms and busts. It began as a city in its own right, milled for its perfect timber and nurtured by the railroad. In 1907 Seattle annexed it, but the small-town feel of its village square (flanked by a colonial

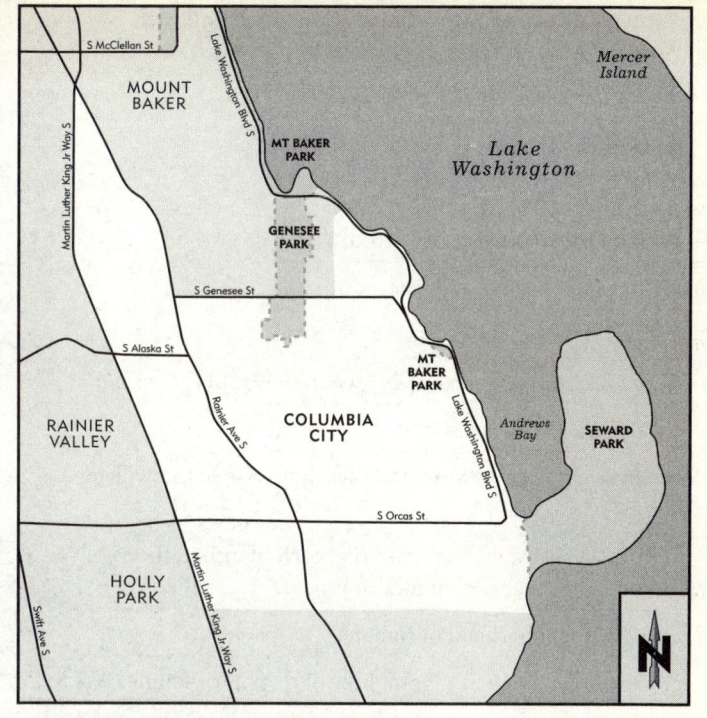

SEWARD PARK/COLUMBIA CITY

Revival **CARNEGIE LIBRARY** and the neo-Palladian **RAINIER VALLEY CULTURAL CENTER**) never left. Unfortunately, hard times fell on the neighborhood as people and businesses fled during the '70s. By 1995 the die-hard residents who love their community refused to accept defeat, preferring to grow their own grassroots renewal. It's an incredible story, different from the similar upturns of the University and the Central Districts, because it was not fueled by business ventures and gentrification so much as a cultural reawakening and a passion for place. Businesses did return—Magic Johnson invested in a Starbucks here, for starters—but even so, they retained local charm as places to gather and feel the pulse of the community rather than places to spend money on the latest and greatest.

Seward Park/Columbia City by the Numbers

Boundaries: S Genesee St; S Willow St; 48th Ave S; Martin Luther King Jr. Wy S

Included neighborhoods: Hillman City, Brighton Beach, Somerville, Sunnyside, Lakewood

NSC: Southeast

Population: 17,996

Median age: 34.3

Median household income: $26,014

Median home sales price: $280,000

Major crimes/1,000: 51

Web sites: www.sewardpark.net, www.columbiacitybeatwalk.org

Media: South Seattle Star

Main drags: Lake Washington Blvd; 47th Ave S; the "village green"

Key dates: Beatwalk, the first Fri of each month in the summer; annual garden tour in June

Motto: "Neighborhood of Nations"

Farmers market: Wed 3–7pm, June–Oct, at 4801 Rainier Ave S

Seward Park/Columbia City Attractions & Institutions

COLUMBIA CITY CINEMA: Housed in a 1921 Ark Masonic Lodge, this fairly new movie theater fills a void: Columbia City endured 20 years without a cinema of its own. 4816 Rainier Ave S, 721-3156, www.columbiacitycinema.org.

LOTTIE MOTT'S: This independent coffeehouse prides itself on its gourmet coffee, tea, and syrups, and operates as a gathering place and community forum. Live entertainment includes old-time fiddling, poetry readings, and whatever else residents want to try. There's enough personality here for the whole neighborhood! 4900 Rainier Ave S, 725-8199, www.lottiemotts.com.

SEWARD PARK: Like an inside-out Green Lake, this park has paths outlined by Lake Washington, brick buildings, Seattle's oldest and largest old-growth trees, and a ton of birds. To truly experience the place, join one of the regular tours on the second Friday of every month. 5902 Lake Washington Blvd, www.ci.seattle.wa.us/parks.

TUTTA BELLA NEAPOLITAN PIZZERIA: Mention Columbia City and people's eyes light up as they talk about Tutta Bella, the first family pizza parlor in this community. And what pizza it is—for pizza to bear the name Neapolitan, it has to pass stringent ingredient and cooking guidelines administered by the Associazione Vera Pizza Napoletana. Only the 114th restaurant in the world to earn the honor, Tutta Bella passes with flying colors. 4918 Rainier Ave S, 721-3501.

UNIVERSITY DISTRICT

With thousands of students constantly moving in and out of the neighborhood, the University District is a community of constant resurgence. One of the oldest neighborhoods in town, it has the youngest inhabitants—even the homeless are in their teens. The campus hogs two-thirds of the neighborhood, but professors and other professionals put down roots on stately 17th Street, made grand by the Olmsted brothers's horse-chestnut trees. Musicians long past the student stage rent houses near campus, their practice sessions a part of the neighborhood hum. This type of diversity—the temporary against the set-in-stone, bohemian versus Gothic, the eager-to-learn challenging the set-in-their-ways—keeps this neighborhood alive.

In 1895 the university moved from downtown to what was then called Brooklyn (a nod to the New York City borough), seeking space for expansion. Few sought residence so far out, since transportation was limited to boat or train. The university streetcar helped, and in 1907 the Wallingford trolley made 45th Street a major east-west thoroughfare. But the real surge to neighborhood status came with the Alaska-Yukon-Pacific Exposition, a fair that brought 4 million visitors in 1909. Just one year later the community had grown fivefold.

Growth continued well into the '30s, but the Great Depression bankrupted several developments, both old and new. Student enrollment dropped to 5,000, then swung back up to 15,000 after World War II, thanks in part to the GI Bill. Traffic came with the returning veterans, and a second shopping district, University Village, threatened the shops on the Ave in 1956. With the slogan "A Department Store Eight Blocks Long" as their battle cry, these businesses defiantly stayed prosperous through 1960.

The beat generation was alive and well here, staging teach-ins and marches, plotting in coffeehouses, and tuning out with psychedelics and grass—the first marijuana bust

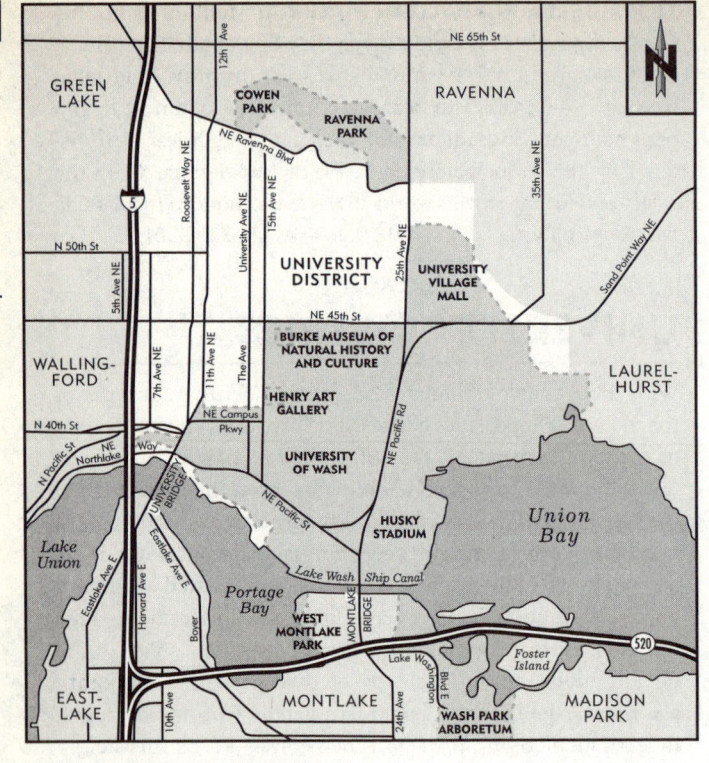

UNIVERSITY DISTRICT

occurred in 1965. When the *University Herald* disapproved of the "District Beatniks," local artists promised in mockery the Second International Bohemian Festival—which, like the first one, never occurred. (Today's **UNIVERSITY STREET FAIR** may be its embodiment with dreadlocks, tie-dye, and drumming.)

Impassioned times led to the Ave's own "Hippie Riot of 1969," a two-night rampage of destruction that resulted, surprisingly, in conciliatory talks. The next year, the Kent State killings caused more protests and three days of rioting that devastated many U-District businesses. In addition, a drug culture had taken root, a habit the neighborhood still cannot shake.

Tensions calmed after the Vietnam War, but the Ave was left both at peace and in pieces. By the turn of the millennium it seemed as if the Ave were shutting down, with its many rows of vacant windows. Instead, it got a new lease (or two). The city invested $9 million in new sidewalks and roads, business is booming again, and exotic teahouses now fill in the gaps between the old staples. A new **AUDIO WALKING TOUR** (pick up tapes and maps at the U-District NSC, 684-7542; UW visitor center, 543-0198; or the U-District library, 684-4063) points out the rich history and culture of this ever-changing neighborhood, such as Richard Beyer's intriguing sculpture at University Playfield (NE 50th and 9th Ave NE), *Sasquatch Pushing Over a House*. A new energy is edging out the old.

Sadly, the spirit of vandalism is slower to leave. In 2004 vandals hacked the steel arm of a beloved sculpture in Peace Park—one that receives constant attention for its humanitarian message. *Sadako and the Thousand Cranes* by Daryl Smith depicts Sadako Sasaki, a real Japanese girl who died at 12 from the effects of the Hiroshima bomb. Her dying wish was to make 1,000 cranes to symbolize peace, but she didn't finish in time. Her classmates took over and brought the 1,000 cranes to her gravesite. Today the sculpture receives a constant supply of crane strings—sometimes so thick you can't even see Sadako. Now *that* is a sign of a loyal neighborhood.

University District by the Numbers

Boundaries: Ravenna Blvd; Portage Bay; 25th Ave NE; I-5

Included neighborhood: Brooklyn

NSC: University District

Population: 22,909

Median age: 24

Median household income: $30,898

Median home sales price: $296,341

Major crimes/1,000: 38

Web site: www.udistrictchamber.org

Media: North Seattle Herald-Outlook, University Herald, The Daily

Main drags: The Ave (University Wy), 15th Ave NE, 45th St

Key date: University Street Fair in May

Farmers market: Every Sat, from spring through autumn, more than 40 vendors bring bread, flowers, and produce to the University Heights Community Center, NE 50th St and University Wy NE

Famous resident: Bruce Lee

University District Attractions & Institutions

BLUE MOON TAVERN: When the U-District was a dry campus, this bar—exactly one mile off campus—was a pretty popular place. Among its many admirers were literati such as Tom Robbins, Theodore Roethke, Dylan Thomas, Allen Ginsburg, and Calvin Trillin. Today the neon-heavy façade has another barfly: a miniature version of the sculpture *Hammering Man*, raising and lowering his beer instead of a hammer. 712 NE 45th St, 545-9775.

BURKE MUSEUM OF NATURAL HISTORY: The tall totems out front start the story of Pacific cultural and anthropological history, and the interior of this natural history museum continues with the biology, paleontology, and geology. From the 2.75 million fossils to the 2,200 amphibian and reptile specimens, this museum packs a lot between its walls. NE 45th St & 17th Ave NE, 543-7907, www.washington.edu/burkemuseum.

GARGOYLES: In keeping with the Gothic theme of the UW campus, this store offers more stone statues and icons of strange-faced creatures than you can count. 4550 University Wy NE, 632-4940.

HENRY ART GALLERY: Don't let that word "gallery" fool you; this is a museum with caliber, one that's not afraid to stretch your idea of art (most of the time for the better). Don't miss the permanent installation of Robert Turrell's *SkySpace*, an intriguing piece that plays with light, space, and acoustics. 15th Ave NE & NE 41st St, 543-2280, www.henryart.org.

SCARECROW VIDEO: The largest video store on the West Coast, this film-lover's haven has 70,000 titles, including rare and obscure films not available elsewhere. 5030 Roosevelt Wy NE, 524-8554, www.scarecrow.com.

UNIVERSITY OF WASHINGTON CAMPUS: The grand design of this Gothic-style campus makes for a pleasant stroll, student or not. The cherry trees lining the main quad burst into bloom in early spring, turning the campus lawn into a romantic picnic area. Nearby, the Suzzallo Library offers a "cathedral of books" behind its gables. Don't miss the Tudor-style reading room, with a ceiling soaring 73 feet and 36-foot-high stained glass windows offering diffused light. Outside, follow a small unofficial path to the left of the fountain into a clearing known as Sylvan Theater. Bruce Lee once practiced kung fu here as a student. The four Ionic pillars are the remains of the original downtown campus. Backtrack and look for a footpath before Stevens Way—it leads to the pharmacy school's medicinal herb garden, filled with 600 plants and operational since 1911. 543-2100, www.washington.edu.

UNIVERSITY VILLAGE: A neighborhood mall that has upgraded to a regional draw. Key stores and restaurants: Fran's Chocolates, Blue C Sushi, Barnes and Noble, Crate and Barrel, Restoration Hardware, among many others. NE 45th St & 25th Ave NE, 523-0622, www.uvillage.com.

WALLINGFORD

Wallingford is a neighborhood of houses—3,335 of them. Condos and apartment complexes flirt with the edges, along Stone Way and the shore of Lake Union, but the interior is all cozy bungalows from the 1920s and earlier. Some house businesses rather than families—a row of houses on NE 45th Street includes two restaurants, side-by-side thrift shops, and a frame store. Wallingford's first library, in 1948, was in the donated home of local Samaritan Alice Wilmot Dennis.

With home ownership comes pride, and this neighborhood is brimming with it. Gardens and yards are well tended and every street is charming—fixer-uppers are rare. Who would guess in today's utopian Wallingford that a cranberry marsh preceded the historic Craftsmans that once housed industrial, blue-collar workers? In the early 1900s soil and air suffered pollution from the nearby gasification plant, as well as from asphalt, ammonia, and tar companies. Of course, the first residents would never have dreamed that their main polluter and employer, the **GAS WORKS**, would become a beloved park, complete with a hill for kite flying and boat views, a sculptural sundial, and a play area near brightly painted machinery. Thank landscape architect Richard Haag for that—his 1970 design around the old rusty Gas Works towers has won international design awards.

Perhaps because of the university influence, Wallingford residents tend to be liberal, educated, and curious. You won't find bookstore chains here, but **NICHE BOOKSTORES** are diverse and plentiful. For travel books there's Wide World Books and Maps; for nautical themes there's Sea Ocean Books on Stone Way, next door to The Seattle Book Center and across

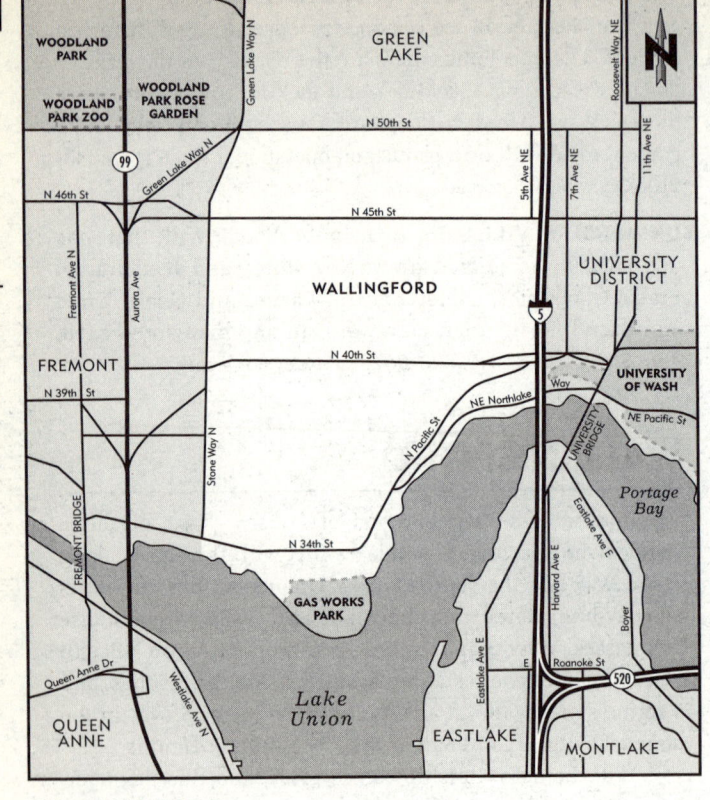

WALLINGFORD

the street from the Episcopal Bookstore. One of only two all-poetry bookstores in the country, Open Books, is on 45th, as is Vandewater Books, specializing in used tomes. Inside the **WALLINGFORD CENTER**, Second Story Books consistently chooses great titles and arranges them enticingly.

Everyone walks here—everything they could possibly need is on 45th or within 10 blocks of home, with plenty of pleasant landscaping, leaded panes, coved ceilings, and dormer windows as decoration along the way. All told, according to the *Seattle P-I*, there are 1,600 businesses in Wallingford, plus 1,600 more operated from home.

As content as these mostly white, affluent homeowners are, they have trouble with boundaries. Being so central, the neighborhood has watched its limbs atrophy as the rest of the city has grown. The Aurora Bridge marks the edge of Fremont, leaving a no-man's land between the Troll and Wallingford. The in-betweeners consider themselves part of Fremont, but ruffled Wallingford residents call it Freford or Wallymont.

Wallingford by the Numbers

Boundaries: N 55th St and McKinley Place N; Lake Union; I-5; Stone Wy N

Included neighborhoods: Edgewater, Latona, and the meandering streets near N 55th and Meridian aka "Tangle Town"

NSC: Lake Union/Fremont

Population: 17,487

Median age: 32.6

Median household income: $56,165

Median home sales price: $307,061

Major crimes/1,000: 22

Web sites: www.wallingfordcenter.com, www.wallingford.org

Media: Seattle Sun, University Herald, North Seattle Herald-Outlook

Main drags: Stone Wy, NE 45th St between Stone Wy and the Ave, Northlake Wy

Key dates: Seafair Wallingford Kiddies Parade in June, Fourth of July celebration at Gas Works Park, Wallingford Wurst Festival in Sept, Pumpkin Push race in the fall

Famous resident: Dave Matthews

Wallingford Attractions & Institutions

DICK'S DRIVE-IN: With more than 50 years under its belt, this beloved local burger chain is thriving—even in vegetarian, hippie Wallingford—when national burger empires are crumbling. The burgers are still cheap, still good, and still served in authentic diner style. Plus, the chain is known for its competitive pay and college scholarship plans for employees. 111 NE 45th St, 632-5125, www.ddir.com.

THE EROTIC BAKERY: Perched on 45th near the University District, this Wallingford institution is the place to go for stag and stag-ette parties—or just to embarrass your grandmother with penis-shaped pasta. Peek past the dizzying array of X-rated party favors into the refrigerated cases, and you'll see startling confections, anatomically accurate beyond belief. 2323 N 45th St, 545-6969, www.theeroticbakery.com.

ESSENTIAL BAKING CO.: This beloved bakery and chocolatier was once the home of the Oroweat factory, which blew its warm scents of baking bread toward the top of the hill in Gas Works Park. Artisan bread still rises here, in a coffeehouse atmosphere. 1604 N 34th St, 545-3804, www.essentialbaking.com.

GAS WORKS PARK: This unique park has hilltop views of downtown and the boats on Lake Union, shoreline beaches, covered picnic tables, play areas, and a twist: industrial detritus turned into brightly painted play pieces and menacing rusty towers that speak of a polluted past. Once called Brown's Point, this sleepy picnic area changed forever when Klondike gold rushers needed better light sources than candles and kerosene. In 1906 the Gas Works took over Brown's Point and produced gas from coal—a filthy, polluting process—until 1937, when oil was all the rage. Those rusty towers once converted raw materials to gas using pressure, heat, and oxygen. After compression, the gas reached homes via pipelines; this was the second-largest utility in the Northwest at the time. For 50 years production—and pollution—continued until the Gas Works shut down in 1956. Natural gas and hydroelectricity made the facility obsolete. Twenty years later, the city hired landscape architect Richard Haag to develop the space rather than sweep the entire 20 acres clean. (Don't chew on the soil—it still contains hydrocarbons.) 2101 Northlake Wy, www.ci.seattle.wa.us/parks.

JULIA'S: This bohemian mecca has dangerously long waits for its creative menu of fairly healthy and vegetarian breakfasts. Buckwheat pancakes, whole-wheat breakfast burritos, and an array of unexpected egg creations make up for the harried but earnest service. 4401 Wallingford Ave N, 633-1175.

WALLINGFORD CENTER: This former primary school closed in 1981 and reopened as two charming stories of stores—plus 24 apartments on the top floor. Like an open-air bazaar with creaking wooden floors, it's a lovely place to browse. (You might even hear a women's choir echoing among the merchandise on Sundays.) 4400 Wallingford Ave S, 547-7246, www.wallingfordcenter.com.

WEST SEATTLE

Great views, dandy parks, nice neighborhood shopping and restaurants, a less hurried pace—those who inhabit the peninsula between the Duwamish and Puget Sound enjoy a lovely quality of life. Homes are more affordable; neighborhood traffic is moderate; schools are good. Furthermore, the entire area retains a sense of independence that derives from the days it was a separate city, like Ballard, until Seattle co-opted it.

West Seattle has spectacular bluff-top manses that enjoy views matching any in Western Washington. There's a long, long stretch of **SALTWATER BEACH** accessible by car. There are also modest neighborhoods in which working families can afford to buy a home, just as they have for the better part of a century. There's a **BUSTLING SHOPPING AND RESTAURANT DISTRICT,** West Seattle Junction (at SW Alaska Street and California Avenue SW). There's even a neighborhood steel mill (Salmon Bay Steel), a down-to-earth distinction no other Northwest locale can claim.

There's just one drawback: If you want to go anywhere except Burien or SeaTac—and we do mean anywhere—you just about *have* to cross the West Seattle Bridge, whose arching passage over the Duwamish is among the most perpetually clogged throughways in the Seattle area. Most mornings between 6:30 and 8, traffic pegs along stop-and-go.

Well, everyone has dues to pay. There are even bypasses savvy residents know (Admiral Wy to Spokane, dodging container trucks). In the summer, when you get home, you can head to **LINCOLN PARK**, watch the sun lower over the Sound and the Olympics, and forget all about traffic.

West Seattle by the Numbers

Boundaries: Elliott Bay; Roxbury St; Puget Sound; Duwamish Waterway

Included neighborhoods: Alki, Fauntleroy, Delridge, High Point, Highland Park

NSC: West Seattle, Delridge

Population: 78,000

Median age: 39

Median household income: $55,000

Median home sales price: $360,000

Major crimes/1,000: 29.2

Web sites: www.westseattle.com, www.wschamber.com, www.wsjunction.com

Media: West Seattle News

Main drags: SW Alaska St, California Ave SW, Fauntleroy Wy, SW 35th St

Farmers market: Sun 10am–2pm at Alaska Junction (SW Alaska St and California Ave SW)

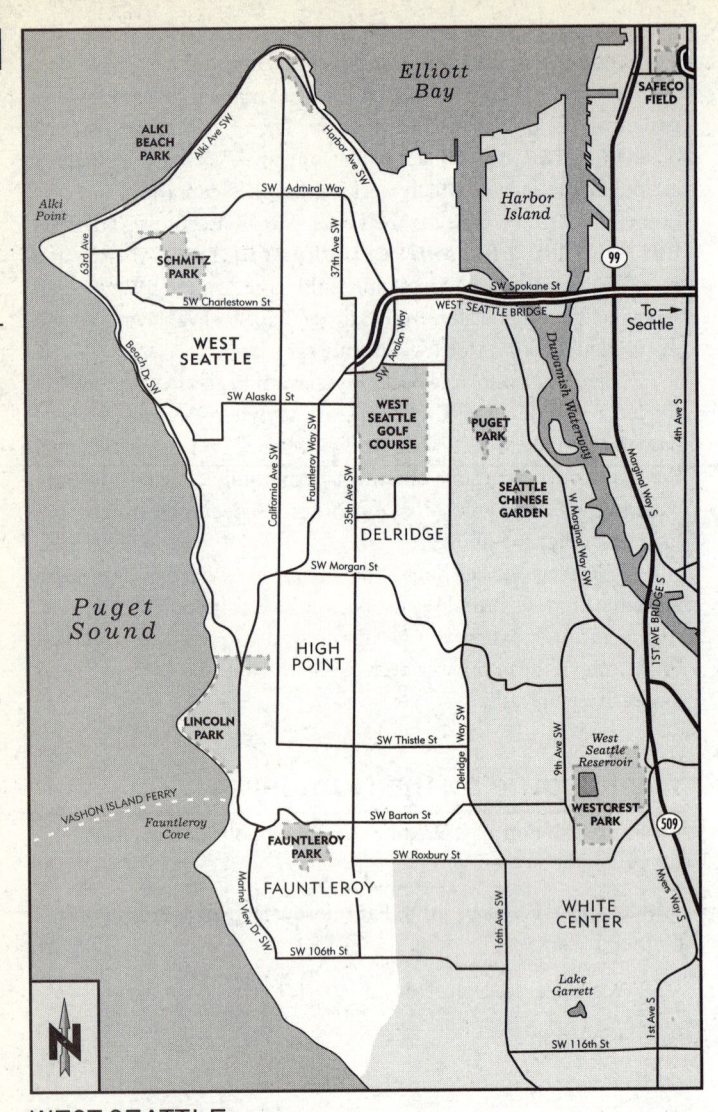

WEST SEATTLE

West Seattle Attractions & Institutions

ALKI BEACH: This is where Seattle's first white settlers set up shop, in November 1851. The weather drove them across Elliott Bay, but today this is a hugely popular promenade for families on sunny, warm days when the universal challenge is, will you get in the water or not? Numerous quirky cafés and shops line the street; behind them are apartment towers with sensational views. Alki Ave SW from Seacrest Marina to 60th Ave SW, www.ci.seattle.was.us/parks.

ALKI LIGHTHOUSE: Though the last resident keeper retired in 1970, this handsome octagonal 1913 structure remains key to navigation, and buildings on the grounds are occupied by Coast Guard personnel. Thus the lighthouse is open to the public only during scheduled tours on summer weekend and holiday afternoons. The area of Puget Sound in front of the lighthouse, with steep drop-offs into deep water, is popular for scuba diving. Alki Peninsula off Alki Ave, 217-6124.

ELLIOTT BAY WATER TAXI: See Chapter 5, "Street Smarts," page 174.

LINCOLN PARK: Besides spectacular bluff-top views across Puget Sound, peaceful paths through quiet woods, and lots of picnic grounds, Lincoln Park has something no other Seattle park does: a heated saltwater pool. The novelty draws huge crowds on hot summer days; get there early. Each afternoon, and especially Fridays, the long lineup of cars along Fauntleroy Wy for the Vashon Ferry creates a memorable traffic snarl. Fauntleroy Wy at Lincoln Park Wy, www.ci.seattle.wa.us/parks.

SALTY'S: This is probably the best view of Seattle's downtown from a restaurant—the whole skyline is right across Elliott Bay, nothing in between. No wonder Salty's is so popular for parties, receptions, meetings, and other confabulations. If only the buffet-line, somewhat greasy seafood were better. 1936 Harbor Ave SW, 937-1600, www.saltys.com.

STATUE OF LIBERTY: The 7-foot replica of Miss Liberty was erected by Boy Scouts in 1953. Never meant to withstand a half-century of the Alki Point weather, it is crumbling and has been vandalized several times. A nonprofit arts organization, Seattle Program for the Arts, is raising money to restore it. On Alki Beach opposite 60th Ave SW, 632-4545, www.northwestarts.org/spa.

WEST SEATTLE GOLF COURSE: One of the oldest, friendliest, and best golf courses in the Northwest was designed by the same fellow, H. Chandler Egan, who laid out Pebble Beach. Seattle's is a much less portentous and much more affordable place to play—weekday greens fees are $26, and tee times are obtainable. The views are great, and the course won't make your head hurt (though your playing still might). SW Genesee St at Avalon Wy, 935-5187, www.westseattlegolf.com.

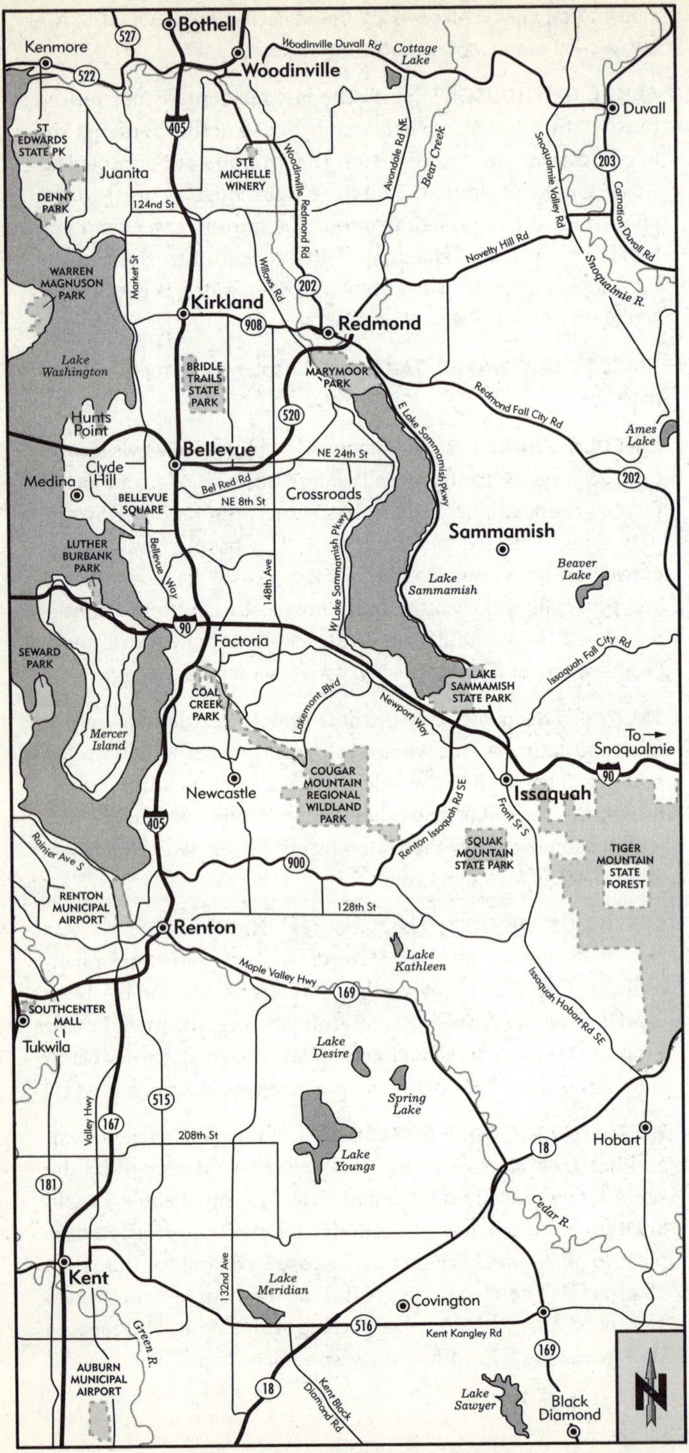
Bothell
Kenmore
Woodinville
Woodinville Duvall Rd
Cottage Lake
Duvall
ST EDWARDS STATE PK
STE MICHELLE WINERY
Juanita
DENNY PARK
124nd St
Woodinville Redmond Rd
Avondale Rd NE
Bear Creek
Snoqualmie Valley Rd
Carnation Duvall Rd
Novelty Hill Rd
Snoqualmie R.
WARREN MAGNUSON PARK
Market St
Willows Rd
Kirkland
Redmond
Lake Washington
BRIDLE TRAILS STATE PARK
MARYMOOR PARK
Redmond Fall City Rd
E Lake Sammamish Pkwy
Hunts Point
Bellevue
NE 24th St
Ames Lake
Clyde Hill
Medina
Bel Red Rd
BELLEVUE SQUARE
NE 8th St
Crossroads
W Lake Sammamish Pkwy
Sammamish
LUTHER BURBANK PARK
Bellevue Way
148th Ave
Lake Sammamish
Beaver Lake
Factoria
SEWARD PARK
COAL CREEK PARK
Lakemont Blvd
Newport Way
LAKE SAMMAMISH STATE PARK
Issaquah Fall City Rd
To → Snoqualmie
Mercer Island
Newcastle
COUGAR MOUNTAIN REGIONAL WILDLAND PARK
Renton Issaquah Rd SE
Issaquah
Front St S
Rainier Ave S
SQUAK MOUNTAIN STATE PARK
TIGER MOUNTAIN STATE FOREST
RENTON MUNICIPAL AIRPORT
128th St
Renton
Lake Kathleen
Maple Valley Hwy
Issaquah Hobart Rd SE
SOUTHCENTER MALL
Tukwila
Lake Desire
Spring Lake
Valley Hwy
208th St
Lake Youngs
Hobart
Cedar R.
Kent
132nd Ave
Lake Meridian
Covington
Kent Kangley Rd
Green R.
AUBURN MUNICIPAL AIRPORT
Kent Black Diamond Rd
Lake Sawyer
Black Diamond
N
527
522
405
203
202
908
520
90
900
169
167
515
181
18
516

CHAPTER 2

Eastside Neighborhoods

Everything Seattle isn't, the Eastside is—glitzy, gated, woodsy suburbia with Microsoft millionaires pulling their Hummers from four-car garages twice a day to go shopping. So goes the myth, anyhow.

And myth it is. The Eastside (everything east of Lake Washington's western shore, roughly) has a good dozen towns that have evolved from exurban outposts to small and medium suburban cities. Microsoft is over here. There are great numbers of prosperous families enjoying quiet lives in newer neighborhoods whose streets curve like Mobius strips.

There are also fine small urban centers (Kirkland, Redmond, and Issaquah, for instance) with just as many nonchain stores and restaurants as any Seattle neighborhood. The metro area's best hiking is here, in the Issaquah Alps. Two exquisite parks bracketing the ends of Lake Sammamish offer endless recreation opportunities. There's even a winery district (in Woodinville) with enough enological heft to warrant a day trip for wine tasting. Does Seattle have that?

Yes, Bill Gates and Paul Allen both built palatial waterfront homes, worth more than the gross national product of some third-world countries, over here. Wouldn't you if you could? The widespread disdain for the Eastside common in some quarters betrays an envy for all the area's advantages. There are many reasons more than a half-million people live over here—and that's more folks than Seattle has. So there.

BELLEVUE

When most Westsiders think of Bellevue, they think of Bellevue Square, luxury cars, and, shall we say, refined tastes? But with a population more than 100,000, the town's makeup is much less homogenized than Seattleites imagine.

In the **CROSSROADS SHOPPING CENTER** common areas you might see an Asian kid hefting a giant chess piece on his way to victory over a grizzled veteran at the center's life-size chess board. Or perhaps you might stroll by a Hispanic family noshing on baklava at the food court. Perusing the magazine racks at the newsstand, you're likely to hear any number of languages as the throngs pass by, an ethnic hodgepodge that defies the Bellevue stereotype.

Diversity doesn't stop at people, either. As one of the larger cities in King County, Bellevue has a wide range of neighborhoods within city limits. House-hunters can find just about any type of abode their hearts desire: ranch starters in Lake Hills, palatial estates on Lake Sammamish, metropolitan condos downtown, two-story family homes in Cherry Crest.

Spanning Lake Washington to Lake Sammamish, the city was once just a quiet little town like all the others on the Eastside. Plucky farmers made their living from strawberry patches and cattle pastures. City slickers would occasionally ferry in from Seattle for a scenic weekend at nearby resorts along waterfronts on both lakes. But it was simply a nice place to visit. The ferry ride, coupled with the long trek from the Kirkland landing, was just too much of a commute for most.

That all changed in 1940, when the ribbon was cut on Lake Washington's first floating bridge. Locals knew this was the big break the town was waiting for—the road from Seattle landed smack-dab on Bellevue real estate.

One of the leading visionaries was Kemper Freeman Sr., a Bellevue businessman who felt a world-class shopping center would be just the thing to put Bellevue on the map. In 1945 he toured the nation looking at shopping centers to use as models. By the next year he was ready to open the doors at the 20 new stores in **BELLEVUE SQUARE**.

Today those stores have blossomed into a destination shopping center that has become the nucleus of Bellevue's downtown. Art galleries, hotels, offices, and condos have all clustered around the busy mall complex. According to estimates from the local chamber of commerce, the city now supports a daily workforce of more than 112,000.

Still, among the Puget Sound family of cities, Bellevue is considered the accomplished but constantly eclipsed younger sibling. During the late '90s the city opened the door to developers to get the jump on Seattle in attracting new Internet businesses to town. Unfortunately, after the high-tech meltdown, "For Lease" signs lined the streets as Bellevue struggled with a commercial vacancy rate above 25 percent. Just across from Bellevue Square, the Lincoln Square project remained as a lonely concrete reminder that even thriving neighborhoods are subject to the fact that all economies, especially real estate, are cyclical. The condominium and retail complex sat unfinished for more than two years while two sets of owners waited out the recession. Unsurprisingly, the owners who righted the ship were none other than the Freemans of Bellevue Square fame. Say what you will about Bellevue, it has long been a family town.

Bellevue by the Numbers

Boundaries: NE 124th Wy; NE 24th St; Evans/Bear Creek Pkwy; 132nd Ave NE

Included neighborhoods: Factoria, Overlake, Cherry Crest, Crossroads, Eastgate, Bridle Trails, Downtown Bellevue, Lake Hills

District Council: Bellevue

Population: 109,569

Median age: 38

Median household income: $62,338

Median home sales price: $299,400

Major crimes/1,000: 41.1

Web site: www.ci.bellevue.wa.us

Media: King County Journal

Main drags: 148th Ave NE, NE 8th St, Bellevue Wy

Farmers market: Thurs 11am–3 pm, Aug–Oct, 1717 Bellevue Wy NE

Bellevue Attractions & Institutions

BELLEVUE ART MUSEUM: The museum operated in Bellevue Square for almost two decades before its ambitious board made the leap of faith to construct a new $23 million facility across the street from the mall. The building got rave reviews when it opened in 2001, but the public didn't care for the abstract and often bizarre exhibits under its new curator. Add a flagging economy to the mix, and the result was a messy bankruptcy only two-and-a-half years later. In late 2004 the museum reopened with a renewed focus on local artists and craftspeople. 510 Bellevue Wy NE, 425-510-0770, www.bellevueart.org.

BELLEVUE BOTANICAL GARDEN: Sweet smells and colorful displays greet visitors daily at the Bellevue Botanical Garden. The 36-acre park is a favorite of wedding photographers and anyone else with aesthetic sensibilities. 12001 Main St, 425-452-2750, www.bellevuebotanical.org.

Medina

When most people think of all the fancy homes and expensive lifestyles in Bellevue, it is possible that they aren't thinking of Bellevue at all. Located between Bellevue and Lake Washington, Medina is the most exclusive neighborhood in the nation.

The Medina zip code has the distinction of having one of the highest median incomes in the entire United States ($133,756). Bill Gates put the area on the map by building his house into a Medina hillside overlooking the lake. To Seattleites, Medina fits the Bellevue profile to a T. But the area is actually a separate municipality from its slumming neighbors in Belle-town.

Maybe visitors are too distracted by the gated drives and the palatial homes to notice the signs announcing city limits. They're easy to miss, considering that the city is completely residential. They might have their own city, but Medina residents still shop in Bellevue.

BELLEVUE SQUARE: There are plenty of malls in Western Washington, but none of them can quite catch up to the popularity of Bell Square. The mall gets close to 16 million visits a year, as shoppers flock to 200 retail stores. Key stores are Nordstrom and Bon-Macy's, with every big-name retailer you can imagine in between. NE 8th St & Bellevue Wy NE, 425-454-2431, www.bellevuesquare.com.

BRIDLE TRAILS STATE PARK: An affection for horses is evident in the Bridle Trails neighborhood shared by Bellevue and Kirkland. Kids still take carrots when they go out for walks, because the stables and pastures have persisted in spite of the high price for land. Right in the middle of this equestrian love-in is the Bridle Trails State Park, an urban stand of trees and trails fit for any filly. NE 53rd St & 116th Ave NE, 360-902-8844, www.parks.wa.gov.

CROSSROADS SHOPPING CENTER: With its concentration of stores, 23 restaurants, a 12-screen cinema, a communal giant chessboard, and live music, Crossroads is aptly known as "the Eastside's living room." NE 8th St & 156th Ave NE, 425-644-1111, www.crossroadsbellevue.com.

KELSEY CREEK PARK: A slice of Bellevue's agricultural past remains at Kelsey Creek Park, a much-visited park best known for its farm. The farm offers tours and children's recreational programs for animal lovers, but it is also a haven for all types of recreational users. It includes more than 150 acres of forest and wetlands, with trails, picnic areas, and a playground available for use. 13204 SE 8th Pl, 425-452-7688, www.cityofbellevue.org.

WADE'S EASTSIDE GUNS & INDOOR RANGE: For years now Wade's indoor shooting range has provided a safe place for gun owners to shoot. Contrary to what some might think, they get all types at the range—even liberals. 13570 Bel-Red Rd, 425-649-8560, www.wadesguns.com.

BOTHELL

The story of Bothell is Puget Sound's own tale of two cities. One of the oldest in the Eastside, this town straddles two counties. To the south, King County's Bothell carries on the town's heritage with well-preserved historic buildings and a main street like they used to make them. To the north, Snohomish County's Bothell points to the future with large strip malls and office complexes for high-tech businesses. The glue that bonds the two together is acres of tract homes and miles of congested freeways.

This is where the average citizen headed when prices in Bellevue, Kirkland, and Redmond started to erupt. Growth centered first around the downtown Bothell core, where more than a century ago pioneers first erected buildings to serve the steamboats that puffed their way up the Sammamish River. Here the neighborhoods expanded organically, each street unique from the next. As demand grew, developers couldn't build affordable housing fast enough, with most buyers moving in the instant the last lick of paint had dried. So the march of development farther north was orchestrated whole subdivisions at a time, with homes neatly lined up in formation.

But whether in Snohomish or King counties, Bothell citizens all have a special something in common: traffic. The city is a notorious bottleneck for both I-405 and SR 522, lanes full of minivans and practical coupes heading where the jobs are. Some lucky residents do manage to avoid the snarls. The Bothell **TECHNOLOGY CORRIDOR** is home to regional offices for such powerhouses as Cingular and Amgen. For some workers it is only a five-minute drive to their work stations and petri dishes.

Of course, this kind of crazy demand eventually diminished the area's original appeal. Housing prices have risen dramatically, and first-time homeowners are being forced to move even farther north to fulfill their dreams.

Bothell by the Numbers

Boundaries: 208th St SE; NE 145th St; 132rd Ave NE; 14th Ave W

Included neighborhoods: Bothell, Wayne

District Council: Bothell

Population: 30,150

Median age: 36

Median household income: $59,264

Median home sales price: $237,700

Major crimes/1,000: 28.3

Web sites: www.ci.bothell.wa.us, www.bothellchamber.org

Media: Bothell-Kenmore Reporter

Main drags: Bothell-Everett Hwy, Bothell Wy

Key date: July 4, Independence Day parade

Farmers market: Fri 10am–3pm, June–Sept, 23732 Bothell-Everett Hwy

Bothell Attractions & Institutions

BOTHELL LANDING: This is the park that city leaders love to brag about. Set alongside the Sammamish Slough, Bothell Landing is a favorite stop for Sammamish River Trail users. It features many of Bothell's first buildings, preserved and moved to the park for posterity. Nearby is a museum to explain their significance. 9919 NE 180th St, 425-486-7430, www.ci.bothell.wa.us.

COUNTRY VILLAGE: A favorite of arty types, Country Village is a boutique mall decked out with country flair. The mall hosts Bothell's farmers market in the summer. 23718 7th Ave SE, 425-483-2250, www.countryvillagebothell.com.

ISSAQUAH

The view from atop Tiger Mountain has changed considerably over the past 30 years. Standing sentinel over Issaquah with its companions Cougar and Squak, Tiger Mountain has for years offered Seattleites hikes close to home and a prime vantage point to watch the area slowly morph.

From the perch above, the occasional home or retail development that dotted the perimeter of the city's core once just looked like flotsam in a sea of farmland. These infrequent specks have now nearly engulfed the scene below. As new residents took refuge from urban crowds in Issaquah's open spaces, their homes and grocery stores began to slowly fill the landscape. Now what remains is a bustling chunk of suburbia that doesn't seem nearly so far in the boondocks as it once did.

Closer to sea level, there are still reminders of the town's bucolic past. The historic buildings on Front Street hark back to the days when Issaquah subsisted on mining, logging, and dairy farms. Along this street visitors can stop in at the old Issaquah railroad depot—now a railway museum—that once served the line that ran up to the Newcastle coal mines. And a few blocks away stands the **DARIGOLD CREAMERY**, which has continuously served Northwesterners dairy products since 1909.

There are other nearby relics of Issaquah's past, too. Adjacent to **LAKE SAMMAMISH STATE PARK** stands the **PICKERING BARN**, the last remnant of the old dairy farm once owned by Washington's territorial governor, William Pickering, in 1878. The park itself hints at the old days of wide-open pastures with its grassy lawns leading to the shoreline.

Just off the I-90 corridor, the **BOEHM'S CANDY FACTORY** also remains as another living piece of history. Julius Boehm opened his little chalet in 1956 to the delight of chocolate lovers around the Sound, and it has stood the test of time. Of course, the little Edelweiss hut now cowers beneath a new I-90 onramp—a fact that Boehm's is none too pleased about. The company sued the state for damages caused by the obstruction of its once-visible signage. Nonetheless, the onramp was much needed by the community. Traffic is notoriously bad throughout Issaquah, and this new conduit to the freeway has done much to alleviate the pressure put on arterials by the neighborhoods that have started to blossom in the hills above the city's center.

Most of the growth has occurred in a new mixed-use development dubbed **"THE HIGHLANDS,"** a project that laid its foundation on some of the last woodland space available and that one day will hold a satellite Microsoft campus, completing the transition from softwood to software.

Issaquah by the Numbers

Boundaries: NE Inglewood Hill Rd/Lake Sammamish; SE May Valley Rd; SE High Point Wy; Renton Issaquah Rd

Included neighborhoods: The Highlands, Downtown

District Council: Issaquah

Population: 11,212

Median age: 37

Median household income: $57,892

Median home sales price: $278,500

Major crimes/1,000: 64.6

Web sites: www.ci.issaquah.wa.us, www.issaquahhistory.org, www.issaquahchamber.com

Media: Issaquah Press

Main drags: NW Gilman Blvd, Front St

Key date: Salmon Days, first weekend in Oct

Farmers market: Sat 9am–2pm, Apr–Oct, 1730 10th Ave NE (Pickering Barn), 425-837-3311

Issaquah Attractions & Institutions

BOEHM'S CANDY: A Puget Sound confectionary staple as much as the fabled Frango mints, Boehm's chocolates are made in the company's chalet just south of I-90. Chocolate lovers can get free nibbles throughout the tour offered at the factory. 255 NE Gilman Blvd, 425-392-6652, www.boehmscandies.com.

COUGAR MOUNTAIN ZOO: It might be smaller than the average zoo, but this community zoo has actually got quite a collection of well-kept animals. For the particularly daring, the zoo offers cougar encounters. For those a little less fearless, encounter their bagged cougar droppings. It helps the zoo pay the bills and keeps deer away from your hostas. 19525 SE 54th, 425-391-5508, www.cougarmountainzoo.com.

GILMAN VILLAGE: A longtime favorite with the boutique-shopping set, Gilman Village offers a range of shops from cute to kitschy. 317 NW Gilman Blvd, 425-392-6802, www.gilmanvillage.com.

ISSAQUAH ALPS: The local joke is "You'd Squak, too, if you were between a Cougar and a Tiger." These three mountains and the surrounding Cascade foothills have been affectionately dubbed the Issaquah Alps by locals who have worked hard over the years to preserve the trees and trails on these slopes for the enjoyment of everyone in and around Issaquah—it's the best hiking in the Puget Sound area. www.issaquahalps.com.

Harvey & Ira

If you were to ask any knowledgeable outdoorsperson who the single most important person to Washington conservation is, odds are it'd be a fifty-fifty split between two men. Harvey Manning and Ira Spring were the granddaddies of outdoors advocacy in the Northwest. They helped form the Issaquah Alps Club, they were vociferous and active members of The Mountaineers, and there wasn't a mountain or tree that they wouldn't stand up to protect.

Some of their best conservation came by way of the printing press. Manning the writer and Spring the photographer were best known for their guidebooks on the area—and they usually found that when they wrote about a trail, authorities were less likely to let it disappear.

Spring passed away in 2003, and Manning has long since retired from the limelight. But their legacy still lives on at the trailhead and on the bookshelf.

LAKE SAMMAMISH STATE PARK: Once the site of Indian potlatch ceremonies, this 512-acre state park on the southern shore of Lake Sammamish is a water-lover's fantasy. The park has 6,858 feet of shoreline, enough for recreational users and wetland creatures to peacefully coexist. 1700 NW Sammamish Rd, www.parks.wa.gov.

XXX DRIVE-IN: The last remaining XXX Root Beer stand in America, this Issaquah hangout still serves its own brew of root beer to both the hometown crowd and those just passing by on their way to and from mountain adventures. 98 NE Gilman Blvd, 425-392-1266.

KIRKLAND

If ever there were a cruising strip on the Eastside, Kirkland's Lake Washington Boulevard would be it. Though there are likely to be more high-clearance SUVs than low-riding Impalas down this **WATERFRONT STRETCH**, it has all the essentials of a good strip: great water views, good eats, beaches and volleyball courts, and plenty of hunks and babes, barely clad, to look at. The city even had a problem involving its police officers and gawking-caused fender-benders years ago.

Heading north on this busy thoroughfare, you'll wend your way through an urban planner's dream street. Corridors of con-

> **GONE BUT NOT FORGOTTEN**
>
> # Issaquah Skyport
>
> Issaquah's farms didn't all just make the jump from pasture to parking lot in one fell swoop. The enthusiasm for technology and development changed the landscape even back in the '40s. It was in that post-WWII era that one of Issaquah's most eulogized institutions was built.
>
> In 1941 developers took advantage of the level terrain afforded by the Pickering Farm to build a flight-school airfield dubbed the Sky Ranch. Responding to demand generated by the GI Bill, the ranch trained pilots for a decade before closing down. It took 10 more years before it was reopened under the guise for which it is most fondly remembered: the Issaquah Skyport.
>
> For a quarter-century, parachutists and skydivers drifted in the skies above the Skyport, an image that most long-time Issaquah residents still remember affectionately. But the scene wasn't meant to last forever. In 1987 the Skyport had its lease terminated so the land's owners could make way for the Pickering Place shopping center.

dos transition to office space and retail as the road closes in on the city center. Joggers and bicyclists line the streets, sweating their way between the public parks scattered along the way.

Before Seattle leaders dredged open the Lake Washington Ship Canal, much of this prime real estate sat underwater. When the project was completed in 1917, the lake dropped 9 feet, leaving a muddy Kirkland shoreline in its wake. At the time the muck was simply an eyesore. Not anymore.

At the heart of the waterfront is **KIRKLAND MARINA PARK**, where the boulevard ends at Central Way NE. This is the true core of the city, the type of place where crusty old-timers gladly rub shoulders with toddling youngsters on a sunny summer day. In the winter the activity simmers down, but it isn't uncommon to see kayakers plish-plashing their way down the water's edge on a rainy day.

This is where the ferry Leschi landed during the days before the floating bridges. In the '30s nearby shipbuilders drew workers from Seattle to help build ships for the war effort. These days destroyer silhouettes have been replaced by a forest of pleasure-yacht masts. But the city hasn't completely outgrown its working-class existence.

Farther inland, Kirkland's **TOTEM LAKE** neighborhood harbors light industrial, manufacturing, and distribution businesses in its warehouses and commercial complexes. Just down the road, **ROSE HILL** still offers affordable housing with its aging ramblers and newer streetside cottages built for those who prefer modest digs.

For those who want more, look back toward the water to find luxury homes in the **JUANITA** area and surrounding the downtown core.

Kirkland by the Numbers

Boundaries: NE 132nd; SR 520; 132nd Ave NE; Lake Washington

Included neighborhoods: Houghton, Rose Hill, Carillon Point, Totem Lake, Juanita, Bridle Trails, Lakeview

District Council: Kirkland

Population: 45,054

Median age: 36

Median household income: $60,332

Median home sales price: $283,100

Major crimes/1,000: 34.8

Web site: www.ci.kirkland.wa.us

Media: Kirkland Courier

Main drags: Lake Washington Blvd, Market St/NE 85th

Farmers market: Wed 11am–6pm, Apr–Oct, Park Ln E between 3rd & Main, 425-893-8766

Kirkland Attractions & Institutions

ARGOSY CRUISES: Argosy offers a Lake Washington cruise to augment its Puget Sound lineup. Though the boat trip usually boasts good views of Mount Rainier and the University of Washington, the number-one reason people buy their tickets is to get a peek at Bill Gates's palatial lakeside home. 1 Kirkland Ave, 800-642-7816, www.argosycruises.com.

KIRKLAND PERFORMANCE CENTER (KPC): The Kirkland Performance Center is one of the most active community performance centers outside Seattle. In addition to a number of dramatic productions every season, KPC also plays host to dance and music performances. 350 Kirkland Ave, 425-893-9900, www.kpcenter.org.

MARINA PARK: Marina Park is the crown jewel among Kirkland's many waterfront parks, no small feat considering the city has preserved more of its waterfront in accessible parkland than any other in the state. Enjoy an ice-cream cone from nearby establishments, chase the ducks at the beach, or just sit at a bench and watch the crowds go by. No matter how you choose to do it, passing time is easy here. Kirkland Ave & Lakeshore Plaza, 425-888-1100, www.ci.kirkland.wa.us.

ST. EDWARDS STATE PARK: Hiking along the cliffs of St. Edwards Park, it is easy to imagine a prospective cleric seeking solitude in nearby trees and faraway vistas. Once the site of a Catholic seminary, this Juanita locale is now a public park, offering fine meditation spots for all. 14500 Juanita Dr NE, 425-823-2992, www.parks.wa.gov.

THIRD FLOOR FISH CAFÉ: This is one of the premier seafood restaurants in the Seattle area. The classy waterfront setting complements an always-fresh menu; take advantage of the restaurant's weekend prix fixe menu to sample the fare. 205 Lake St S, 425-822-3553, www.fishcafe.com.

MERCER ISLAND

Unlike most of the Eastside neighborhoods that started out as working-class farming towns, Mercer Island has upper-crust roots. One of the first developments on the island was built to draw wealthy Seattleites over the water. Opened in 1887, the Calkins Hotel was a three-story, turreted affair with lavish grounds and an unheard-of 100-slip boathouse. The hotel didn't last for long—a personal tragedy caused the owner to abandon it, and just as it was reopened, it burned to the ground. But its legacy of extravagance lives on.

The high demand for real estate here is ironic, considering that 150 years ago the island was uninhabited. The local Indians believed that evil spirits lived on the island and that each night the land mass sank into the lake, only to bob up at sunrise each day.

They'd be surprised if they paddled around the island nowadays. The shoreline is ringed with estates, sun shining on windows looking out to million-dollar views, decks, docks, and yachts. Most notable among them is the home of Microsoft co-founder Paul Allen. The 40,000-square-foot fortress is rumored to be valued at $69 million.

The bar may be set a little high for the average millionaire neighbors to keep up with the billionaires, but that doesn't keep 'em from trying. Most of the 6-square-mile island is a testament to conspicuous consumption. A typical family home anywhere else would be a tear-down here.

But there is still a comfortable neighborhood hiding under the lavishness. Beyond the cars in the parking lots, the shops and restaurants look like those in any other small town. People love pizza here, they drink their lattes in paper cups, and they don't wear tuxedos through the McDonald's drive-through. Gucci, maybe.

Mercer Island by the Numbers

Boundaries: Lake Washington

District Council: Mercer Island

Population: 22,036

Median age: 44

Median household income: $91,904

Median home sales price: $573,900

Major crimes/1,000: 17.8

Web sites: www.ci.mercer-island.com, www.mercerislandchamber.org

Media: Mercer Island Reporter

Main drag: Island Crest Wy

Mercer Island Attractions & Institutions

I-90 BIKE TRAIL: Some avid cyclists might argue that Mercer Island, and not Redmond, is the true bicycle capital of the Northwest. Its rolling hills, quiet streets, and pretty homes make for a swell ride. The popular I-90 pedestrian path makes for a good extension of this ride, as well as providing easy access to the island from Seattle. www.metrokc.gov/parks.

LUTHER BURBANK PARK: Islanders pride themselves on their greenery. The city's park system maintains over 475 acres of land, with Luther Burbank Park reigning as the park centerpiece. The waterfront park sees heavy use from joggers, cyclists, kayakers, and even a thespian or two. Luther Burbank's amphitheater plays host to Wooden O Theater Production's Shakespeare in the Park series every summer. 2040 84th Ave SE, 296-4232, www.ci.mercer-island.wa.us.

ROANOKE INN TAVERN: Built in 1914, the Roanoke Inn has survived the test of time and redevelopment to remain one of the traditional hangouts for island citizens. During prohibition the Inn was whispered to have sold illegal brew in coffee cups. Now islanders just get it in a pint glass as they shoot the breeze with their neighbors. 1825 72nd Ave SE, 232-0800.

ROBERTO'S PIZZA AND PASTA: This mom-and-pop pizza shop has had dough flying in its kitchen since the '70s. 7619 SE 27th, 232-7383.

REDMOND

Known round the world as the home of **MICROSOFT HQ**, Redmond blends its high-tech present with its pastoral past. The city is undeniably a Microsoft company town, but unlike most such, it manages to maintain a sense of identity independent of its corporate citizen. At the city's core you can find an upscale shopping center laden with trendy chains—and you can also visit a sawdust tavern, an outdoor equipment shop that knows the best local fishin' holes, and a local coffee shop that roasts its own beans.

On the way there's a good chance you'll hear the clicking of gears shifting; the city proclaims itself the **"BICYCLE CAPITAL OF THE NORTHWEST."** It's got plenty of shops and trails to prove it and each July holds a festival to celebrate cycling.

Much of the city's buzz occurs downtown on Redmond Way and Cleveland Street, a pair of parallel one-ways that thread downtown. The intersection at Leary Way and Cleveland Street is a good starting point. On three of the four street corners brick buildings still stand from the era of the McRedmonds.

In 1851 Luke McRedmond and his family started a wholesome settlement off the banks of the Sammamish River. Among his children's generation of architectural legacies is the Bill Brown building, the town's former tavern and house of ill repute. Upstairs, "professional" women have been replaced by, well, professional women (and men), but you can still get a pint of brew and some rowdy conversation downstairs at Big Time Pizza.

Just a stone's throw away the summertime **SATURDAY MARKET** still pays homage to the town's agricultural roots. Vendors from both Western and Eastern Washington offer everything from canned salmon to fresh strawberries, as well as arts and crafts.

In its infancy Microsoft was lured to Redmond by a favorable tax climate and affordable land. Taxes have stayed reasonable; real estate has not. Nevertheless, there are still some enclaves of older ramblers scattered among the high-priced subdivisions. And for those desperate for a new home within their means, the city recently courted developers to build **REDMOND RIDGE**, a mixed-use community that features cottage homes for more affordable living. Developers had people camping out to buy these units, but Redmond residents are reserving judgment about the success of the project until they see how well the local government can handle the strain on nearby roads. If it works, though, Redmond Ridge's builders may be back to add more homes to the development.

Redmond by the Numbers

Boundaries: NE 124th Wy; NE 24th St; Evans/Bear Creek Pkwy; 132nd Ave NE

Included neighborhoods: Grass Lawn, Willows, Education Hill, Sammamish Valley, Overlake, Union Hill, Novelty Hill

District Council: Redmond

Population: 45,256

Median age: 34

Median household income: $66,735

Median home sales price: $269,400

Major crimes/1,000: 42.3

Web sites: www.redmond.gov, www.redmondchamber.com

Media: Redmond Reporter

Main drags: Avondale, Redmond Wy, Bear Creek Pkwy, 164th Ave NE

Slogan: "Bicycle Capital of the Northwest"

Key date: Redmond Derby Days bicycle festival, second week of July

Farmers market: Sat 9am–3pm, May–Oct, 7730 Leary Wy, www.redmondsaturdaymarket.homestead.com

Redmond Attractions & Institutions

CELTIC BAYOU: This relatively new establishment offers hot Cajun food with its mugs of custom-brewed Irish ale. Opened by a pair of Microsoft retirees, the place was an instant hit with their brethren. Parking can be tricky on weekends. 7281 W Lake Sammamish Pkwy, 425-869-5933, www.farwestirelandbrewing.com.

FARREL MCWHIRTER PARK: A favorite with the preschool set, the park's petting zoo is home to a number of barnyard animals. 19545 Redmond Rd, 425-556-2311, www.ci.redmond.wa.us.

MARYMOOR PARK: There is something for everyone at this major regional park, including an off-leash dog-romp section, a climbing rock, a radio-control airfield, a Velodrome bicycle track, and numerous ballfields and tennis courts. A controversial rule change to allow businesses on county parklands may open Marymoor to more activities—it already boasts a new amphitheater, and talks are under way for a golf driving range. By the way police are wise to the temptation to use the park as a shortcut to SR 520 during morning and evening rush hour—if they don't get you, the 700 speed bumps will. 6046 W Lake Sammamish Pkwy NE, 205-3661, www.metrokc.gov/parks.

MICROSOFT MAIN CAMPUS AND MUSEUM: A mecca for Asian tourists and ambitious job seekers, Main Campus is where (most of) the high-tech magic happens. Visit the Microsoft Museum in Building 127 for the company word on software history. 4420 148th Ave, 425-703-6214, www.microsoft.com.

REDMOND TOWN CENTER: A sterling example of new-generation malls—a bit smaller, more selective, and user-friendly. Key store: REI. 16495 NE 74th St, 425-867-0808, www.redmond towncenter.com.

THENO'S DAIRY: Over the decades urbanization has shrunk Theno's Dairy from a full-blown dairy farm to a roadside ice cream stand. Despite the subdivision encroachment, this shop manages to offer a slice of Americana à la mode. 12248 156th Ave NE, 425-885-2339.

VICTOR'S CELTIC COFFEE CO: Walk into Victor's anytime of day and you'll likely find someone reading a C++ book in one corner and Proust in another. The cozy café serves up coffee brewed from its own beans, roasted in back, to a uniquely Redmond crowd. 7993 Gilman St, 425-881-6451.

WILLOWS RUN: One of the premier golf complexes in the region. Willows offers two 18-hole courses, a pitch-and-putt, a driving range, and a Northwest-themed putting course. 10402 Willows Rd NE, 425-883-1200, www.willowsrun.com.

SAMMAMISH

One of the newest cities on the Eastside, Sammamish was a city born out of necessity. While transplants and natives alike were enjoying home-equity windfalls during the high-flying '90s, developers busily scoured the region looking for places to put roofs over their heads.

One favorite was an out-of-the-way swath of woods and fields between Redmond and Issaquah, called the **SAMMAMISH PLATEAU** (or simply "The Plateau"). There, acres and acres of homes went up, lawns and play sets and all. Things seemed to be going well for a while, until longtime residents and newcomers began to realize that though the county was green-lighting new projects by the dozen, it was doing little to construct the necessary infrastructure demanded by these mushrooming developments.

So in 1999 the City of Sammamish incorporated to put a little more control in the hands of residents. The city they put together is a prototypical bedroom community, less a municipality than one big extended neighborhood. From the eastern shore of **LAKE SAMMAMISH** all the way up to the higher ground on the Plateau, cul-de-sacs and training wheels abound. Local services have sprung up here, but little commercial exists beyond the neighborhood strip mall or gas station—and City Hall is in a shopping center. It all adds up to a quiet existence of near perfection.

Despite incorporation, the need for road improvements has been Sammamish's challenge. With only a few years under their belts, city leaders are still working to find ways to accommodate traffic from Sammamish neighborhoods.

This high concentration of residents and low concentration of good roads has contributed to one gnarly traffic problem. Major thoroughfares off the Plateau are scarce, and the closest freeway is miles away. As a result, many people in the area must fight their way through more than an hour of traffic to get to their workplace in the morning. E Lake Sammamish Parkway and NE 228th are particularly bad sticking points for commuters into Redmond and beyond.

But the area's skyrocketing real estate prices indicate there are still plenty of people willing to give up their time on the road for a bit of tranquility at home.

Sammamish by the Numbers

Boundaries: Redmond Fall City Rd NE; SE 43rd Wy; Redmond Fall City Rd SE; Lake Sammamish

District Council: Sammamish

Population: 34,104

Median age: 35.3

Median household income: $101,592

Median home sales price: $362,900

Major crimes/1,000: 18.1

Web site: www.ci.sammamish.wa.us

Media: Sammamish Review

Main drags: Fall City Rd, E Lake Sammamish Pkwy, 228th Ave SE

Slogan: "What traffic?"

Sammamish Attractions & Institutions

PINE & BEAVER LAKES: Just a few blocks from one another, Pine Lake and Beaver Lake used to be little, out-of-the-way destinations visited by families in Redmond or Issaquah. Now they act as community swimmin' holes and recreational gathering spots for the locals. Pine Lake: 2400 228th Ave SE; Beaver Lake: 25201 SE 24th St; 425-836 7907.

SAHALEE COUNTRY CLUB: Sahalee has been one of the region's finest golf establishments since 1969. Rated as one of the top 100 golf courses in the nation, Sahalee played host to the 1998 PGA Championship and the 2002 World Golf Championship–NEC Invitational. It's private—yes, that means private. www.sahalee.com.

SNOQUALMIE VALLEY

Feeling claustrophobic? Need fresh air? How about some relief from traffic? Maybe you need to step out into the backyard . . . Seattle's backyard, that is.

Nestled against the foothills of the Central Cascades, Snoqualmie Valley is one of the last bastions of tranquility in the

Seattle metro area. Farmland and forests link together a number of small communities that manage to retain their **RURAL LIFESTYLE** even as suburbia creeps closer.

From north to south, Duvall, Carnation, Fall City, Preston, and Snoqualmie all balance growth with their residents' need for breathing room. It is a tall task considering that the valley is pinched between suburban enclaves on the west and undevelopable mountain land to the east. With the cost of homes and land rising elsewhere, it is only inevitable for families to look to the Valley for refuge.

Both Snoqualmie and North Bend have already started to succumb to expensive subdivisions—land there has skyrocketed in value since 2000. Because of their close proximity to I-90, these two areas were prime targets for people with city jobs who couldn't afford anything else on the Eastside. Now their properties are worth what those Bellevue homes were once selling for.

Farther north near Carnation and Duvall, more affordable developments have sprung up to accommodate the average Joe. And in those spaces between each town, it is still possible to buy a piece of the country at a reasonable price.

Despite the growth in each town, Snoqualmie Valley is still known more for its **OPEN SPACES** than its housing developments. Livestock still graze along the country roads that wind their way through this area. People still come to check out the scenic beauty of **SNOQUALMIE FALLS.** And hikers still muddy their boots on the **NUMEROUS TRAILS** that wind through the abundant public land in the Valley.

Snoqualmie Valley by the Numbers

Boundaries: NE Cherry Valley Rd; South Fork of the Snoqualmie River; Snoqualmie Pass; Fall City Rd

Included neighborhoods: Snoqualmie, North Bend, Fall City, Preston, Carnation, Duvall

Population: 14,524

Median age: 34

Median household income: $61,507

Median home sales price: $221,840

Major crimes/1,000: 23

Web sites: www.cityofduvall.com, www.ci.carnation.wa.us, www.ci.north-bend.wa.us, www.ci.snoqualmie.wa.us, www.snovalley.org

Media: Snoqualmie Valley Record

Key date: Snoqualmie Railroad Days, first weekend in Aug

Farmers markets: North Bend: Sat 9am–1pm, June–Oct, 411 Main Ave S; Carnation: Tues 3–7pm, June–Oct, Hwy 20, Tolt Ave & W Bird St

Snoqualmie Valley Attractions & Institutions

MOUNT SI: Travel anywhere around North Bend and you'll find it is pretty hard to escape the mountain. The city rests right at the base of the 4,167-foot Mount Si, one of the highest Cascade foothills. A mecca for all local hiking enthusiasts, Mount Si's 4-mile trail can be a doozy for some beginners. Mount Rainier climbers use this steep trail as a training ground; ordinary citizens consider it a gaspingly difficult climb to a mind-boggling view. www.mountsi.com.

REMLINGER FARMS: Kids love it. Adults love it. Families love it. This is one of the pioneers of the U-pick, destination-farm industry and still one of the best, with everything from apples to zucchini. Bring your appetite and enough room for plenty of sacks of fresh, luscious things to eat. East of Carnation (get directions online). 425-333-4135, www.remlingerfarms.com.

SALISH LODGE & SPA: Perched just above the Snoqualmie Falls that David Lynch was so enamored with, the similarities to *Twin Peaks's* Great Northern Hotel end at the door. Inside you'll find a world-class establishment that is as well-known for its expansive, Asian-style spa, massage treatments, and sumptuous meals as it is for its luxurious rooms. Valentine's Day is peak season here, when dinner and a room can be had for about the same price as a small car. 6501 Railroad Ave SE, 800-272-5474, www.salishlodge.com.

SNOQUALMIE FALLS: When the river is at full flood, you can hear the thunder of Snoqualmie Falls long before you approach them. Dropping an impressive 276 feet into its icy-cold splash pool, the falls have been a gathering spot for gawkers since even before Seattle's birth—Snoqualmie Indians regarded the spot as sacred. Best viewing is from a small observation platform just west of Salish Lodge.

SNOQUALMIE VALLEY TRAIL: A former railroad grade, this bucolic treasure starts near Snoqualmie Falls and wends its way downhill through peaceful woods into the valley, intersecting the edge of Carnation on its way to Duvall. It's one of the best biking trails in the Seattle area, a special treat in October when the maples and cottonwoods are in color. 296-8687, www.metrokc.gov/parks.

WOODINVILLE

"Country living, city style" isn't just Woodinville's motto, it's also the town's way of life. The place is steeped in the farm heritage of the Sammamish River Valley, but explosive regional growth has necessitated constant blurring of the line between city and country.

Ira and Susan Woodin first settled the fertile valley in 1871. Moving from their Columbia City home, you might say they were one of the first couples to suburbanize the Eastside. But theirs was a simpler existence, and for more than a century the area developed slowly as a small agrarian community.

Once Seattle began to feel the crunch of expansion in the 1980s, people began streaming to Woodinville's countryside for its spacious setting. Inevitably, residential growth spawned commercial development, but longtime residents have fought fiercely to defend its **RURAL CHARACTER**.

It took three tries before the town could even get an incorporation measure to pass, with the final ballot slimly getting a thumbs-up in 1992 when a compromise was struck to set city boundaries for only a few square miles. As a result, much of what is considered Woodinville is actually unincorporated King County—on paper Woodinville's population hasn't seemed to swell the way neighboring cities have.

But don't let the numbers fool you. Hidden between the **HORSE PASTURES AND P-PATCHES**, plenty of housing developments are still sprouting up in Woodinville zip codes. Officials estimate that there are close to 50,000 residents living in the combined area of incorporated and unincorporated Woodinville.

In spite of this, most would say neighborhood leaders have done a good job maintaining the pastoral setting. The town still boasts the distinction of keeping more horses per capita than anywhere else in the nation. In many areas in the valley you can still find plenty of people that grow their own food. And on any given day at the Woodinville Post Office, you're as likely to see a muddy pickup truck as a BMW convertible.

This isn't to say that the finer things in life aren't appreciated here. Many of Woodinville's amenities now surpass its neighbors' offerings. Beer and wine aficionados frequent the

REDHOOK BREWERY and the numerous wineries in the area. The stressed-out and burned-out can escape to the spa facilities at nearby **WILLOWS LODGE** or sup on the cuisine offered by the adjacent **HERBFARM** and **BARKING FROG** restaurants. And outdoor enthusiasts can while the time away on the **SAMMAMISH RIVER TRAIL** or aloft in one of the many **HOT AIR BALLOONS** that dot the sky on sunny days.

Woodinville by the Numbers

Boundaries: SR 522; NE 124th Wy; W Snoqualmie Valley Rd; 124th Ave NE

Included neighborhoods: Hollywood Hill, Leota, West Ridge, The Wedge

District Council: Woodinville

Population: 9,194

Median age: 35.7

Median household income: $68,114

Median home sales price: $270,300

Major crimes/1,000: 52

Web sites: www.ci.woodinville.wa.us, www.woodinvillechamber.org

Media: Woodinville Weekly

Main drags: NE N Woodinville Wy, Woodinville-Duvall Rd, Woodinville-Redmond Rd

Key date: All Fool's Day Parade, last weekend in Mar

Farmers market: Sat 9am–4pm, Apr–Oct, 17401 133rd Ave NE, 546-7960

Woodinville Attractions & Institutions

ARMADILLO BARBECUE: This is the hole-in-the-wall of choice for most Woodinville residents. It offers Texas-style cuisine without any pretension. 13109 NE 175th St, 425-481-1417.

CHATEAU STE. MICHELLE: Woodinville estimates that 1.5 million tourists visit the town every year, and it is a good bet most of them make a stop here. The winery is the destination of the popular Washington Dinner Train, and in addition to winery tours and tastings it hosts an annual summer concert series. A dozen other wineries in the neighborhood make this a day-trip destination. 14111 NE 145th St, 425-488-1133, www.ste-michelle.com.

THE HERBFARM: Once upon a time a small herb farm near Snoqualmie Falls decided to start serving meals based on its homegrown ingredients. From those humble beginnings grew one of the most conspicuous gourmet restaurants in the Seattle area, a national food shrine whose costly prix fixe dinners are lengthy, exotic affairs booked months in advance. After a fire at the original site, the restaurant reopened in classy quarters on the grounds of Woodinville's Willows Lodge in the Eastside's nascent winery district. If you want to see what the rep is all about, call far, far in advance—six months for summer evenings. 14590 NE 145th St, 425-485-5300, www.theherbfarm.com.

MOLBAK'S: First started in 1956 as a little wholesaler of cut flowers, Molbak's has blossomed into the region's leading gardening center and a destination stop for green thumbs around Puget Sound. The annual poinsettia show before Christmas is a holiday wonder: There are literally thousands. 13625 NE 175th St, 425-483-5000, www.molbaks.com.

OVER THE RAINBOW BALLOON RIDES: Woodinville's hot air balloons are as much a fixture in the landscape as its horses. Over the Rainbow offers rides twice a day between May and September from its headquarters near the winery district. 14481 Woodinville-Redmond Rd, 425-861-8611, www.letsgoballooning.com.

REDHOOK BREWERY: Just a few paces away from Chateau Ste. Michelle is its unruly sibling, the Redhook Brewery. Like the winery, the brewery offers tours and tastings. 14300 NE 145th St, 425-483-3232, www.redhook.com.

WILLOWS LODGE: Though the grapes grown in the area are far more decorative than productive, Woodinville's winery district has something the Yakima Valley does not—a first-class resort. Stone and Douglas fir mark the Northwest contemporary structure, surrounded by huge gardens; all the 88 rooms have fireplaces; and the hotel's **BARKING FROG** restaurant (425-424-2999) offers Northwest/Mediterranean cuisine focusing on Washington wines. Aside from its appeal to execs in the high-tech industry, the Willows is giving Salish Lodge some competition for romantic getaways within reach of Seattle. 14580 NE 145th St, 425-424-3900 or 877-424-3930, www.willowslodge.com.

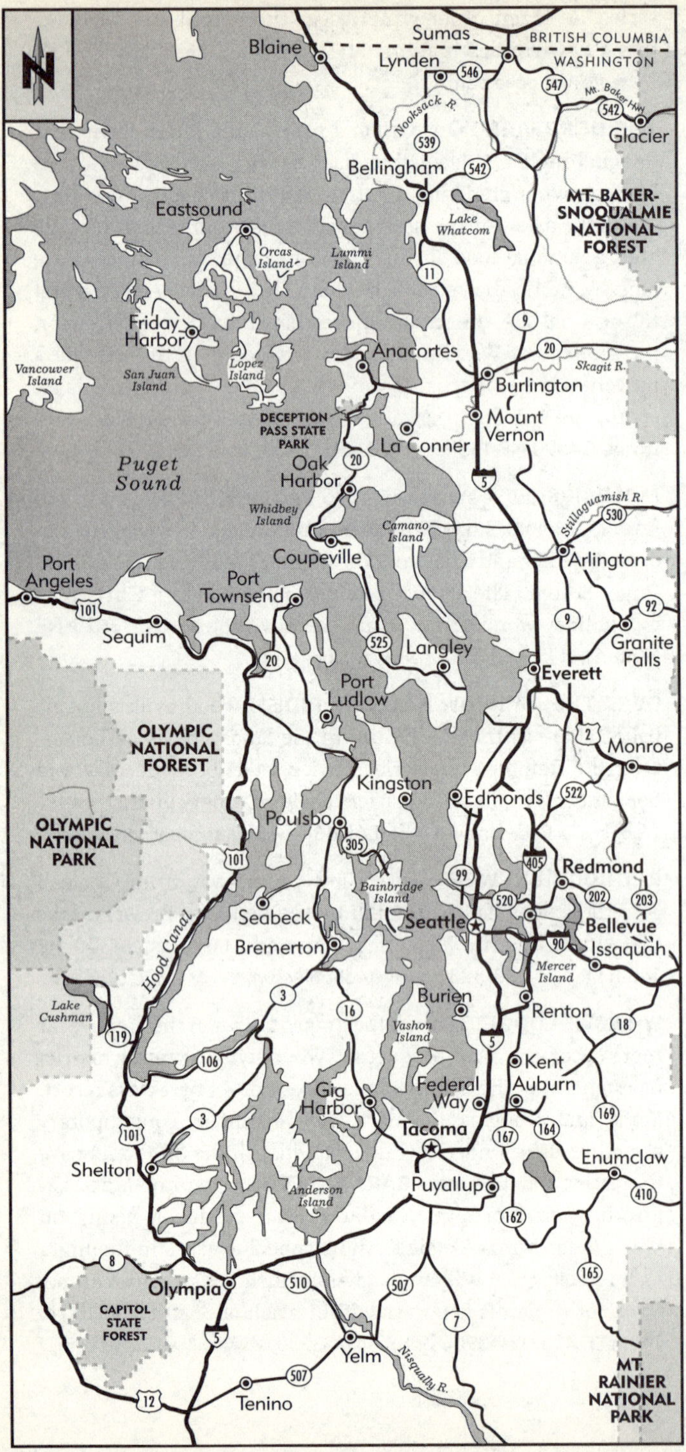
N
BRITISH COLUMBIA
WASHINGTON
Blaine
Sumas
Lynden
546
547
Mt. Baker Hwy
542
Glacier
Nooksack R.
539
Bellingham
542
MT. BAKER-SNOQUALMIE NATIONAL FOREST
Lake Whatcom
Eastsound
Orcas Island
Lummi Island
11
9
Friday Harbor
20
Anacortes
Skagit R.
Vancouver Island
San Juan Island
Lopez Island
Burlington
DECEPTION PASS STATE PARK
Mount Vernon
La Conner
Puget Sound
Oak Harbor
20
5
Whidbey Island
Stillaguamish R.
530
Camano Island
Coupeville
Arlington
Port Angeles
Port Townsend
101
92
9
Sequim
525
Langley
Granite Falls
20
Everett
Port Ludlow
OLYMPIC NATIONAL FOREST
2
Monroe
Kingston
Edmonds
522
OLYMPIC NATIONAL PARK
Poulsbo
305
405
Redmond
101
99
Bainbridge Island
520
202
203
Seabeck
Seattle
Bellevue
90
Issaquah
Hood Canal
Bremerton
Mercer Island
Lake Cushman
3
16
Burien
Renton
119
Vashon Island
5
18
106
Kent
Federal Way
Auburn
Gig Harbor
3
169
Tacoma
101
167
164
Shelton
Enumclaw
Puyallup
410
Anderson Island
162
8
165
Olympia
510
507
CAPITOL STATE FOREST
7
5
Yelm
Nisqually R.
507
MT. RAINIER NATIONAL PARK
12
Tenino

CHAPTER 3

Nearby Burgs

Once upon a time there was no highway network circling Puget Sound, and all the basin's cities and towns were linked by a flotilla of small tugs, transports, and ferries: the "Mosquito Fleet," it was nicknamed. Today the Puget Sound megalopolis encompasses several dozen cities and suburban municipalities adding up to almost 3 million people, and almost all of them serve in part as bedroom communities for other nearby areas. As with many other West Coast cities, the classic metropolitan model—a large business and jobs center surrounded by satellite suburbs—does not really apply.

There are thousands of folks, for instance, who live in Seattle and Eastside neighborhoods but commute to Boeing plants and other industrial facilities in South King County—just *try* to travel south through Renton on I-405 at 6:30am. Plenty of high-tech workers live in Seattle and commute eastward across Lake Washington to Redmond's Overlake area. Tacomans and Puyallupians (yes, we made that up) commute to Seattle and Kent. North Seattle and Lynnwood residents head north to Everett and another huge Boeing facility. And thousands of people live across Puget Sound entirely, thronging onto Washington State ferries for their commute. It's a remarkably pleasant way to get to work and one with a heritage of which most are blithely unaware: The ferry system was born when the state took over the unsafe remnants of the Mosquito Fleet in the '50s, and it did so largely as transportation for residents, not tourists (though it serves both today).

Though the cities in the Seattle area share much in common—we all use the same airport, experience much the same climate, watch the same local TV stations—each has its own identity. Nearly every community has an annual fair or festival; most have a "downtown" of some sort; each has a distinct claim to fame.

AUBURN

Seems like the farther south you go, the lower the home prices, the lesser the opinion Seattle residents have of the place . . . and the more likely an inferiority complex lurks about. Well, Auburn has its own symphony orchestra. Redmond doesn't have *that*, does it?

True, Auburn also has a **MEGASIZE OUTLET MALL** that opened with a rather ridiculous depiction of Mount Rainier erupting out front. Elsewhere, Auburn has a quiet, user-friendly downtown, with a performing arts center that brings in remarkably prominent and diverse shows and artists, and lots of modest neighborhoods in which working families live comfortably.

Auburn by the Numbers

District Council: Auburn

Population: 45,000

Median age: 34

Median household income: $41,000

Median home sales price: $192,000

Major crimes/1,000: 38.3

Web sites: www.ci.auburn.wa.us, www.auburnareawa.org

Media: King County Journal

Main drags: Main St, C St

Key date: Auburn Good Ol' Days, early Aug

Auburn Attractions & Institutions

EMERALD DOWNS: When the late, long-lamented Longacres was sold to Boeing, the Northwest horse-racing community stretched heaven and earth to make sure this sparkling racetrack replaced it. Horse racing has seen its heyday come and go, but Emerald Downs is a magical place for anyone who loves the pounding of hooves, Thoroughbred style. The season runs early April through September, and the annual $250,000 Longacres Mile is the premier horse race north of LA. SR 167 at 15th St NW, 253-288-7000, www.emdowns.com.

MUCKLESHOOT CASINO: The Muckleshoots have been in the gambling business a long, long time, starting out with bingo back when Indian casinos were just a gleam in most tribes' eyes. Today it's got 2,000 machines, 70 tables, 5 restaurants, a piano lounge, and on and on. But it hasn't forgotten its roots: You can still play with pennies here. 2402 Auburn Wy S, 800-804-4944, www.muckleshootcasino.com.

SUPERMALL OF THE GREAT NORTHWEST: The world's largest outlet mall encompasses 12 million square feet, but sheer size doesn't describe it. Nordstrom Rack, Ann Taylor, Liz Claiborne, Kenneth Cole, Tommy Hilfiger—this isn't your grandma's outlet mall. There's even a more-or-less concierge (Guest Services). OK, there's also a Sam's Club. SR 167 (Valley Freeway) at 15th St SW, 253-833-9500 or 800-SAY-VALU, www.supermall.com.

BAINBRIDGE ISLAND

Though fame came to Bainbridge at the hands of one of its most famous residents, David Guterson, the island directly across from Seattle remains a determinedly peaceful, low-key place. Winslow, its dock-town (the whole island is an incorporated municipality, but Winslow is the "town"), is still a small bayside village ideal for strolling. Favorite stops along the main drag include the classic '70s landmark the **STREAMLINER DINER** (397 Winslow Wy E, 842-8595), **BLACKBIRD BAKERY** (210 Winslow Wy, 780-1322), and **EAGLE HARBOR BOOKS** (157 Winslow Wy, 842-5332). Excepting a few roadside strip malls, the rest of the island is a pastoral expanse of field, garden, and forest—and the people who live here come for exactly that.

Guterson set his novel *Snow Falling on Cedars* on a very Bainbridge-like island. In the novel racial prejudice provides the dramatic tension. Today the island's schoolkids are among the few American pupils who learn the unvarnished truth about the "relocation" of Japanese Americans to prison camps during World War II. Back then Bainbridge was a truck-farming center. Today it is a high-end residential enclave whose residents treasure their privacy, the island's serenity, and the relatively easy access to downtown Seattle, which is just 35 minutes by ferry.

Bainbridge by the Numbers

District Council: Bainbridge	
Population: 21,600	
Median age: 43	
Median household income: $72,100	
Median home sales price: $350,000	
Major crimes/1,000: 7.5	

Web sites: www.ci.bainbridge-isl.wa.us, www.bainbridgeisland.com, www.bainbridgechamber.com

Media: Bainbridge Island Review

Main drags: SR 305, High School Rd NW

Key dates: Island Homes Tour and Winslow Art Walk, early May; Island Days Festival, late June–early July

Farmers market: City Hall Plaza, Sat 9am–1pm, Apr–Oct

Bainbridge Attractions & Institutions

BAINBRIDGE GARDENS: This destination nursery sprawls over 7 acres with a fine selection of woody plants, theme gardens for herbs, perennials, grasses, water plants, and shade plants. The restored Harui Memorial Garden showcases bonsai trees, and a nature trail loops through native woods. There are education programs on sustainable gardening, as well as a small outdoor cafe. 9415 Miller Rd NE, 842-5888.

BAINBRIDGE ISLAND VINEYARDS & WINERY: Unlike most other Puget Sound wineries, this one grows its grapes on-site, and thus specializes in such cool-climate North European varietals as Müller-Thurgau, siegerrebe, madeleine angevine, pinot noir, and pinot gris. There's a fragrance garden for picnics, and the wines are sold only at the winery. It's a short walk from Winslow. 682 SR 305, 842-9463.

BISTRO PLEASANT BEACH: The island's best-known restaurant is right in Winslow, a short stroll from the ferry dock. Its Mediterranean menu incorporates Moroccan elements and Northwest ingredients. The tables on the brick patio outside are highly sought after. 241 Winslow Wy E, 842-4347, www.bicomnet.com/bistropb.

BLOEDEL RESERVE: The French-style chateau here belies the character of the 67-acre estate, which is largely natural woodlands. Though it was once owned by a timber tycoon, the focus of the reserve is distinctly low-key, providing people with a place to enjoy nature through walks in gardens and woodlands. 7571 NE Dolphin Dr, 842-7631, www.bloedelreserve.org.

HERONSWOOD NURSERY: One of North America's chief finders, importers, and popularizers of exotic landscape plants. A visit during one of the nursery's open times (call ahead for an appointment) is an adventure in horticultural wonder, best combined with a trip to Bloedel Reserve. 360-297-4172, www.herons wood.com.

BURIEN

Though the community is more than a century old, Burien didn't incorporate until 1993, when the municipality coalesced around opposition to Sea-Tac airport expansion plans. Before that it was a hodgepodge of residential and small commercial districts; today it is a locale for families to start residential life. Among other things, the city has more than 100 Neighborhood Block Watch groups and a program to certify apartment complexes crime-free.

Burien by the Numbers

District Council: Burien

Population: 31,800

Median age: 38.4

Median household income: $43,000

Median home sales price: $192,000

Major crimes/1,000: 35.3

Web sites: www.ci.burien.wa.us, www.swkcc.org

Media: Highline Times

Main drags: Ambaum Blvd, 1st Ave S, SW 152nd

Farmers market: Thurs 11am–6pm, May–Oct, 4th St SW & SW 150th Ave

Burien Attractions & Institutions

SEAHURST PARK: Once a King County Park, this broad expanse of beach was given to the city in 1996 after it incorporated. With 2,000 feet of sandy beach, it is a rarity along Puget Sound and can get crowded on warm summer days. On low-tide weekends volunteer naturalists are often on the beach to answer questions about intertidal life. Long ago this was all a 185-acre private estate. 140th Ave SW & 16th Ave SW, www.ci.burien.wa.us/parksrec.

ENUMCLAW

Perched on a plateau at the north foot of the Mount Rainier massif, Enumclaw is a pastoral place that has become a bedroom community for Tacoma, South King County, and determined Seattle workers. (The commute is an hour each way in good traffic.) The name derives from a Native American phrase that means "strong wind" or "thunderous noise." Indeed, the occasional downslope easterlies for which the term "chinook" was coined strap the Enumclaw plateau periodically, crashing tall trees to earth and prompting Seattle weathercasters to explain why atmospheric pressure differentials cause air to slide down mountains, speed up, and warm up.

Once Enumclaw was a farming and logging center, with a few coal miners thrown in for spice. Today it is a peaceful, pleasant place to live, with one outstanding characteristic: a drop-dead, full-on **VIEW OF MOUNT RAINIER** 30 miles away. When the sky is clear, that is. It rains more up on the plateau, and since it's higher, it is colder than Seattle. It's often warmer in summer, too.

The plateau is one of the premier Thoroughbred breeding areas in the country, and a drive around the area reveals dozens of paddocks with long-legged foals gamboling about.

Enumclaw by the Numbers

District Council: Enumclaw

Population: 11,000 (40,000 entire plateau)

Median age: 35.1

Median household income: $43,820

Median home sales price: $175,000

Major crimes/1,000: 10.4

Web sites: www.ci.enumclaw.wa.us, www.enumclawchamber.com

Media: Enumclaw Courier-Herald

Main drags: Potter St, Griffin Ave, Roosevelt Ave (SR 410)

Key dates: King County Fair, mid-July; Scottish Highland Games, early Aug

Enumclaw Attractions & Institutions

KING COUNTY FAIR: Yes, county fairs are wonderful everywhere, and King County's is one of the best, but how many others offer "Logger Rodeo"? Top that, bull riders. There are also regular rodeo performances, scones and fry bread, nightly entertainment, and all the other fair staples. 296-8888, www.metrokc.gov/parks/fair.

SCOTTISH HIGHLAND GAMES: Feeling an urge to see large, red-faced fellows heave logs? The caber toss joins pipe bands and other highland frivolities at this annual event, the largest of its kind in the United States. At the fairgrounds in early Aug, www.sshga.org.

EVERETT

Founded, like so many Western cities, in the late 1800s in the belief that the transcontinental rail line would end up here, Everett has been an industrial center ever since. Long reliant on extractive industries—mainly timber, some mining—the city experienced deep decline during the Depression, was reborn with World War II and the postwar need for timber products, then declined again until Boeing chose it as the site for its wide-body jet assembly plant in the '70s.

BOEING itself proved only cyclically prosperous, and Everett's fortunes have never totally stabilized. The opening of a major naval base in 1994 added a more constant element to the local economy, but the city center still struggles. Everett neighborhoods are classic pre- and postwar collections of bungalows, many with Craftsman elements. The city occupies a ridge along Puget Sound that enjoys **SPLENDID VIEWS** of the Sound and the Olympics.

Everett by the Numbers

District Council: Everett

Population: 97,000

Median age: 32.2

Median household income: $42,200

Median home sales price: $184,000

Major crimes/1,000: 31.2

Web sites: www.ci.everett.wa.us, www.everettchamber.com

Media: Everett Herald

Main drags: Pacific Ave, Rucker Ave, Everett Ave, Marine View Dr

Farmers market: Rockefeller & Wall, across from the county courthouse, Wed 10am–2pm, June–Sept, www.snohomishmarkets.org

Everett Attractions & Institutions

AQUASOX: Real grass, real fans, real hot dogs—the AquaSox have it all, including a lime-green frog mascot named Webbly. Watching this Class-A farm team of the Seattle Mariners is always worth the drive to Everett's 4,500-seat Memorial Stadium, which attracts a loyal cadre of fans from mid-June through early September. Tickets usually can be purchased at the gate. 39th St & Broadway, 425-258-3673, www.aquasox.com.

BIRINGER FARM: Its corn and pumpkin fields plainly visible from I-5 north of Everett, Biringer is one of the pioneers of the destination U-pick farm industry. Its key offerings are strawberries, raspberries, tayberries, and such; a visit to the farm with the kids in October to pick a pumpkin is great fun. It's a bit hard to get to—best to get off at the Marysville exit and backtrack south, following the signs. 425-259-0255, www.biringerfarm.com.

BOEING EVERETT PLANT: The world's (erstwhile) largest commercial jets are made here in the world's largest building, a massive hangar south of Everett in which 747s, 767s, and 777s are assembled (parts arrive from elsewhere around the world). Visitors tour the plant Mon–Fri; you have to reserve a spot, and don't bring a camera, they won't allow it. It is truly astounding to stand beneath one of these behemoths and get a ground-level perspective on them. 544-1264 or 800-464-1476, www.boeing.com.

EVERETT HOMEPORT: The first new major navy facility on the West Coast in decades (1994) is home to a carrier group, including one nuclear-powered aircraft carrier, one destroyer, and three frigates, with about 6,000 sailors based here. It's the most significant event in the Everett economy since Boeing arrived in the '70s. Security concerns make tours rare, but they can be done. 425-304-3261, www.everett.navy.mil.

FEDERAL WAY

The name of this city derives from construction of Federal Highway 99—the "federal way"—in the 1920s. It was unofficial until adopted by the local chamber in the early '50s but was not the name of a city until it incorporated in 1990, one of a spate of South King County cities to do so that decade under growth pressures.

The community was given its modern character by two events, both in the '70s: Weyerhaeuser left Tacoma behind for its new headquarters in the woods east of I-5 in 1971, and a few years later the SeaTac Mall opened. (It was recently renamed **THE COMMONS** at Federal Way.) Residential and strip commercial growth followed rapidly, and when Federal Way incorporated it was Washington's sixth-largest city.

Today it is a distinctly suburban place—the area around the mall is its "downtown," and many of the jobs inside the city are retail and service. Commuters head to Tacoma, the Kent Valley, and Seattle daily. Like most other south county cities, it is quite multicultural; one-third of the residents are nonwhite or Hispanic.

Federal Way by the Numbers

District Council: Federal Way

Population: 82,200

Median age: 32.5

Median household income: $42,300

Median home sales price: $210,000

Major crimes/1,000: 26.2

Web sites: www.cityoffederalway.com, www.federalwaychamber.com

Media: Federal Way News

Main drags: SW 320th St, Pacific Hwy S (SR 99), 1st Ave S

Farmers market: The Commons parking lot, Sat 9am–1pm, June–Oct

Federal Way Attractions & Institutions

DASH POINT STATE PARK: Easily one of the most spectacular parks along Puget Sound, Dash Point has more than 3,000

feet of sandy beach, along with a campground and lots of trails and other amenities within its 397 acres. Beachcombing and swimming are particularly popular, though clamming is not recommended (toxic deposition issues). 5700 Dash Point Rd, 888-2216-7688, www.parks.wa.gov.

RHODODENDRON SPECIES BOTANICAL GARDEN: There are more than 800 species of rhodies on earth and countless thousands of varieties—and many of them are here. The 22-acre garden, nestled in fir and hemlock woods, holds 10,000 rhodies, plus companion plants such as heathers, maples, and ferns. The companion Pacific Rim Bonsai Collection is more circumspect, but intriguing. The garden is free Nov–Feb, and there are a few rhodies in bloom in the winter. 2525 S 336th (on the Weyerhaeuser grounds), 253-838-4646, www.rhodygarden.org

WEYERHAEUSER: Nestled like a fallen ledge in a broad ravine, the timber company's HQ building is one of the most striking corporate facilities in the Northwest, a melded-into-the-landscape edifice (the architects called it a "groundscraper") with strong hints of Frank Lloyd Wright. Outside, vines cascade from the various levels. Inside, an open office environment prevails—even the president occupies what's basically an overgrown cubicle. 33663 Weyerhaeuser Wy S, 253-924-2345, www.weyerhaeuser.com.

WEYERHAEUSER KING COUNTY AQUATIC CENTER: Built for the Goodwill Games, this training facility has two separate swimming areas ("natatoriums"), with seating for 2,500 spectators by the competition pool. Try your hand (or foot) at synchronized swimming. 650 SW Campus Dr, 206-296-4444, www.federalway.org/aquatic.

WILD WAVES WATER PARK: A wave pool, raging rivers, giant water slides, and attractions known as Cannonball and drop slides—if only the swimming season were longer than, well, two months. The adjacent thrill park has the largest wooden roller coaster in Washington. 36201 Enchanted Pkwy S, 253-661-8000, www.sixflags.com/parks/enchantedvillage.

KENT

King County's second-oldest municipality (1890) began life as a hops-farming center—the valley's fields, flooded often by the **GREEN RIVER**, were incredibly fertile. Later, truck farming took over: Kent was the "Lettuce Capital of the World" in the '20s, before Salinas seized the title forever.

The Howard Hanson flood-control dam on the upper reaches of the Green changed all that in 1963. The flat valley floor proved even more fertile for warehouses and industrial plants. Boeing arrived in the late '60s—Kent is the home of the **BOEING SPACE CENTER**—and literally hundreds of warehouses followed. The Kent Valley is a commercial real estate district known nationally as a bellwether area.

This is where Green River Killer Gary Ridgway's first victim was found in 1983, beneath a street bridge in Kent. It doesn't typify the city, however, which is a moderate, safe, and unassuming place. (By the way, the Green River and the Duwamish River are one and the same.)

Kent's other side is, literally, on its other sides: the plateaus east and west of the valley, which have become suburban residential areas in the midprice range. Thousands of workers pour off the plateaus each morning headed for the valley floor—not unlike the floods that once swept down the Green.

Kent by the Numbers

District Council: Kent

Population: 84,275

Median age: 31.8

Median household income: $48,000

Median home sales price: $217,000

Major crimes/1,000: 31.4

Web sites: www.ci.kent.wa.us, www.kentchamber.com

Media: King County Journal

Main drags: James St, Meeker St, West Valley Hwy

Key dates: Cornucopia Days, mid-July; Canterbury Faire Arts Festival, mid-Aug

Farmers market: Kent municipal parking lot, 4th Ave N & Smith, Sat 10am–3pm, June–Sept, 253-852-5466, www.kentlionsclub.org

Kent Attractions & Institutions

GREAT WALL MALL: Like the suburban Asian malls in Richmond, BC, this is the satellite "Chinatown" of King County, with dozens of vendors offering everything from ginseng preparations to durian and teak furniture, and representing a dozen Asian/Pacific cultures. The key draw is the 99 Ranch Market, a Uwajimaya-like Asian grocer. 18320 E Valley Hwy, 425-251-1600, www.greatwallmall.com.

OBERTO SAUSAGE: Seattle's homegrown Italian sausage company moved its operations to the Kent Valley decades ago, just like so many other firms in search of warehouse space; the factory store is near the headquarters. Beef jerky is now the company's lead product. Bring a product label to the Seafair hydro races and get a ticket for the "Oh Boy! Oberto" pit tour. 310 Washington Blvd N, 425-859-8472, www.oberto.com.

REGIONAL JUSTICE CENTER: This is a satellite King County Courthouse, with everything citizens might need from their government, except short waiting times. 401 4th Ave N, 205-2501, www.metrokc.gov/kcsc/rjc.

RIVERBEND GOLF COMPLEX: Tucked into oxbow bends of the Green River, this is one of the nicest municipal golf clubs in King County, with an 18-hole course, a 9-hole course, 3 pro shops, and something you definitely won't find at more highfalutin golf venues: a miniature golf course. The views of Rainier are great. 2019 Meeker St, 253-854-3673, www.ci.kent.wa.us/riverbend.

LYNNWOOD

This is a pleasant, medium-size, medium-priced suburban residential area just over the Snohomish County line. There is a nice 18-hole municipal golf course, a full-scale athletic complex and skate park, and a popular shopping center (**ALDERWOOD MALL**). In other words this is middle America to a T.

Other than that, Lynnwood is distinguished as the place where the "Puget Sound convergence zone" most often parks overhead. This is the line where air currents sweeping around the Olympic Mountains from north and south meet, creating an unstable atmosphere that erupts in rain showers. Many are the days you can leave Seattle in sunshine, reach rain at the county line, and drive back into sun by the time you're past Everett.

Lynnwood by the Numbers

District Council: Lynnwood

Population: 34,500

Median age: 34.9

Median household income: $44,100

Median home sales price: $212,000

Major crimes/1,000: 19.5

Web site: www.ci.lynnwood.wa.us

Main drags: SR 99, 196th SW

Lynnwood Attractions & Institutions

ALDERWOOD MALL: The big news at this regional mall is a recent (2004) expansion and renovation that brought a Nordstrom to Lynnwood, plus 35 other new retailers, including an Apple Computer store and an REI with a climbing wall. 3000 184th SW, 425-771-1211, www.alderwoodmall.com.

PUYALLUP

Puyallup-ites grow tired of explaining to outsiders how to spell and pronounce their city's name and its provenance (a Coast Salish term meaning "generous people"). Variations range from *Puwallyip* to *Pooh-ah-loop*; residents, when they want to be sarcastic, say they live in *P-yooei-loops*. You can win many, many party games with Puyallup trivia.

It is, withal, a peaceful and pleasant small town. A modest regional mall, **SOUTH HILL MALL**, perches on a ridge above town; house prices are reasonably affordable; and the Puyallup River Valley is still the home of small berry, bulb, and fruit farms, many of which offer **U-PICK HARVESTS** in the summer.

Unless you are actually going *to* **THE FAIR**, don't go to Puyallup *during* the fair. The whole town is taken over by this production, which is the major economic enterprise in the city.

The city's location directly downstream from one of the most likely faces of Rainier to melt and head down in an eruption (more trivia: this is called a pyroclastic flow) is Puyallup's other, more sensational claim to fame. But fear not—if it ever happens, Orting, a half hour up-valley, will go first, and the muck-slide won't reach Puyallup for several hours. Plenty of time to grab the scone mix and go.

Puyallup by the Numbers

District Council: Puyallup

Population: 35,400

Median age: 34.1

Median household income: $47,300

Median home sales price: $175,000

Major crimes/1,000: 21.5

Web sites: www.ci.puyallup.wa.us, www.puyallupchamber.com

Media: Puyallup Herald

Main drags: Pioneer Ave, Meridian St

Key dates: **Daffodil Festival,** early Apr; **Puyallup fair,** mid-Sept

Farmers market: Pioneer Park, Sat May–Oct, Sun June–Sept

Puyallup Attractions & Institutions

"THE FAIR": The Western Washington Fair is a feel-good, aw-shucks Puget Sound institution that is also the major force in Puyallup and far more technologically advanced than it may seem (witness its Web address). Its two-week, three-weekend run in mid-September brings more people to town than live there; some nearby residents pay for their vacations every year by selling parking space in their front yards. Those who "do the Puyallup" enjoy entertainment that ranges from the Beach Boys to barely pubescent rap groups, with the requisite half-dozen country stars thrown in. Pro rodeo, Fisher scones, Indian fry bread, curly fries, exquisitely groomed pigs, and kitchen-device hucksters are other reliable favorites. Pierce County Transit mounts special bus service to "the Puyallup"—if you do the fair, do this. Unless you like waiting in long, long lines of cars on suburban freeways. 253-841-5045, www.thefair.com.

MEEKER MANSION: Ezra Meeker, one of the West's most colorful personalities and an Oregon Trail pioneer, founded Puyallup in 1877 and set its early industry, agriculture, in motion with his advocacy of hops cultivation. His mansion is a yellow, quasi-Italianate Victorian structure, one of the finest late-19th-century homes in Western Washington. 312 Spring St, 253-848-1770, www.meekermansion.org.

RENTON

The vast majority of Seattle-area residents experience Renton as a sturdy industrial area where they sit in traffic fumes in the inevitable slowdowns on I-405 at the notorious **S-CURVES** (see Chapter 5, "Street Smarts," page 163). This identity is so ingrained that the city's own slogan tacitly acknowledges it, while attempting to overcome the image: "Ahead of the Curve."

That curve might be the cost of living in the Seattle area, as Renton is one of the more economical places within hailing distance of Seattle proper. The city is a popular settling spot for newer Americans (Asian/Pacific, 15 percent; Hispanic, 8 percent). Seventy-five percent of its residents rate Renton a great place to live; 93 percent feel safe.

Some things don't change, though—Renton is still industrial. As the home of Boeing's assembly plants for its smaller planes (737s), it is a factory town. But that's not a bad thing: The 737 is the best-selling commercial jet of all time and likely to remain so for decades.

Renton by the Numbers

District Council: Renton

Population: 54,900

Median age: 34

Median household income: $46,000

Median home sales price: $195,000

Major crimes/1,000: 35.1

Web sites: www.ci.renton.wa.us, www.renton-chamber.com

Media: King County Journal

Main drags: Grady Wy, Rainier Ave S, S 2nd St

Key date: Renton River Days, late July

Farmers market: Renton Piazza, Tues afternoons mid-June–mid-Sept, www.ci.renton.wa.us/attract/fmarket.htm

Renton Attractions & Institutions

IKEA: Wal-Mart has nothing on the original huge warehouse purveyor of economical lifestyles. IKEA has become such a force in Renton that it now sponsors the city's annual festival and performing arts center. The Swedish company's inventory ranges from bunk beds to napkin rings; visitors (it's as much like a family entertainment center as anything else) wend their way through on a designated path, with road signs indicating occasional shortcuts. The café's specialty is Swedish meatballs, yum, and three parking garages handle the crowds. 600 SW 43rd, 425-656-2980, www.ikea.com.

JIMI HENDRIX'S GRAVE: Hendrix found fame elsewhere, lived elsewhere, and died elsewhere. But his memory burns brightest here in his hometown. Technically, that's Seattle, but he is buried in Renton's Greenwood Cemetery, and the grave attracted so many visitors that the family built a memorial with a 30-foot granite dome, a statue of Jimi, and other enhancements. Fans still leave flowers and other mementos. Greenwood Memorial Park, 350 Monroe Ave NE, 425-255-1511, jimihendrixmemorial.com.

SOUTHCENTER MALL: With 500 retail stores and a huge surrounding commercial district, this is the major shopping area for South King County. Key stores: Sears, Bon-Macy's. Intersection of I-5 S & I-405, Tukwila, www.cricorp.com/southcenter.

SEATAC

Formed in 1990, SeaTac has two regionally notable claims to fame: It's the home of our airport, **SEATTLE-TACOMA INTERNATIONAL**, and the headquarters of Alaska Airlines. Naturally, the city's information page features a prominent photo of an Alaska plane coming in to land.

Not to foster confusion, though: The airport's actual name is Seattle-Tacoma, with a hyphen, abbreviated Sea-Tac. The city's name has no hyphen.

SeaTac by the Numbers

District Council:	SeaTac
Population:	25,500
Median age:	33.9

Median household income: $42,500

Median home sales price: $198,000

Major crimes/1,000: 35.5

Web sites: www.ci.seatac.wa.us, www.seattlesouthside.com

Main drag: International Blvd (Pacific Hwy S, SR 99)

SeaTac Attractions & Institutions

BAI TONG: Once upon a time, Thai food was ultra-exotic, and even Seattleites thought "Chinese" when the topic of Asian food was broached. Then an enterprising Thai Airways flight attendant dreamed up the notion of serving her native land's food to crews on layover in Seattle. At first it was known only to (and open only to) the flight crews, but after a year she moved to a former root beer drive-in, opened to the public in 1990, and word spread. Thai Airways dropped Seattle years ago, and more inventive restaurants have since raised Thai cookery to much higher levels, but this is still a fine place for lunch or dinner on your way to or from the airport. The name means "banana leaf." 15859 International Blvd, 431-0893.

SEA-TAC AIRPORT: Why is our airport here? Because in 1948, when it was built to replace Boeing Field, this plateau had plenty of available ground—and it experiences less fog than the low-lying location of Boeing Field. The airport is the obvious economic powerhouse in SeaTac. 433-5388, www.portseattle.org/seatac.

TACOMA

Tacoma residents are tired of hearing about the "aroma from Tacoma." The city's pulp mill, which long ago did indeed spew somewhat noxious smoke into the regional atmosphere, has cleaned up its emissions significantly. But, skeptics say, you can still see the plume. And smell it. Yes, it does have visible water vapor, and the odor of wood chips cooking is unmistakable and penetrating. But this is a microscopic fraction of the pollution created daily by vehicle emissions in, say, Bellevue; nor does it smell any worse than the 10,000 diesels that ply I-5 daily delivering those all-important battery-lit basketball shoes to Southcenter Mall.

Tacoma has long had an inferiority complex. History helped create it. The "City of Destiny" was Puget Sound's leading urban area until a ship from Alaska chanced to dock in Seattle with the first gold from the Klondike. Happenstance, that. Tacoma still had the first transcontinental railroad (1873) to reach Puget Sound, and if you want to bandy millionaires about, Tacoma attracted a doozy: Frederick Weyerhaeuser was a Midwest timber tycoon who decided to come west and buy a few trees. In 1900 he sat down in a hotel lobby in Tacoma, took title to 900,000 acres of timberland, and wrote what was at that time the largest check ever written: $1 million.

The **WEYERHAEUSER** Corporation set up shop in Tacoma, and its wealth soon translated into some of the finest homes in Puget Sound, lining the bluffs overlooking **COMMENCEMENT BAY**. Weyerhaeuser has since moved to Federal Way (see listing earlier in the chapter), and downtown Tacoma declined until the 1990s, when the city quite deliberately set about reconfiguring itself—cleaning up its famed crime area, Hilltop; encouraging local industry to clean itself up, including the pulp mill; and encouraging the installation of miles and miles of fiber optic cable. Thus the city's claim to be "America's #1 Wired City," with which it is assiduously wooing King County businesses looking for a more economical and more amiable home.

Tacoma has dozens of **LOVELY RESIDENTIAL DISTRICTS** in which well-kept older homes, ranging from Victorian manses to postwar bungalows, line quiet streets. The **PROCTOR NEIGHBORHOOD** in the North End is particularly well-known; this is where "Frugal Gourmet" Jeff Smith lived before fame lured him to Pike Place Market.

Tacoma by the Numbers

District Council: Tacoma	
Population: 197,000	
Median age: 33.9	
Median household income: $37,879	
Median home sales price: $155,000	
Major crimes/1,000: 42.9	
Web sites: www.cityoftacoma.org, www.wiredcityusa.com	
Media: Tacoma News Tribune	
Main drags: Ruston Wy, Pacific Ave, 6th Ave	

Key date: Daffodil Parade, early Apr

Farmers market: Downtown, on Broadway between 9th & 11th Aves; Thur 9am–2pm, June–mid-Oct; www.tacomafarmersmarket.org

Tacoma Attractions & Institutions

ASARCO SMELTER: Once one of the most toxic and best-known Superfund sites on the West Coast, this arsenic-laden piece of Commencement Bay shoreline is slowly being cleaned and reclaimed. You still don't want to eat the dirt in the immediate neighborhood (along Ruston Wy west of Tacoma's Old Town), but hey, there are plenty of good eateries nearby. Cleanup information center, 253-756-5436.

BROADWAY PERFORMING ARTS DISTRICT: Those who marvel at the restored Paramount Theater in Seattle had best reserve their superlatives until they see Tacoma's Pantages Theatre. This glistening, white, 1916 neoclassical fantasy is opulent on a European scale, with brass, gilt, tile, and friezes everywhere you look. It and the nearby **BEAUX ARTS RIALTO THEATER** (1918) are home to four symphonies, opera, ballet, and numerous touring performance series. Tickets—and parking—are more economical and easier to come by than anything in Seattle. 901 Broadway, 253-591-5894 or 800-291-7593, www.broadwaycenter.org.

FRISKO FREEZE: With uncompromising old-fashioned greasy burgers and fries, this famous drive-in is Tacoma's answer to Seattle's Dick's. The name refers to the milkshakes, which are also not lowfat substances. 1201 Division Ave, 253-272-6843.

MUSEUM DISTRICT: By far the best and most compact cultural neighborhood in Puget Sound (sorry, Seattle), this stretch of eastern downtown Tacoma represents the community's determination to transform itself. What was once a rundown, unsafe industrial district now has three of the best museums in the state. The **WASHINGTON STATE HISTORY MUSEUM** (1911 Pacific Ave, 253-272-3500 or 888-be-there, www.washingtonhistory.org) came first, with an admirable depiction of the human history of the state, from Native bands to rock bands. The arresting **MUSEUM OF GLASS (MOG)** (1801 E Dock St, 253-284-4750 or 866-4-MUSEUM, museumofglass.org), designed by famed Canadian architect Arthur Erickson, features working glass artists in a "hot shop" contained within a distinctive cone designed to mimic the traditional hog fuel burners of old-time Northwest timber mills. MOG includes work by native son Dale Chihuly, including the sensational Bridge of Glass that connects it to the history museum. The **TACOMA ART MUSEUM** (1701 Pacific Ave, 253-272-4258, www.tacomaartmuseum.org), the district's newest arrival, has an excellent, mostly modern, and mostly American collection, with works by artists ranging from Mary Cassatt to Andrew Wyeth.

POINT DEFIANCE PARK: Tacoma's municipal pride and joy is a 1,000-acre expanse of old-growth forest (some of the last remaining along Puget Sound), undeveloped shoreline, gardens, and attractions; the main route through the park, Five-Mile Dr, winds past it all. Within the park are a restaurant complex, marina, ferry dock, logging museum, pioneer fort replica, and a dandy small zoo and aquarium, **POINT DEFIANCE ZOO**, known for its work with beluga whales (253-591-5337, www.pdza.org). The park's rose and dahlia gardens are especially fine. 253-305-1000, www.metroparkstacoma.org.

THE SPAR TAVERN: A venerable brick institution in Tacoma's Old Town, the Spar has the best pub food in the South Sound: great fish and chips, Caesar salads, soups, and sandwiches. Occasionally there's live entertainment. 2123 N 30th St, 253-272-2122.

TACOMA DOME: One of the largest wooden dome structures on earth—surely that harks back to Tacoma's heritage as a timber town—is the home of rock concerts, ice-skating extravaganzas, tractor pulls, boat shows, and high school sporting events. Several minor-league sports teams have come and gone within its confines. 253-593-7617, tacomadome.org.

TACOMA RAINIERS: The Seattle Mariners's AAA minor-league affiliate is just down the road in Tacoma, a fact that proves handy for both sides. The Rainiers play in Cheney Stadium, a medium-size baseball park that fans say offers everything good about being down on the farm—moderate prices, fan-friendly atmosphere, the chance to see the game up close. The team's name honors the old Seattle AAA team that longtime residents remember fondly, no matter how well the Mariners do. 253-752-7700, www.tacomarainiers.com.

UPS/PLU: Tacoma's blue-collar, gritty image is belied by the presence of not one but two exceptional liberal arts colleges. **PACIFIC LUTHERAN UNIVERSITY** (253-535-7457, www.plu.edu)

is known for its bookish atmosphere and a football team whose legendary coach, Frosty Westering, enjoyed such success (innumerable league championships) that the position was, literally, passed on to his son Scott. **UNIVERSITY OF PUGET SOUND** (253-879-3900, www.ups.edu) is best known for its extravagantly beautiful campus of Tudor Gothic brick and stone buildings, as well as exceptionally high admission standards, with Rhodes and Oxford scholars among its enrollees.

VASHON ISLAND

First of all, there is no bridge. You get to the island and off it by ferry—or not at all. This doesn't bother residents a bit, though grousing about ferry service is the national pastime on Vashon. Second, there are two islands here. Vashon, the larger, more northwesterly island, is connected to **MAURY**, the smaller southeasterly islet, by a narrow land bridge that was dredged up from a tideflat long ago. Thus the bumper stickers you see that urge "Free Maury Island," as if Maury's 2,000 or so residents would rather swim their cars across. (Actually, there's a legitimate reason for the idea: Cutting off the tide circulation has changed the saltwater regime in Quartermaster Harbor, where shellfish are now often not safe to eat.)

Vashon/Maury islanders are fervently committed to their laid-back, pastoral lifestyle. Though quite a few commute to Seattle, it is by and large a pleasant trip—a peaceful country drive, a ferry ride, then a bus ride or walk on the mainland. Islanders tend to spend as much time on the island as possible; many residents get by doing pickup work as carpenters, and many are artists and craftspeople. The vast majority of homes on the island are on acreage in the country.

Vashon is a determinedly eclectic community—possibly the only place on earth where a petition urging Ellen DeGeneres to come out on network TV was posted on the bulletin board of the local weightlifting/athletic club. Though not incorporated (an effort to do so was squashed by county political heavyweights in the early '90s), the community council can exercise some influence. At one session in the late '90s, county planners showed up to seek feedback on installing a stoplight in the center of the island's town (also called Vashon). At community council meetings everyone present gets to vote: The result was a unanimous 127–0 against a stoplight. The county officials rolled up their plans and left, and there is still no traffic light on the island.

The highlight of the annual **STRAWBERRY FESTIVAL** in July is the parade, which features the local Thriftway's marching grocery-cart drill team and usually includes such other island groups as the corgi club, the belly-dancing club, and sometimes the marching kazoo band. Top that, Fremont.

Vashon by the Numbers

District Council: Vashon Community Council

Population: 10,100 (12,000 in summer)

Median age: 34

Median household income: $60,000

Median home sales price: $240,000

Major crimes/1,000: NA (negligible)

Web site: www.vashonchamber.com

Media: The Beachcomber

Main drag: Vashon Hwy

Key date: Vashon Island Strawberry Festival, mid-July

Farmers market: Vashon Island Growers Association, center of town, Sat 9am–1pm, May–Oct

Vashon Attractions & Institutions

POINT ROBINSON LIGHTHOUSE: One of the most oft-photographed and painted points in Puget Sound, this gravel promontory on the east end of Maury Island has lots of pleasant space along the beach for picnics and a drop-dead view of Rainier in the background. The 1915 lighthouse is still an automated navigation beacon. At the end of Pt Robinson Rd, www.vashonparkdistrict.org.

SOUND FOOD: It's hard to get a meal here that doesn't have carrots somewhere in it. (Even breakfast, in the vegetarian omelets and muffins.) A holdover from the counterculture era of the '70s, one of the island's most beloved institutions has a bakery and a delightful outdoor patio shaded by wisteria, and serves splendid soups, salads, sandwiches, and pastas. All just as wholesome as can be. There's a natural foods market (Minglement) next door. 20312 Vashon Hwy SW, 463-3565.

CHAPTER 4

No Place Like Home

Seattle has some of the highest housing costs in the country, thanks to a red-hot real estate market that continued to see values appreciating going into 2005. The city is not even the most expensive place in the Puget Sound region to buy or rent a home—in Bellevue, a four-bedroom, 2,200-square-foot home costs an average of $490,000, about $150,000 more than a typical house of the same size in Seattle. The run-up in prices has diminished considerably from the late '90s, when house-hungry buyers flush with stock-option cash were bidding on houses the minute they came on the market, transforming the asking price from a ceiling to a floor.

Relatively low mortgage interest rates have continued to make these higher-priced homes accessible to people earning at least the area median income of $59,000 per year. Whatever high income and low interest rates can't cover, distance can: The farther you are willing to live from downtown Seattle, generally, the lower the home price. According to the Seattle–King County Association of Realtors, the **MEDIAN HOME SALES PRICE** in King County topped $300,000 for the first time in late 2004; in Snohomish County, $250,000; in Pierce County, $200,000. There are usually 6,000–10,000 active listings in King County and 3,000–4,000 in Pierce and Snohomish.

At the same time, high-end homes have been particularly hot sellers throughout the area. Luxury home sales between $1 million and $3 million went up almost two-and-a-half times in the summer of 2004, compared with a year earlier. The rate was even higher for homes above the $3 million threshold. In June 2004 nine houses and a luxury condominium sold above that astronomical price, compared with just one in the same time period in 2003. On average, high-cost homes spend fewer than two months on the market.

POSH CONDOMINIUMS are sprouting like dandelions both in downtown proper and in the transitional neighborhoods on the outskirts of the central core, such as Fremont, Queen Anne, and even Ballard. By some estimates, over the course of the 1990s, **DOWNTOWN HOUSING** grew faster than anyplace in the country besides Houston. In the first half of 2000, eight major new residential projects went up in downtown's Belltown district. The gentrification of the formerly low-end neighborhood has produced some striking contrasts, with the office of *Real Change*—a weekly newspaper produced and sold on the streets by current and formerly homeless vendors—located just blocks away from some of the newest and most expensive high-rise housing in the city. Even before construction was complete on Avenue One, a 58-unit condo complex near the northern end of the neighborhood, the apartments were being snapped up at the rate of almost two a day, most in the range of $250,000 to $1 million.

Seattle neighborhoods hold every type of housing imaginable, with older styles closer in—Victorian on Capitol Hill; Arts & Crafts and Craftsman in Fremont, Ballard, and Green Lake; mid-century brick bungalows north of Green Lake and along Lake Washington. The Eastside is largely housing stock less than 50 years old and even sports its own style, a modern faux-chateau two-story called "Bellevue French."

Daunting as home prices may be in the Seattle area, those who manage to squeeze into their own homes can take comfort in the fact that real estate has appreciated steadily, with few slumps, over the past half-century. That's because we live in a desirable locale—and in real estate, as the saying goes, location is everything.

BUYING A HOME

In most instances a real estate agent represents the seller, who is responsible for paying the commission out of the sale price. That's the way it has been for decades, and it continues to be so. The standard commission rate is 6 percent, but there are a number of agents offering discount rates as low as 4.5 percent or less, in an effort to attract customers.

The proliferation of buyer's agents in the late '90s prompted a reconfiguration of state law and real estate regulations, which basically say that an agent working with a homebuyer represents the seller, unless the agent is the listing agent or all parties explicitly agree the agent represents the buyer. For an agent to represent both sides a legal acknowledgement of that must be prepared.

Confusing? It can be. Best to simply link up with an agent under the clear understanding that he or she works for you. (There are a few agents who specialize as buyer's agents.)

A buyer's agent's goal will be to get his or her client the best house for the least money at the most favorable terms. The agent might show not only properties included in the local Mul-

The Top Two

Unlike other metropolitan areas, Seattle's two leading real estate firms, based on 2003 sales volumes, are homegrown: **WINDERMERE REAL ESTATE**, founded in 1972, has 90 offices and 3,300 Puget Sound–area agents, with an annual sales volume around $14 billion. The company usually represents the higher end of the market. 527-3801, www.windermere.com.

JOHN L. SCOTT REAL ESTATE, founded in 1931, has 58 offices with 2,000 agents representing about $6 billion in sales volume. 230-7600, www.johnlscott.com.

---

tiple Listing Service inventories, but also For-Sale-By-Owner homes. Some buyer's agents will expect buyers to enter into an agreement making them an exclusive representative. Buyers may agree to pay a flat fee, an hourly rate, or (most often) to include the agent's commission in the purchase offer. Buyer's agents can also ask for what they would have earned in a traditional commission structure, though their fee may work out to less than that of a traditional agent on more expensive homes. Increasingly, though, buyer's agents work on an hourly basis or for a set fee negotiated in advance.

Some of the things that a buyer's agent can do include developing a comparable-sales market analysis that shows similar properties in the area by price and features (this is similar to what an appraiser does). A buyer's agent can find and pass on information about the seller and concessions the seller may be ready to offer. Most important, a buyer's agent approaches the essential market-sifting with his or her clients' needs in mind first.

The best way to find an agent is through a personal reference from friends, co-workers, family members, and the like. Otherwise, several large groups offer Realtor-search options. House.com is an Internet matching service connecting home buyers with prescreened and customer-rated real estate agents in a specific area.

The **NORTHWEST MULTIPLE LISTING SERVICE,** which encompasses essentially all Realtor-listed properties, has a comprehensive Web site that features home listings, useful information for buyers and sellers, and links to Seattle community and school information and other real estate sites at www.nwrealestate.com.

Though not all real estate agents are Realtors, the vast majority are, and they are all members of Realtors associations. To search these groups by agent area, experience, and specialty, visit www.realtor.com/seattle. The site for the local branch, the **SEATTLE-KING COUNTY ASSOCIATION OF REALTORS**, is www.nwrealtor.com. This is the professional organization to which you should direct complaints about agents, if a problem arises.

Property Taxes

King County property taxes are, not surprisingly, the highest in Washington State. Assessments vary by municipality, fire, school, and other districts; every homeowner receives an assessed valuation statement each year. The actual tax is transparent to most homeowners as the levy is paid by the mortgage servicing company, which collects a monthly fee. (Why do banks do this? To be sure their secured property isn't seized by the county.) Those homeowners who do pay their taxes directly receive a statement early each year with the annual tax bill. It's due in two installments, by April 30 and October 31. (Postmarked on that day, if you pay by mail; the following Monday if either day falls on a weekend.)

You can pay online, by mail, or in person (at the courthouse downtown, 500 4th Ave, or at county service centers in Kent, Renton, Bothell, Fall City, Sammamish, Cottage Lake, and Vashon). What you cannot do is pay late; miss by one day and the county will send your check back, and you'll have to repay with interest. Make sure your check is in the mail the day before. Property tax abatements and reductions are available to seniors and disabled persons who meet income guidelines; call 296-3850 or 800-325-6165; www.metrokc.gov/finance/treasury/kctaxinfo.

If you want to find out more about why you owe what you do in property taxes compared with your neighbors, visit the Public Information Unit of the assessor's office on the seventh floor of the King County Administration Building. The information available covers everything from the parcel number and a property's characteristics to the history of a parcel's assessed value. The same information is available at the Web site of the King County Assessor's Office; you'll need your property's parcel number before getting started because you can't look it up on the site.

Each of King County's 7 million pieces of property is assessed every year and assessors visit your property every five years. Valuations are based on sales figures for similar pieces of property, how much it would cost to replace the existing structure if it's new construction, and, in the case of business or rental property, the amount of income it's expected to generate.

About 7,000 valuations are appealed every year with a 60 percent success rate. You can appeal by contacting the Board of Appeals/Equalization within 30 days of the date you received the assessment, or July 1, whichever is later. The best way to support your case is to use comparative value estimates from area real estate agents and show how the condition and maintenance of your property differs from similarly assessed properties. The board typically makes its decision within 6 to 12 months. If the board agrees, it will recommend a new

The Home Owners Club

This 45-year-old organization provides prescreened referrals to members for plumbing, electrical, repair, remodeling, contractors, etc.—including emergencies like broken pipes and arranging bids for remodeling projects. Annual dues are $48. 1202 Harrison St, 622-3500; www.homeownersclub.org.

assessment. If not, you can take your case to the State Board of Appeals. King County Assessor's Office: 296-7300, www.metrokc.gov/assessor; County Board of Appeals/Equalization: 296-3496; State Board of Appeals: 360-753-5446.

That Valuable View

Seattle real estate buyers value a vista more than most metropolitan dwellers. Mount Rainier; Puget Sound; Lakes Washington, Union, and Sammamish; the Cascades; the Olympics (the latter particularly valued for their sunset color display)—all add to the enjoyment of inhabiting a house. And they add to the home's price as well, sometimes substantially. Rainier and the Olympics are the most desirable views; even a corner-window glimpse of Rainier from an upstairs bedroom will appear in a for-sale listing as a "Rainier view" and add $10,000 to the price tag. A full-expanse view of Rainier, the Olympics, Lake Washington, and the Cascades, or something similar, can add $50,000 or more to a home's value.

Sometimes the view mania seems a bit excessive. "Territorial view" is the term invented for what you see from a home that overlooks almost anything, including your neighbors' yards. "Water view" covers Lake Washington and, well, a seasonal pond in a drainage marsh. If a view is an important criterion in your home search, it's a good idea to nail down exactly what view a home offers before you dash off to see it, or you'll be looking at literally hundreds of "views."

Before you buy a house with a view, it's best to keep in mind that you may not get to keep it. Very few properties are situated so that nothing will ever, ever block the view—remember, we live in a temperate rain forest where the native trees can and do grow 5 feet a year. View easements are possible but uncommon; otherwise, there is little or no general legal protection for a view. This includes construction of taller buildings in downtown areas, though size and height codes apply in residential zones. The best idea, if the view you want is crucial to your enjoyment of the property, is to make sure you control the land on which something might intervene—that means waterfront or atop a steep slope that you own.

People do occasionally go to extremes to "protect" their view, such as the judge not long ago who paid a tree-faller to cut down some trees on city property. Homeowners occasionally do it "accidentally" on neighboring properties. This is illegal, unjust, and unethical.

Home, Buoyant Home

Floating homes date back to Seattle's beginnings—logging crews lived in boom-mounted bunkhouses. That brawny group of folks evolved into a bohemian community of freethinkers and students, then into more upscale but independent residents who treasure their exotic lifestyle next to downtown on the water. Immense cachet was conferred on the idea by *Sleepless in Seattle*, which was set on a Lake Union houseboat.

Today there are fewer than 500 houseboats left, all more or less "grandfathered" in place—no new moorages are available, part of the reason one such residence sold for $2 million. The community's interests are ably and zealously represented by the **FLOATING HOMES ASSOCIATION**, which has mounted numerous court challenges to anyone trying to beach the remaining homes. Association members sometimes offer tours of the community. 325-1132, www.seattlefloatinghomes.org.

HOME INSPECTIONS

Almost all real estate transactions these days are accompanied by a home inspection. Once upon a time this was the detail sellers resisted and buyers demanded; now, most reputable agents require it, just to settle any questions on the sale and alleviate the need for the two sides to tussle over it. (After all, if the sale blows up, the agent loses the commission.) Most sales contracts these days make an inspection a condition of sale.

Inspectors assess everything from a home's structural soundness to the efficacy of its insulation. Electrical systems, plumbing, heating, foundation, durability—everything that goes into making a home durable and useable falls within the inspector's purview. You can direct that particular concerns be addressed, such as the stability of a steep slope. The inspection result will be a thick report detailing your home's condition; usually the buyer is welcome to accompany the inspector while he or she looks at the home.

A **NATIONAL HAZARD DISCLOSURE STATEMENT** is also required. That form covers potential problems from fire and flood to earthquakes—all of which have been known to happen in Seattle. In 2001, for instance, the Nisqually Earthquake shook the northwestern part of the state pretty severely. While most of the damage occurred 60–100 miles south of the city, a number of older masonry buildings were rendered uninhabitable until repairs could be made.

Also consider that **MUDSLIDES** can be a problem in parts of Seattle. Neighborhoods like Capitol Hill, Queen Anne, and Magnolia, which are on steep hills, have seen some houses' foundations undermined following particularly heavy rains in the wintertime.

Federal law now requires sellers to disclose any known **LEAD** hazards. For the most part these come from the use of lead-based paints and so are of concern primarily in homes built prior to 1978, when the last of the lead-based paints were removed from the consumer market.

None of these requirements obligate the seller to hire an engineer to cover their property with a fine-tooth comb to find potential problems. For a savvy buyer, paying a good inspector a fee of $400 or so to give the home a careful going-over before the papers are signed and money changes hands can ultimately save thousands in headaches and possible legal bills later.

There are dozens of home inspectors. It's wise to hire one who has been in the business a while and, most important,

> ## Rx for Rot
>
> Given our soggy weather, mold, mildew, and rot are typical Seattle house ailments. Some types can even cause respiratory ailments.
>
> **CAUSES:** Weather from outside seeping in through leaks, especially in basements that aren't sealed and from leaky roofs, and moisture generated from inside that can't get out.
>
> **SIGNS OF IMPENDING DOOM:** Blistering paint, mildew or dampness on walls, and sweaty windows. If you aren't sure if you have rot, push an ice pick or screwdriver into suspect wood and see if it goes in easily.
>
> **SOLUTION:** You need ventilation, especially in the attic, kitchen, bathroom, and crawl spaces. Install fans and vents, and get that basement sealed. Cut back on houseplant watering and aquariums in the winter. Make sure your roof is ship-shape.

knows the particular territory—the issues that pertain to exact locales are often little known and little publicized. An East King County home inspector, for instance, will know things about coal-shaft subsidence (yes, really) that a downtown Seattle inspector won't, while the latter will have expertise in earthquake vulnerability the former won't.

One good way to find an inspector is through your mortgage loan officer or Realtor, if you have a buyer's agent. Most reputable home inspectors are licensed by the **AMERICAN SOCIETY OF HOME INSPECTORS**, www.ashi.org.

PROPERTY TITLES

Title companies are an essential part of the home-buying process, as is purchasing title insurance. Simply put, the title search is a way to ensure that there are no outstanding liens, loans, or other encumbrances on the property before plunking down a bunch of money. The fee for the title search is small, generally $25–$50, depending on the price of the home. Title insurance, which may run as high as several hundred dollars, is a way to guarantee there are no problems if something unexpected comes up after the title search has been completed.

Given the headaches that can arise from unresolved claims, it is a small price to pay. As a rule the buyer and seller divide the cost of the title insurance. The most prominent local title firms are **STEWART TITLE** (770-8700, www.stewarttitle.com), **PACIFIC NORTHWEST TITLE** (622-1040), and **CHICAGO TITLE** (628-5666, www.chicagotitle.com).

REAL ESTATE ATTORNEYS

People love to hate lawyers until they need one. And real estate transactions are one of those occasions when just about everyone is glad to have the services of a good attorney. The lawyer's role is to make sure the terms are clear to all and that all the legal requirements are being met. Every contract with as much riding on it as the purchase of a home should be looked over by a competent real estate attorney at least once.

ATTORNEYFIND at www.attorneyfind.com is a directory of law firms that lists a directory of real estate attorneys. If you have a complaint about a real estate transaction or an agent's conduct, contact the **SEATTLE-KING COUNTY ASSOCIATION OF REALTORS** at www.nwrealtor.com. The Better Business Bureau handles complaints about business transactions of all types; 431-2222, www.thebbb.org.

DID YOU FEEL THE EARTH MOVE?

Seattle actually gets a lot of earthquakes—it's just that we don't notice most of them. The **PACIFIC NORTHWEST SEISMOGRAPH NETWORK** reports that around 1,000 earthquakes occur every year in Washington and Oregon, but only one to two dozen of those are felt by anyone on the surface. Damaging quakes are far less frequent, but they do happen (see "What's Shakin'," below).

Though the 2001 Nisqually Earthquake was frightening and disruptive for many, its outcome seems rather benign when one recalls the results of California's 1989 Loma Prieta earthquake, which was of similar magnitude (7.1): more than 60 deaths and over $6 billion in damage in Santa Cruz County and the San Francisco Bay Area. Why did the Puget Sound area get off so easy? The depth of the Nisqually quake is commonly regarded as its saving grace—it occurred about

What's Shakin'?

THE PACIFIC NORTHWEST SEISMOGRAPH NETWORK: Archived data on Pacific Northwest earthquakes, big and small. www.ess.washington.edu/recenteqs/latest.htm

SEATTLE EMERGENCY MANAGEMENT: Details on Seattle's vulnerability to earthquakes and landslides, including maps. www.cityofseattle.net/emergency_mgt/hazards/earthquakes.htm

---

30 miles down. (The Loma Prieta quake, by contrast, had a focal depth of only 11 miles.)

The city has devoted a fair amount of effort to preparing homes and schools for future earthquakes. **SEATTLE'S PROJECT IMPACT** focuses on "retrofitting" homes and schools and mapping areas vulnerable to earthquake hazards. For those interested in protecting their homes against future earthquake damage, Project Impact offers two-hour courses in home retrofitting for a $10 tuition fee. Call 382-2159 for a list of times and dates, or visit www.cityofseattle.net/projectimpact.

To Insure, or Not to Insure

Earthquakes happen. The Nisqually quake proved that. While significant damage was confined mostly to Pioneer Square, it left a nagging question for millions of homeowners: Should we be insured? There's no easy answer. Earthquake coverage is expensive, up to $300 a year per $100,000 of house value. Deductibles are high. Many likely catastrophes are excluded, such as landslides. Many homes don't qualify whatsoever, such as those on steep slopes. Should a severe quake strike Seattle, federal disaster assistance is certain, though that is usually in the form of low-interest loans, rather than the outright payments insurance coverage provides.

For all these reasons even knowledgeable residents such as geologists forgo quake coverage and concentrate on quake preparation: secure tie-downs between house and foundation; chimney bolsters; water-heater straps; latched cabinets for china and glassware. It may be a better investment to spend $200 on an inspection to find out how to quake-proof your house is than twice that on an insurance premium.

IT PAYS TO BE ENERGY EFFICIENT

That little crack next to your bedroom window is worth: $7,800. That faucet drip? A couple hundred bucks over the years. Those old single-pane metal windows? Thousands of dollars. Over the lifetime of the average home, the tiniest inefficiencies cost, in the current energy market, huge amounts of money.

Numerous local agencies and companies are willing and able to help Seattle-area residents upgrade their windows, homes, appliances, and furnaces. New equipment in all these cases can reduce energy use enormously, saving you money and our society environmental costs.

Seattle residents can take advantage of **SEATTLE CITY LIGHT** programs to upgrade clothes washers and dryers, buy high-efficiency light fixtures and bulbs, and even, in pilot neighborhoods, have their homes weatherized at subsidized rates. Programs range from advice to purchase rebates up to $100, to outright loans; call 684-3800 or visit www.cityofseattle.net/light/conserve. **PUGET SOUND ENERGY (PSE)**, the other major power provider in King County (once this was known as Puget Power, and many still call it that) offers many of the same services for homeowners, including free "energy audits" of your house. Since it took over Washington Natural Gas, PSE also is happy to help homeowners convert to gas heating and cooking, including low-cost loans; see www.pse.com/yourhome.

There are also lots of very simple things anyone can do to conserve energy, without spending a dime: turn off lights; open curtains on sunny days, keep them closed on cold, cloudy days; turn down the heat when you leave for the day; turn down your water heater when you travel. Tips are available from both City Light and Puget Power.

PERMITS

Renovations, no less than new construction, require a permit before any actual work is begun—and this applies to nearly anything that involves structural work in or around a house, ranging from a new sidewalk to a backyard deck.

The city's **DEPARTMENT OF PLANNING AND DEVELOPMENT (DPD)** administers construction and land use regulations for all properties within the Seattle city limits. Permits must be obtained from DPD for construction projects, projects involving new or changed uses of property, and other building and design elements. DPD issues two main types of permits—land use and construction—and they may be applied for either separately or together. Land use permits ensure that structures meet zoning requirements and comply with environmental regulations.

Construction permits allow the city to review structural and safety elements of the project. Construction-related permits include either building a new structure or adding on to an existing building, demolition (a must if someone is planning to erect a new home on an existing lot or to remove an old garage, shed, or other standing structure on the property), and grading, for reshaping the grounds or adding a driveway, for example. DPD also administers electrical, energy, and mechanical codes, and side sewer codes. Plumbing permits are approved on-site at DPD by Seattle/King County Health Department staff. The DPD is located in the Key Tower building in downtown Seattle at 700 5th Ave, Suite 2000; 684-8850, www.ci.seattle.wa.us/dpd.

Permit fees are based on a number of components that depend on the nature and scope of any given project or situation. Fees are not ultimately determined until a permit is issued. But people applying for a building permit who know the square footage and occupancy of what they are planning to build can get an estimate from a permit specialist. Specialists are available to meet with prospective permit applicants at the DPD Applicant Services Center during normal business hours. They can also be contacted by phone at 684-8850 from 1 to 4:30pm, Monday through Friday.

IN THE ZONE

A man's home may be his castle, but until the city recognizes individual monarchies, he'll still have to comply with single-family zoning regulations that cover almost everything but the moat, including:

LOT USAGE: A house and other structures may only take up 1,750 square feet or 35 percent of the property, whichever is greater. Below-ground swimming pools and decks shorter than 18 inches are excluded.

YARDS: The front yard should either have 20 feet between the property line and the house, or have the average distance between house and property line of parcels on either side of it, whichever is smaller. There must be 25 feet (or 20 percent of the lot depth) from the rear property line to the house foundation. Storage sheds and chicken coops are acceptable as long as they don't cover more than 40 percent of the back yard. Side yards must be at least 5 feet wide.

Want to tear it all down and rebuild? It will cost you. **DEMOLITION PERMITS** are $225 from the Seattle Department of Planning and Development Applicant Service Center. 684-8850 or 684-8600 (24-hour info), www.cityofseattle.net/dclu.

HARDWARE HELP

Though Seattle has a healthy share of Home Depot outlets, the city is also home to a more rare, more interesting, and often essential institution—the **NEIGHBORHOOD HARDWARE STORE**. Many of these have been open for decades, and they offer both materials and expertise you can't find at the big-box stores. Like, how to replace an aging brass doorknob fixture in an early Craftsman house; and what to do with a stuck counterbalance pulley in an old wood casement window. More notable practitioners of this valuable art include Crown Hill Hardware, 784-0016; Limback Lumber, 782-3487; Madison Park Hardware, 322-5331; Rainier Hardware, 448-9415; Stoneway Hardware, 545-6910; Compton Lumber, 623-5010; and Magnolia Hardware, 282-1916.

Seattle also has an excellent set of **BUILDING SALVAGE OUTLETS**. The marvels you can encounter during a stroll through these stores is remarkable—leaded-glass windows, old wood cook stoves, wrought-iron railings, entire stairways, banisters, and kitchen cabinets. If you are the proud owner of a home as old the New Deal, these are likely the best places for you to find appropriate remodel/replacement materials: Rejuve Seattle, 382-1901; Earthwise, 624-4510; The Restore, 297-9119; and Second Use, 763-6929.

The unique Environmental Home Center (628-7332) offers "green" building materials for building and decorating homes, including nontoxic paint, sustainable wood products, and natural carpets.

FOR THE LOVE OF TREES

For a city in which few of its original trees remain, Seattle guards its trees, new and old, zealously. Trees on public property, or within the public right-of-way (such as the planting strip in front of your house) may not be pruned or removed without a permit. Other regulations govern what may be done in the planting strip, restricting plant height, for instance. And the **CITY ARBORIST** is both an information resource for homeowners (check out the list of recommended trees when you're landscaping) and an advocate for trees, should you see someone taking a saw to an old cedar. 684-7649, www.ci.seattle.wa.us/transportation/arborist.htm.

RECYCLING

Seattle was once among the nation's leaders in recycling, with an average approaching the official municipal goal of 60 percent (by weight of waste produced). Alas, it's now down to 40 percent—well above the national average of 27 percent, but still low enough that the city ships to its Eastern Oregon landfill 72,000 tons of discarded paper a year. That equals 1.2 million trees.

Just do it

What happened? Blame whichever societal trend you wish, the recycling slump tosses a wrench in the usually reliable theory that cost incentives will drive public behavior. Recycling costs about half what garbage collection does, but even famously progressive Seattleites are apparently willing to pay to be lazy. That's why the city has adopted a radical new hard-line stance. Garbage with recyclable material in it—paper, cans,

---

Potholes, mudslides, and flooding, oh my!

The city can be your best resource when you need help when something goes wrong, from potholes in the alley to debris and downed trees in the street. The **ROAD MAINTENANCE OFFICE** is divided into two regions, so if you live north of Denny Wy, call 684-7508; if you live south of there, call 386-1218. For water-related problems like sewer backups, flooding, and general drainage problems, call the city water department's 24-hour hotline at 386-1800.

bottles, plastic, and such greater than 10 percent—will not be collected. That's right: The garbage truck will pass you by. You'll get a note from your collector explaining the problem; businesses and multifamily complexes will pay fines. All the details are explained at 732-9253, www.ci.seattle.wa.us/util/services. It remains to be seen whether the traditional theory on garbage will apply: If the city won't take it, refuse will simply pile up in vacant spaces. If you abide by the new rules, your garbage is picked up once a week, and you pay according to the size can you regularly fill.

Yard waste goes in special "green waste" containers and is picked up twice a month, on collection days that alternate with recyclable pickup. Recyclables need not be sorted—pitch them all in the big container and set it by the curb. It couldn't be simpler. Most other King County cities follow similar policies, though details vary.

Tossing Toxics

As always, toxic materials and appliances cannot be tossed—no batteries, paint, computers, kerosene, or plutonium by-products, please. Oil, batteries, tires, paint, and such are accepted by numerous retail outlets that sell such things. For all else, there are two hazardous waste drop-offs in Seattle; the north one is open by appointment (296-4692), the south one Thursdays, Fridays, and Saturdays 10am–4pm. King County has a **WASTEMOBILE** that travels the rest of the county; for the schedule, call 296-4692.

RENTING A HOME

The fact that even a "starter home" in Seattle costs $200,000 or more helps explain why better than half the households in Seattle are renters. Whether you're looking for a house, an apartment, or a shared living situation, there are numerous resources to help: classified ads in the daily newspapers and two alternative weeklies; agencies such as Apartment Finders; *For Rent* magazine, which focuses on apartment complexes around the Sound; and a plethora of Internet sites, including Craig's List (www.craigslist.org) and www.homerentalads.com, a free searchable database that includes home rentals, condos and townhouses, duplexes, lofts, and other Seattle properties for rent, lease, lease option, or rent-to-own. **SEATTLE RENTALS** (284-2554, www.seattlerentals.com) also has hundreds of listings for Seattle apartments, condos, or rental houses.

What's Your Budget?

Where to look for apartments and rental houses:

HIP & HIGH-PRICED: Queen Anne, Capitol Hill, Belltown, Alki, Overlake

MODERATE: Magnolia, Delridge, West Seattle, Kent, Factoria, Redmond

ECONOMY: Renton, Auburn, Kent, Federal Way, Tacoma, Everett.

Washington has modest legal protections for renters. State law prohibits rent-control ordinances. Efforts to revise the law to exempt the largest cities (or even just the single largest—aka Seattle) from the regulations have consistently been blocked by lawmakers in Olympia. After a number of instances when new owners of apartment buildings raised rents 60 to 200 percent with 20 or 30 days' notice, the Seattle City Council adopted some rules to make things a little easier for tenants while preserving the landlord's right to set the basic terms and conditions.

Seattle landlords are now required to give tenants 60 days' notice when they plan to increase rents more than 10 percent in a 12-month period. The Landlord-Tenant Act does not limit how much rent can be raised, or how often. However, the landlord cannot raise the rent to retaliate against a tenant.

Signing a Lease

From the tenant's perspective, the best assurance of a stable rental situation is had by signing a lease. Under the law rents cannot be raised during the lease period, which is typically one year or less, and in return the tenant agrees to stay for the length of the agreement, to limit the number of unrelated people living in the house or apartment without prior permission, and to maintain the property in reasonable order.

In addition to leases, which cover a fixed period and offer guarantees of stability for both sides, the state allows for rental agreements short of a lease. Unlike a lease, which is always in writing and signed by both parties, rental agreements can be either written or verbal agreements. While they can extend over time, most rental agreements are for month-to-month occupancy. Even in that case, though, there is a minimum

20-day-notice policy for terminating a month-to-month tenancy and notice must be given in the first 10 days of the rental period. There are very limited exceptions to this policy, usually having to do with emergencies or unsafe conditions.

Renter's Rights

In addition, renters do have a number of basic rights under state law, and for the most part landlords and tenants deal with each other on reasonable terms. The **LANDLORD-TENANT ACT** expressly prohibits any agreement to waive basic rights; not to contest a lawsuit filed by the other party; to limit the landlord's responsibility in case of injury, accident, or damage; or to pay legal fees in situations that are not expressly allowed in the landlord-tenant law. If both sides agree to submit a problem to binding arbitration, the landlord cannot legally require a tenant to accept a particular arbitrator.

There are also a number of clauses that, while not expressly prohibited by the Landlord-Tenant Act, are still unenforceable. Whether or not the rental agreement or lease says it is allowable, landlords cannot legally take someone's property if they fall behind in their rent; charge a tenant for all damages, regardless of fault; or demand that a tenant who has been taken to court pay more than the courts require.

As a rule, tenants must give the landlord or manager reasonable access to the property with 48 hours' notice, or in some cases, such as if a landlord is showing the building to potential buyers, 24 hours' notice. Tenants should approve the visits, but they cannot unreasonably try to keep the landlord away. On the other hand, the house or apartment is still the renter's home, and managers or landlords cannot enter the premises without fair notice or permission.

In most of the state, property owners can apply a "no-children policy" on 60 days' notice, but in the city, discrimination against children is illegal.

Information on landlord-tenant issues from the tenant's perspective is available from the **TENANTS UNION**. The Tenants Union information and education hotline is open for people to speak to a counselor Wednesdays between the hours of noon and 3pm (no appointment necessary). To make an appointment for in-person or phone consultation, call on Tuesday or Thursday between noon and 1pm. Appointments can only be scheduled for Mondays between 3pm and 6pm or for Thursdays between 9am and noon. 723-0500, www.tenantsunion.org.

PETS

While Seattle does protect families and prohibit discrimination against children, pets are a different matter entirely. Whether and how many pets are allowed in a rental, for instance, is a matter between the owner and the renter, within the limits set by law. Like most of the other cities within King County, Seattle has adopted pet ordinances that mirror the county's rules.

Do They Need Licenses?

Yes. Regardless of other conditions, all dogs and cats must be individually licensed. License fees vary depending on whether the pets are spayed and the age of the owner. For most residents pet licenses run about $15 a year, although senior citizens can buy a lifetime license for $10 per pet.

When licensing a dog or cat, a spay or neuter certificate has to be shown to get the preferred rate. Low-cost spay-neuter clinics are held periodically around the county, and vouchers are available for low-income residents to get their pets fixed. Staffed by a licensed veterinarians and technicians, **SEATTLE'S MUNICIPAL SPAY AND NEUTER CLINIC** helps with spays and neuters for Seattle dogs and cats. Surgeries are by appointment only; call 386-4260.

How Many Animals Can I Have?

There is no set legal limit on small indoor pets kept in aquariums, terrariums, or cages, as a general rule. Otherwise, there is a limit of five small animals, excluding indoor cats, per household. The number of small animals kept outside, including adult cats and dogs, is limited based on the size of the lot, with a maximum of three per household on lots of less than 20,000 square feet, five per household on lots of up to 35,000 square feet, with an additional one per half-acre, up to a maximum of 20.

Inside Seattle proper, however, the limit for a single-family home is three small animals, including pot-bellied pigs. Chickens do not count against that limit, so a person can have up to three chickens along with his or her other pets. Whether roosters are included in the mix depends largely on how tolerant the neighbors are about crowing at the crack of dawn. For the most part these regulations are all policed on an honor system unless there is a complaint over specific conditions.

If You're Feeling Pastoral

You'll need to live outside the city in King County, where more dogs and cats and large animals may be kept if you have the space. If you want more than three dogs or cats, you must obtain a hobby kennel license ($50), though that doesn't mean you must have any actual kennel. For horses, cows, sheep, goats, and other domestic livestock, you must have a lot larger than 35,000 square feet, and the number of animals you can have increases as your property size does, at roughly three animals per acre.

Animal Care

There are a number of organizations in the Seattle area dedicated to the well-being of dogs, cats, and other animals:

THE HUMANE SOCIETY FOR SEATTLE/KING COUNTY: The classic, mainstream animal welfare and adoption organization has its offices, clinic, and shelter in Bellevue. 425-641-0080, adoption center 425-649-7563, www.seattlehumane.org.

KING COUNTY ANIMAL CONTROL: This is where your dog or (rarely) cat winds up if it is unlicensed, lost, or a nuisance. 296-7387, www.metrokc.gov/lars/animal.

PROGRESSIVE ANIMAL WELFARE SOCIETY: An activist group in Lynnwood with a no-kill philosophy, firm commitment to animal husbandry and pet neutering, and many animals to adopt. 425-787-2500, www.paws.org.

SEATTLE ANIMAL SHELTER: The city's home for lost, seized, or unwanted animals, with many available for adoption. 386-4254, www.cityofseattle.net/animalshelter.

PESTS

When it comes to pests, Seattle is better off than most places. For whatever reason, cockroaches are all but unheard of in the Pacific Northwest. The same can be said for most of the flying biters like mosquitoes. Although it would be an exaggeration to suggest that Seattle never has mosquitoes, they do not last through the cooler seasons, and it is seldom hot enough for long enough in temperate Seattle for them to become the serious problem they are in much of the country. Ants and other colonizing insects are found throughout this area, as they are nearly everywhere else on the planet, but they, too, seldom make an appearance here. (However, powderpost beetles and carpenter ants particularly like mold and damp wood, so if you see signs of them—little piles of sawdust at the base of wood posts in older homes—call a pest control company.)

Other pests range from fleas—easily controlled these days with modern veterinary prescriptions—to termites, an occasional but serious home hazard. The yellow jackets that are so common in late summer are not a great threat unless you are dangerously sensitive; yellow jackets, hornets, and wasps rarely nest within houses. We do not have poisonous snakes or black widow spiders in Western Washington, no termites, no weevils or roaches, or any of the other omnipresent aliens homeowners in much of the rest of the country must beware.

Oh, Rats!

Rats, however, can be a problem. People store food, and mice and other rodents try their best to come in from the cold and share what they can of it. Fortunately, rats are easily deterred. The primary thing that attracts them to an area is the prevalence of open garbage cans with food waste. Make sure garbage cans are made of gnaw-proof materials (like galvanized steel) and have a tight-fitting lid. This also tends to discourage most other trash-hunting pests, including raccoons and the neighbor's dog.

Check out the county Public Health Department's information and advice on pest control at www.metrokc.gov/health; the page on rat control is the department's third-most-popular link.

Get Control

For more active interventions there are numerous professional pest-control companies that will spray and set traps. Please hire environmentally responsible firms, and ask them to use the least toxic method that will be effective—most pests can be controlled with minimal use of chemicals.

One Last Word

Coons. They are not the cute, cuddly bumblers they seem to be. They are, in fact, efficient predators, like bears, that can and do occasionally take a family pet. *Do not* feed raccoons; even if you don't care about the consequences, your neighbors do.

CHAPTER 5

Street Smarts

Driving in Seattle? The rules are simple: don't honk your horn; pedestrians have the right of way; allow an extra hour (you may not need it, but when you do, you really do); and don't get on the freeways unless you have a full gas tank and an empty bladder.

Although **SEATTLE TRAFFIC** is famously bad—in the late '90s, some measures tied us with the LA area—the economic collapse that struck Puget Sound in the early part of the new millennium had the ironically salutary effect of diminishing congestion. Now, in general terms we are one of the more congested large metro areas, on a par with San Diego, Denver, and Phoenix, but much better than Atlanta and much worse than Kansas City, Pittsburgh, and Las Vegas.

Seattle's Clogged Arteries

CARS REGISTERED IN KING COUNTY: 1.2 million (3.8 million statewide)

DAILY VEHICLE MILES: 30,465,000

DAILY PASSENGER MILES, PUBLIC TRANSIT: 2,845,000

ANNUAL DELAY PER TRAVELER (ABOVE NORMAL COMMUTE): 46 hours (Los Angeles, 93 hours; New York, 50; Portland, 41; Las Vegas, 27)

EXCESS FUEL CONSUMED: 110 million gallons

COST OF CONGESTION: $1.175 billion

AVERAGE RUSH HOUR TRAVEL TIME:

　　SeaTac to Seattle, 23 minutes

　　Tukwila to Bellevue, 30 minutes

　　Bothell to Bellevue, 19 minutes

(Source: Texas Transportation Institute/Texas A&M 2004 Urban Mobility Study; WA State Department of Transportation)

Eight Seconds

It takes a car thief only eight seconds to steal a car—and they keep busy in Seattle. In 2004 there were more than 8,400 auto thefts reported to the Seattle Police Department. The good news is that the SPD recovers up to 86 percent of stolen vehicles (data given is from 2002, when 8,308 cars were stolen). To prevent theft, keep all valuables out of sight, always lock your car, never leave a running car unattended, and park in well-lit areas.

Nationally, we're 18th worst, better than all the supermetro areas except Philadelphia.

How to explain this? The **CHALLENGES OF GEOGRAPHY** cause problems: Seattle is hemmed in by two large bodies of water, one of which is crossed by just two bridges, the other by none. Steep hills also pin down highway corridors; transportation officials often point out that any plans to expand I-5 through downtown are blocked by simple lack of ground.

Atop lack of land is lack of action. No major highway construction (except carpool lanes) has taken place for two decades, and although there is talk of expansion—especially on the 520 floating bridge and along I-405—neither concrete plans nor money to execute them have materialized. The same problem afflicts construction of alternatives such as regional light rail. Voter-approved tax-limitation measures have impaired progress on both issues, so in effect we are swallowing our own poison on a daily basis.

Thus travel in the Seattle metro area proceeds much as it has since the mid-'70s, with two improvements: Air pollution has been significantly lessened by cleaner cars and cleaner fuels. And bus service is better.

Furthermore, the obvious geographic advantages and unique cultural attributes of the city contribute considerably to the flavor of travel in the region. Can there be any better way to commute or go for a simple day trip than on a Washington State ferry? Few places are better suited to bike riding: Seattle is likely the most **BIKE-FRIENDLY** metropolitan area in the United States. And drivers, however slow their travels may be, are frequently presented sights available nowhere else: the morning sun painting the Olympic Mountains persimmon; Mount Rainier shining bright white to the south. There is often a slowdown on SR 520 at the point eastbound drivers top the western high-rise and catch their first glimpse of Rainier.

Numbers to Know on the Go

Emergencies: 911, no matter where you are

State Patrol: Seattle area, 800-283-7865; Tacoma, 800-283-7801; Everett, 800-283-7807; wsp.wa.gov

Non-emergency calls: Seattle, 206-684-8923; Bellevue, 425-452-6917; Redmond, 425-556-2500; King County, 206-296-3311

Traffic conditions: 368-4499 or 800-695-7623, www.wsdot.wa.gov/pugetsoundtraffic

Report aggressive drivers: 911 or the local State Patrol number

Drunk driver hotline: 800-22DRUNK or 911

Litter hotline: 866-LITTER-1

Carpool lane violations: 206-764-HERO

Pass reports and weather conditions: 511, www.wsdot.wa.gov/traffic/pass

As for Seattle's **FAMOUS AUTOMOTIVE COURTESY**, it is both real and baffling to outsiders. Cultural anthropologists believe it may derive from the courteous, orderly ethos brought by the area's early Scandinavian settlers; wherever it came from, it is definitely not OK to honk your horn in an unseemly fashion, if at all, and cutting lines is also not OK. But stopping to let people into a line gets you brownie points. And if someone is crossing the street on foot, you also stop to let them go by, whether it's an intersection or not.

Courtesy is the story on city streets. On the freeways just about anything goes—or stops, depending on traffic and weather conditions.

HOW TO COMMUTE YOUR SENTENCE

OK, you have a job in Seattle and a home in Kirkland. Or a job in Redmond, home in Fremont. Or home in Bellevue, job in Kent. Whatever—if you're getting on the Seattle-area freeways, you are entering a twilight zone of clogged arteries, gawkers' blocks, and S-curves stop-and-go. Most of the time the system works creakily but serviceably; commutes range from a half hour to more than an hour, and stop-dead jams are relatively rare.

But the exceptions are memorable. When it's raining, and a fender-bender takes place on I-5 under the convention center at 5:30 the same night as a concert at Key Arena and a Mariners game at Safeco Field, traffic can back up well past the city limits in both directions, and you might wish you had *War and Peace* on tape.

A few things distinguish Seattle rush hour. First, because there is such a large workforce at Boeing plants in South King County and Everett, where shifts begin earlier than the average business office, rush hour starts earlier in several areas—before 6am headed south into the Kent Valley and north into Everett. Second, the rise of the high-tech industry on the Eastside created a countercommute, from Seattle to Redmond, that sometimes equals the traditional suburb-to-city rush.

Add all these factors together and there is hardly a freeway in the Seattle area that doesn't jam up, sometimes in both directions at once (such as SR 520). Some key tips:

USE THE CARPOOL LANES. Find someone to share your misery. There are numerous programs, public and private, to boost carpooling—the top of the line is the **METRO VANPOOL** program, which supplies vehicles to commuters and stickers that get you choice parking spots in downtown Seattle. Metro will also help you connect with other carpoolers in your neighborhood.

There are 57 miles of carpool lanes (also called HOV lanes, for "high-occupancy vehicles") in the Seattle area; all require two people in a car for use, except SR 520 between the I-405 interchange and Lake Washington, which requires three people to qualify. All passengers of any sort count, though there has been heated controversy over whether children should qualify (the lanes are meant for working commuters, goes the argument). Motorcycles qualify; buses too, of course, but not heavy trucks. Some lanes have been opened to use by any vehicle in nonpeak hours. 888-814-1300, www.wsdot.wa.gov/hov, www.rideshareonline.com, www.transit.metrokc.gov/tops.

USE THE PARK & RIDE LOTS AND TAKE THE BUS. There are more than 200 such lots in King, Pierce, and Snohomish counties; pretty much all of them have direct bus service to key employment centers. Commuting by bus is remarkably pleasant, reasonably time-efficient, and economically sensible. For more information on regional bus service, see "Alternative Transportation," page 165. (A complete list of Park & Ride lots is on www.transit.metrokc.gov.) A few, such as the Issaquah

It's All in the Timing

The state tracks average travel times for a dozen common routes in the Puget Sound region, in five-minute intervals. You can pick your route, find the "95 percent reliable" travel window, and plot the most advantageous moment to leave your house and reach your destination on time. www.wsdot.wa.gov/pugetsoundtraffic/traveltimes.

lot, fill up by the end of morning rush hour, but street parking is usually available for stragglers. Security has been an issue at some lots; be sure to follow the usual precautions—lock your car, don't leave valuables in view, don't commute in a car with a $10,000 custom A/V system.

COMMUTE OFF-HOURS. Rush hour starts at 6am or before, lasts till 8:30 or so, then recommences at 2:30 or 3pm. Why the early surge? Shift change at Boeing plants in Renton, Kent, Auburn, and Everett takes place at 7am and 3pm. If you're working in South King County, you can ease your commute considerably by traveling after 8am and 6pm. But if you work downtown, you'd do best to arrive before 7am or after 9am. Daily rush hour encompasses 7.6 hours; if you can travel outside those times, do it.

TAKE THE TRAIN. The Sounder train that links Everett, Tacoma, and South King County to Seattle is the closest thing to light rail we have so far. Three trains a day run from Tacoma to downtown Seattle with stops in Puyallup, Sumner, Auburn, Kent, and Tukwila; one train a day runs from Everett to Seattle. At $3 a trip or $30 a week, it's a bargain. 398-5000, www.sounder.org.

Highway Stretches to Avoid if You Can

- I-405 Bellevue south to Renton, 6–8am; the reverse, 3–6pm
- SR 167 (Valley Freeway) south to Auburn, 6–8am; the reverse, 3–6pm
- SR 520 westbound into Seattle, 7–9am; the reverse, 4–6pm; (I-90 is almost always a better choice.)
- I-405 into downtown Bellevue, both directions, 7:30–9am; the reverse outbound, 4–6pm
- I-5 Southcenter Hill (Tukwila to Midway), 3–6pm
- I-5 through downtown Seattle, Boeing Field to Northgate, 7–9am and 4–6pm

Navigation

Finding your way around King County is easy. Almost.

The entire county subscribes to a numbered, directional street-naming system that tells you exactly where any address is. Divided in quarters, with downtown Seattle more or less the zero point, avenues run north-south, streets run east-west, and the quadrant designation precedes street numbers and follows avenue numbers. Thus 15279 NE 202nd is a house on NE 202nd Street just past 152nd Avenue NE. Simple, even if it produces some bizarre results, such as the road numbers approaching 400 that first-time visitors invariably remark on in Federal Way and North Bend.

Within Seattle, the grid is further divided, like a tic-tac-toe board—SE, E, NE, N, NW, W, SW, S. Same principles apply as out in the county. Easy, eh?

Alas, it's not quite that simple. A glance at the map of Seattle reveals any number of cockamamie streets running willy-nilly across and around the nice, symmetrical grid; and the grid itself is canted at odd angles to Elliott Bay and neighboring areas. What happened? Early feuds among cranky pioneers? Old wagon tracks made into city streets? Yep.

And some outlying cities have expressed their independence by refusing to adopt the countywide numbering system. SE 128th, for instance, does fine in East King County—until it strikes the Renton city limits, when it transforms into NE 4th Street. Same piece of asphalt. The same phenomenon occurs in downtown Kent, Auburn, Issaquah, and Kirkland, where, just to be especially perverse, avenues run east-west and streets north-south.

A few particularly confounding roadways combine both eccentricities. Martin Luther King Jr. Way is a perfectly well-behaved north-south arterial in northeast Seattle, but as it heads south, it veers across the grid like a dairy cow wandering a pasture, ultimately making a slight southeasterly turn and becoming Renton Avenue—until it actually arrives in Renton, whereupon it turns again and becomes Airport Way.

These sorts of conundrums led the authors of a study (Sperling's Best Places.com, 2004) on ease of navigation to declare the Seattle area the eighth-most-confusing city to find your way around in. (Boston was worst.)

Hooked on Mnemonics

JCMSUP is the tried-and-true acronym for the street order downtown—Jefferson, James, Cherry, Columbia, Marion, Madison, Spring, Seneca, University, Union, Pike, Pine. Remember it thus: Jesus Christ Made Seattle Under Protest (a fact Republicans have oft suspected). Of course, it only covers the downtown core, but it's cool.

Shortcuts and Go-Arounds

SR 99/SR 509: Best way to the airport from downtown, Ballard, Fremont, Green Lake, and most of North Seattle. Possible hitches: 1st Ave S Bridge is up; Mariners or Seahawks game traffic.

SR 99/SR 599: Best way south through the city when I-5 is plugged up under the convention center or in the Boeing Field stretch; route spills you out on I-5 just north of Southcenter. Hitches: 1st Ave S Bridge; Mariners or Seahawks traffic.

SR 99/AURORA AVE N: Best way into and out of downtown from most of North Seattle west of I-5; also an alternate when I-5 itself is blocked. Use 105th and Northgate Wy to reach I-5 (don't continue north on 99).

MADISON EXIT COLLECTOR/DISTRIBUTOR: When I-5 is blocked northbound under the convention center, you can veer right as if you're getting off at Madison, but stay to the left and merge back on I-5 a bit farther north.

I-5 TO I-90 COLLECTOR/DISTRIBUTOR: Another short veer around balky traffic on I-5 southbound. Take the exit under the convention center marked for I-90, but stay right and whiz on down back to I-5 near Safeco Field.

ELLIOTT AVE/15TH AVE/HOLMAN RD: Ultra-alternate route in and out of downtown from the north, if both I-5 and 99 are blocked. Sorry, Ballard residents, we have to share this secret.

BROAD/VALLEY/EASTLAKE AVE: Best way to and from downtown and the U-District; don't use I-5.

1ST AVE S/SPOKANE/AVALON WY: Alternate route to and from West Seattle when the West Seattle Bridge is blocked. Stay alert for Harbor Island container truck traffic.

1ST AVE S/ALASKAN WY: If the 99 viaduct is slow, you can travel surface streets to get north/south through downtown. Lots of other people know this go-around, but it will get you through.

E MARGINAL WY: Alternate route to the airport if the 1st Ave S Bridge is up or worse, stuck. Also a backup route south out of town if I-5 is blocked.

2ND AVE: This is the best route southbound through downtown. Lots of buses, but the lights are well timed and the buses stay to the right (mostly).

50TH/GREEN LAKE WY: Don't use 45th, which has innumerable lights, to get to and from I-5 to Fremont, Ballard, Green Lake, and other points west.

12TH & 15TH AVES: Both parallel Capitol Hill's Broadway, which can be virtually impassable on weekend evenings.

RAINIER AVE/RENTON AVE: Back way to Renton if I-5 is blocked. You might even take an hour and stop for dim sum along the way in Skyway.

W VALLEY HWY: Alternate way north/south through the Kent Valley from Tukwila to Auburn, if SR 167 is blocked.

SAMMAMISH PKWY/LEARY WY: Traffic bunches at the end of 520 in Redmond, as drivers try to make their way up onto the Sammamish Plateau. Get off one exit early, just before the Sammamish Slough Bridge, at the exit for Marymoor Park/Sammamish Pkwy. Head left at the light, then right at Leary Wy into downtown Redmond and Town Center.

E LAKE/W LAKE SAMMAMISH PKWY: Not high-speed routes, but they are shortcuts from I-90/Issaquah to Redmond/Overlake. On the east lake route there's a reason everyone is observing the 35 mph limit—it's a City of Sammamish speed trap.

SR 167/SR 512: Best way from the Eastside south toward Olympia/Portland. An alternate for everyone if I-5 is blocked.

Speed Traps, Island Turns & Other Oddities

THE TRAFFIC ISLANDS in the middle of residential intersections are there for the obvious reason: to deter speeding. To go straight, you have to go around. But to turn left, you can cut in front of the island if there are no other cars at the intersection.

THE SPEED LIMIT, unless otherwise marked, is 25 mph on residential streets and 30 mph on arterials. Arterials have yellow center lines and controlled intersections—stop signs, yield signs, or traffic lights.

UNPROTECTED INTERSECTIONS where residential streets cross (there are many in Seattle) call into play old-fashioned traffic rules and customs. Basically, if two cars arrive at the same time, the car to the right goes first. Who arrived first? It's not a contest; be courteous (and safe).

STILL TOO MANY SPEEDERS on your street? The city lends out radar devices to clock drivers under its Neighborhood Speed Watch program; offending drivers are all too often neighborhood residents who receive warning letters from the city. Police patrols are often pulled in to follow up. Contact Seattle Engineering, 684-7577, www.cityofseattle.net/transportation. Many other Puget Sound cities have similar programs.

RIGHT TURN ON RED: yes (unless posted otherwise). Left turn onto a one-way: yes, with caution.

SPEAKING IN TONGUES: TRAFFIC JARGON

The most reliable traffic reports are on AM stations KIRO 710 and KOMO 1000, both every 10 minutes. Each station employs on-staff reporters, including aerial trackers in choppers and planes.

BOEING FIELD: The general aviation airport south of downtown; the runways stretch about a mile along I-5. A reference point frequently used in reports, though it has no effect on traffic.

Hurry Up and Wait

Seattle's bridges open on demand for boats, except during weekday rush hours. All three ship canal bridges are closed to smaller boats Mon–Fri 7–9am and 4–6pm; the First Ave S bridge is closed Mon–Fri 6–9am and 3–6pm.

THE BREWERY: The old Rainier Brewery south of downtown along I-5, now a Tully's roasting plant marked with a large neon *T*. Backups coming into downtown frequently begin here. Sometimes now referred to as "the roaster."

BUS BARN: A bus-only exit off I-5 at N 175th St.

COLLECTOR/DISTRIBUTOR LANES: Approach lanes along I-5 downtown that divide traffic headed various ways, including onto I-90. Get in the wrong set of lanes and you're headed 90 degrees from where you want to go. Drivers subsequently slow down, and guess what that causes?

CONVENTION CENTER: The Washington State Convention & Trade Center is perched directly above I-5 in downtown Seattle; the profusion/confusion of merging and exiting lanes here, along with the plunge into darkness, slows traffic most hours day or night.

EXPRESS LANES: Northbound on I-5 out of downtown, all the way to Northgate; eastbound across Lake Washington on I-90 through Mercer Island.

FLOATING BRIDGES, OR JUST "THE BRIDGES": The I-90 and SR 520 crossings of Lake Washington. The latter is also known as the Evergreen Point Floating Bridge. Yes, the bridges are made of concrete pontoons and do float.

HIGH-RISES: The points at each end of the 520 and I-90 floating bridges where the highways climb on pilings so boat traffic can pass underneath. Traffic often bunches up at these points.

MERCER ISLAND LID: Across Mercer Island I-90 traverses a below-grade "tunnel," a half-billion-dollar highway enhancement built to minimize the freeway's impact on the island's serenity.

MIDWAY: Spot in Kent along I-5, home of an old landfill, and theoretically halfway between Tacoma and Seattle.

S-CURVES: The 1-mile stretch of I-405 where the road loops around the toe of some hills in northeastern Renton, above Lake Washington. The state spent millions back in the mid-'90s "straightening" the S-curves, but traffic still slows here.

SOUTHCENTER HILL: I-5 climbs from the Duwamish Valley near Tukwila to the Kent Plateau near Midway; each afternoon the whole stretch backs up from the top of the hill.

THE TUNNEL: SR 99 dives under Belltown, emerging near Lake Union. Sharp turns into and out of the tunnel often slow traffic; if an accident closes the tunnel, the snarl's effects spread for miles.

THE VIADUCT: SR 99 through downtown Seattle, from Safeco Field to Lake Union.

DRIVER'S LICENSES

Washington State newcomers must obtain driver's licenses within 30 days after establishing residency.

Adult (older than 18) driver's licenses are good for five years; the initial fee is $35. First-time drivers must pass both a knowledge test and a driving test, and demonstrate adequate vision. Teens 16 and older must show they have completed a driving instruction course and have their parents' approval; learner's permits (licensed driver must be in the car) can be obtained at age 15 and a half, or 15 if the teen is enrolled in a driving course. License renewals are $25; online renewal was instituted in 2004.

There are numerous **LICENSING OFFICES** in the Puget Sound region, including five in Seattle. www.dol.wa.gov/drivers.htm.

REGISTRATION & PLATES

Vehicle registration used to be charged according to the value of the vehicle, a sensible system that promoted tax fairness. When initiative 695 was adopted in 1998, the fee theoretically became a flat $30, though various cities and jurisdictions have tacked on other fees and surcharges. Today it averages $50 to $70.

Ironically, where some Washington residents used to adopt various forms of subterfuge to register their high-priced cars in Oregon (a practice both states censured), the arrival of artificially low registration fees unleashed a spate

GONE BUT NOT FORGOTTEN
Bridging the Gap

The Puget Sound region is painfully dependent on the bridges that cross its lovely bodies of water. Occasionally the wind blows, a lot; the bridges suffer.

The first to go was the old Tacoma Narrows Bridge, the only roadway crossing of Puget Sound itself. A 1940 windstorm set up a freak harmonic vibration that literally caused the bridge to shake itself apart. Captured on film by an enterprising camera buff, it is one of the most widely seen natural disaster movies. The bridge was nicknamed "Galloping Gertie" and rebuilt (and redesigned) in 1950.

The Hood Canal Bridge, one of our three floating bridges (longest in the world on saltwater), came next: A gale in 1979 flung it in two. Rebuilt three years later, it is now opened (to the waves, but closed to traffic) during high winds to prevent a recurrence.

The I-90 floating bridge followed 16 years later during another gale, the famed 1995 Inauguration Day storm. Wave agitation flooded the pontoons, and part of the bridge sank. The effect on Seattle area traffic was pretty close to catastrophic.

Though all these spans have been redesigned and reinforced to prevent further such disasters, windstorms still play havoc with highway water crossings, as the wind-driven spray easily crests the side rails and wets pavements and windshields alike. Traffic slows to a crawl. Surprise: Nature still rules.

---

of Washington registrants from Oregon. What people won't do to save a hundred bucks!

Like you, **YOUR CAR MUST BE REGISTERED** within 30 days of establishing residency in Washington. Sure, you can drive around for a long time with a plate from Guam and hope you don't get caught; if you do get caught, the fine is $330. To title and register your car in Washington, you need your registration and title from elsewhere, or the same from the previous owner. There are about two dozen licensing offices in King County. Some are operated by independent agents and have oddball hours; www.dol.wa.gov/cars.htm.

Vehicle license renewal can be accomplished both online or by mail—the renewal postcard will arrive about 45 days before the fee is due. *Do this.* (Waiting in line at the licensing offices is better than a poke in the eye with a sharp stick, but not much.)

Personalized plates are $44. Most of the obvious ones are already taken. The state won't issue off-color plates; you'll have to confine vulgar or offensive remarks to bumper stickers.

EMISSIONS TESTS

Emissions tests are required every two years for most cars in most areas of King, Pierce, and Snohomish counties. These are widely available at licensed **TESTING STATIONS**; they cost $15 and take about a half hour. If it really bugs you (clean air is a hassle?), buy a gas/electric hybrid vehicle. 800-272-3780, www.ecy.wa.gov/programs/air.

ALTERNATIVE TRANSPORTATION

Get on the Bus, Gus

Though lacking light rail, the Seattle area does have pretty good bus service. You can get almost anywhere within an hour or so, for $2 or less. Buses are clean, comfortable, and largely piloted by amiable drivers and ridden by courteous, well-behaved passengers, especially during commute hours. Bus culture generally eschews boom boxes, discourtesy, and obnoxious behavior (and bus system rules prohibit such), though there are some routes that attract transients who use them as rolling nap-nooks. Fares range from $1.25 to $2, depending on the distance (King County is divided into two zones) and time, as peak-hour fares are higher. Seniors, kids, and students get a discount. Monthly passes are a bargain, if you ride the bus daily.

By far the largest transit provider, **METRO TRANSIT** was once an independent public agency that was subsumed by

Boat Licenses

Boats have to be licensed unless you paddle the thing yourself or it's under 16 feet and is only used on nonfederal waters. The fee is $25. Boat trailers and snowmobiles have to be licensed, too. By the way, state law prohibits boating under the influence.

King County back in the '90s. Metro operates 1,300 vehicles on more than 100 routes serving 100 million riders a year.

Tips for using Metro (most apply to other systems too):

PLANNING: The Web site trip planner (see "Metro Contacts," below) is a much better information source than the customer service line, whose operators ask for the exact addresses of your origin and destination.

STOPS: Buses stop only at designated, signed bus stops. Drivers pass you by elsewhere, not because they're mean, but because they are forbidden to stop at other points.

EXPRESS BUS routes are different from the regular routes, both in number of stops and course of travel. The #17 express, for instance, runs straight downtown from Sunset Hill/Ballard, while the regular #17 wanders along the foot of Queen Anne. Look carefully at bus-stop signs to see if express buses stop at that intersection.

TIMING: Buses do run late, but never early. (Pretty much.) That's why drivers have to park and wait at certain checkpoints if they are ahead of schedule.

NO CHARGE: The Ride Free Zone extends between Battery St and S Jackson St, and between 6th Ave and the waterfront, and is in effect between 6am and 7pm. Bicyclists should know that they can't load/unload their bikes in the Ride Free Zone unless it's on the first or last stop (i.e., Battery or Jackson).

Metro Contacts

General info: 553-3000, www.transit.metrokc.gov

Automated schedule info: 287-8463, or on www.tripplanner.metrokc.gov (this site also covers Pierce and Snohomish counties)

Customer service: 553-3060

Pass and ticket-book sales: 553-3090

Service centers for tickets and information: Westlake mezzanine in the bus tunnel; King Street Center at 201 S Jackson St.

Carpool ride-matching and Metro Vanpool: 625-4500

NO CHANGE: The Borrowers took one of the quarters you were sure you had in your pocket? Most drivers will let you slide a few nickels' worth, but not the whole fare.

COURTESY: Debarking passengers get off first. Then new passengers get on. All buses have lifts for wheelchair users and other disabled individuals.

TRANSFERS are usually valid for four to six hours. Metro says two hours, but most drivers set them further ahead than that (though not enough for both ends of a normal commute).

PAYMENT: You pay as you embark, on some routes at some times; otherwise, as you disembark. Watch for the signs on the paybox as you enter the bus.

VISITORS: Aunt Edna's in town from Muskogee? Get her a Metro visitor pass, which is $5 and covers all Seattle-area transit options (except Sound Transit) for a full day.

Regional Buses

SOUND TRANSIT: This separate regional agency (its main role is to foster a Puget Sound light rail system) operates connecting routes to serve trips Metro can't easily handle. Chief among them are commuter routes linking employment centers and routes to Sea-Tac airport from West Seattle, Bellevue, Pierce County, Renton, and South King County. Fares are $2; frequency is less than most Metro routes. 888-889-6368, www.soundtransit.org.

PIERCE COUNTY TRANSIT: This transit system operates express buses to and from downtown Seattle to Tacoma and other points in Pierce County. 252-581-8000, 800-562-8109, www.ptbus.pierce.wa.us.

SNOHOMISH COUNTY: Community Transit operates express buses to and from downtown Seattle and numerous points in Snohomish County, such as Everett, Lynnwood, Mukilteo, Edmonds, and Mill Creek. 425-353-RIDE or 800-562-1375, www.commtrans.org.

Trains

AMTRAK: Trains run regularly north- and southbound, and eastbound over the Cascades. The service to Vancouver, BC and Portland is especially popular; fares are $30 to $40. Trains load and unload at King Street Station, S King St & 2nd Ave, near Seahawks Field. 382-4125 or 800-872-7245, www.amtrak.com.

Streetcars

WATERFRONT STREETCAR: Meant mostly as a tourist attraction, these cars were actually brought here from Australia in the mid-'70s, so they're historic but not indigenous. The line runs from the north end of Alaskan Wy almost to the International District, so it's a good option to get from, say, the Bell Harbor cruise ship dock to King Street Station. Trolleys run approximately every 20 minutes; fare is $1.25.

Pedal Power

Bicycle commuting in Seattle is by and large simple, feasible most of the year, embraced by a fair number of people—and a heck of a lot of fun. Commuting to downtown within an hour or less is possible from Ballard, Green Lake, Fremont, the U-District, Magnolia, Madison Park, Capitol Hill and Queen Anne (there's a steep climb going back up), Madrona, and Mercer Island. Many of these commutes can be accomplished mostly on paved, protected bike trails. Other routes are quite feasible, too: Ballard to the U-District; Kirkland to Redmond; Issaquah to Redmond. As many as 8,000 workers commute by bike in Seattle, and recreational ridership encompasses hundreds of thousands of King County residents.

Few ways to get to work are as enjoyable as following a bike trail, out of traffic, in the fresh air. Riders are amused by nonbikers who wonder about the time it takes—and then sit in their cars for as much as two hours a day. Most folks who balk at trying it are blocked by misimpressions, such as the overall difficulty and the danger. Most of those who do try it are charmed by the fun and aesthetic appeal.

Countywide there are 14 major paved bike trails separated from roadways; Seattle has in addition 22 miles of painted bike lanes and 90 miles of signed bike routes. Every Metro and Sound Transit bus has a bike rack on the front that will hold two bicycles; riders must load their bikes themselves, but otherwise they are treated the same as any other passenger. The only hitch is that you can't load a bike in the downtown **FREE RIDE ZONE** from 6am–7pm; www.seattle.gov/transportation/bikeprogram.htm, www.metrokc.gov/bike.htm.

Bicycle riders must wear helmets throughout King County; the fine is $30 for failure to do so. Bike riders on city streets are considered vehicle operators and must obey traffic regulations; bikes are not allowed on interstates in King County. For more information on biking guidelines, and for a free map of area bicycle routes, call the city's **BICYCLE & PEDESTRIAN SAFETY PROGRAM** at 684-7583.

There are organizations devoted to helping new bike commuters learn the ropes—they'll put you in touch with someone familiar with your route who can mentor you. Contact the **BICYCLE ALLIANCE OF WASHINGTON** (224-9252, www.bicyclealliance.org) or the **CASCADE BICYCLE CLUB** (522-3222, www.cascade.org). The latter offers classes on the basics of bike maintenance, commuting, and safety. For more about recreational biking in King County, see Chapter 9, "Get Out & Play," page 260.)

Flexcar

Need a car just twice a month to go to snowboard clinics? Flexcar is practical, economical, and politically correct: You sign up and reserve a community car for the time you need it. Fuel, insurance, taxes, depreciation, maintenance—even wash-and-wax—are all included in the rate. It's $35 a year for membership, then $9 an hour to use the car. Volume plans are available (like cell phone calling packages, e.g., 50 hours for $350), and discounts are available through the University of Washington and PCC Natural Markets. There are more than 100 cars poised at strategic locations throughout the Seattle area. 323-3539; www.flexcar.com/seattle.

AFOOT IN SEATTLE

Like most Americans, Seattleites do not realize how much simple getting-around can be accomplished on foot, particularly downtown. It's good for you, opens up infinite exploration possibilities, and helps immensely with the parking challenge (see "Parking," below).

The whole of downtown is foot-friendly, and the distances are not as forbidding as they seem. (If the pioneers got here on foot, cross-continent, 150 years ago, surely we can get from Westlake to the Opera House the same way.) Travel times are quite manageable if you allow for them—the entire distance from Safeco Field to the foot of Queen Anne can be traversed in less than an hour. In fact, residents of Queen Anne and Capitol Hill can sensibly walk to work downtown (though few, alas, do).

Best routes north-south are along Alaskan Way (use the Harbor Steps, the Market Climb, or Bell Harbor to get up the hill into the market or commercial district); First Avenue, which has numerous buses to grab in the free-ride zone if your bunions act up; or Third Avenue, which passes most of the shopping destinations such as Westlake. Best east-west routes are Pike and Pine Streets.

Other areas that lend themselves admirably to walking are the U-District, downtown Ballard, Fremont, Wallingford, downtown Kirkland, Issaquah, downtown Redmond/Town Center, and downtown Tacoma/Museum District. All of these can be traversed in 20 minutes.

In Seattle **PEDESTRIANS HAVE THE RIGHT OF WAY** at intersections and along most streets by custom. There are crosswalks protected by overhead signs and lights at numerous places along Alaskan Way, though the hurry-up drivers trying to cut through downtown fairly often ignore them; be watchful.

Seattle police have abandoned their long-standing practice of paying no attention to jaywalkers; you may find yourself cited if you cross against a light or in the middle of a block in traffic.

PARKING

Parking in downtown Seattle is a challenge. City Hall staffers acknowledge that unofficial city policy is to discourage bringing your car downtown whatsoever. ("Parking is a sin, simple as that," a planning official once sardonically told us.) Rates at metered curbside spots and in most commercial parking lots range from $1 to $2 an hour, depending on the location, time of day, proximity of a special event, and so on. That puts Seattle on a par with the most expensive cities in the United States for parking.

Furthermore, most of the free parking spots once found in or near central downtown have disappeared like dodo birds. They are either metered now or have been transmogrified into loading zones, landscape strips, and such.

That's the bad news, and people do go on about it. The good news is that a little foreknowledge, combined with a bit of practice, can make things somewhat easier. A willingness to walk a few blocks can make things immensely easier.

There are numerous commercial lots on lower Queen Anne, for instance, that offer all-day parking for $3 or less for those who arrive before 9am. From there it's a 15-minute walk nearly anywhere in Belltown. The same is true south of downtown, in the Safeco Field area, and toward Lake Union along 7th Avenue, from which it's just a 10- to 15-minute stroll to Westlake, the convention center, and much of central downtown.

Then there are the **METERED SPOTS** savvy residents head for: under the Alaskan Way viaduct and along Western Avenue, in the fringes of Belltown, on the upper-east end of downtown. All these are limited to two hours.

There are also some central parking garages that offer particularly good rates, most famously the large city-owned Pacific Place garage at Sixth Avenue and Pine Street, which offers an hour for $3, two hours for $5, and an evening rate of four hours for $5; 405-2655, www.pacificplaceseattle.com. Another convenient, relatively affordable garage is in the IBM Building at 1200 Fifth Avenue, just up from the Fairmont Olympic Hotel; 623-2675.

Quite a few merchants in various shopping districts participate in the **CITYPARK PROGRAM**: buy $20 of goods and you get a $1 token you can use at most attended lots or in some self-park lots. Downtown, Pioneer Square, Pike Place Market, Belltown, International District, U-District, and Capitol Hill, among others, are included.

Some special areas and considerations:

PIKE PLACE MARKET: Look for metered spots along Western Avenue north and south of the market. Your best bet is before 10am, or sometimes midafternoon. Otherwise, the various garages associated with the market are the best choice—all have entrances along Western. *Don't even think about* driving your car on Pike Place; you'll "park" for an extended period just waiting for traffic to move. Someday the city will have the courage and vision to close the street to regular traffic. A better bet: The garage at 1531 Western Avenue connects via elevator and skybridge to the market, and if you're in and out under 1 hour your parking is free.

NEIGHBORHOOD PARKING ZONES: Some Seattle neighborhoods where the contest for parking is particularly fierce, such as Capitol Hill and around the University of Washington, have been designated Neighborhood Parking Zones in which only residents with stickers can park in certain areas at certain times (usually overnight). Permits range from free to $31. 684-5086, www.ci.seattle.wa.us/transportation/parking.

MARINERS/SEAHAWKS GAMES: The metered spots underneath the Alaskan Way viaduct are free after 6pm. Zillions of people know this—thus the crawl of cars in the northbound-only parking loop next to Alaskan Way—and during tourist season you have about as much chance at a free spot as you do at Huskies season tickets. If you do get lucky and spy one at about 5:30, which is more possible in April/May and during NFL season, you can pay for the half hour and enjoy the rest of the evening free.

There are also a couple hundred free spots along Alaskan Way and under the viaduct south of Pioneer Square, as well as south of Safeco Field along Occidental Avenue. These are no secret either, and they start filling up two hours before game time—which, in the evenings, is just as daytime office workers are getting in their cars to go home. It creates a charming game of musical cars. Your best bet is to get there at 5:20, scout out a spot, and head off for dinner before the game.

SONICS GAMES/SEATTLE CENTER EVENTS: Use the Opera House parking garage on the north side of Mercer (between 3rd and 4th Aves). It can usually handle most of the cars—particularly for operas and other concerts and plays—it's usually only $5, and access is easy in and out. If you insist on a free-parking expedition, check lower southwest Queen Anne, west of First Avenue; enjoy the competition with seasoned local residents all scouting for a free overnight spot.

NATIONAL FOREST PASSES AND SNO-PARK PASSES: See Chapter 9, "Get Out & Play," page 263.

Tickets, Tow Trucks & Traffic Court

Tickets for meter violations and most other everyday infractions are $35 to $38. That's more than 16 hours (two days) of paid parking—and patrols are frequent. Figure that every meter is checked three to four times a day. It's against the law, by the way, to drop a coin in a stranger's meter just as a parking officer is getting set to write a citation.

Other parking violations are more costly (parking in a handicapped spot, for instance: $250) and carry other travails. If you're parked too near a corner (30 feet is the supposed maximum, though usually it's 20), you'll not only receive a citation, a tow truck will be called. Should you arrive just as the truck driver is hooking your car up, he'll often tell you he is forbidden to unhook it; this is a fabrication these companies use to boost their receipts if they can. Make a fuss and threaten lawsuits; they'll usually unhook after a while, claiming it's the biggest favor they've done anybody in years.

> ### Park and Pay
>
> According to a recent study by the Puget Sound Regional Council, Seattle's central business district has 5,723 more parking spots today than it did in 1999. If you're lucky enough to find one, you'll be paying more for it: Overall average cost of parking for a day in downtown Seattle is now $14.52 ($200 a month). Lower Queen Anne is a bargain at $6.52 a day, or only $106 a month.

Is it worth it to contest a ticket? The time involved is usually three to four hours, including getting to court, waiting, and then arguing your case; the magistrate may or may not reduce the fine, depending on how good your story is; there is no effect on your driving record or insurance. So—what's your time worth? The larger the fine, of course, the greater the potential reward, but also the tougher it is to sway a magistrate. You'd better have a very good reason for parking in a handicapped space, for instance. You must request a hearing within 15 days of the ticket's issuance, or pay; a hearing is usually scheduled within 20 days after your request is received. By the way, ticket scofflaws are reported to the state vehicle licensing division; when license renewal comes around, you'll have to pay the tickets before your tabs are renewed. Orwellian, but effective.

You can pay tickets online, by phone, or in person downtown or at the city's neighborhood service centers. Seattle Justice Center, 600 5th Avenue, 684-5600, www.ci.seattle.wa.us/transportation/parking.

FERRIES

Washington State Ferries has four main routes serving the Seattle area: West Seattle Vashon/Southworth; downtown to Bremerton; downtown to Bainbridge; Edmonds to Kingston. Schedules are complex, but there is roughly one boat an hour daily from 6am to 11pm. All these routes serve thousands of commuters during morning and evening travel times; walk-on commuters use the car ferries or the Vashon Island passenger boat, which links the island to Colman Dock downtown. Crossing times range from 15 to 35 minutes.

Ferry lines are long on Friday evenings headed westbound and on the concluding afternoon and evening of three-day weekend holidays. If you're going to Port Townsend, say, for Memorial Day, allow two to three hours for ferry-line waits.

How to get to Colman Dock (Pier 52) to catch the Seattle-Bremerton and Seattle-Bainbridge ferries? From the north, head south on Alaskan Way, turn right into the entrance opposite Yesler Way. Occasionally there is a barrier here to protect the high foot traffic along the sidewalk; in that case you have to proceed south along Alaskan Way, follow the signs, and loop back around on a circuitous path designed by traffic engineers to burn as much gas as possible. From the south, get on First Avenue S anywhere south of Safeco Field, then cut over west to Alaskan Way at Royal Brougham.

Fares range from $10 to $18 for a car and driver, depending on the route, season, and time of day. Regular commuters can buy discount books of 10 tickets, or monthly passes, which can be combined with Metro passes for foot commuters. 464-6400 or 888-808-7977, www.wsdot.wa.gov/ferries.

The **ELLIOTT BAY WATER TAXI** is a small jitney that crosses between Seacrest Park on Alki and Pier 55 downtown. It operates daily in the summer and on special occasions the rest of the year. Crossing takes 12 minutes and costs $2 one way. 205-3866, www.transit.metrokc.gov.

Ferry Etiquette

Harsh words have been exchanged. Fists shaken. There have even been a few incidents when weapons were brandished, though no shootings have taken place. The etiquette of ferry travel—particularly the business of getting and staying in line—is well developed, and breaches are not popular.

First and foremost: Go to the end of the line. Stay in your spot, and stay in your car. This is particularly important at the West Seattle (Vashon) and Edmonds (Kingston) ferry docks, where the lines form along arterial roads, and often stretch well back from the dock. At West Seattle any service disruption can create an afternoon/evening line miles long along Fauntleroy Way up past Lincoln Park and toward California Avenue. Many of these cars are occupied by commuters going home; they do not feel kindly toward line-cutters.

Hopeful cheaters pull up along the line, turn on their signal, and ask to be let in. Greeted by refusal, they'll pretend they're actually turning into Lincoln Park or a driveway. "I'm from out of town, how would I know?" (As if line-cutting is OK in Peoria.) Those who do sneak into line will be accosted by drivers behind. If they refuse to go to the end of the line, regulars will smile darkly, wait till the line reaches the dock, inform ferry officials about the line-cutter—who will then be tossed out of line and sent back to the end, losing all the time they spent so far in line.

(Any exceptions? Police officers in official cars and a few rare people who have state-issued temporary letters recognizing medical transport needs.)

Say the wait is long and you go for a walk: Be alert. If the line moves suddenly (it does), there will be no pity, and you'll lose your place.

Once you've reached the dock, go where the ferry workers tell you. Position on the boat is not a user option. Most of the time the boat is loaded front to back, lower deck to upper, and unloads in the same way at the other side: first on, first off. Set your brake. No SMOKING. Turn your engine OFF, and don't turn it on again once the boat docks; wait until car movement reaches your part of the boat. The folks behind you don't want to breathe your exhaust for 10 minutes.

TAXIS & LIMOS

Taxi drivers are licensed by King County (which also handles the chore for Seattle). Drivers are trained in courtesy, routes, and regulations, and must pass several tests to demonstrate their abilities.

Rates are $1.80 per drop, $1.80 per mile, 50 cents per minute waiting. There is a flat rate of $25 from the downtown hotel district to Sea-Tac airport (see "Getting To and From Sea-Tac," below).

For taxi complaints call the King County hotline set up for that purpose, 296-TAXI. The Seattle-area community of cab drivers is reasonably fair and amiable, and complaints are extremely rare—just eight in 2003.

LIMOUSINES: For-hire vehicles that charge per trip, not per mile—are numerous. Regular users, such as those frequently needing to get to the airport, often establish a relationship with a particular driver; the best are eager to give you their cards for frequent calls. Unfortunately, turnover is high.

HAILING TAXIS: There are very few places in Seattle—most of them downtown—where you can hail a taxi by standing on the curb. Taxis do hang around the Colman Dock ferry terminal; at King Street Station; near Safeco Field, Seahawk Stadium (Qwest Field), and Key Arena after games; and near

Seattle Center and Benaroya Hall following concerts. Bellhops at major hotels can get cabs quickly. Otherwise, your chances of reliably flagging down a cab are poor, even on major thoroughfares downtown. (This is not New York. Get over it.)

CALLING A CAB: No matter which major cab company you call, the dispatcher will want to know the address at which you'll be picked up and a phone number. It helps if you have a cell phone; among other things, it offers the cab driver some certainty you are a real passenger he or she can call to check for whereabouts.

STAND-UPS: The companies grouse that they receive too many calls from "customers" who disappear; regular users complain that all too often they will call a cab that never shows—not a happy moment if you're trying to get to Sea-Tac to catch a plane. Outlying ferry docks, such as in West Seattle, are a particular problem; no-shows by both cabs and customers are a regular occurrence. If you cannot afford to have the cab or limo not show, stress this point with the dispatcher—they will usually concede a problem if they are stretched thin. Then you can try another company.

MAJOR COMPANIES: Yellow Cab/Graytop (same company, largest in Puget Sound with 330 cabs): Seattle, 622-6500; Eastside, 425-455-4999; Tacoma, 253-872-5600, www.yellowtaxi.net; Far West, 622-1717. There is little, if any, difference in cost; if you find one company more consistently reliable and customer-friendly, stick with it.

ALL ABOUT THE AIRPORT

Seattle-Tacoma International Airport enjoys several distinctions that are both good and bad. First opened in 1948, it is close to downtown—savvy travelers can usually get there in 20 minutes. But that also means it is landlocked, with precious little room for expansion: The airport's massive project to build a new (third) runway requires that literally millions of tons of gravel and fill be hauled in to build up what was an unusable, ravine-riddled slope.

Difficult and costly as that is, it's eminently more sensible than early '90s harebrained alternatives such as settling an entirely new airport south of Chehalis, almost halfway to Portland. The new runway (theoretically set for completion in 2008, though the Port of Seattle, which runs the airport, has stopped advertising an exact date) will ease one of the airport's more pressing problems: the fact that planes now must take off and land more or less single file during bad-weather, low-cloud conditions. The travel slump spurred by 9/11 eased the problem quite a bit, but continuing recovery in the air travel industry will exacerbate it. The question is whether it will reach a crisis point once again before the third runway is done.

Strapped and crowded though it is, Sea-Tac is reasonably user-friendly (been to JFK lately?) for those who know their way around. And we are lucky to have an airport that is the main hub for a major airline (Alaska), a secondary hub for several more (United, American), and offers nonstop flights to all of North America, Europe, and Asia. You can get anywhere on earth from Sea-Tac with just one plane change.

By the way, planes in holding patterns rarely circle the airport any more. When your jet throttles back over Walla Walla or Corvallis, that's an air traffic slowdown. Sea-Tac info: 433-5388, www.portseattle.org/seatac.

Getting To and From Sea-Tac

Sea-Tac is about a half hour from downtown and 45 minutes from most places on the Eastside, in decent traffic.

BY CAR: If you're coming from downtown, the only sensible way is to get on the Alaskan Way viaduct, cross the First Avenue S Bridge, and head up the hill on SR 509. If the bridge is not up, 20 minutes is an average travel time. If you're coming from north of downtown, I-5 or SR 99 are equally good choices, depending on traffic.

BY BUS: There are two main services. One is vastly preferable: Metro's #194 express bus downtown. This costs $2 or less, makes a quick run with no stops between the busway and Sea-Tac, and winds up in the bus tunnel, thus reaching basically all the significant points downtown. It runs roughly every half hour and takes about that long in transit. Tip: Don't make a mistake and get on the #175, which also heads downtown—stopping at every other corner along the way on Pacific Highway.

Sound Transit runs buses to Bellevue, West Seattle, South King County, and Pierce County from the airport, roughly once an hour, for $2.

The Gray Line Airport Express bus, which draws many passengers who don't know about the Metro #194, serves all the major downtown hotels. It actually takes a bit longer than the #194 and costs more ($8.50), but the buses are nicer and have baggage compartments. The stop is also about 100 feet closer to the terminal, if you happen to be smuggling gold bars; 626-6088 or 800-426-7505, www.graylineofseattle.com.

BY TAXI OR LIMO: Leaving the airport, the port's taxi-limo monopoly, STITA, offers the only at-your-beckon service available. It's on the third floor of the parking garage; trips downtown cost about $30, with tip; to the Eastside, $40 or more. The port claims that having its own taxi agency offers better service, though frequent travelers have trouble detecting the difference; 246-9999, www.portseattle.org/seatac/ground.

Inbound, any taxi or limo can bring you to Sea-Tac. They are not supposed to pick up fares once they have dropped off an inbound passenger, though occasionally they will if you are standing on the upper-level drive.

BY SHUTTLE: The two main shuttle services offer door-to-door transport, but there's a caveat—you have to allow a significant amount of extra time inbound to the airport for pickup of the other three or four passengers. Dispatchers do not always mention this, and even if they do, they'll sometimes add another pickup after you've booked your trip. Rates vary, by distance and number of passengers, from $20 to $50; Shuttle Express, 425-981-7000 or 800-487-7433, www.shuttleexpress.com; Airporter, 360-380-8800 or 866-235-5247, www.airporter.com.

Various independent shuttles serve most Western Washington outlying areas—check Sea-Tac's Web site for a listing of them all: www.portseattle.org/seatac/ground.

Airport Parking

Innumerable expansion projects have turned Sea-Tac's on-site parking garage into a monster facility that hardly ever fills up. There is a short-term parking area on the bottom floor; floors four to eight are for general parking. Rates range from $2 per half hour to $20 a day; monthly passes are available. There's also a valet service at $20 an hour for budget-free people.

The key to getting a good space in the garage is to go up. Floors four and five are invariably full; nonetheless, people waste huge amounts of (paid) time driving back and forth looking for that one spot. You can head straight up to the top floor, park within 20 feet of the elevator, admire the view of Mount Rainier, and invest far less time.

All parking is paid by taking a ticket as you enter the garage, then feeding the machines (credit cards or currency) on the fourth floor when you head back to your car. Forget to use the self-pay machines? There are a couple lanes with cashiers at the exit, but cars sometimes bunch up.

The rule for remote parking is pretty much distance equals money—the closer in, the more expensive. Lots are operated by hotels, parking companies, even rental car companies. Expect to pay $10 a day close in, $5 a day farther out. Allow about 15 minutes extra to get to the airport. Rates go up around holidays. Major holidays and spring break, call ahead to be sure the lot isn't full.

Several hotels near Sea-Tac offer extended parking with an overnight stay. If you're headed out of town on vacation and have an early flight, this is a great bargain—parking can be as long as eight days, and the room as little as $100, so you've just about covered the cost of leaving your car and simplified your morning dash to the airport considerably. Check the Yellow Pages for airport hotels and call.

Getting Through Sea-Tac

All the airlines, the federal government, and anyone else with an official position wants you to walk in the doors at Sea-Tac two hours before your flight. Unless you're heading overseas, you can shave that near an hour if you use a bit of savvy.

E-TICKETS: Still using paper tickets? Must be interesting in that cave you inhabit. Sea-Tac and its airlines—particularly Alaska, American, and United—have been pioneers in electronic ticketing. Get a code and use the electronic check-in machines: You'll almost always spare yourself 10 to 15 minutes standing in line. If you use the now common Web check-in programs and print your boarding pass beforehand, it will save another 5 minutes. (There's little to be gained by using the curbside baggage check, by the way. These checkers do not work for the airlines, have painfully slow computer access, and can't help you with any special requests such as pleading for an exit-row seat.)

USE ANY SECURITY CHECKPOINT: There are signs that explain this and the TSA guards try to direct people; still, folks bunch up in one or two lines (usually the A, C, or D concourse checkpoints, depending on flight schedules) while other checkpoints have little or no wait. Once you are through security, all the concourses are connected and you can get to any gate.

PAY ATTENTION TO THE GATE ANNOUNCEMENTS. Gate assignments change constantly, and the overall information-stimulus level at the airport is high.

TAKE CARE OF BUSINESS AFTER YOU GO THROUGH SECURITY: Newsstands, burger joints, coffee stands—all are available on the concourses past security. Get there, then relax.

Time in the Airport Tube

Surfers believe time in the tube is infinite. Time at the airport can seem that way, too. Though never exactly enjoyable, there are a few tricks to make it better. Our tips:

YOU WILL LISTEN TO CNN: Don't want to? Too bad. The airport's Big Brother series of overhead video displays is omnipresent, and the corollary speakers are even more so—good luck finding a silent corner. There are a few, in remote nooks of the C, N, S, and A concourses—look behind gate check-in booths. Another option is to buy a burger at one of the many lovely gourmet cafés and relax in Formica-land.

A PLACE FOR PEACE: There is, by the way, an airport meditation chapel, on the mezzanine level in the center of the main terminal. No music, no news, no high-octane execs on cell phones.

FINDING AN OUTLET: You want to plug in your laptop/cell phone/handheld game or, say, portable defibrillator? Good luck. Most of the airport was built back in the days only vacuum-wielding janitors needed electric outlets. Look along the baseboards behind the seat rows—or look for other people using their computers who may be plugged in, as each outlet has two plugs.

BECOME AN ART FAN: The airport has on display more than two dozen works by some very well-known artists, including Louise Nevelson, Robert Rauschenberg, Frank Stella, and Northwest favorites William Morris and James Seawright. Wander the hallways and see what you find.

💼 CHAPTER 6

A Hard Day's Work

Seattle has always had a zigzag jobs economy. After all, the city sprang up as a major stop on the way to the Klondike gold rush and depended for decades on such cyclical industries as timber, fishing, aerospace, and recently high-tech. Just as in the 1890s, new workers flocked to Seattle in the 1990s, lured by the brief but blinding prosperity of the **DOT-COM GOLD RUSH**. Jobs really did grow amid the trees, and millionaires spawned by Microsoft had been inflating the local economy for a decade. But the new millennium brought a huge hangover—the dot-coms disappeared, and almost simultaneously Boeing slumped. With unemployment at a painful 7.7 percent in 2003 (it had approached 2 percent in the late '90s), Seattle was the third-worst economy in the nation. All of a sudden workers who had been fielding recruitment calls on a weekly basis were hauling out their résumés.

Such economic chaos means that if you live in Seattle, you'd better know how to job-hunt. It's not arcane magic: To succeed, you have to devote some 35 hours a week (15 if you have a job already) to your search. In many ways it's like running a small business: You, Inc. You have to assess your strengths and weaknesses, improve in areas that need it, communicate effectively, network, and keep to your budget—all while dealing with the conflicting emotions of job loss or job stress.

Some searches have stretched past two years, and tried-and-true tactics of the old days don't always work anymore. Ironically, in the post–dot-com landscape, the Internet has become a primary tool to retrieve the very employment all those URLs evaporated.

Before the Internet revolution, job-hunting meant numerous trips to Kinko's and the post office with stacks of résumés. Now most people apply for work from their home office or the library. Sending an application takes a matter of seconds. But by saving applicants so much time, employers have more résumés to sort through and thus take longer to respond, if at all. A few send automatic responses, but most make it impossible for you to check back. Sending a list of your credentials into a nonresponsive ether can seem futile and lonely. Luckily, Seattle-area residents have had lots of practice with job-hunting, and there are plenty of resources to help you succeed, network, communicate with real people, and even hone new skills.

Dress to Regress

Seattle has always had a reputation for casual dress. When Nirvana's Kurt Cobain sang "Come as You Are," he not only described the attitude of most outdoorsy, natural-living Seattleites, but also spawned a new fashion era called "grunge." Even before that, legends told of businessmen sporting long ponytails and businesswomen who walked to work in skirts and sneakers. The dot-com era took everything a step further, making every day "casual day." Jeans, T-shirts, piercings, even shorts were all fair game, as long as they helped keep young tech workers comfortable, motivated, and creative.

When hip dot-coms infiltrated staid office towers filled with law offices and accountants, clothing cultures clashed in the elevators. Executives in button-down suits looked down their noses at the nose rings, pink hair, and sandals of the tech workers. That is, until the techies became their clients. One business valuation firm so strict that it outlawed open-toed shoes relented when tech clients balked at the trappings of their corporate culture. Gone were the suits and ties; in came the polo shirts and sandals.

Much of the corporate world has reclaimed the business-suit look, but even now dress codes in Seattle stay somewhat more lax than the national norm. Recruiters for tech firms advise clients not to wear full suits to interviews; some have been known to confiscate ties before introducing candidates to interviewers. Just use your best judgment. If you are interviewing at Microsoft or a small dot-com, a blazer sans tie is fine. If you're interviewing at a bank, law office, or other business in a long-established industry, you'd best put on a tie or nylons. If you have a recruiter or know someone at the place where you are interviewing, ask them what they think is appropriate.

Always make sure you look polished, clean, confident, and pressed, no matter what you wear. No jeans or sweatpants for an interview—even if that's what your interviewer is wearing.

JOB-HUNTING CENTRAL

The best place to start is **WORKSOURCE WASHINGTON**, a state-sponsored network of 33 resource centers and affiliates that provides everything you need, from workshops and classes to databases and job counselors. Only one WorkSource Center is in Seattle proper (on Aurora, in North Seattle; 440-2500). However, there are affiliates downtown, at South Seattle Community College, and in Park Lake. Many of the resources you need are accessible online through www.go2worksource.com, which offers a résumé-posting service, links to all the local classifieds, a database of online newspapers, labor market information, wage estimates honed from a sample of 24,000 employers, links to training programs, a career-event calendar, and informative articles on interviewing. Another state site with helpful resources is access.wa.gov.

NEWSPAPERS

Once the bastion of job-hunting, newspapers still offer classified ads (and classified ad volume is still considered a key economic measure). However, the Department of Labor has determined that only 15 percent of all available jobs are advertised. (During the dot-com fallout the classified section of local papers sometimes consisted of a scant few pages.) The classifieds are merely a place to start, but they can't be overlooked. The largest section, Northwest Classifieds from the *Seattle Times–P-I*, is available in paper form and also online. Online searches allow you to find listings more quickly with key words. And since most classifieds now refer job seekers to Web sites and online applications, it's easier to get there from the computer.

If you want to do it the old-fashioned way—there is something intrinsically hopeful about a fresh cup of coffee and the morning paper—the same ads run in both the *Times* and the *P-I*, the former daily and the latter every day but Sunday. The online ads Web site is classifieds.nwsource.com/jobs. Another local jobs publication, *Today's Careers*, is available as a free paper in numerous locations around town or online: www.todays-careers.com.

WORD OF MOUTH

If ads only tell 15 percent of the job-market story, what about the other 85 percent? You'll have to talk to people to find out. Most jobs, especially in the Seattle professional community, come the old-fashioned way: inside contacts, networking, referrals, and word of mouth. Send e-mails to all your friends and business contacts stating what you are looking for and politely asking them to keep you in mind if they hear of anything. Attach your résumé in PDF form or in the text of your e-mail to make sure it is accessible to all operating systems. You would be surprised how much help you'll get from people who already know your skills.

ASK THE EXPERTS

Perhaps you are so overwhelmed by the emotions of needing a job and financial stability that you can't think straight. Or maybe you are so deadened by a job you hate that you can't see a path to other positions. Seattle has a great community of career counselors, people who will help you sort out your goals, form a plan, fix your résumé, leave your downtrodden emotions at the door, and interview like a pro. Many of them are nationally known, so look for their seminars around town or self-motivate with their books. If your severance package or savings allow, spend some personal time with these gurus. If money is scarce, talk to the job counselors at the WorkSource centers and affiliates. Their advice is free. Either way, experts can give you the kick-start you need and point you toward specific resources. Here are some top local career counselors:

- Linda Carlson, author of *How to Find a Good Job in Seattle*; 284-8202, www.lindacarlson.com

- Regina Pontow, author of *Proven Resumes: Strategies That Have Increased Salaries and Changed Lives*; 425-398-7378, ProvenResumes.com

- Robin Ryan, author of *60 Seconds and You're Hired!* 425-226-0414, www.robinryan.com

- Tom Washington, author of *The Hunt: Complete Guide to Effective Job Finding*; 425-454-6982, www.cmr-mvp.com

JOB FAIRS

Another way to overcome the sense of sending your list of skills into a void is to personally place your résumé in the hands of dozens of employers. Job fairs gather employers from similar industries in one spot. Dress as if for a job interview, carry your résumés in a folder or case to keep them crisp, look people in the eye, and be ready to shake a lot of hands. The key to working a job fair is not to be discouraged by the crowd scene. Especially in a down economy, many employers collect résumés even though they don't have positions. And while all the employers are in one place to make it easier for you, all the job seekers are in one place, too. So keep yourself competitive and follow up with every employer you greet at a job fair.

For upcoming job fairs, check the following sites:

- www.todays-careers.com
- www.nwcareerexpo.com (the site for the Northwest High-Tech Career Expo)
- www.accessnw.org (every October, ACCESS holds a job and technology fair for people with disabilities)
- www.go2worksource.com

WEB SEARCHES

There is no shortage of job listings on the Internet—and while such sites as hotjobs.com, careerbuilder.com, craigslist.org, and www.monster.com all allow you to search for local jobs from a national database, there are quite a few Seattle-specific sites. Some of these allow you to post your résumé and sign up to receive automatic e-mails for jobs in your field, but for others, checking jobs should be part of your daily routine. While more jobs appear online than in the papers, all is not ideal in cyber-hunting: As soon as you post your résumé on a job site, you become a target for spam from headhunters and executive search firms. Keep in mind that reputable executive search consultants never collect a fee beforehand from job seekers and are usually paid by employers. Be wary: The desperation that accompanies a job hunt can leave you vulnerable to pressure sales tactics from less professional operators.

Local sites include the following:

- www.seattlerecruiter.com
- seattle24x7.com/jobs
- www.411seattlejobs.com
- www.localwashingtonjobs.com
- www.jobdango.com
- www.northwestjobs.com
- www.seattlejobs.com
- www.todays-careers.com
- www.thingamajob.com
- www.go2worksource.com

While you're at it, check out these sites for how-to articles, job-hunting events, and links to everything from job banks and résumé doctors to personality tests and recruiter directories:

- www.washjob.com
- seattle.employmentguide.com
- www.spl.lib.wa.us
- www.rileyguide.com
- www.skagit.edu
- www.metrokc.gov/kcdot/jobs
- access.wa.gov

IT'S ONLY TEMPORARY, RIGHT?

One way to get out of the house, add to your income, enhance existing skills, or learn new ones is to accept temporary positions through an agency. In Seattle high-tech temping has become a legendary way of life, but few people call themselves "temps" or even refer to their agencies as "temp agencies." Most people call themselves "contractors," or "permatemps" (see sidebar, page 189), a term coined by WashTechs, the closest thing to a union for the many tech workers in long-lasting "temporary" jobs. Agencies are referred to as "recruiters." Two- to three-month tech contracts can be lucrative stopgaps that often turn into longer contracts and occasionally even full-time positions. The length of contracts and pay make them desirable, but the process of getting one is often complicated.

Of course, there are also the classic temp jobs: clerk, receptionist, warehouse worker, day laborer. These positions range from one day to six months, and in the incarnation brought to prominence by Manpower in the '80s, sometimes even offer marginal benefits.

Temp opportunities ebb and flow with the economy, just as jobs do. Right after the dot-com bubble burst, recruiters and temp agencies turned many discouraged candidates away. A few years later, in 2003, contract work had once again become all the rage, so temping became a growth industry again. Recruiters welcome new résumés with open arms, often telling candidates they have the perfect position for them, or will soon. Usually this translates into a few interviews for positions that don't match the skills on your résumé or missing out on positions that do match. Why? Because recruiters have so many résumés buzzing around in their brains at any moment, not to mention the extremely subjective hiring particulars of the many managers they serve. They work for their managers first, since their paychecks depend on placing candidates—any candidates, not necessarily you—instead of losing out to competing agencies. Rather than looking for a match between your skills and a job's requirements, they are often comparing your skills against another candidate's skills, which is not quite the same thing. So sign up, but prepare to wait quite some time for the right match. Checking in constantly and recommending positions (easily accessible in the online classifieds) can boost your chances. But don't rely on just a recruiter or temp agency to find work.

Here is a small sampling of recruiters and temp agencies, some national, some regional:

ADAMS & ASSOCIATES, INC.: 447-9200, www.adamsandassoc.com

AVAILABLE PERSONNEL SERVICES: 405-3839, www.availablepersonnel.com

MANPOWER: 425-827-2952, localsites.manpower.com/mppro/seattle

MOLLY BROWN TEMPS, INC.: Seattle, 628-0598; Bellevue 425-883-2427; www.mollybrowntemps.com

OFFICE TEAM: Seattle, 749-9060; Bellevue 425-455-3860; www.officeteam.com

PACE STAFFING NETWORK: Seattle 623-1050; Bellevue 425-454-1075; www.pacestaffing.com

PARKER SERVICES, INC.: Seattle, 447-9447; Bellevue, 425-462-8050; www.parkerservices.com

SNELLING PERSONNEL SERVICES: Bellevue, 425-289-0830, www.snelling.com

S&T ONSITE (one of the big Microsoft staffers): 632-6931, www.sakson.com

TEMPORARILY YOURS: 386-5400, www.tempyoursseattle.com

VOLT SERVICES GROUP (another major player in professional/technical staffing): 441-2929, jobs.volt.com

UNEMPLOYMENT

Seattle has long been a city of frequent layoffs, even before the dot-com economy. The state also charges higher taxes to offset the large amount of benefits it pays out. If you have lost your job, unemployment benefits can help defray the cost of living while you sort out your future and get back on your feet. The challenge is navigating the complex maze of rules and procedures.

Claiming unemployment in the Seattle area means applying via phone or online, waiting a week for processing, and then calling in to a telecenter every week by a certain time and answering a string of questions via touchtone numerals. You then receive in the mail a weekly check for up to 70 percent of your former income (unless you have changed jobs and/or incomes in the year and a half prior to your unemployment claim; the state calculates your amount from your annual earnings starting six months before the claim). For most people this is easy. But if you are freelancing or accepting self-employment, things get tricky.

Many freelance projects pay weeks, sometimes even months after the work is done, but you have to claim the money the week you invoice, which probably means you won't receive a benefit check that week. If you worked for any employer during the week, you must claim your earnings, which reduces your benefit payment for that week, but doesn't affect the overall amount of your benefits. Temp work causes all sorts of problems with claims as well, and it can take away from the time it takes to job-search properly. Although the WorkSource centers encourage taking part-time jobs to prolong your benefits, the stern, complicated claim system discourages temp-

Permatemps

Nowhere is temping more controversial than in Seattle, where large employers such as Microsoft and Boeing have so many fluctuating short-term projects that they employ entire agencies to hire **CONTRACTORS** for them. On the Microsoft campus in the '90s, tensions flared and raw feelings festered among workers segregated by the color of their badges: "Blue Badges" were full-time Microsoft employees with benefits and access to the athletic fields and other corporate facilities; "Orange Badges" were temps, regardless of the fact that some had worked there as long as 10 years. They got no benefits, no vacation, no sick days, no privileges, limited access to corporate facilities, and no respect. Even now, Microsoft prohibits them from listing "Microsoft" as an employer on their résumés. In other words they are full-time employees in every way but name and status.

Hence the name "permatemps," coined by WashTech, the **WASHINGTON ALLIANCE OF TECHNOLOGY WORKERS**, which formed in 1998. So many disgruntled temps joined the alliance that in just two years, it had 260 members and 1,700 newsletter subscribers. WashTech was instrumental in securing rights for permatemps in several court cases. The courts ruled that longer-term temp workers were entitled to the same stock options and benefits as full-time temps (although as a rule Microsoft no longer offers stock options). So Microsoft gave the burden of providing health care and benefits to its recruiting agencies. And since the law states that the person giving raises is the legal employer, Microsoft also gave recruiters the responsibility of performance reviews. Things did get better—Microsoft started hiring a significant number of its permatemps, which make up a third of its work force and number roughly 6,000.

But Microsoft still had troubles. Beginning in 1990, the IRS got after the company regarding who was keeping track of taxes for the permatemps. Eventually, in the mid-'90s, Microsoft came up with the now-famous "100 days" plan. No permatemp is allowed to work for Microsoft for more than a year, at which time they must take a 100-day break before they can be hired back.

ing, self-employment, and those same small jobs. It can be best to choose one or the other: unemployment and a serious job search, or temping and/or self-employment.

The State of Washington also requires that a job seeker make three job contacts a week. You must keep—and sometimes turn in—a log of these contacts, and the state is very specific about what counts and what doesn't. In certain industries and during downturns there may not even be three appropriate job openings to apply to in one week. In that case you can attend certain workshops or take tutorials on software programs at a WorkSource center in lieu of your three contacts.

To learn more about unemployment, make a claim online, or even calculate how much your weekly benefits would be, go to these sites: www.cityofseattle.net/personnel/transitions, www.worksourcekc.org/seekers, and www.go2ui.com.

Finding Legal Help

What if you were fired, and your former employer has made it a mission to deny you your benefits? A vindictive or wronged employer can create a case against you that will complicate your pursuit of benefits—although the system and its counselors favor the fired worker more often than not. If denied, you may need a lawyer. Here are two Web sites that can help you research your rights and locate legal counsel: www.prosavvy.com, a database of more than 2,000 prequalified unemployment insurance consultants, and www.unemploymentlawproject.org.

RESOURCES FOR PEOPLE WITH DISABILITIES

What if you want to work, but you have a physical or mental disability that makes most jobs difficult for you? The Seattle area has quite a few networks, nonprofits, and programs set up to help you find work where you can succeed. The following Web sites link to a valuable community of disability resources:

- The Washington State Division of Vocational Rehabilitation site includes a downloadable guide to occupations in the state, labor information, and community resources for people with disabilities; www1.dshs.wa.gov/dvr/jobseekers/jobseekers.htm.

- ACCESS (Allying Companies, Communities, and Employees with Skills for Success) holds a job and technology expo every October; www.accessnw.org.

- A thorough national database of disability employment information is at www.ilr.cornell.edu/library/subjectGuides/disabilityAndTheWorkplace.html.

- The Job Accommodation Network offers information for low-cost job-site accommodation; janweb.icdi.wvu.edu.

- Learn all about the Americans with Disabilities Act (ADA) at www.adata.org.

- This national database allows you to post résumés and offers ADA and job-search information: www.jobaccess.org

Some disabilities may be harder to define than others. For instance, what if you are stuck in a domestic violence situation with no financial recourse if you leave? The Unemployment Insurance for Battered Women Project, supported by the Legal Assistance to Victims grant program administered by the U.S. Department of Justice's Office on Violence Against Women, is affiliated with the Unemployment Law Project and Seattle University: www.law.seattleu.edu/accesstojustice/projects/batteredwomen.

Worker's Comp

If your disability resulted from an accident or incident on the job, you could be eligible for workers compensation. Find out from your employer how to make a claim. The following agencies offer resources for finding lawyers and understanding your rights, should you need to take your case to court:

- www.workerscompensationinsurance.com

- www.disabilitysecrets.com/workers-compensation-washington.html

- Washington State Bar Association, 727-8200, www.wsba.org

- lawyers.findlaw.com

SEATTLE INC.

Seattle's business economy is based on a combination of fortuitous location and equally fortuitous circumstance. The city's first industry, timber processing, resulted not only from the vast forest resources the first white settlers found, but from the relative ease of shipping out of Elliott Bay. The last advantage remains as crucial as ever: The overall value of international trade to the Washington economy is more than $100 billion, most of which passes through the ports of Seattle and Tacoma.

That first circumstance—timber—brought west several key characters. One was Frederick Weyerhaeuser, an already-wealthy Midwest lumberman who sat down one day in Tacoma in 1900 and made out the largest check ever written to that point in time. He paid $1 million for thousands of acres of Western Washington timberland, land still managed today by the company that bears his name. A few years later another wealthy timberman, William Boeing, decided to get into the fledgling aviation business using Seattle as his base.

Some of the biggest companies that started in Seattle have since left. UPS began as a bicycle delivery service in the Pioneer Square area; the delightful Waterfall Garden Park at 2nd Avenue and Main Street marks the spot today. (The company is headquartered in Atlanta now.) United Airlines began life as a Boeing subsidiary, but federal antitrust regulators forced the two to split, and the airline HQ wound up in Chicago. Ironically enough, that's where Boeing sent its own headquarters at the dawn of the 21st century. A bit later another local trade and transportation heavyweight, Airborne Express, was bought by DHL.

The two most visible Seattle companies at the dawn of the new millennium, though, have become Microsoft and Starbucks. Both are global business stars, their names known worldwide. Both have registered a quarter-century of uninterrupted growth. Both earn almost daily mention in the *Wall Street Journal*. And Microsoft has grown to the point that it gives Boeing a run for its money in the, well, regional money department: Economists figure the software giant accounts for about 7 percent of the local economy, when you figure the direct and indirect impact of its payroll and purchasing.

But Boeing remains the top economic driver and the largest private employer. Fears that its headquarters' move to Chicago would knock the stuffing out of the local psyche proved unfounded. In fact, the high-tech collapse of the early years of this century did much greater damage, with more than 50,000 high-paying jobs vanishing. So Boeing, which accounts for about 10 percent of the region's economy, is still number one.

However, that's a far cry from the days of the late '60s, when Boeing was responsible for *a third* of the region's economy. Next time you hear someone gripe about Microsoft, mention economic diversification.

GONE BUT NOT FORGOTTEN
Microsoft Millionaires

Once upon a time, Seattle prospered beyond its wildest dreams. The dream of the self-made millionaire sprang to life for thousands of high-tech workers as everyone from the lowliest clerk to the loftiest programmer suddenly found themselves stock-struck. The setting was Microsoft, one of the first companies to offer its employees stock options. Many of the workers hired in the '80s were given large blocks of options, and when the company's stock soared and split multiple times—at one point $10,000 in Microsoft stock in the mid-'80s was worth more than $1 million in the late '90s—suddenly, a slew of worker bees were richer than they could ever have imagined. Janitors and middle managers alike cashed in, clocked out, and let their fortunes change their futures. Though Microsoft was by far the most prominent wellspring of stock wealth, many other companies followed suit: Amazon, Immunex, and Infospace, to name a few.

After the tech stock market crashed and the economy followed, Microsoft stopped offering stock options to its employees and temps—and the company's stock stalled once it became embroiled in the federal antitrust case—but the 10,000 millionaires created during the stock-option era have made a hefty impact on the Seattle area. From 1995 to 2002, $30 billion in options entered the local economy, according to Washington State Employment Security.

Few people talk about Microsoft millionaires anymore. Most of us have stopped dreaming that we, too, could sign on with a start-up tech company, work hard for a decade, retire at 38, and "pursue other interests." But we all benefit from the $5 billion to $9 billion of options wealth invested in the area each year starting in the late '90s. The Seattle Public Library's $3 million reference section with 132 computers and wireless communication devices; donations to the University of Washington totaling $284 million; Paul Allen's Experience Music Project; local ownership of the Mariners, the Seattle Sounders, the Seahawks, the Portland Trailblazers, and the Golf Course at Newcastle; $766 million in venture capital investments in the year 2000; and a $7.5 million penthouse in Belltown—these are but a few of the legacies Seattle gained from Microsoft millionaires.

At the top of the heap is the Bill and Melinda Gates Foundation. With its endowment based on Gates's Microsoft stock, it has given billions of dollars to philanthropic endeavors around the world—including more than $1 billion in the Pacific Northwest.

Get the Scoop

The *Puget Sound Business Journal* is an admirably comprehensive, weekly observer of the Seattle area business scene, printing everything from broad trend stories to detailed compilations of real estate transactions, new business incorporations, and the like. A year's subscription is about $80. Every year, the *PSBJ* also publishes its "Book of Lists," a catalog of rankings for enterprises of all sorts, from attorneys to web designers; it's $35. Both the paper and the "Book of Lists" are peerless resources for anyone engaged in business in the Seattle area; 583-0701, seattle.bizjournals.com/journal.

And if you need truly knowledgeable information and analysis, economist Dick Conway has been tracking the Seattle-area business economy for decades (and provided some of the background for this chapter); he offers independent consulting work (324-0700).

PUBLIC COMPANIES

Each entry ends with approximate annual sales, employees, stock ticker symbol, phone, and URL.

ALASKA AIRLINES: Seattle's hometown airline traces its roots back to bush pilots in Alaska, but it has leveraged strong customer loyalty into a national presence with its new-millennium expansion across the United States. The company's biggest boo-boo in the recent past was an ill-fated attempt to

---

Chart Toppers

Biggest office building: Bank of America tower (Columbia Center), 701 5th Ave, 1.5 million square feet

Biggest shopping mall: Southcenter, Tukwila, 1.38 million square feet

Biggest residential real estate firm: Windermere, $14 billion annual sales

Biggest home builder: Quadrant (arm of Weyerhaeuser), 1,000 homes/year

Biggest law firm: Perkins Coie, 600 lawyers, represents Boeing

Biggest hotel: The Westin, 890 rooms.

> ## Join the Club
>
> Want to hobnob with the best and brightest of the Seattle business community? Wangle yourself a membership in the Rainier Club or the downtown Rotary. Or both, if you really have juice. Seattle Rotary #4 (meaning it was the fourth Rotary club on earth): 623-0023, www.seattlerotary.org, about $800/year; Rainier Club, 296-6848, www.therainierclub.com, $4,000 year.

get rid of the Eskimo face on the tails of its planes, which went over like New Coke. The face remains, and you can now fly Alaska as far east as Miami. The umbrella corporation, Alaska Air Group, also owns and operates Horizon Air. $2.5 billion, 11,000, ALK, 870-6062, www.alaskaair.com.

AMAZON: Naysayers said it couldn't be done when Internet pioneers promised multibillion-dollar companies within years. In most cases the cynics were right, but Amazon, under the high-profile leadership of founder Jeff Bezos, has carved out an enviable online retail presence. Skeptics have often scoffed at Bezos's strategy of selling everything on earth, but Amazon actually started earning a profit in 2003. $6 billion, 7,500, AMZN, 266-1000, www.amazon.com.

BOEING: Despite the fact the country's biggest aerospace company got where it is by taking some of the biggest gambles in business history—building the 747 when it looked like no one wanted it, for instance—some folks still call it the "Lazy B." Its notorious up-and-down cycles torment the Puget Sound economy; one Boeing bust was the genesis for the famous billboard in 1971 asking, "Will the last person leaving Seattle please turn out the lights?" Among other innovations Boeing brought to the Seattle area were card keys, which company workers started sporting long before anyone heard the term "Microsoft millionaire." Erstwhile CEO Phil Condit moved the headquarters to Chicago, but the heart of the company, its commercial airplane plants, remains here, and no one will be surprised if the HQ moves back someday, too. $52 billion, 150,000, BA, 766-2910, www.boeing.com.

COSTCO: This warehouse staples company has such fervent fans that some drive hundreds of miles and pack their cars floorboard to ceiling. Costco's impact on retailing even prompted Wal-Mart, the biggest company in the galaxy, to

GONE BUT NOT FORGOTTEN
A Barrel of Air

"Roll out the barrel," advises the old polka tune, "we'll have a barrel of fun." That's just what legendary test pilot Tex Johnston had in mind when he took Boeing's new commercial jet prototype, the "Dash 80," aloft over Lake Washington during the Seafair hydroplane races on August 7, 1955. Earlier commercial jets made in Europe had broken apart in midair, and public fear of such planes was high. Boeing boss Bill Allen was hosting aviation industry executives at the races, and Johnston figured he would prove the new jet's airworthiness in a fly-by over the lake: At less than 1,000 feet, he put the Dash 80 in a barrel roll, then turned back and did it again, in full view of 300,000 people. The plane performed admirably; built out as the 707, it launched the jet travel era. Bill Allen, however, was less than pleased: The next day he icily told Johnston never to do anything so outlandish again. The famous barrel roll is now reckoned the most significant moment in Seattle industrial history, and it's one of the most notorious stunts in the history of aviation.

---

create its competing Sam's Club. Costco has more than 40 million members and is approaching 450 stores. $42 billion, 92,000, COST, 425-313-8100, www.costco.com.

EXPEDITORS INTERNATIONAL: A global freight handler and forwarder (when you have a customer in Singapore who wants a dozen crates of your huckleberry jam, call Expeditors), with special expertise in the Pacific Rim. $3.2 billion, 8,000, EXPD, 674-3400, www.expd.com.

MICROSOFT: Founders Bill Gates and Paul Allen believed that the future of information technology would be driven by software, not hardware. If you've ever compared the retail price of a full suite of Microsoft products to the price of a midline home computer, you'd have to concede their point. Another famous comparison: what $10,000 invested in Microsoft in 1986 has turned into today (enough to start your own industry). The actual cost of producing software is modest, so the Redmond company's famous cash hoard, which approached $50 billion at one point, reflects its enviable profitability. More than 90 percent of all the computers on earth run Microsoft software. $36 billion, 51,000, MSFT, 425-882-8080, www.microsoft.com.

NORDSTROM: Gone are the days that, when you told someone in a distant city you were from Seattle, they'd get a wistful look and exclaim, "Oh, you can shop at Nordstrom!" Now, with more than 150 stores in 28 states, almost anyone can sample Nordstrom's legendary service and tony ambience. The company's annual shoe sales reflect its prosaic beginnings as a 1901 Seattle shoe shop. $6.5 billion, 45,000, JWN, 628-2111, www.nordstrom.com.

PACCAR: Get a handle on that road hog there, pardner, this Bellevue company makes big rigs, namely Kenworths and Peterbilts. It wants everyone to spell its name in all caps, but hardly anyone does. One of its biggest plants is in Renton. $8.5 billion, 16,000, PCAR, 425-468-7400, www.paccar.com.

PUGET SOUND ENERGY: They'll keep the lights on for you. The company's old moniker, Puget Power, was forsaken when it merged with Washington Natural Gas; now it cooks your food, lights your bulbs, heats your water, and sends crews scurrying everywhere to lop tree limbs when the region's annual windstorm comes along. $2.5 billion, 2,100, PSD, 425-454-6363, www.pse.com.

SAFECO: It was big, big news in the corporate fashion world a while back when Safeco relaxed its dress code to allow business casual attire. Gadzooks! It remains a very staid, mainline insurance and financial services company that really, really doesn't like earthquakes, hurricanes, and such. $7.3 billion, 12,000, SAFC, 545-5000, www.safeco.com.

STARBUCKS: Critics say this company charges too much for selling boiled milk it adds to burned coffee. Fans say when you happen to be in Keokuk—or Kyoto—it's the most reliable place for a cup of joe. Both viewpoints are arguably true—but what is inarguable is that Starbucks almost singlehandedly spurred the worldwide visibility of gourmet coffee. As late as 1990 there were fewer than 100 stores; now the company is headed for 10,000 stores, and company poobah Howard Schultz owns the SuperSonics. $5 billion, 62,000, SBUX, 447-1575, www.starbucks.com.

WASHINGTON MUTUAL: Once upon a time this was your typical old-line local savings and loan, its roots dating back to the late 19th century in Seattle. Now it's the largest S&L in the country, with 2,400 branches nationwide. WAMU's takeover of a couple California S&Ls in the mid-'90s exemplified the city's economic ascendancy at the time. $280 billion (assets), $20 billion (revenue), 54,000, WM, 461-2000, www.wamu.com.

Bill Gates & Paul Allen

William Henry Gates III was raised in Seattle—his father was a prominent attorney—and became fascinated by computers as a teenager. After forays in and out of college (including two years at Harvard) and the business world, Gates and his chum Paul Allen founded a programming company in 1975 in New Mexico. They called it Microsoft and gained a firm foothold for Gates's business model in 1980 when IBM awarded them a contract to create the operating system for the big company's new personal computers. That system was DOS—still the foundation of most PC operating systems—and it was the fulcrum for creation of a technology behemoth. The company moved to Seattle in the '80s, setting up a corporate campus in Redmond (see Chapter 2, "Eastside Neighborhoods," page 100), and Gates's and Allen's stock holdings made them both among the world's wealthiest individuals, with fortunes in the tens of billions. Allen left Microsoft to form his own investment company, Vulcan, which backs everything from redevelopment in the downtown Seattle perimeter (Pioneer Square and Lake Union) to private space exploration. Allen also owns the Seahawks and footed the bill for the Experience Music Project. Gates and his wife, Melinda French Gates, and their children live in a 37,000-square-foot, high-tech mansion on the shores of Lake Washington. Their philanthropic foundation, with an endowment of billions of dollars, donates money around the world, chiefly to help eradicate childhood disease. The Gates Foundation has also donated more than $1 billion to Northwest causes.

WEYERHAEUSER: Many are the small countries not as large as the timberlands owned or managed by the Federal Way firm—43 million acres worldwide. Though long associated with Seattle in the public mind, it was founded in Tacoma and has never had a presence in Seattle proper. Yes, it's a timber company, but one of the most progressive ones, adopting environmentally minded techniques long before most of its brethren in the industry. Former governor Booth Gardner is one of the founding family's heirs. $25 billion, 57,000, WY, 253-924-2345, www.weyerhaeuser.com.

OTHER NOTABLE LOCAL COMPANIES

AMGEN: Biotech pioneer, used to be Immunex; www.amgen.com

CRAY: Supercomputers, but not super success; www.cray.com

DRUGSTORE.COM: One of the last Internet survivors; www.drugstore.com

EDDIE BAUER: Rugged casual clothing; www.eddiebauer.com

EXPEDIA: Microsoft's booming castoff; www.expedia.com

GETTY IMAGES: Owns a zillion photographs; www.gettyimages.com

PLUM CREEK TIMBER: Erstwhile clear-cutting dynamo that has reformed; www.plumcreek.com

REAL NETWORKS: Another Internet holdout; www.real.com

REI: Everything for outdoors, one of the nation's biggest cooperatives; www.rei.com

SEATTLE TIMES: Iconoclastic family-owned journalism; www.seattletimes.com

SERVICES GROUP OF AMERICA: Restaurant supplies, owned by Republican stalwart Tom Stewart; www.fsafood.com

SIMPSON INVESTMENT: Large family-owned timber company; www.simpson.com

TULLY'S: The anti-Starbucks; www.tullys.com

VULCAN: Paul Allen's investment holding company; www.vulcan.com

WESTFARM FOODS: Darigold; www.westfarm.com

STARTING A BUSINESS

While 90 percent of businesses in Washington are classified as "small," negotiating the regulations, paperwork, licenses, and fees required to start a business in Seattle is no small affair. Even if your business is making and selling bead jewelry on the weekends, you must start by thoroughly researching all that's required for running a business in Seattle.

The Very First Starbucks

Back in 1971 a trio of UW graduates was casting about for careers (that was the height of one of Seattle's Boeing-fueled slumps) and recalled an intriguing coffee bar in Berkeley founded by a Dutchman named Alfred Peet. Peet roasted his own beans in back and, as he explained it, let the aroma serve as advertising as it drifted out on the street. The young entrepreneurs apprenticed to Peet for a few months, then returned to Seattle and opened their own store in Pike Place Market, roasting coffee and selling espresso drinks. Starbucks store #1 is still there, at 1912 Pike Place, and though it hasn't expanded an inch from its beginnings, it does remind you of the saying about what can grow from tiny acorns.

There are plenty of resources to help you lay the groundwork. A good starting place is the Seattle Chamber of Commerce's resources for **SMALL BUSINESS DEVELOPMENT**. Their Web site covers everything from writing a business plan to payroll considerations and unemployment insurance; 389-7200, www.seattlechamber.com. The City of Seattle and State of Washington web sites (see "The Basics," below), also have more details and FAQs to guide you through the process.

The Basics

SEATTLE BUSINESS LICENSE: If you're conducting business within city limits, you'll need one of these. For 2005, the license fee was $90 (or $45 if you open your business after June 30). If your business makes $20,000 or less in gross income, you pay only $45 for the annual fee. Download application forms at www.seattle.gov/rca/licenses/licmain.htm, or call 684-8484 for more information.

UBI NUMBER: The Unified Business Identifier, or tax registration number, is required by the State of Washington for all businesses for state tax purposes. (It's also how you register the trade name of your business.) The annual fee is $15, and master applications are available online at www.dol.wa.gov/mls/startbus.htm. There are also links to other city, state, and federal resources that can assist small business owners. For more information, call 360-664-1400.

CHAPTER 7

School Daze

It's hard to tell if it's the large number of bookstores throughout town, or the U.S. Census Department's finding that Seattle is one of the country's best-educated cities, but there's no question about the community's commitment to education. It's evident in the school district's willingness to try different approaches to get the job done. The district may not have magnet schools, for instance, but it does boast alternative schools emphasizing particular all-embracing subjects. There's an elementary school that uses its focus on the environment and arts to teach basic skills, a program from nursery school through middle school that emphasizes African American culture, and a high school where students, rather than receiving letter grades, set up their own plans of instruction and are evaluated on their ability to complete them.

In fact, **SEATTLE PUBLIC SCHOOLS (SPS)** was so willing to try something different that it once took the controversial step of hiring a retired army major-general with no education experience to head the district. Although Superintendent John Stanford improved and invigorated the school system, the district faltered after he died of leukemia three years later (see sidebar, page 205). SPS stumbled when Stanford's successor resigned following the revelation of a $33 million budget shortfall. The appointment of another noneducator, Raj Manhas, to the superintendent slot has helped restore confidence in the system, however.

Other King County districts—there are 19 in all—offer a level of educational attainment that ranges from superb to good. And the Seattle area, with one of the country's major public universities, numerous top-notch private schools, and a comprehensive network of community colleges, is among the best places in the country to obtain an education. There is a wrinkle, though. The federally imposed requirement for accountability in schools led to the imposition of the **WASHINGTON ASSESSMENT OF STUDENT LEARNING (WASL)**, a comprehensive series of achievement tests administered to students in grades 3, 4, and 5. Because each district's funding and reputation depend in part on WASL scores, and graduation requirements are linked to WASL results, the state's educational system has shifted its focus to test-passing. Critics say some teachers are now teaching how to pass the test, rather than focusing on curriculum.

The umbrella agency aiding and overseeing schools in Washington State is the Superintendent of Public Instruction, 360-725-6000, www.k12.wa.us.

COMPARING TEST SCORES

Thanks (or, depending on your opinion, no thanks) to the Bush administration's push for school accountability, test results for every school in the state are easy to find, either through the individual district or through the state. In Seattle, for instance, you can visit the district Web site (www.seattleschools.org) and click on the "test scores" tab on the home page—or call 252-0140. This obtains demographic and academic achievement results for every school in the district, as well as other data such as faculty profiles and a school "value added" report.

If you really want to "shop" schools, much of the same data for every district—and every individual school—in Washington is available through the Superintendent of Public Instruction, whose Web site (reportcard.ospi.k12.wa.us) allows you to search by district or school name.

Though obtaining the information is simple, interpreting the data is another matter entirely, as test scores do not take into account innumerable subjective factors such as arts programs, school "friendliness," and athletics. Furthermore, as Seattle's much discussed school-choice program is in flux, the only way to absolutely ensure your child is able to attend a particular school is to live in its core enrollment area. Aside from that, if you want to apply to a nearby school, the best bet is to get your application in early (so-called open enrollment is January and February). The other selection criteria the district uses—proximity, sibling enrollment, academic potential—are otherwise largely out of your hands.

SEATTLE PUBLIC SCHOOLS

Groucho Marx may have refused to join any club that would have him as a member, but Seattle children don't have much choice. If their parents support public education or don't want to shell out big bucks to go private, Seattle schools are the only game in town. Luckily, the system offers numerous options.

Students don't have to attend school in their own neighborhood if they'd rather go elsewhere, as long as they can get into the school of their choice (see "School Choice at a Glance," page 206). The choices include alternative programs for children with different learning styles and special programs ranging from Native American studies at the elementary level to marine biology and biotechnology at the high school level.

Seattle Public Schools by the Numbers

Main office: 2445 3rd Ave S

Phone: 252-0000

Web site: www.seattleschools.org

Enrollment: 47,000 at 106 schools

Annual budget: $437 million

Student-teacher ratio: 23:1

Percentage of 10th-grade students meeting WASL standards (2003–04): reading, 55.1%; math, 38.6%; writing, 54.5%; science, 28%

The ABCs of Seattle Public Schools

AFTER-SCHOOL PROGRAMS: Most of the district's middle and high schools offer late-afternoon activities ranging from sports to origami and orchestra. Contact individual schools for information.

ALTERNATIVE SCHOOLS: When most people hear the phrase "alternative school," they think of "problem" children. Although the tag has long been seen as a designation for schools that take slow learners and juvenile delinquents, that's not necessarily so in Seattle. While some programs are designed to help students with disabilities or other issues including language or cultural barriers, other programs offer nontraditional techniques, curricula, or teaching philosophies. For a list of these schools, see "Alternative Schools," page 212.

ATHLETICS: Many middle and high schools have sports teams for the athletically inclined. Choose from middle school sports such as wrestling, co-ed Frisbee, boys' and girls' soccer and basketball, girls' volleyball, and co-ed track. High school activities include football, golf, soccer, tennis, baseball, and basketball. Offerings vary; for more information, contact individual schools.

COMMUNITY LEARNING CENTERS: The district has partnered with a range of organizations such as the YMCA to provide programs for families; these include English as a Second Language, parenting, computers, and how to help students study. Contact the school district's Office for Community Learning (www.seattleschools.org/area/ocl) for more information.

DAY CARE: Some schools have partnered with organizations that provide before- or after-school programs on a fee basis within the facilities or at separate units on school grounds. For more information, contact individual schools.

ENROLLMENT: Although the occasional bedraggled parent might disagree, school officials believe it's easy to navigate the system via a simple process with just a few steps. First, know the rules. Parents can apply for their children to attend any school in the district, but odds are best at the schools that are in the neighborhood as long as students apply during the open-enrollment period. (Transportation may be an issue if a student is attending a distant school.) Next, register early. Families that apply during the open-enrollment period early in the year have the best shot at getting the assignments they want because they have a higher priority than latecomers. And pick schools in order of preference: Choose at least three schools in case a spot in the first isn't available. And finally, fill out a registration form. The form should be accompanied by a photo ID; a parenting plan, if necessary; two additional documents verifying home address (such as utility bills, court papers, or mortgage documents); the child's birth certificate or passport for preschool, kindergarten, or first grade; as well as a Certificate of Immunization Status form.

IMMUNIZATIONS: Parents must be able to provide the dates of a variety of immunizations before a child will be admitted into the school system. Requirements are subject to change, but students should have immunizations for diphtheria/tetanus/pertussis, polio, measles/mumps/rubella, and hepatitis B. For more information about the latest requirements, contact the district or check out the Student Enrollment page on the district's Web site at www.seattleschools.org.

LUNCH PROGRAMS: Families on limited income—basically, those that meet federal food stamp guidelines—are eligible for free or reduced cost school lunches; for information, call 252-0685. Otherwise, elementary school lunches are $1.50 a day, and middle and high school lunches cost $1.75 a day. The

> ### GONE BUT NOT FORGOTTEN
> # John Stanford
>
> Although he was superintendent of Seattle Public Schools for just three years, John Stanford left such a lasting mark on the face of education in Seattle that the district named its administration building after him. The decision to hire the retired army major-general initially proved controversial because he didn't have professional experience in education. What he did have was a passion for public service that quickly turned his doubters into supporters. Within a week of starting his job, he called for higher academic standards, announced a "reading offensive," promised to finish the district's building projects "on cost and on time," and announced that employees who provided poor customer service would be subject to dismissal.
>
> One reform seemingly followed another as Stanford made the district more responsive to parents' needs, promised to make the schools safe for children, suggested a four-day work week for teachers to allow for a training day, and gave principals more control over their schools. As a result of his tireless crusading for children and his endless hours of work, test scores improved, performance gaps between the races decreased, and the district's bureaucracy seemed manageable.
>
> Alas, his tenure was a short one. Stanford announced he had been diagnosed with leukemia in early April 1998. Although he came back to work with the cancer in remission after a month of treatments, the disease returned, and he died on November 28, 1998.

school district has been shifting its menus toward healthier meals, with more fruits, fruit juices, and whole vegetables, and less starch.

PARENTAL INVOLVEMENT: The district encourages participation in a number of areas, including volunteering in classrooms, tutoring, escorting classes on field trips, and serving on school committees. For more information, contact your school.

SEATTLE SCHOOL BOARD: The seven-member school board serves as the district's board of directors. Each member represents a geographic district and serves four years. Meetings are held at 6pm on the first and third Wednesdays of the month in the auditorium at the John Stanford Center for Educational

Excellence. 2445 3rd Ave S, 252-0040, www.seattleschools.org/area/board.

SECURITY & CRIME: Public schools are required to report weapons confiscated at their school as well as security incidents (arson, assault, bombs, burglary, disturbances, drugs, harassment, sex offenses, vandalism, etc.). Each school's annual report and outcome summary include data on suspensions and expulsions, though this does not break the infractions down by type. For specific information, call the individual school or the school district's main office (for Seattle, 252-0000).

SCHOOL CHOICE AT A GLANCE

Although the district may change the way assignments will be made in 2006, the current system works this way: No matter his or her grade, every child living in the district lives within the attendance area (or "reference area") of a specific school based on the student's home address. If a student requests the reference-area school during the early registration period at the start of the year, he or she will be high on the list, second only to kids who already have siblings enrolled there. Students who request distant schools are lower on the pecking order and may not get their first request if space runs out.

When space is limited, applicants from the open-enrollment period are subject to a series of tiebreakers. First priority is given to children who already have a sibling attending the school. A child's distance from the school may also be a potential tiebreaker. If the tiebreakers don't resolve the situation, the district then assigns applicants random three-digit numbers and holds a drawing to resolve the deadlock. Children who don't get in on the first try go on a waiting list and have the application reprocessed for the next choice. The process continues until all students have a school assignment. If they can't get into any of the schools they want, they will be assigned to the reference-area school or the closest school where space remains.

There is an appeals process, but it's used only in exceptional situations such as the need for a particular school based on a child's psychological or medical condition or other unusual circumstances.

Alternative and nontraditional schools are the only exception to the rule. Elementary students in some areas may get an assignment priority to those schools.

The process may be tangled, but there is one bit of good news: Students don't have to go through it every year. They only face it when they are ready to graduate to middle or high school.

MAJOR PUBLIC SCHOOL DISTRICTS*

* WASL scores based on the percentage of 10th-grade students meeting WASL standards, 2003–2004

Auburn School District by the Numbers

Phone: 253-931-4900
Web site: www.auburn.wednet.edu
Enrollment: 13,657 at 19 schools
Annual budget: $169 million
Student-teacher ratio: 22.5:1 (includes counselors and librarians)
WASL scores: reading, 60.1%; math, 40.8%; writing, 55.9%; science, 29.7%

Bellevue School District by the Numbers

Phone: 425-456-4000
Web site: www.bsd405.org
Enrollment: 15,743 at 27 schools
Annual budget: $129 million
Student-teacher ratios: K–3rd, 21:1; 4th–5th, 23:1; middle school, 26.3:1; high school, 26.3:1
WASL scores: reading, 82.5%; math, 65.7%; writing, 81.4%; science, 57.2%

Edmonds School District by the Numbers

Phone: 425-670-7000
Web site: www.edmonds.wednet.edu
Enrollment: 20,727 at 37 schools
Annual budget: $146.7 million
Student-teacher ratio: 17.5:1
WASL scores: reading, 68.4%; math, 47.6%; writing, 72.2%; science, 29.7%

Federal Way Public Schools by the Numbers

Phone: 253-945-2000
Web site: www.fwps.org
Enrollment: 22,462 at 36 schools
Annual budget: $152,883,000
Student-teacher ratios: K–2nd, 20:1; 3rd, 24:1; 4th–6th, 29:1; middle school, 24.5:1; high school, 26:1
WASL scores: reading, 66.4%; math, 42%; writing, 70.1%; science, 24.3%

Highline Public Schools by the Numbers

Phone: 433-0111
Web site: www.hsd401.org
Enrollment: 17,711 at 31 schools
Annual budget: $138.5 million
Student-teacher ratio: 17.6:1
WASL scores: reading, 59.6%; math, 34.6%; writing, 59%; science, 24.4%

Issaquah School District by the Numbers

Phone: 425-837-7000
Web site: www.issaquah.wednet.edu
Enrollment: 15,009 at 21 schools
Annual budget: $109 million
Student-teacher ratios: K–2nd, 20:1; 3rd–5th, 24:1; 6th–8th, 29:1; 9th–12th, 31:1
WASL scores: reading, 82.4%; math, 65.7%; writing, 84.4%; science, 53.5%

Kent School District by the Numbers

Phone: 253-373-7000
Web site: www.kent.k12.wa.us
Enrollment: 26,891 at 39 schools
Annual budget: $204,188,382
Student-teacher ratios: K–3rd, 22:1; 4th, 23:1; 5th–9th, 29:1; 10th–12th, 30:1

WASL scores: reading, 66.5%; math, 50.6%; writing, 69.6%; science, 35.6%

Lake Washington School District by the Numbers

Phone: 425-702-3200
Web site: www.lkwash.wednet.edu
Enrollment: 23,660 at 48 schools
Annual budget: $172 million
Student-teacher ratio: K–1st, 19:1; 2nd–3rd, 24:1; 4th, 25:1; 5th–6th, 27:1; 7th–12th, 29.5:1
WASL scores: reading, 81.4%; math, 65.2%; writing, 79.9%; science, 50.8%

Mercer Island School District by the Numbers

Phone: 236-3330
Web site: www.misd.k12.wa.us
Enrollment: 4,024,460 at 5 schools
Annual budget: $32,851,436
Student-teacher ratios: elementary, 22.7:1; middle school, 26.7:1; high school, 25.4:1
WASL scores: reading, 90.2%; math, 79.1%; writing, 93.3%; science, 71.8%

North Shore School District by the Numbers

Phone: 425-489-6000
Web site: www.nsd.org
Enrollment: 18,828 at 32 schools
Annual budget: $157.5 million
Student-teacher ratios: K–1st, 22.8:1; 2nd–3rd, 24.3:1; 4th, 24.8:1; 5th–6th, 26.5:1; 7th–9th, 25.4:1; 10th–12th, 25.7:1
WASL scores: reading, 80.3%; math, 68.1%; writing, 81.2%; science, 53.8%

Renton School District by the Numbers

Phone: 425-204-2300
Web site: www.renton.wednet.edu
Enrollment: 13,000 at 22 schools

Annual budget: $100 million
Student-teacher ratios: K–5, 23.2:1; 6th–12th, 29:1
WASL scores: reading, 58.9%; math, 37.3%; writing, 62.1%; science, 23.4%

Tacoma School District by the Numbers

Phone: 253-571-1000
Web site: www.tacoma.k12.wa.us
Enrollment: 31,128 at 54 schools
Annual budget: $274,160,251
Student-teacher ratio: 17.7:1
WASL scores: reading, 52.8%; math, 29.4%; writing, 53.4%; science, 20%

PRIVATE SCHOOLS

ANNIE WRIGHT SCHOOL: This internationally known Tacoma school is co-ed from pre-K through 8th grade, then serves as an all-girls day and boarding school from 9th through 12th grades.
Address: 827 Tacoma Ave N, Tacoma
Phone: 253-272-2216
Web site: www.aw.org
Grades: pre-K–8, co-ed; 9–12, girls
Enrollment: 437
Annual tuition: $8,080–$31,270

BERTSCHI SCHOOL: This Seattle school's goal is "challenging children to become academically confident and creative thinkers."
Address: 2227 10th Ave E, Seattle
Phone: 324-5476
Web site: www.bertschi.org
Grades: pre-K–5
Enrollment: 204
Annual tuition: $13,285

THE BUSH SCHOOL: This co-ed college prep school's goal is to prepare students to become good community members and to succeed in life beyond college. The Seattle school believes that students learn best when their interests are engaged.
Address: 3400 E Harrison St, Seattle
Phone: 322-7978

Web site: www.bush.edu
Grades: K–12
Enrollment: 560
Annual tuition: $14,150–$19,210

CHARLES WRIGHT ACADEMY: The only private, independent co-ed college prep school in south Puget Sound (Tacoma). Not related to Annie Wright School.
Address: 7723 Chambers Creek Rd W, Tacoma
Phone: 253-620-8300
Web site: www.charleswright.org
Grades: Pre-K–12
Enrollment: 680
Annual tuition: $14,110–$15,935

EASTSIDE PREPARATORY SCHOOL: Focuses on teaching critical and creative thinking skills; students are given information to question, analyze, and make decisions.
Address: 8005 SE 28th St, Mercer Island
Phone: 425-822-5668
Web site: www.etcinc.org
Grades: 6–8
Enrollment: 45
Annual tuition: $16,700

LAKESIDE SCHOOL: This Seattle school has a global service learning program in which students go to other countries for a few weeks to participate in projects in the communities they visit. Famed as the place Bill Gates was schooled.
Address: 14050 1st Ave NE, Seattle
Phone: 368-3600
Web site: www.lakesideschool.org
Grades: 5–12
Enrollment: 757
Annual tuition: $18,550–$19,320

SEATTLE ACADEMY: An independent, private college prep school for 6th–12th graders with a four-building urban campus and a strong arts program designed to engage both sides of the brain.
Address: 1201 E Union St, Seattle
Phone: 324-7227
Web site: www.seattleacademy.org
Grades: 6–12
Enrollment: 528
Annual tuition: $17,610–$18,506

UNIVERSITY PREP: An independent, private college prep school for 6th–12th graders that emphasizes small class size and social responsibility.
Address: 8000 25th Ave NE, Seattle
Phone: 523-6407
Web site: www.universityprep.org
Grades: 6–12
Enrollment: 458
Annual tuition: $17,587–$18,694

ALTERNATIVE SCHOOLS

AFRICAN AMERICAN ACADEMY AT MAGNOLIA ELEMENTARY SCHOOL: Curriculum is taught from an Afrocentric perspective, but students of any race may attend.
Address: 8311 Beacon Ave S
Phone: 252-6650
Web site: www.seattleschools.org/schools/aaa/
Grades: K–8
Enrollment: 394

ALTERNATIVE SCHOOL #1: Students of all ages share class space in this open-concept school, where the emphasis is on experience-based learning rather than linear teaching methods, grade level, or letter grades. Students have more than 80 days of field trips. Interview required before enrollment.
Address: Pinehurst Bldg, 11530 12th Ave NE
Phone: 252-4600
Web site: as1.seattleschools.org
Grades: K–8
Enrollment: 265

ALTERNATIVE ELEMENTARY #2 (AE2) AT DECATUR ELEMENTARY: Open-concept school focusing on individualized project-based instruction. Instead of receiving letter grades, students are evaluated in parent-teacher conferences based on their project portfolios.
Address: 7711 43rd Ave NE
Phone: 252-5300
Web site: www.seattleschools.org/schools/ae2
Grades: K–5
Enrollment: 300

JOHN MARSHALL HIGH SCHOOL: Focuses on at-risk students, underachievers, students reentering school after suspension/

expulsion, and teenage parents (day care available). The evening program offers an option for students who cannot attend school during the day and helps students complete graduation requirements.
Address: 520 NE Ravenna Blvd
Phone: 252-4700; 252-4680 (evening program)
Web site: www.seattleschools.org/area/main/ShowSchool?sid=950
Grades: High school
Enrollment: 200; evening program: 300

KIMBALL ELEMENTARY: Open-concept school with a team-teaching approach emphasizing reading, math, and language arts. Outreach to bilingual students.
Address: 3200 23rd Ave S
Phone: 252-7280
Web site: www.seattleschools.org/area/main/ShowSchool?sid=288
Grades: K–5
Enrollment: 519

MIDDLE COLLEGE HIGH SCHOOL: Education for at-risk 16- to 21-year-olds, emphasizing completing high school and preparing for higher education.
Address: 401 NE Northgate Wy
Phone: 366-7940
Web site: www.seattleschools.org/schools/middlecollege/index.html
Grades: 11–12
Enrollment: 100

NOVA: The school relies on highly individualized teaching with students evaluated based on their ability to complete a contract covering their plan of instruction.
Address: 2410 E Cherry St
Phone: 252-3500
Web site: www.novaproj.org
Grades: High school
Enrollment: 280

ORCA: Basic skills, arts, and environmental sciences are the main focus. Parental involvement is encouraged.
Address: 3528 S Ferdinand St
Phone: 252-6900
Web site: www.seattleschools.org/schools/orca
Grades: K–5
Enrollment: 242

PATHFINDER (FORMERLY ALTERNATIVE SCHOOL #4): West Seattle's only alternative public school. Multicultural education with a focus on Native American culture.
Address: 5012 SW Genesee St
Phone: 252-9710
Web site: www.seattleschools.org/schools/pathfinder
Grades: K–8
Enrollment: 400

PROYECTO SABER: This program designed for Latino and Chicano students provides tutoring and support services at some schools in the district, including Denny Middle School as well as Ballard, Chief Sealth, and Denny High Schools.
Address: 2600 SW Thistle St
Phone: 252-8550 (Chief Sealth)
Web site: www.seattleschools.org/schools/chiefsealth

SALMON BAY (FORMERLY ALTERNATIVE SCHOOL #5, COHO/NOMS): Hands-on, cooperative-style learning and project-based education with student evaluation based on student portfolios.
Address: 1810 NW 65th St
Phone: 252-1720
Web site: www.salmonbay.seattleschools.org
Grades: K–8
Enrollment: 604

SOUTH LAKE HIGH SCHOOL: Focuses on at-risk students, underachievers, people reentering school after suspension or expulsion, and teenage parents (private day care on-site).
Address: 8825 Rainier Ave S
Phone: 252-6600
Web site: www.seattleschools.org/area/main/ShowSchool?sid=960
Grades: High school
Enrollment: 150

SUMMIT K–12: Focuses on arts and physical education at the district's only K–12 alternative school.
Address: 11051 34th Ave NE
Phone: 252-4500
Web site: www.seattleschools.org/schools/summitk-12
Grades: K–12
Enrollment: 740

TOPS (THE OPTION PROGRAM AT SEWARD): Arts, music, and basic skills are emphasized as well as investigating the

urban environment beyond the school. Some grades have waiting lists.
Address: 2500 Franklin Ave
Phone: 252-3510
Web site: www.seattleschools.org/schools/tops
Grades: K–8
Enrollment: 527

HIGHER EDUCATION

Aside from being home to one of the largest and most prominent state universities in the country, the Seattle area offers postsecondary education in many forms, ranging from exceptional small liberal arts colleges to highly effective and affordable community colleges.

Colleges and Universities

ANTIOCH UNIVERSITY SEATTLE: Antioch's main focus is on graduate programs in such areas as psychology and education. Its Center for Creative Change prepares people to be effective leaders while managing sustainable change and offers courses in four areas: environment and community, management, organizational psychology, and whole systems design.
Phone: 441-5352
Web site: www.antiochsea.edu
Enrollment: 1,806
Annual tuition: $7,800

ARGOSY UNIVERSITY SEATTLE: Top undergraduate programs include bachelor's degrees in business and psychology. This local branch of a network of schools also offers a master of arts in mental health counseling.
Phone: 283-4500
Web site: www.aspp.edu
Enrollment: 300
Annual tuition: $9,100

BASTYR UNIVERSITY: Bastyr is one of only four accredited natural health science schools in the country. The Eastside school's top programs are naturopathic medicine, acupuncture, and Eastern medicine, as well as nutrition.
Phone: 425-602-3330
Web site: www.bastyr.edu
Enrollment: 2,000
Annual tuition: $14,016

CORNISH COLLEGE OF THE ARTS: Cornish is the Northwest's leading performing arts school. Many Seattle musicians and actors were educated here, and its students offer numerous live performances to the public.
Phone: 726-5151
Web site: www.cornish.edu
Enrollment: 650
Annual tuition: $20,000

THE EVERGREEN STATE COLLEGE: If colleges had the equivalent of an alternative school, this legendary Olympia institution would be it. Students pick a single program and use an interdisciplinary approach to study aspects of the subject. No letter grades are given, just written evaluations from both faculty and student.
Phone: 360-867-6000
Web site: www.evergreen.edu
Enrollment: 4,410
Annual tuition: $4,134

PACIFIC LUTHERAN UNIVERSITY: This private Lutheran school's goal is the "integration of liberal arts studies and professional preparation." The Tacoma school's top programs include business, nursing, education, biology, and psychology.
Phone: 253-535-7457
Web site: www.plu.edu/external
Enrollment: 3,643
Annual tuition: $20,790

SEATTLE PACIFIC UNIVERSITY: This private Christian school describes its mission as "the scholarly pursuit of truth, guided not by scientism or relativism, but by a prayerful listening to Scripture, a careful study of God's creation, and a responsible engagement with the issues of our world." Top programs include teaching, business administration, and psychology.
Phone: 281-2000
Web site: www.spu.edu
Enrollment: 3,728
Annual tuition: $20,139

SEATTLE UNIVERSITY: Long known for its tradition of academic excellence, this Jesuit school on First Hill is also home to a prestigious private law school. Other top programs include business and economics, nursing, engineering, and theology.
Phone: 296-6000

Web site: www.seattleu.edu
Enrollment: 6,810
Annual tuition: $20,070

UNIVERSITY OF PUGET SOUND: A private liberal arts college in Tacoma emphasizing an interdisciplinary approach to each of its 40 major programs. Graduate programs include education, occupational therapy, and physical therapy.
Phone: 253-879-3100
Web site: www.ups.edu
Enrollment: 2,782
Annual tuition: $25,190

UNIVERSITY OF WASHINGTON: The UW is the state's largest public university and has been #1 in federal research funding among all public institutions for the past 30 years. Among the school's top programs are health sciences, including nursing; environmental studies; and the Henry M. Jackson School of International Studies.
Phone: 543-2100
Web site: www.washington.edu
Enrollment: 27,732
Annual tuition: $5,290

UW–BOTHELL: Top offerings at this upper-level Eastside campus are computing, education, and nursing. Because of the high level of competition for spots and class space at the main UW campus, some students actually transfer here.
Phone: 425-352-5000
Web site: www.uwb.edu
Enrollment: 1,608
Annual tuition: $5,190

UW–TACOMA: Primarily a commuter school, this branch campus features the Milgard School of Business, which grants undergraduate and MBA degrees. The Institute of Technology offers a BS in computing and software systems. Since all undergraduate programs start at the junior level, many students have transferred from community colleges.
Phone: 253-692-4400
Web site: www.tacoma.washington.edu
Enrollment: 2,100
Annual tuition: $5,190

WASHINGTON STATE UNIVERSITY: It may be because of the chance to escape an urban setting, the number of alumni who are residents of Seattle, or the opportunity to run away from home, but many Seattleites opt for this Pullman university in eastern Washington over the larger UW campus. Top programs include agriculture, science, and communications.
Phone: 509-335-5586
Web site: www.wsu.edu
Enrollment: 18,500
Annual tuition: $5,154

WESTERN WASHINGTON UNIVERSITY: Bellingham's WWU is home to Huxley College of the Environment, one of the country's oldest environmental colleges, and the car design program at the Vehicle Research Institute, plus many liberal arts programs.
Phone: 360- 650-3000
Web site: www.wwu.edu
Enrollment: 11,374 (undergraduate)
Annual tuition: $4,452

Community Colleges & Vocational Schools

ART INSTITUTE OF SEATTLE: Nestled against the Alaskan Wy Viaduct, this school's top programs are graphic design, animation, and video production.
Phone: 448-0900
Web site: www.ais.edu
Enrollment: 2,000
Annual tuition: $12,960

BELLEVUE COMMUNITY COLLEGE (BCC): In addition to offering programs in health science and interior design, BCC also has a fast-track information technology program for people who want to get back into the job market quickly.
Phone: 425-564-1000
Web site: www.bcc.ctc.edu
Enrollment: 22,200
Annual tuition: $2,384

HIGHLINE COMMUNITY COLLEGE: The Des Moines school's top programs include nursing and a nationally recognized paralegal program. Highline added a computer forensics program in 2004.
Phone: 878-3710
Web site: www.highline.edu

Enrollment: 10,000
Annual tuition: $2,172

NORTH SEATTLE COMMUNITY COLLEGE: The majority of the school's students are enrolled in transfer programs that will allow them to earn enough credits to switch to a state university within two years. The rest are in workforce development programs such as business, accounting, and information technology. The school also has the only certified watch-making program west of the Mississippi.
Phone: 527-3600
Web site: www.northseattle.edu
Enrollment: 8,856
Annual tuition: $2,160

RENTON TECHNICAL COLLEGE: A classic trade school, Renton Technical trains people with specific skills so they are prepared to take a job upon graduation. Top programs include licensed practical nursing, and medical and dental assistant.
Phone: 425-235-2352
Web site: www.renton-tc.ctc.edu
Enrollment: 3,500
Annual tuition: $2,154

SEATTLE CENTRAL COMMUNITY COLLEGE: Located on Broadway in the heart of Capitol Hill, the school's top programs are nursing, biotechnology, culinary arts, and information technology.
Phone: 587-3800
Web site: www.seattlecentral.org
Enrollment: 10,000
Annual tuition: $2,160

SEATTLE VOCATIONAL INSTITUTE: The Central District school's top programs train people for positions as network technicians, health unit coordinators, medical assistants, and dental assistants.
Phone: 587-4950
Web site: sviweb.sccd.ctc.edu
Enrollment: 506
Annual tuition: $2,455

SHORELINE COMMUNITY COLLEGE: Top programs at this north Seattle school are automotive, nursing, dental hygiene, and music.
Phone: 546-4101

Web site: www.shoreline.edu
Enrollment: 14,200
Annual tuition: $2,163

SOUTH SEATTLE COMMUNITY COLLEGE: Although the school is best known for its culinary program, it also offers wine studies, aviation maintenance, nursing, and landscaping.
Phone: 764-5300
Web site: www.southseattle.edu
Enrollment: 3,600
Annual tuition: $2,160

THE SEARCH FOR THE GRAIL: DECENT CHILD CARE

As parents almost everywhere will tell you, good child care is hard to find. Longtime residents might work their connections only to find out nothing is available, while newcomers may lack the resources to point them in the right direction. Fortunately there is a nonprofit agency to help natives and newcomers alike: **CHILD CARE RESOURCES** (329-5544, www.childcare.org). The organization has a database of more than 2,000 child-care facilities throughout King County and provides searches over the phone or on the Internet for a modest fee (or free for certain income levels). The list includes licensed family child-care providers, child-care centers, and preschools.

Even if you conduct the search yourself, it's important to **KNOW STATE LICENSING REQUIREMENTS**. Under state law child-care centers serving 12 or more children require licenses. So do family child-care centers where people provide the service in their own homes. Nannies, part-day preschools, and baby sitters do not require licenses, however. Staff members must have training in child care, early learning, first aid for infants and children, CPR, and HIV/AIDS, and they must have received a background check by the Washington State Patrol. Requirements also cover the use of positive discipline, planned activities, safety, and communication with families.

Rates vary widely, depending on the city or area of the county, the type of care, and the age of the child, according to Child Care Resources. In Seattle, for example, a week at a child-care center costs $242 for an infant, $201 for a toddler, and $164 for kids 30 months to 5 years. Eastside rates are comparable; North and South King County rates are lower.

There are a few programs to help low-income families in Seattle with the high price of child care. **WORKING CONNECTIONS CHILDCARE** (341-7433, www.washingtonparentpower. org) is operated by the Washington Department of Social and Health Services, which requires families to make a monthly co-pay of anywhere from $20 to several hundred dollars per month, depending on income and family size. The family must be earning less than 200 percent of the poverty level and working at least 20 hours a week to be eligible. **COMPREHENSIVE CHILD CARE PROGRAM** (386-1050, www.cityofseattle.net/humanservices) is a Seattle program open to low-income families not aided by any other subsidy; the breadwinner must be in a training program that leads to employment within two years.

Other cities in the region may also have child-care scholarships available from their federal block grants. For more information, contact Child Care Resources.

Resources for Parents

THE PARENT EDUCATION PROGRAM at North Seattle Community College offers cooperative preschools, online parenting classes, and more. 528-4625, northonline.northseattle.edu/parented/.

PARENTMAP: Free monthly newsmagazine for Seattle and Eastside parents. Look for it at area bookstores, grocery stores, museums, libraries, etc. 709-9026, www.parentmap.com.

PEPS (Program for Early Parent Support) is a nonprofit organization designed to guide and educate parents about all things related to raising children. Groups meet regularly in neighborhoods across the metro area to share in the "concerns, successes, issues, and joys" that come along with being parents. 547-8570, www.pepsgroup.org.

SEATTLE'S CHILD: Free monthly newsmagazine covering issues and events relevant to area families. Available at libraries, community centers, and businesses serving families. 441-0191, seattle-city.parenthood.com.

CONTINUING EDUCATION

Seattle Arts & Lectures offers the unique **WEDNESDAY UNIVERSITY**, three courses a year for continuing education in the arts and humanities. Past subjects have included the Belle Epoch, silent film, Greek myths, and Renaissance Italy. Classes are held at the Henry Art Gallery. 621-2230, www.lectures.org/wed.html.

DISCOVER U is an educational and recreational organization that offers hundreds of classes in personal and professional development. Subjects run the gamut, from photography and dance classes, to relationships and career training—even how to plan your next Italian vacation. 365-0400, www.discoveru.org.

CHAPTER 8

That's Entertainment

Like Nashville, Austin, and Memphis, Seattle has had a disproportionate impact on the cultural life of the United States. We sent Jimi Hendrix out into the world to change the face of rock music, though he was long gone by the time he achieved fame. Kurt Cobain stayed right here when he and Nirvana set the music world on its ear once again. *Sleepless in Seattle* and *Frasier* imprinted indelible images of Seattle on the public—now everyone thinks we all live along Lake Union or up on Queen Anne, kayak on our lunch hour, and are kinder, gentler, and more highly evolved than the average soul. (True, yes?)

This preeminence is not confined to music. Dale Chihuly and the Pilchuck School helped turn an obscure craft, glass-blowing, into one of the most prominent modern art forms worldwide. Seattle is a national theater center, with both playwrights and actors honing their crafts here. David Guterson's *Snow Falling on Cedars* was a national literary sensation, invoking for millions of readers the image of a mist-clad island in the Sound near Seattle.

It's a bit unfortunate that most of these bright lights of Seattle culture are somewhat overblown—Hendrix and Cobain are legendary partly because they did themselves in, Chihuly is an unabashed Warhol-style self-promoter, and *Sleepless in Seattle*, however clever it was, had about as much intellectual heft as Elliott Bay fog.

This is ever the story with popular culture, though, and it means those of us who live here have ample opportunity to discover and savor the equally excellent work of less-conspicuous artists. Wander the galleries of Pioneer Square and you can marvel at the glasswork of Ginny Ruffner and the dynamic American modernism of painter Jacob Lawrence. Stop in a music store and pick up a CD by rock pioneers the Wailers or grunge pioneers the Melvins. Check out *The Fabulous Baker Boys*, a most interesting movie set and filmed in Seattle.

Maybe the vibrant cultural life of Seattle will inspire you to pick up a pen, paintbrush, or guitar. If not, you'll still never lack for something to go see or hear.

MUSIC

There's as much speculation about the genesis of Seattle's musical prominence as about its coffee addiction. Maybe both represent sheer circumstance. Maybe the two are intertwined: Our long, dark winters lead to introspective indoor pursuits. Alas, we still await the first hit song about coffee.

Performance-wise, the Seattle universe is broad. Many national tours make a stop in or near Puget Sound, any number of bands come here to record, and the regional music scene is as good as any in the country. You could listen to good, interesting music almost every night of the year—when you aren't busy kayaking Lake Union at sunset, of course.

All Things Classical

BELLEVUE PHILHARMONIC: This Eastside orchestra plays in Meydenbauer Center, with a full program of classical and orchestral pop. 325-6500, www.bellevuephil.org.

BENAROYA HALL: Opened in 1998 after a remarkable fundraising campaign that garnered $159 million from the Seattle community, Benaroya was the most significant local addition until the new library was built six years later. Benaroya's glistening glass façade, discreet outdoor gardens, Sound-view lobby, and exceptional 2,200-seat main performance hall make it one of the finest such facilities in the United States (though critics find its sound a bit more cool than warm). The best seats, visually and acoustically, are in the lower balcony. Benaroya's 500-seat recital hall is a splendid place to see a more intimate performance. The hall, including non-symphony performances, is managed by its chief tenant, the Seattle Symphony (see below). 200 University St, 215-4747, www.seattlesymphony.org/benaroya.

EARLY MUSIC GUILD: For more than 25 years the EMG has helped make Seattle a center of historically informed early music performance. Among other performances, look for its popular International Series, five concerts of medieval, Renaissance, baroque, or other classical music featuring top international ensembles. 325-7066, www.earlymusicguild.org.

MCCAW HALL: When the Seattle Symphony vacated the Opera House in 1998, its prime tenant, Seattle Opera, set about a campaign to create a new home too. But in this case what was done was a snazzy, 70 percent refurbishment of the early-'60s

Opera House, a World's Fair artifact that had wonders like orange-tone carpet. The result, opened in 2003, is a nifty performance hall with an airy lobby, a fountain-splashed courtyard, rejuvenated acoustics, and discreet décor that improve the hall significantly. Though still called the "opera house" by locals, it's officially Marion Oliver McCaw Hall (much of the renovation money was fronted by the namesake's tech-billionaire sons). Located at the north side of Seattle Center. 305 Harrison St, 684-7200, www.seattlecenter.com.

NORTHWEST CHAMBER ORCHESTRA: Offering up small-scale classical works for more than 25 years, this orchestra has adapted masterfully to the bright acoustics of Benaroya's small recital hall. Each season the group performs seven mainstage concerts, five showcase events, and a Music in the Park series at Volunteer Park. 343-0445, www.nwco.org.

NW SINFONIETTA: This Tacoma-based orchestra makes periodic forays to Seattle and provides a lively, smaller orchestra approach to the classical repertoire. 253-383-5344, www.nwsinfonietta.com.

SEATTLE BAROQUE ORCHESTRA: This group offers period instruments and instrumentation for renditions of Bach, Handel, Vivaldi, and so on, usually at Benaroya. 332-3118, www.seattlebaroque.org.

SEATTLE MEN'S CHORUS: Openly gay, wonderfully rehearsed, and wildly popular, the Men's Chorus presents several concerts a year with a deep vocal timbre one rarely hears. It's the largest gay men's chorus in the world and the largest community chorus in the United States. The group's highlight is the annual series of holiday music concerts. 323-2992, www.seattlemenschorus.org.

SEATTLE OPERA: Under the innovative hand of Texas transplant Speight Jenkins, Seattle Opera (SO) has vaulted to international prominence, chiefly on the towering framework of Richard Wagner's music. SO is one of the few companies in North America to have offered all 10 of Wagner's major works, and it is best known for the *Ring* cycle, the long, intense, and haunting four-opera set that for most people is a once-in-a-lifetime experience. SO produces the *Ring* every four years, usually in the summer, and devotees literally come from around the world. The 2001 series sold out *one year* in advance. It's scheduled again in 2009 and 2013; other Wagner pieces, including the rare *Parsifal*, appear in intervening sum-

Cheap Seats

Can't afford the price of admission? Many theaters welcome **VOLUNTEER USHERS:** pass out programs for half an hour and see the show for free. Larger venues will often hold **PREVIEW PERFORMANCES** the week before a show opens that carry a cheaper ticket price. (These vary by venue and can disappear fast, so call well in advance.) **TICKET/TICKET** offers half-price tickets to same-day performances (324-2744), and several area museums offer one day a month with **FREE ADMISSION**.

mers. Seattle Opera also has a regular winter-spring season of four mainstream operas. 389-7676 or 800-426-1619, www.seattleopera.org.

SEATTLE SYMPHONY ORCHESTRA (SSO): Under the direction of Gerard Schwarz for the past two decades, the SSO has achieved national prominence, largely because of Schwarz's advocacy of the music of such American composers as David Diamond, Howard Hanson, and Seattle's own Alan Hovhaness (see sidebar, page 232). The symphony's recordings have several times made the classical best-seller lists. The SSO offers about 30 programs a year, mid-September through mid-July. Most programs run Thursday, Friday, and Saturday nights, with a Sunday matinee. In addition, the symphony traditionally presents a holiday music series in early December, Handel's *Messiah* in mid-December, a New Year's Eve ball, and Beethoven's *Ninth Symphony* in early January.

Aside from SSO concerts, visiting orchestras and recital stars frequent Benaroya under the SSO banner, including some of the biggest stars in the musical firmament, such as Pinchas Zukerman and Andre Watts, plus pop stars like Arlo Guthrie. 215-4747, www.seattlesymphony.org.

Musical Theater

CREPE DE PARIS: Classic cabaret in a dinner theater downtown. 623-4111.

FIFTH AVENUE THEATRE: Seattle's Broadway outpost for musical theater brings in four or five national touring companies a year, and the resident troupe produces a few more shows. It's an intimate place to see a production, by Broadway standards. 1308 5th Ave, 292-ARTS, www.5thavenuetheatre.org.

KIRKLAND PERFORMANCE CENTER: An intimate venue programming folk music, dance, children's theater, light theater, and such. 350 Kirkland Ave, 425-893-9900, www.kpcenter.org.

MEANY THEATER: The University of Washington's performance venue schedules a comprehensive and diverse season of performances, ranging from classical music to aboriginal dance to progressive theater. The programming is better than the hall itself, which could use a renovation. 4001 University Ave NE, 543-4880, www.uwworldseries.org.

THE MOORE & PARAMOUNT THEATERS: These two old-line downtown gems are owned and operated by the Seattle Theater Group, which invested quite a bit of money in restoring the Paramount to its 1920s glamour. Touring dance, music, and occasional drama performances come to both venues; the Paramount (911 Pine St) is larger and snazzier, and the Moore (1932 2nd Ave) is a bit funkier. 467-5510 (theater group), 292-ARTS (tickets), www.theparamount.com.

TEATRO ZINZANNI: This dinner theater is one of the city's greatest theatrical successes. Its unlikely mix of Northwest cuisine, cabaret, and European-style circus acts often makes it one of the most popular tickets in town (read: waiting list). 2301 6th Ave, 802-0015, www.dreams.zinzanni.org.

Pop/Rock

CHATEAU STE. MICHELLE: You have to admire the marketing savvy that led the folks at this Woodinville winery to start an outdoor concert series back in the late '80s. Garrison Keillor, B. B. King, the Dave Matthews Band, and Buffy Ste. Marie are the sorts who play here. 14111 NE 145th St, Woodinville, 425-415-3300, www.ste-michelle.com.

CONCERTS AT THE PIER: Uniquely Seattle, Pier 62/63 is one of the loveliest places anywhere to see a musical performance: The venue is small and intimate, the fresh breeze washes off the Sound, and the sun sets over the Olympics in the background. Quite a few artists, such as Chris Isaak, Lyle Lovett, and the Indigo Girls, visit here every summer simply because they like the venue so much. Alas, in 2005 the concerts moved to a temporary location on South Lake Union while structural restoration work began on the piers. Expect the same rock, blues, jazz, pop, and R&B talent—just a different view. S Lake Union Park, 281-7788, www.summernights.org.

EMERALD QUEEN CASINO: An enterprise of the Puyallup Indian tribe, this casino near Tacoma brings in notable established artists such as Merle Haggard, Joan Jett, and others whose music endures but no longer can fill major arenas. The Diamonds here are evergreen—the Neil Diamond imitators, that is. And the Beatles, and Creedence, and so on. 2024 E 29th St, 888-831-7655, www.emeraldqueen.com.

THE GORGE AMPHITHEATER: Perched at the edge of the Columbia River valley, east of Ellensburg, near George, this outdoor arena is one of the nation's most prominent homes for big acts ranging from the Dead to Ozzy Osbourne. It's set in the middle of potato-farm country, the weather is dependable, camping is available, and the drive from Seattle is about three hours. The season runs May through September. 628-0888, www.gorgeconcerts.com.

MARYMOOR PARK: The concerts at Redmond's Marymoor are similar to those at the Woodland Park Zoo, both in ambience and programming, with a tendency toward world music; the park was host to WOMAD USA several years in a row. 628-0888, www.concertsatmarymoor.com.

THE MOORE & PARAMOUNT THEATERS: See listing under "Musical Theater," above.

WHITE RIVER AMPHITHEATER: The Muckleshoot tribe's new outdoor arena, a sort of mini-Gorge, draws national touring pop and rock acts. 360-825-6200, www.whiteriverconcerts.com.

WOODLAND PARK ZOO: The zoo runs a series of outdoor summer concerts, Zoo Tunes, where folk, country, and blues predominate. Bring a blanket, a picnic basket, and your laid-back summer psyche to Phinney Ridge. 684-4800, www.zoo.org.

Clubs

A healthy selection of smaller venues regularly bring in artists of regional or national stature. The **CROCODILE CAFE** (2200 2nd Ave, 441-5611, www.thecrocodile.com) programs alternative rock. **SHOWBOX** (1426 1st Ave, 628-3151, www.showboxonline.com) is a showplace for indie rock and is considered the grande dame of Seattle music venues. Ballard's **TRACTOR TAVERN** (5213 Ballard Ave NW, 789-3599, www.tractortavern.com) veers toward bluegrass, country, roots rock, and blues. **CENTURY BALLROOM** (915 E Pine St, 324-7263, www.centuryballroom.com) has added a dining section, making Seattle's best dance hall into a supper club as well. **RE-BAR**

GONE BUT NOT FORGOTTEN

Hendrix, Cobain & Grunge

Jimi Hendrix (1942–1970) reconfigured the face of rock 'n' roll, applying matchless showmanship and infinite skill to guitar-driven rock. Raised in Seattle, he was a backup musician (for B. B. King, among others) until he rocketed to fame as a solo performer at the Monterey Pop Festival in 1967. After that he flashed across the musical landscape like a meteor, creating a musical genre that has not been expanded much since. But drug addiction led to his death in London. His burial site in Renton's Greenwood Cemetery is now a much-visited shrine (see Chapter 3, "Nearby Burgs," page 126). Zobrist Music, on 1st Ave, is where he supposedly bought his first electric guitar. For information, see www.jimihendrix.com.

Kurt Cobain (1967–1994), born and raised in the gritty Washington coast town of Hoquiam, came to Seattle to pursue musical fame and, unlike Hendrix, did not have to leave. As a member of Nirvana—and the band's chief musical force—he pushed rock into a raw, visceral direction that, in Cobain's hands, was nonetheless musically sophisticated. Though it was called "grunge," Nirvana's work has a musical complexity unusual for popular culture. Other Seattle grunge bands that leaped to success include Soundgarden and Pearl Jam. Read more about Cobain's story at www.cobain.com.

Worldwide fame came Cobain's way, and he, too, flared across the musical sky for a brief three years. Tormented by drug addiction, he killed himself in his Seattle home. His widow, the spiritually peripatetic Courtney Love, is rumored to have scattered his ashes in an Olympic Peninsula river.

(1114 Howell St, 233-9873) has distinguished itself among the city's many hipster-friendly clubs by playing host to theater events, rock musicals, and performance-art events. Local DJs spin house, old-school, and soul on the off nights. There are dozens of other venues, too: Check *The Stranger* weekly music listings for the best roundup.

A group of taverns and restaurants in Pioneer Square, all of which have live music on weekends, have banded together to offer patrons a universal cover charge: One cover gets you in everywhere. So if you find the zydeco at the **NEW ORLEANS** too

"Louie Louie"

Though this song was first brought to prominence by a Seattle band, the Wailers, in the late '50s, it later vaulted to national fame at the hands of Portland's Kingsmen. The tune was actually penned by a Los Angeles writer, Richard Berry, who sold the rights not long after he first recorded it. When Seattle's Wailers picked it up a few years later, their rendition became a regional, but not a national, hit.

Then, in 1963, two bands in Portland—the Kingsmen and Paul Revere and the Raiders—recorded "Louie Louie" within a few weeks of each other. These did become national hits, particularly the Kingsmen's version, which has probably been played at more than a million high school parties at which young dudes proclaimed their interpretation of the lyrics. (In reality, they are not about sexual proclivities; it's a quasi-calypso love song about a guy who misses his girl.) Supposedly more than a thousand versions of the song have been recorded over the years. None of them benefited Berry, who died in 1997; see www.louielouie.net.

"Louie Louie" is the seventh-inning stretch song at Safeco Field and was once quite seriously proposed as Washington's official song.

---

bouncy, you can shift over to blues at the **CENTRAL SALOON**. Other clubs include the **BOHEMIAN, DOC MAYNARD'S, FENIX UNDERGROUND, J&M CAFÉ & CARDROOM, JUAN O'RILEY'S, LARRY'S BLUES CAFÉ, THE OLD TIMER'S CAFE,** and **TIKI BOB'S**. It doesn't include drinks or food, of course, and things do get a bit rowdy after 10pm or so. (Unescorted women would be wise to depart Pioneer Square well before midnight.) It's a real scene on Halloween, Mardi Gras, and after Mariners and Seahawks games.

World/Jazz

DIMITRIOU'S JAZZ ALLEY: Seattle's ultimate supper club brings in the very best of North America's jazz artists, such as Jane Monheit, Diana Krall, and Marian McPartland. The food is surprisingly good, too. 2033 6th Ave, 441-9729, www.jazzalley.com.

MARYMOOR PARK: See listing under "Pop/Rock," above.

TRIPLE DOOR: A refined, gracious new venue for such artists as Richie Havens and Nancy Sinatra; two other smaller stages showcase local and regional musicians. The pan-Asian dinner menu is by upstairs neighbor Wild Ginger. 216 Union St, 838-4333, www.thetripledoor.net.

TULA'S: This Belltown hotspot offers a jazz-inflected lineup. 2214 2nd Ave, 443-4221, www.tulas.com.

DANCE

ON THE BOARDS: Long the source of cutting-edge works that merge dance, music, theater, and visual media, and an important local showcase for local choreographers. The sellout New Performance Series (Oct–May) brings internationally known contemporary artists. 100 W Roy St, 217-9888, www.ontheboards.org.

PACIFIC NORTHWEST BALLET (PNB): Seattle Center–based PNB is one of the nation's leading ballet companies. The ballet's holiday production of *The Nutcracker*, designed in collaboration with famed children's book artist Maurice Sendak, has been an annual sellout for years. 441-2424, www.pnb.org.

SPECTRUM DANCE THEATER: Founded in 1982, this classical jazz company offers two mainstage concert series at Meany Theater at the UW every fall and spring, as well as informal Dance in the Making studio performances that include audience Q&A sessions. Family-friendly, with instructional classes for kids and adults. 800 Lake Washington Blvd, 325-4161, www.spectrumdance.org.

UW WORLD DANCE SERIES: Six world-renowned dance groups come to town every year as part of this series, held October through May at Meany Theater. Top draws include Merce Cunningham's dance company, the Alvin Ailey American Dance Theater, and Seattle-boy-done-good choreographer Mark Morris. 543-4880 or 800-859-5342, www.uwworldseries.org.

VELOCITY DANCE CENTER: A popular venue for catching recitals and performances by local choreographers. 915 E Pine St, 325-8773, www.velocitydancecenter.org.

GONE BUT NOT FORGOTTEN

Hovhaness & Lawrence

Alan Hovhaness and Jacob Lawrence are the two brightest stars in the Seattle cultural firmament—and each, alas, is less well-known than he should be in his hometown. Both made national contributions to their art; both enjoyed early success but later overcame midlife obscurity; both spent the last third of their lives in Seattle enjoying national prominence that often exceeded their local visibility.

Prolific composer Hovhaness (1911–2000) was born in Brooklyn to Armenian immigrants and joined the between-wars creative explosion that shaped American classical music, consorting with Leonard Bernstein, Leopold Stokowski, and Samuel Barber. But he fell out of favor for his refusal to embrace atonal styles, preferring instead to meld long melodic themes with ultra-traditional forms such as fugues. His second symphony, *Mysterious Mountain*, is the most famous example of that, a soaring, sweeping river of music.

After a late-'60s stint as composer-in-residence with the Seattle Symphony, Hovhaness settled here in 1973 to be near the mountains that he loved. Under Gerard Schwarz, the SSO became a leading advocate of Hovhaness's music, and its recordings of the composer were classical bestsellers. The composer himself appeared several times at Benaroya in the '90s to hear performances of his work, receiving thunderous waves of approbation from the capacity audience when Schwarz directed the spotlights to him.

Lawrence (1917–2000) was born in New York, also, and as a young man experienced the heady days of the Harlem Renaissance in the '30s. He found fame with a series, "Migration of the Negro," devoted to the long exodus of America's black people from south to north after the Civil War. His canvases, which incorporate elements of cubism and of Mexico's master muralists, are vivid, powerful, and deeply colored works with an instantly recognizable personal style. He moved to Seattle in 1971 to accept a teaching position at the University of Washington, and his works are available in local galleries.

THEATER

ACT: A Contemporary Theatre emerged from financial near-disaster a few years back to reclaim its role as Seattle's edge-bending mainstage company. Its long-running, ever-popular *Late Night Catechism* is an affectionate but unflinching comic look at Catholicism. 700 Pine St, 292-7676, www.acttheatre.org.

BATHHOUSE: Set in a most intimate space in a renovated Green Lake bathhouse, this active semiprofessional company offers original comedy, holiday shows, and family dramas. 524-1300, www.seattlepublictheater.org.

BOOK-IT: Book-It's scripts are largely expanded readings of prose fiction. 216-0833, www.book-it.org.

FIFTH AVENUE THEATRE: See listing under "Musical Theater," page 226.

INTIMAN: Intiman focuses on progressive drama, old and new, from *Our Town* to *Angels in America*. Its pinnacle came when it premiered a series, *The Kentucky Cycle*, that eventually won the Pulitzer Prize. Major national stars such as Seattle's Tom Skerritt often star. 269-1900, www.intiman.org.

PARAMOUNT THEATER: See listing under "Musical Theater," page 227.

SEATTLE CHILDREN'S THEATRE: Plays for kids (6–12, mostly) in a fine venue at Seattle Center. 441-3322, www.sct.org.

SEATTLE REP: Seattle's mainstage professional repertory company is of national stature and has premiered plays by, among others, August Wilson and Wendy Wasserstein. It won the Tony for regional theater in 1990. Its schedule includes independent productions of Broadway sensations—sometimes better here than there. 443-2222, www.seattlerep.org.

SEATTLE SHAKESPEARE COMPANY: Aside from the fact that everyone needs a little Bard in their lives, this Seattle Center–based group is distinguished among local troupes by the fact it operates on a fiscally sound basis, in the black. Maybe that's because, much as purists protest, it offers user-friendly shows such as a "chamber" Othello, distilled from its original length and density. The four-play season runs November to June. Center House Theater, 305 Harrison St, 733-8222, www.seattleshakes.org.

Ticket Madness

Seattle's arts and performance community is firmly in the grasp of **TICKETMASTER**, the giant national ticket broker people love to hate. Sports, theater, music—nearly all sell through the big T, which means you'll have to try to navigate their demanding Web site ("enter blood type here") or speak to the barely functional voice-response computer. For these privileges you pay fees and add-ons that can exceed 10 percent of the ticket price. But there is often little choice; 628-0888, www.ticketmaster.com.

There are other alternatives, especially for those who work in downtown Seattle. Most of the major venues have their own box offices at which the seat selection and fee-free pricing are both better—Benaroya Hall, the Opera House, the Moore and Paramount Theaters, Seahawks, Mariners, Sonics, and so on.

There are also a couple of notable ticket services. **SEATTLE TIXX** is a ticket exchange and resale marketplace that covers most of the major venues and genres; 425-778-5522, www.seattletixx.com. **TICKETWEB** offers tickets online for numerous independent performance events; www.ticketweb.com. And **TICKET-TICKET** has discount ducats (usually half-price) to many events on the day of performance—booths are at Pike Place Market, Broadway Market on Capitol Hill, and the Meydenbauer Center in Bellevue; 324-2744.

TAPROOT THEATRE: This small but active company presents traditional drama (Shakespeare, for instance) and more modern plays reflecting Judeo-Christian values. 781-9707, www.taproottheatre.org.

VILLAGE THEATER: This professional troupe in Issaquah presents productions of such classic American dramas as *Oklahoma*. 425-392-2202, www.villagetheatre.org.

MUSEUMS AND OTHER ATTRACTIONS

BURKE MUSEUM OF NATURAL HISTORY & CULTURE: Seattle's natural history museum is associated with the University of Washington. The Burke has been a key player in the controversy over Kennewick Man, human skeletons found in Eastern Washington and claimed by both Native tribes and scientific researchers. Its explication of the Pacific Coast environment is admirably comprehensive. 17th Ave NE & NE 45th St, 543-5590, www.washington.edu/burkemuseum.

CENTER FOR WOODEN BOATS: See Chapter 1, "Seattle Neighborhoods," page 28.

EMP: Paul Allen's homage to rock music in general, and Jimi Hendrix in particular, the Experience Music Project may be more noteworthy outside than in. The Frank Gehry no-straight-line, painted metal structure is one of those love-it-or-hate-it public buildings that will be universally considered a monument a half-century from now. The collection itself is most meaningful to those who came of age in the '60s. A steep admission price ($19.95) dilutes the nostalgic joy of inspecting old posters, guitars, and film clips. The museum's concert venues, including a vast hall called "Sky Church," regularly schedule performers of every vintage and genre. The ancillary **SCIENCE FICTION MUSEUM & HALL OF FAME** is for anyone who's read Tom Swift. 5th Ave between Broad & Thomas Sts, 367-5483 or 877-367-5483, www.emplive.com.

FRYE ART MUSEUM: The Frye, created by its namesake family, represents an East Coast phenomenon: the heavily endowed free museum. It offers a light but intriguing survey of American and European art. 704 Terry Ave, 622-9250, www.fryeart.org.

KLONDIKE GOLD RUSH MUSEUM: Gold rushers heading over Chilkoot pass in 1898 were required to haul a ton of supplies with them, lest they starve or freeze or both. If you want to see just how much that ton was, a daunting diorama at this compact Pioneer Square museum illustrates it. Why is this here in Seattle? The Alaskan Way waterfront is where the vast majority of Klondike hopefuls embarked; the other branch of the museum (it's actually a U.S. national park) is in Skagway, Alaska. 117 S Main St, 553-7220, www.nps.gov/klse.

MOHAI: The Museum of History and Industry honors Seattle's past as an industrial center. Yes, there was a time when hardware—the rivets and sheet metal on World War II bombers—represented Seattle to the world. 2700 24th Ave E, 324-1126, www.seattlehistory.org.

MUSEUM OF FLIGHT: In 1917 a visionary lumber tycoon named William Boeing set up shop in Seattle to make airplanes. The famed "red barn" in which he did so is now incorporated in this glorious museum, which also includes other choice artifacts such as an old Air Force One, World War II planes made in Seattle, and fascinating displays about the development of aviation and space travel, exploring Seattle's key role in both. Perched next to Boeing Field, the museum's 20,000-item collection is one of the finest in the world. 9404 E Marginal Wy S, 764-5720, www.museumofflight.org.

NORDIC HERITAGE MUSEUM: See Chapter 1, "Seattle Neighborhoods," page 5.

ODYSSEY MARITIME DISCOVERY CENTER: Explains why and how waterborne enterprise remains economically and culturally vital to the Seattle community. Pier 66, 374-4000, www.ody.org.

PACIFIC SCIENCE CENTER: Some of the attractions here are classic science: the dinosaur exhibit. Some are hands-on technology: working with robots. Some are simply fun, such as the room full of ping-pong balls into which you can leap. The IMAX screen is bigger than the average house, and so are the panoramas it offers of Mount Everest and such. This is one of those rare good-for-you places that kids and adults enjoy equally. 200 2nd Ave N (Seattle Center), 443-2001, www.pacsci.org.

SEATTLE ART MUSEUM (SAM): The new SAM isn't so new any more, having left its old Volunteer Park home (now the Seattle Asian Art Museum) in 1992 for downtown digs on First Avenue. The impressive kinetic sculpture out front, "Hammering Man" (by Jonathan Borofsky), is one of the city's modern icons, meant to reflect Seattle's industrial past. SAM's collection includes a healthy representation of local artists Morris Graves, Dale Chihuly, and Jacob Lawrence, as well as a representative catalog of First Nations art. It does an admirable job of bringing in international touring exhibits to supplement its small holdings of European and modern art. The Lusty Lady peep show (a legendary women-owned business) across the street offers another sort of art, and many Seattleites find the juxtaposition entertainingly appropriate. 100 University St, 654-3100, www.seattleartmuseum.org.

SEATTLE ASIAN ART MUSEUM: An adjunct of SAM, this 1933 art deco stone building in Volunteer Park is an imposing home for the museum's deep collection of art from across the Pacific; particularly noteworthy are Japanese calligraphy and watercolors, and Chinese statuary. 1400 E Prospect St, 654-3100, www.seattleartmuseum.org.

TACOMA MUSEUMS: The City of Destiny has lately transformed itself into the city of legacy with its museum district just east of downtown. (See Chapter 3, "Nearby Burgs," page 129.)

Art Walks

Seattle's prime gallery district is in Pioneer Square, with many galleries set along a lovely, tree-lined plaza between heritage stone buildings on Occidental Square. On the first Thursday of each month is "Art Walk," from 6–8pm, with galleries offering late hours, special shows, coffee, wine, and pastries. The following neighborhoods also have Art Walks: Fremont (first Fri of each month, 6–9pm), Ballard (second Sat, 6–9pm), Capitol Hill (first Sat, all day), and Kirkland (second Thurs, 6–9pm).

Animal Attractions

COUGAR MOUNTAIN ZOO: This is a small but lovely facility outside Bellevue, concentrating on North American animals. And yes, there are cougars. 5410 194th Ave, Issaquah, 425-391-5508, www.cougarmountainzoo.org.

NORTHWEST TREK: An adjunct of the Point Defiance Zoo, this sprawling complex in the foothills of Mount Rainier is one of the best family attractions in the West. Housed on hundreds of acres of natural Cascades landscape, the elk, bears, cats, and other animals here are definitely at home, while the people are unobtrusive visitors. Special attractions for kids are overnight stays and feeding-time journeys into the habitats with zookeepers. Eatonville, 360-832-6117, www.nwtrek.org.

POINT DEFIANCE ZOO: This Tacoma zoo is the official survival and breeding center for the most endangered mammal in North America, the red wolf (the program has grown its population from 14 in 1980 to 300 today). In the aquarium don't miss the seals, sea lions, and white beluga whale. 5400 N Pearl St, 253-591-5337, www.pdza.org.

SEATTLE AQUARIUM: Somewhat confined by its waterfront site on Alaska Way, this is a compact facility devoted largely to Pacific marine life, including its own salmon run. Pier 59, 386-4300, www.seattleaquarium.org.

WOODLAND PARK ZOO: Blessed with ample room and innovative management, Seattle's zoo has been one of the world's pioneers in creating natural habitats for its denizens. Its African savannah and Northwest coast habitats are particularly noteworthy. 5500 Phinney Ave, 684-4800, www.zoo.org.

FESTIVALS

BITE OF SEATTLE: What began as a friendly daytime city picnic, where visitors could sample tidbits from local chefs, has mushroomed into a late-July extravaganza that draws huge crowds—and we do mean crowds: close to a half-million people jam into the Seattle Center grounds for the three-day event. You do the math; the 60 or so participating restaurants are preparing very fast food indeed. Withal, it's a great place to try out dishes ranging from ostrich burgers to Ethiopian stews. Be sure to bring at least $30 (it's no longer a bargain event), and don't make your wedding dinner plans based on the food here. www.biteofseattle.com.

BUMBERSHOOT: Summer's wrap-up comes Labor Day weekend at the Seattle Center, with a high-octane affair that brings in major national rock and pop acts, along with blues, country, jazz, classical, dance, theater, visual arts, fashion, film, and literary events. There are dozens of venues, many occupied simultaneously; crowds are huge; and you have to get in line very, very early for the big-name acts. "Bumbershoot" is a British word for umbrella, and there is a reason this festival is so named. 281-7788, www.bumbershoot.com.

FOLKLIFE: The festival season kicks off Memorial Day weekend at the Seattle Center with this down-home affair devoted to folk, ethnic, literary, and dance performances of all sorts. More than just an entertaining event, Folklife is a vital part of the Northwest folk arts scene with few big stars, but lots of populist culture. 684-7300, www.nwfolklife.org.

SEAFAIR: Pirates trundle along downtown streets. Parades and community fairs crop up in towns throughout King County, culminating with the Torchlight parade downtown. The Blue Angels roar over downtown and Lake Washington, and innumerable thousands of folks head to Seward Park to guzzle beer and peer uncertainly in the distance at the hydros. Ah, Seafair—it's Seattle's own, for better or worse. (Some folks use it as an occasion to leave town.) The climax is either the last weekend in July or the first one in August, which is statistically the moment it is least likely to rain. www.seafair.com.

WOODEN BOAT FESTIVAL: As if there wasn't enough to do July 4th, each year the weekend closest to it draws more than a hundred classic boats to the south end of Lake Union for this friendly celebration sponsored by the Center for Wooden Boats. Visitors to the free festival can stroll the docks and admire the handsome, polished craft; learn how to build their own boats; watch kayak and canoe races; and visit the *Virginia V*, the last of Puget Sound's famed Mosquito Fleet. For anyone who admires true craftsmanship, this is an aesthetic treasure. 382-2628, www.cwb.org.

READINGS & LECTURES

ELLIOTT BAY BOOK COMPANY: See listing under "Bookstores," below.

HUGO HOUSE: This Capitol Hill institution has an admirable mission, to foster the written (and spoken) word in Seattle culture. Its programs range from author appearances, usually by poets (as Hugo himself was) to prison writing workshops. Aspiring writers can learn and gain spiritual sustenance here. 1634 11th Ave, 322-7030, www.hugohouse.org.

SEATTLE ARTS & LECTURES: At the top of the local literary food chain is this evening lecture series, founded in 1987, which runs fall through spring. The list of guests reads like a veritable who's who of modern writers: Gary Wills, Salman Rushdie, Michael Ondaatje, Margaret Atwood, and Philip Roth, to name just a few. Don't leave early or you'll miss the equally entertaining postlecture audience Q&A sessions. Tickets for popular lecturers can be as hard to come by as Mariners playoff tickets, so plan ahead. Benaroya Hall, 200 University St, 621-2230, www.lectures.org.

THIRD PLACE BOOKS: See listing under "Bookstores," below.

TOWN HALL: The annual series of presentations and lectures at this former Christian Science church on First Hill is guaranteed to edify you and improve your perspective. There are also musical and performance events. 8th Ave & Seneca St, 652-4255, www.townhallseattle.org.

BOOKS, BOOKS, BOOKS

Seattle is a city devoted to reading: One of our key cultural statistics is that we check out more library books per capita than any other U.S. city. (Attributable to the number of gray days endured in winter, no doubt.) Several of our local literary landmarks, such as the Elliott Bay Book Company, are national leaders and quintessential Seattle institutions.

Libraries

SEATTLE PUBLIC LIBRARY: The library's stunning new central facility at 1000 Fourth Avenue replaced a spiritless '60s hulk—it opened in 2004 to almost universal critical acclaim. Rem Koolhaas's controversial glass-plate design has facets and angles every which way, and consists of a long downward spiral of sloping floors. The layout can be a bit hard to navigate for the uninitiated—just try to make your way directly from top to bottom without using the overtaxed elevators—but the staff is exceptionally helpful. (To arrange a tour, call 733-9609.) There are branches in almost every neighborhood in Seattle, and any proof of Seattle residence, such as a utility bill, will suffice to obtain a library card. 386-4636, www.spl.org.

Library Fines

The daily fine for an overdue book or videocassette from the Seattle Public Library is 15 cents a day, with a maximum of $6. If you keep the book or video for more than 40 days, however, you'll owe them the item's replacement cost.

KING COUNTY LIBRARY: One huge advantage to the county's library system is that its cards are good at any one of three dozen branches. Though each branch may have limited titles on the shelves, the system is exceptionally efficient at forwarding books on request from one branch to another. There are five regional libraries, with large collections and a full range of services:

- Bellevue, 425-450-1765
- Bothell, 425-486-7811
- Federal Way, 253-838-3668
- Kent, 253-859-3330
- Redmond, 425-885-1861

There are numerous branches throughout the area; for a full list, visit www.kcls.org.

UNIVERSITY OF WASHINGTON LIBRARY: The UW library system is an incomparable academic research resource, with individual libraries representing disciplines from art to physics. The main Suzzallo-Allen undergraduate library is a vast facility with a seemingly limitless collection of periodicals and an especially serene, attractive reading room. 543-0242, www.lib.washington.edu.

WASHINGTON CENTER FOR THE BOOK: Each year the Seattle Public Library and the Washington Center for the Book undertake the ambitious If All of Seattle Read the Same Book program—now called simply "Seattle Reads"—in which one lucky author becomes the subject of numerous book groups, lectures, and radio discussions. 386-4650, www.spl.org.

Bookstores

BAILEY/COY BOOKS: This friendly bookshop is geared to the diverse expectations of its Capitol Hill neighborhood. 414 Broadway Ave E, 323-8842.

BEYOND THE CLOSET: Books and periodicals for the gay and transgender community. 518 Pike St, 322-4609.

ELLIOTT BAY BOOK COMPANY: Seattle's quintessential bookstore is a Pioneer Square warren of shelves lined with an

Information, Please

All three of the major library systems in the Seattle area offer quick information desks whose staffers will attempt to answer any question you have, from grammatical and mathematical quandaries to the identity of Paul Revere and the Raiders's lead singer. The Seattle Public Library **ANSWER LINE** is 386-4636; King County is 425-462-9600 or 800-462-9600; the University of Washington's is 543-0242. If you really want to have some fun with the diverse nature of knowledge, run the same question by all three and see what happens. The Seattle Public Library's answer line, which fields an average of 8,000 calls a month, now answers questions by online chat weekdays 10am–4pm: Go to www.spl.org, then click the blue "ask a question" button.

exceptionally well-chosen inventory of fiction, poetry, travel, culture, and cooking and gardening books. Every tour of Seattle for the newcomer or out-of-town visitor should include a stop here. Its downstairs café is a favorite place to meet for coffee and quiet discussion, and is the leading Seattle venue for readings from such authors as Barry Lopez, Anne Rice, and Martin Amis, to name a few. 101 S Main St, 624-6600, www.elliottbaybook.com.

FLORA & FAUNA: A Pioneer Square shop devoted exclusively to gardening and natural history titles. 121 1st Ave S, 623-4727.

HALF-PRICE BOOKS: The inventory, largely new editions, is sold at the namesake price; there are eight local branches. 547-7859, www.halfpricebooks.com.

LEFT BANK BOOKS: All things radical and antiestablishment line the shelves at this Pike Place Market institution, which labels itself a "collective" (when was the last time you heard that term?). 622-0195.

METSKER MAPS: Seattle's foremost resource for finding your way is a wonderful place in the Pike Place Market to pore over maps of distant climes and dream of fabulous journeys. They have plenty of travel books, too. 1511 1st Ave, 623-8747, www.metskers.com.

THIRD PLACE BOOKS: The Eastside's best bookstore and venue for author readings. 17171 Bothell Wy NE, 366-3333, www.thirdplacebooks.com; Ravenna branch at 6504 20th Ave NE, 525-2347.

TWICE SOLD TALES: Can't sleep? Seattle's biggest used book emporium has a half-price sale from Friday midnight to 8am Saturday in the U-District. 905 E John St, 545-4226, www.twicesoldtales.com.

UNIVERSITY BOOKSTORE: Aside from the fact this is a full-fledged book vendor with much more than just textbooks, it is also the prime spot for Husky fan gear. Other stores are located in Bothell, Bellevue, downtown Seattle, and Tacoma. 4326 University Wy NE (and branches), 634-3400, www.ubookstore.com.

WORLD WIDE BOOKS & MAPS: Everything you need to research and plan your next trip to a far-flung exotic destination. Books are organized by region: USA, Pacific Northwest and Canada, AustralAsia, Latin America, Africa, and Europe. 4411 Wallingford Ave N, 634-3453, travelbooksandmaps.com.

REEL OPTIONS

Most people bring to mind *Sleepless in Seattle* when they think of Seattle on film, but over the years dozens of productions have featured Seattle locations, including *Singles*, *10 Things I Hate About You*, *Little Buddha*, and *Say Anything*. A more thoughtful and prototypical Seattle picture is painted by a cult classic, *Trouble in Mind*, which never names its real-life setting but is clearly the Emerald City. Only a few, bigger cities have broader offerings. The art-house cinema community on Capitol Hill and near the U-District is extensive, and the Seattle International Film Festival is one of the biggest and best in North America.

BLUE MOUSE THEATRE: This is the oldest continually operating movie theater in Washington, open in Tacoma since 1923. In addition to other movies, the theater plays *The Rocky Horror Picture Show* every Saturday night. And in case you're wondering, part-owner Dale Chihuly supplied the little glass mice that run along the upper part of the theater. 2611 N Proctor St, 253-752-9500, www.bluemousetheatre.com.

CINERAMA: Paul Allen bought this massive movie palace in the late '90s and refurbished it. The huge screen remains a matchless venue for big movies—chief among which in recent years were the three installments of *The Lord of the Rings*, which ran for many months. 2100 4th Ave, 441-3080, www.cinerama.com.

THE CREST: If you don't mind waiting a few weeks to see a first-run film, the Crest in north Seattle is for you. Admission to all shows is $3, parking is relatively easy, and the movie selections are top-notch. 16505 5th Ave NE (at 165th St), 781-5755.

FREMONT OUTDOOR CINEMA: A quintessential Seattle summer experience, the cinema shows classic and cult films outside, in a Fremont parking lot. Bring a blanket—or an old sofa—and a picnic supper, and cheer on Harrison Ford, Harry Potter, and Humphrey Bogart. N 35th St & Phinney Ave, www.outdoorcinema.net/seattle.

LANDMARK THEATRES: This Seattle company operates the majority of the independent and art-house cinemas in the city, including the Egyptian and Harvard Exit on Capitol Hill; the Guild 45 in Wallingford; and the Metro, Neptune, Seven

Gables, and Varsity theatres in the U-District. Programming ranges from first-run releases to independent and foreign films of all types. 285-1022, www.landmarktheatres.com.

SEATTLE INTERNATIONAL FILM FESTIVAL (SIFF): This late May/early June annual event is one of the premier cultural affairs in the Northwest and has achieved considerable prominence in the film industry. Each year's lineup includes both major-studio and independent releases, and crowds throng to the director showcases. Tickets for the most desirable showings are best acquired months in advance. Multiple venues, 384-9997, www.seattlefilm.com.

READ ALL ABOUT IT

Newspapers

SEATTLE TIMES: The great gray eminence on Fairview Avenue takes itself very, very seriously, aspiring to be one of the top newspapers in the country. It isn't, though it is a locally owned voice that offers decent arts coverage, a few Northwest columnists such as James Vesely and Jerry Large, and a Sunday edition that will consume most of a morning with coffee. The paper's content and circulation were damaged by a silly, debilitating editorial strike in 1999 that left both workers and management worse off. It's owned by the founding Blethen family—51 percent owned, that is—the other 49 percent is Scripps-Howard, so there is outside pressure for profitable management. The *Times* has been locked in a bitter court battle to cancel its Joint Operating Agreement with the *P-I* (see listing below). 464-2111, seattletimes.nwsource.com.

SEATTLE POST-INTELLIGENCER: Seattle's other daily survives, barely, at the behest of a Joint Operating Agreement under which its printing, production, circulation, and advertising functions are performed by the *Times*. Yep, that leaves just editorial, and here the *P-I*, as it is universally called, outshines the *Times*—more interesting, more scrappy, more liberal. Its columnists, such as Art Thiel (sports), Bill Virgin (business), and Joel Connelly (Northwest affairs), are superior to the *Times*. 448-8000, seattlepi.nwsource.com.

SEATTLE WEEKLY: Seattle's first alternative newspaper is more than 30 years old now and has settled into a comfortable role in which it thrives: comprehensive, thoughtful, and sprightly coverage of arts, food, and culture; and news features that politely kick the shins of the establishment (including the *Times*, a favorite target). Their annual "Best of Seattle" poll is a colorful snapshot of the city's mood. The *Weekly* is part of Village Voice Media Inc., owned by Stern Publishing, along with the *Village Voice*, *LA Weekly*, and the *Nashville Scene*. Free distribution throughout the Seattle area. 623-0500, www.seattleweekly.com.

THE STRANGER: It's the alternative to the alternative, a no-holds-barred, hip weekly that pushes the mainstream newsprint envelope as far as it will go. Its coverage of alternative music, art, and performance is unmatched, and its "Savage Love" column by editor Dan Savage offers an utterly unvarnished perspective (often eminently wise) on sex in the new millennium. The personals are anything goes, period. Some of the news features will leave you scratching your head with their abstruse viewpoint, but you'll never be bored. Free distribution throughout Seattle. 323-7101, www.thestranger.com.

KING COUNTY JOURNAL: The *Journal* offers some local coverage of Bellevue, Redmond, Kirkland, Renton, Kent, and Auburn that you won't find in the Seattle dailies, but it's definitely a secondary information source. 425-455-2222 or 253-872-6600, www.kingcountyjournal.com.

ROBINSON NEWSPAPERS: The biggest and best community newspaper chain in the Seattle area has papers in Ballard, West Seattle, White Center, Highline (Burien), Des Moines, and Federal Way. All are fair, locally minded, and notably professional. www.robinsonnews.com.

THE JEWISH TRANSCRIPT: News, features, and events for the regional Jewish audience; biweekly and online. 441-4553, www.jtnews.net.

REAL CHANGE: This weekly newspaper is a voice for the poor, homeless, and marginalized in Seattle. It also provides a steady income to the more than 200 vendors who sell the $1 paper on city streets (look for official vendor badges). 441-3247, www.realchangenews.org.

Magazines

COLORS NW: This engaging monthly devotes itself to promoting and enhancing Seattle's multicultural character. It's found in free distribution boxes throughout the metro area. 444-9251, www.colorsnw.com.

SEATTLE HOMES & LIFESTYLE: *Seattle Magazine*'s competitor is more frankly devoted to glistening kitchens, blossom-perfect gardens, and all the finer things in upscale life. Subscription and newsstand. 322-6699, www.seattlehomesmag.com.

SEATTLE MAGAZINE: This was originally an offshoot of the late, lamented *Pacific Northwest*. It survived where its parent did not, offering lightweight coverage of design, fashion, food, and events in the city, becoming "the magazine Seattle lives by." It is owned by the same company that publishes *Seattle Bride*. Subscription and newsstand. 284-1750, www.seattlemag.com.

WASHINGTON CEO: The state's business magazine has clung to its narrow niche for more than 15 years now. It is heavy on executive profiles and economic development news. Subscription and newsstand; 441-8415 or 888-860-9495, www.washingtonceo.com.

TELEVISION

Seattle's broadcast community has been as much affected by the national consolidation trend as other cities—the only major station with any semblance of local ownership anymore is KOMO, whose parent, Fisher Broadcasting, is headquartered here.

Seattle's four main commercial TV stations are all stalwarts, none enjoying any huge advantage over the others. All feature stable, longstanding local talent lineups, though there is some tendency for reporters to migrate among stations. The overall approach is pleasantly low-key and sensible, except for the annual half-dozen occasions when snow seems possible, in which case "StormWatch" hysteria grips the newsrooms. CNN's Aaron Brown, by the way, cut his broadcasting teeth here in Seattle.

Nearly all of Seattle and King County is supplied cable service by **COMCAST** (888-266-2278, www.comcast.com), one of the country's megalithic broadcast providers. The city has been fussing with the company for years to improve its service ethic, with little success, Ultra-basic stripped-down service is about $20 a month and includes the major local channels.

Stations

KING (NBC), CHANNEL 5: Jean Enerson and Don Porter are both longtime Seattle broadcast veterans. (KONG, channel 16, is a sports subsidiary.) 448-5555, www.king5.com.

KIRO (CBS), CHANNEL 7: Former home of Harry Wappler, tireless dean of Seattle weathercasters. Harry's chair is now occupied by his son Andy. (See Chapter 12, "Weather Wise," page 318) Newscaster Steve Raible is a former Seahawks wide receiver turned on-air personality. 728-7777, www.kirotv.com.

KOMO (ABC), CHANNEL 4: Kathi Goertzen and Dan Lewis are a pair of long-term local anchors. Herb Weisbaum is one of the nation's leading consumer-affairs reporters, and Ken Schram is by far the most outspoken TV commentator in Seattle. 404-4000, www.komotv.com.

KCPQ (FOX), CHANNEL 13: Even Northwest news gets the Fox down-home, slightly rightward once-over. 674-1313, www.kcpq.com.

KCTS (PBS), CHANNEL 9: Financial difficulties have plagued our local nonprofit broadcast outlet, but it perseveres. At least *Riverdance* has dropped from the pledge cycle. 443-6677, www.kcts.org.

KSTW (UPN), CHANNEL 11: 441-1111, www.upn11.com.

RADIO

On Seattle radio it used to be the Mariners ruled: Whichever station had the rights to Mariners broadcasts won the ratings. That remains true in the news niche—KOMO vaulted past KIRO when it took over the Mariner schedule in 2002—but the rest of the radio band is so diverse and fragmented that the leading station is, well, er, a modern-country format. The landscape among the 30 or so local stations is, as in most major markets, constantly shifting, with ownership, call letters, format, and on-air personalities bouncing around like pinballs.

Dave Ross, now a member of Congress, was a long-term talk-host/commentator on KIRO. The best news and local traffic reports are on KIRO and KOMO. Unique among the lot is KING-FM, a nonprofit classical station that returns a large share of its proceeds to the Seattle music community. NPR can be found on KUOW, 94.9 FM, and KPLU, 88.1 FM.

Mixing It Up

KEXP 90.3 began as a college radio station out of the University of Washington in the early '70s, and has, thanks to listeners around the world who tune in via streaming audio, established itself to near-cult status. The station has since separated from the university and is now completely funded by its members. KEXP plays an eclectic mix of rock, hip-hop, country, world, and blues—music combinations you don't hear on commercial radio. KEXP is also committed to giving unknown—but promising—bands airtime. (Check out www.kexp.org for instructions on how to submit your demo.) The Web site also offers a streaming archive where you can catch up on your favorite shows, like John in the Morning or DJ Riz.

Top 20 radio stations

KMPS-FM, 94.1, modern country
KUBE-FM, 93.1, top 40
KOMO-AM, 1000, news and sports
KRWM-FM, 106.9, adult contemporary
KIRO-AM, 710, news, sports, and talk
KWJZ-FM, 98.9, smooth jazz
KZOK-FM, 102.5, classic rock
KBSG-FM, 97.3, oldies
KTTH-AM, 770, talk
KCMS-FM, 105.3, Christian
KBKS-FM, 106.1, pop hits
KISW-FM, 99.9, rock
KVI-AM, 570, talk
KJR-FM, 95.7, classic hits
KQBZ-FM, 100.7, talk
KMTT-FM, 103.7, adult hits
KNDD-FM, 107.7, alternative rock
KING-FM, 98.1, classical
KLSY-FM, 92.5, adult contemporary
KIXI-AM, 880, adult standards

(Source: Arbitron; ratings by listenership)

SINGLE IN SEATTLE

Whether deserved or not, Seattle has a reputation of being a hard place to be single. Perhaps it's because the city attracts independent outdoor-types who spend their free time in the mountains or on the water—places where it's particularly hard to mingle.

That said, however, there are plenty of resources to fill any lonely heart's social calendar. National dating clubs like eHarmony.com, Match.com, and Matchmaker.com are perennially popular choices, but there are also many clubs designed specifically for Seattle singles. The clubs listed below vary widely in the level of selectivity; audience (some clubs are open to couples); price (some are free or pay-as-you-go activity clubs; others require membership fees and monthly dues); and location (Seattle or greater Puget Sound). The one thing they have in common is activities, activities, activities—everything from snowshoeing and wine tasting to Mariners games, cooking classes, professional networking, and vacations abroad.

EVENTS & ADVENTURES: 425-882-0838, www.eventsandadventures.com

HAUTE MONDE: 333-4632, www.hautemonde.org

MAGNETIC: 800-ATTRACT, www.bemagnetic.com

THE MOUNTAINEERS: 284-6310, www.mountaineers.org

SEATTLE PLAY DATE: 728-6733, www.playdateseattle.com

SPACE CITY MIXER: www.spacecitymixer.com

CHAPTER 9

Get Out & Play

The sky is leaden and lumpy. Driblets of rain peck downward. The sun made a brief appearance at dawn, crimsoning the blanket of overcast, and will do likewise eight hours later at dusk. It seems like no time for anyone to be outdoors—yet there we are, thousands and thousands of Seattleites tucked into Columbia or Filson rain gear, pedaling along the Burke-Gilman Trail, kayaking Lake Union, cheering on local college students at Husky Stadium. What gives?

What's up is a Seattle phenomenon: Few major cities can claim residents as fervently committed to outdoor sports and recreation as Puget Sounders are. Those who move here from drier, warmer climes are informed that you simply grow accustomed to practicing your avocation, whatever it is, in inclement weather. And when the weather does happen to be nice—Ah! Is there any better place to be than the upper deck at Safeco Field, watching both the Mariners and the sun setting over the Olympics? Well, sure: Out on Lake Washington, running a sailboard toward Medina in a stiff northerly. Or up on Rattlesnake Ledge, peering at the alpenglow starting to appear on Rainier. Or simply setting a picnic at Seward Park.

The key to getting outdoors in Seattle much of the year is to heed the old Norwegian axiom: "There is no bad weather, only poor clothing." A modern addendum: Layering. Whether you are biking along Sammamish Slough in Redmond or sitting in the end zone at the Seahawks' Qwest Field, you might in the space of a few hours experience blazing sunshine, blustery winds, horizontal mist, and spates of rain. To adapt, all you need to do is peel off or add on wind pants, parkas, rain slickers, duck boots, ball caps. (Duck boots are an absolutely essential item in every Seattle-area mud room.)

With adequate preparation, there is hardly a day year-round that you can't get outdoors. We'll let those wimpy elsewhere-denizens huddle inside when the weather is marginal. They do, you know. But we're tough—and very well waterproofed.

SPECTATOR SPORTS

It used to be incontrovertible: **HUSKIES** rule. Oh, sure, the **SEAHAWKS** were exciting; the **MARINERS** were our own loveable losers; the **SONICS** brought home the only world championship the city has known (1979, for those of you who can't remember prehistoric events). But the heart and soul of the Seattle sports scene was the University of Washington Huskies. More than 72,000 rabid fans fill Husky Stadium for all six home games each fall. Huskies bumper stickers outnumber political, social, and humorous ones combined.

That's the way it is, has been, and always will . . . wait a minute.

Then the Mariners ignited the baseball world with their improbable run to the playoffs in 1995, and the team's succeeding eight years of success made it the most conspicuous sports draw in Seattle. (At the same time, rules infractions at UW drove the football program into decline.) And the Seahawks finally made rumbles toward football prominence with playoff showings in 2003 and 2004. Trumping them all was the **SEATTLE STORM** women's basketball team, however, which won the world championship in 2004, playing before delirious sellout crowds at Key Arena.

All in all, Seattle sports fans have proven themselves much like those almost everywhere else—we like winners best.

Mariners

The Mariners seized the sad-sack title from the New York Mets and Chicago Cubs as soon as they began play in 1977 and did not relinquish it until their first winning season 17 years later. With a few wrinkles the team's level of success has since placed it among baseball's best; alas, many of the Mariners' most notable stars have departed the modest stage of Puget Sound for bigger platforms—think Randy Johnson, Alex Rodriguez, Ken Griffey Jr. Thankfully, the lasting icons of Mariners vintage—Jay Buhner, Edgar Martinez, all-time single-season hits leader Ichiro Suzuki—are also made of finer material.

The most consistent performer in Mariners history—play-by-play announcer Dave Niehaus—is also the best at his profession in all of baseball. He'll be in the Hall of Fame one day, and if there's any justice, Safeco Field will be renamed in his honor. Meanwhile, he's the reason all those fans at the game are listening to the radio while they watch. Tune him

> **GONE BUT NOT FORGOTTEN**
>
> ## Junior & Sweet Lou
>
> These two baseball icons—Ken Griffey Jr. and Lou Piniella—both found their greatest notoriety during their years with the Mariners. Piniella, who played for and managed the Yankees (and won a World Series in the Bronx) was a no-nonsense old-school scrapper whose umpire-induced and obviously deliberate tantrums were legendary. Highlight films of his years as Mariners manager (1993–2002) invariably include footage of him ripping up a base and flinging it about the field, kicking dirt.
>
> Griffey, son of the Cincinnati Reds legend, came up through the Mariners farm system and became an All-Star for his hitting and fielding exploits. He had a classic left-handed power swing and could run down a long drive to left-center field like a gazelle. His Mariners career (1989–1999) was marked by long injury respites, however, and he was often accused of being a malingerer (failing to run out routine ground balls, for instance). Few tears were shed when he was traded to Cincinnati.

in—you'll discover an erudite, articulate, unconstrained fan who isn't afraid to tell the truth about the team's play.

The franchise is owned by Japanese interests (basically the family behind Nintendo), who adhere to an almost completely hands-off philosophy and leave management to Seattle-based executives. Safeco Field seats about 47,000, and sellouts were universal until the team began to sag in the 2004 season; season ticket packages start at 20 games for a fairly reasonable $200 or so. 622-HITS, www.mariners.org.

Mariners Game Tips

BEST BARGAINS: Rows 8–12 of the third-deck "View Reserved" sections and Monday-night promotions throughout the season, when tickets are half-price.

BEST SEATS: The box seats on the first- and third-base sides, about 10 rows back. (For some reason there are almost always better seats available on the third-base side than on the first.)

FAMILY SECTION: Section 342 on the third deck, third-base side, is an alcohol-free zone.

The Scoop on Scalping

Though ticket scalping—selling an event ticket for more than its face value—is illegal in Seattle (a misdemeanor, $5,000 fine), anyone who ventures to Safeco Field or Qwest Stadium is likely to encounter guys outside, looking stereotypically shifty, offering tickets for sale. What's up? Seattle police, on city time, have better things to do than corral the trade. Occasionally, the Mariners instruct off-duty officers they've hired for security to crack down on scalpers, but that's rare; and one such miscreant sued in 2004, pointing out that Mariners season ticket holders sell their own tickets, online, on the Mariners' own Web site, for premium prices. A judge bought that argument and threw out the charge. At any rate, so few events in Seattle are in high demand—usually when the Yankees are in town—that you have to be woefully ill-prepared to need to buy scalped tickets. If you simply must sit behind home plate, that's another matter.

HYDRO RACE: Whichever boat first gets in trouble and flips off the course will return later in the race and win. Works about 85 percent of the time.

"MEET AT THE MITT": The huge stainless-steel baseball glove sculpture at the southeastern corner of Royal Brougham and 1st Ave S is a popular and handy place to tell people to meet you.

ROLLING THE RETRACTABLE ROOF: Can be done slowly or quickly, depending on the imminence of bad weather. Watching the roof roll (a quick transit takes about four minutes) is an impressive sight.

ROWDINESS: Neither Seattle custom nor Mariners management tolerates the sort of brain-free behavior often exhibited at stadiums in other cities we won't name. If a fan near you is drunk, belligerent, or interfering with other fans, you can find a security guard and have him removed. And they *will* remove him.

TICKET WINDOW: The box office on the south side of the stadium, along Atlantic a half-block east of 1st Ave, has a better seat selection than Ticketmaster, and you don't have to pay the latter's annoying fees.

TRADITIONS: Garlic fries, available at a half-dozen locations throughout the stadium; fish and chips from Ivar's on the third-deck promenade, near which is a lovely eating area overlooking Elliott Bay; and the Hot-Dog Man, who can lob a wiener (wrapped) from behind his back to a precise location 20 rows away. You may be indifferent to hot dogs, but his prowess is worth investing in a pork sausage at least once.

TRAIN WHISTLE: The long wail of the freight trains that chug through town just east of Safeco Field has become the stadium's signature sound. When the All-Star Game was held here in 1999, Major League Baseball asked the city and the Mariners to pressure Burlington Northern to silence its locomotives; city and team officials told the league to get over it.

Seahawks

When Mike Holmgren was lured away from the Green Bay Packers to Seattle by Paul Allen, his mission was to lead the Hawks to the promised land (a Super Bowl appearance), and thus maybe overcome the Huskies' long hold on Northwest football affections. If that hasn't happened by the time you read this, it remains true that the Hawks have been a better team under Allen's ownership and Holmgren's tutelage—in fact, the team would be gone from Seattle were it not for Allen. Seattle's abrupt departure from the AFC West for the NFC West, lopping longstanding rivalries with Oakland and Denver, made the NFL's 2003 season somewhat colorless. Tickets have been easily available for years, but Holmgren's recent successes have changed that somewhat. A game at Qwest Field runs about $60 for two. 622-4295, www.seahawks.com.

SODO Game Tips

SODO is an acronym for "South of the Dome," a reference to that beloved Seattle icon, the Kingdome (see sidebar, below). Though the dome is gone, the area from Qwest Field south, roughly to Starbucks headquarters, is known as SODO.

DRIVING to the game? The best approach is from the south, up 1st or 4th Aves. There is even free parking to be found along side streets south of the stadiums under the Alaskan Way viaduct, and along Alaskan Way itself—if you get there early. Plan to arrive more than an hour before game time.

BUS SERVICE is excellent (Metro provides dozens of extra buses), but remember that for an hour or so after games all traffic is blocked from traversing 1st Ave along Safeco Field. Bus routes that must go that way, don't.

GONE BUT NOT FORGOTTEN

The Kingdome Kingdom

The Kingdome was, depending on your point of view, either a detestably ugly monstrosity or an eminently practical acknowledgment of the Northwest climate. Opened in 1976 to host the Mariners and the Seahawks, the concrete bubble occupied the spot that now holds the Seahawks stadium (aka Qwest Field). The building covered 9.3 acres, and the roof itself spanned 7.8 acres. The Dome seated 60,000 fans (66,000 for football) and could be a world-class din of noise when the local team was doing well, as in a few Seahawks glory years in the late '80s under coach Chuck Knox ("Ground Chuck," he was called, for his fondness for running the football) and during the Mariners's improbable run to the playoffs in 1995. Decibel levels sometimes reached past 120.

Baseball purists objected to the idea of indoor ball, though it had been pioneered years before in Houston at the Astrodome. The Kingdome was known as a hitter's park: With no wind and drier air, the ball tended to sail. During one memorable confrontation in 1994, Mark McGwire launched a Randy Johnson fastball to the base of the Dome itself in left-center field, the longest ball ever hit there. And football purists objected to making the game clean, dry, and warm. Both parties have had their perspectives honored at their respective new stadiums.

The Kingdome was leveled on March 29, 2000, in a timed explosion broadcast live throughout the Northwest. The leftover concrete was, in true Seattle fashion, recycled into the new stadium.

FINDING FOOD: There are a good dozen fine restaurants in the area around Qwest and Safeco Fields, mostly to the north in Pioneer Square (FX McRory's, for instance). Pyramid Brewery, directly across from Safeco, has excellent pub food. But, hey, you have to get down there in plenty of time if you want a table. Otherwise, there are a handful of insta-dine barbecue joints—and a large number of surprisingly decent food vendors in the stadiums themselves.

Sounders

The Sounders are a long-established, consistently excellent, and highly regarded A-League soccer team that plays, unfortunately, to crowds regularly below 10,000 at Qwest Field. A game costs about $25 for two. 622-3415, www.seattlesounders.net.

Storm

The Storm's 2004 crusade to the pinnacle of women's basketball was the city's first professional championship since the Sonics accomplished the same feat in 1979. Stars Sue Bird and Lauren Jackson are among the most conspicuous female athletes in the world; to some folks, the brand of basketball practiced by WNBA performers offers more finesse and is much more accessible than men's hoops. Alas, attendance, broadcast revenue, and community interest lag behind men's sports. Wouldn't it be great if women's games sold out and the men's didn't? A night at a Storm game runs $20–$50 for a pair of tickets. 217-WNBA, www.wnba.com/storm.

SuperSonics

The Sonics (and also the women's basketball team, the Storm) are owned by Starbucks tycoon Howard Schultz, who set himself the task of creating a winning team while endeavoring to employ NBA stars who are a bit more thoughtful, mature, and selfless than the norm. That doesn't necessarily translate to wins, though. Withal, NBA basketball is raucous, fast, heady, and intense; those who like it find a night at Key Arena invigorating, win or lose. But it's a far cry from the days that Fred Brown (now a banking executive), Jack Sikma, Lenny Wilkens, and Paul Silas led the team to the championship in 1979. The Sonics' surprising success in 2004–05 reflects a return to that team philosophy that brought the franchise's long-ago title.

Key Arena seats more than 17,000. $20–$50 for a pair of tickets. 281-5800, www.nba.com/sonics.

Tacoma Rainiers

The Mariners' AAA affiliate plays in Cheney Stadium, a friendly ballpark in Tacoma. Many are the stars who have passed through here, either on their way up to the big leagues or on injury-rehab assignments. It's a great place for kids to snag autographs. $10–$25 for a pair of tickets. 253-752-7700 or 800-281-3834, www.tacomarainiers.com.

Thunderbirds

Tired of watching overpaid professionals swat each other around the arena in major-league hockey? The T-birds are in the minors, yes, but their games are adrenaline baths—rowdy, intense, and loud—and their skating skill is astounding. Don't follow them on the road, though, unless you really want to find out what's doin' in Moose Jaw. Here, they play at the Key Arena; a night at a game runs about $40 for a couple. 448-PUCK, www.seattlethunderbirds.com.

COLLEGE SPORTS

University of Washington Huskies

FOOTBALL: In case you didn't know, the Huskies shared the national championship (with BYU) in 1991. That's why the coach at the time, Don James, is universally known around town as the "Dawgfather." Had he run for president, he'd have received thousands of grateful Husky votes. Things have deteriorated since then, but Husky games remain one of the major autumn events in Seattle. The Huskies play in the PAC-10 conference, with such perennial powerhouses as USC and UCLA. Aside from Washington State (see below), the biggest annual rivalry is with Oregon. One quintessentially Seattle twist—boat owners are welcome to anchor near Husky Stadium to attend games (by permit), and the university runs a water shuttle to bring fans to shore. 543-2200, gohuskies.collegesports.com.

BASKETBALL: Husky teams rarely made a blip in either the PAC-10 or, heaven knows, the national scene, until Lorenzo Romar took over and the roundball Huskies made it to the NCAA playoffs in 2004. Under the leadership of the former Huskies player, the team is a serious contender. 543-2200, gohuskies.collegesports.com.

SOFTBALL: The UW women's softball team has made it a habit to reach the national playoffs. 543-2200, gohuskies.collegesports.com.

CREW: UW is one of the national centers for college rowing, and the annual Windermere Cup (in May) is one of the sport's premier events. Watch it for free along the Montlake Cut. 543-2200, gohuskies.collegesports.com.

Washington State Cougars

The name of this university, located across the state in another universe called Pullman, is pronounced "Waz-zu." Graduates of WSU are commonly encountered in Seattle—many have even left Pullman behind to live, work, and play here on the "wet side." They maintain their collegial loyalty, however: WSU often opens its football season with a game at Qwest Field that approaches a sellout almost every year. The annual UW–WSU Apple Cup, which is the last game of the regular season, alternates between Seattle and Pullman and is one of the fiercest such rivalries in the country. Those planning a trip to Pullman (it's in the Palouse, one of the most beautiful places in Washington, if not on earth) are in for a five-hour drive. Hang your heads, Husky fans—the Cougs have been to the Rose Bowl more often lately. WSU also fields a consistently top-notch college baseball team. 800-462-6847, wsucougars.collegesports.com.

OUTDOOR RECREATION

Puget Sound's natural environment is the key to Seattle's recreational lifestyle. Compared with folks in other cities, we are both more active and outdoor-oriented; in fact, many of the most notable recreational pursuits of American life have found expression here first. **THE MOUNTAINEERS**, for example, is one of the oldest outdoor recreational clubs in the country and has played a key role both in opening urban eyes to the value of wilderness activity and in helping preserve the wilderness in which to be active.

With the possible exception of coconut-palm climbing, there is almost no outdoor activity that cannot be accomplished within a day's reach of Seattle. Naturally, mountain- and water-oriented pursuits are the most popular. The city is one of the few places an energetic and dedicated individual can accomplish a sporting trifecta: ski, golf, and sail all in one day. Doing so would be way more compulsive than the Seattle character, though—why don't you just take our word for it?

Burke-Gilman/Sammamish Trail System

One of the first such trails in the nation—now past 30 years old—the Burke-Gilman follows for most of its length an old railroad grade that wends its way along the Lake Washington Ship Canal, through the University of Washington, then northeast along Lake Washington to Kenmore, where it joins the Sammamish Slough Trail. The latter follows its namesake streambed all the way to Marymoor Park in Redmond, the whole forming a 27-mile dedicated right-of-way, most of which is entirely off-vehicle roads. There are a number of street crossings, but there are also long stretches free of any worries other than dodging the occasional bike-jock hotdogs who barrel through.

The Burke-Gilman is truly one of the treasures of Seattle, a pioneering amenity that showed other cities around the nation the potential for such trails. The city is planning to extend it westward to the Ballard Locks, then up along the Sound to Golden Gardens Park. One key stretch in Ballard lacks funding and faces property-owner opposition; a local group, Friends of the Burke-Gilman Trail, welcomes citizen support. www.burkegilmantrail.org, www.metrokc.gov/parks.

Biking

You can bike in Seattle year-round—we all see hardy souls bundled in Gore-Tex wrappings braving the road spray of Second Avenue to get to work on December mornings. The rest of us—and there are innumerable thousands—head out on nice days from April to October to the many trails and back streets around the Seattle area for long rides on one of the best bike path networks in the country. Because the trails tend to follow river valleys, they are for the most part level and easy to navigate, passing lots of parks and picnic areas.

Both the city and county publish bike-trail maps, and the two major bike clubs offer information, classes, and guidance for riders just starting to learn the ins and outs of biking in the area. They also sponsor numerous training events and group rides. The **CASCADE BIKE CLUB**'s (522-BIKE, www.cascade.org) 5,000 members are an active bike advocacy group as well as an instructional and recreational association. The **SEATTLE BIKE CLUB** (www.seattlebicycle.com) is a largely recreational group that focuses on sponsoring rides and other biking events. Mentors are even available to teach new riders safe and practical routes to and from work, if you want to combine commuting with recreation; see www.metrokc.gov/bike.

The best recreational biking in the area is found along the Burke-Gilman/Sammamish trail system (see sidebar), the Duwamish Trail in South King County, and on Bainbridge and Vashon Islands. If high velocity is your thing, the Marymoor Park Velodrome is for you. Children and adults must wear a helmet throughout most jurisdictions in King County; the fine for failure to do so is $30.

The region's major bike "races" (most participants are recreational rather than competitive) are among the best and best known in the nation:

CHILLY HILLY: Sponsored by the Cascade Bike Club, the Chilly Hilly is a late-winter ride around Bainbridge Island that is aptly named. The 33-mile route includes 2,700 feet in elevation change, and its (usually) February running is, well, not for sun bunnies. www.cascade.org/eandr/chilly.

SEATTLE TO PORTLAND BICYCLE CLASSIC: *The* major ride in the Northwest is a two-day double-century—that is, it spans 200 miles. Up to 8,000 riders participate in the Group Health–sponsored event. www.cascade.org/eandr/stp.

TREK TRI-ISLAND: A benefit for the American Lung Association, this three-day September ride traverses the islands and waterside communities of North Puget Sound; one itinerary focuses on the San Juans, the other veers over to Victoria. Unless your bike is amphibious, several ferry crossings are included. It's about 135 miles. 441-5100, www.alaw.org.

Fishing

Salmon fishing is king in Seattle. Though the Sound's runs have been severely depressed over the past half-century, seasons are still open every year for all the four major species, and a sockeye run that reaches Lake Washington in the fall is also usually open to sport anglers. Anglers who know what they are doing regularly catch very nice fish.

But salmon is not the whole story. The light-equipped anglers jigging in Elliott Bay from the various piers are catching squid, and long-term fishing enthusiasts enjoy the smelt runs that ply local streams in the spring. More zealous adherents test the limits of hypothermia fishing for steelhead in winter months. Rainbow and cutthroat trout are found in numerous lakes and streams in the Cascades.

It can take great diligence to navigate all the various regulations for the different types of fish, and it matters whether you are fishing in freshwater or saltwater. Different permits and licenses are necessary for specific fish, areas, and seasons. For information, call 360-902-2700 or visit wdfw.wa.gov.

Charters leave from both Fishermen's Terminal and Elliott Bay moorages, and more exotic trips utilize seaplanes to reach the salmon-rich waters up in British Columbia.

Golf

Though Seattle is not quite the golf center that the rest of the West Coast is, there are more than enough courses of every type, difficulty, and cost to keep golfers busy for years, including a couple of national-caliber layouts (Newcastle, Sahalee, Snoqualmie Ridge) and some old-fashioned, low-key municipal layouts that are surprisingly challenging. The best overall guide to golf in the area can be found at www.seattlegolfguide.com, which has a rundown of notable public and private courses.

The city of Seattle maintains four fine courses. The Interbay complex north of downtown on 15th Avenue is a nine-hole, par-3 "executive" course with a large driving range. The Jackson Park, Jefferson Park, and West Seattle courses are 18-hole layouts with user-friendly fees and atmospheres, and very nice course designs; www.ci.seattle.wa.us/parks.

Hiking

Mountains on both horizons and a lowland climate in which snow is a rarity—Puget Sound seems like a hiker's heaven. And if you dress properly, it is; few other places in the country offer year-round hiking possibilities. The key is appropriate gear—it's lovely to climb up into alpine meadows on the shoulder of Rainier in late July to stroll through limitless acres of wildflowers, but you'd best be prepared to be both hot and sun-shy—or to don storm gear and sit out a snow squall. In the lowlands a trek through an **OLYMPIC RAIN FOREST** of moss-clad old trees is a serene and spiritually satisfying January respite—but if you aren't thoroughly waterproofed, you'll be miserable.

Some of the best hiking in and around Seattle can be found in Discovery Park, the Washington Park arboretum, Lincoln Park, Marymoor Park, the Issaquah Alps (Cougar, Tiger, and Squak Mountains), along I-90 east to Snoqualmie Pass, and at Tacoma's Point Defiance Park.

Don't Forget Your Parking Pass

There's no such thing as free parking around Seattle—even in the mountains. You'll need to buy a **NATIONAL FOREST SERVICE PASS** to park at trailheads on Forest Service land. Day passes are available for $5; annual passes are $30. Purchase them at area outdoor retailers or online at www.fs.fed.us/r6/mbs/passes.

In winter, snowshoers and cross-country skiers who park in a designated Sno-Park lot need a Washington State **SNO-PARK PASS**. Daily passes are $9; buy them at outdoor retailers or online at www.parks.wa.gov/winter/permits.asp. To access groomed trails requires a seasonal pass for $21. To access ungroomed trails, you'll need to buy a separate pass, also $21. Both can be purchased at outdoor retailers or by sending a check to Winter Recreation Program, P.O. Box 42650, Olympia WA 98504-2650.

Of special note is **MOUNT SI** (www.mountsi.com), the sheer granite face directly east of North Bend, 30 miles from downtown. This forbidding haul climbs 3,700 feet over 4 miles and is widely used as a training route for serious climbers and backpackers. The view of Puget Sound Basin from the top is breathtaking. A more user-friendly alternative nearby is **RATTLESNAKE LEDGE** (www.issaquahalps.org), a hike up a flank of the Issaquah Alps southeast of Issaquah to a bluff affording sensational views of the Eastside, the Cascades, and Mount Rainier. This hike climbs a more merciful 1,170 feet over 4 miles, and the trail was reconstructed in 2003.

The most **POPULAR NEARBY WILDERNESS HIKES** are in the Alpine Lakes Wilderness east of Seattle, a spectacular high-country basin of lakes and snowclad peaks so popular that permits are needed; the Glacier Peak Wilderness northeast of Everett; the Goat Rocks and William O. Douglas Wilderness on the southeast flank of Rainier; and Mount Rainier National Park itself.

The **WONDERLAND TRAIL** is a 93-mile circuit around Rainier within the park that takes up to a week to travel. The **PACIFIC CREST TRAIL,** which starts its West Coast journey at the United States–Mexico border, traversing the spine of the Cascades from Oregon to BC, offers a weeks-long wilderness trek. Both of these hikes are for expert wilderness travelers only.

The **OUTDOOR RECREATION INFORMATION CENTER** at the downtown REI store (222 Yale Ave N, 470-4060, www.

The Mountaineers

Founded in 1906 by local outdoor enthusiasts, largely climbers, the Mountaineers began life as a club devoted to its namesake pursuits. Early figures included photographer Asahel Curtis and the UW's Edmond Meany. The club's first activity was a walk to the West Point Lighthouse in what is now Discovery Park, but far more challenging treks quickly ensued. The 1907 climb of Mount Olympus drew 65 club members on a journey that is not much less difficult today. Since then Mountaineers members have made innumerable first ascents of West Coast peaks and pioneered hundreds of wilderness trails.

With about 25,000 members the Mountaineers today fulfills numerous other functions, ranging from education to social facilitation to advocacy. The list of Mountaineer-sponsored activities ranges from singles hikes to wilderness-protection petition drives. Its Web site is one of the best overall guides to outdoor activity in Western Washington, and its book-publishing arm offers a long list of titles on hiking, biking, and boating in the Northwest.

Despite the addition of scores of activities over the years, from sea kayaking to orienteering, the club hews to an explicitly nonmechanical focus: If you're going to do something with the Mountaineers outdoors, it will be on your own two feet. Aside from the main Seattle club, there are branches in Bellingham, Everett, Kitsap, Olympia, the Eastside, Tacoma, and Wenatchee. Membership is $61 a year. 284-6310, www.mountaineers.org.

---

fs.fed.us/r6/mbs) is staffed by a rotating staff of national park, state park, and forest service personnel who can answer almost any questions about trails, camping, and hiking in the Northwest.

The chief membership and advocacy organization for Seattle-area hikers is the **WASHINGTON TRAILS ASSOCIATION** (625-1367, www.wta.org), which offers information, outings, and trail guides. Most important, its members perform a huge amount of trail construction and maintenance, benefiting everyone who ever sets foot on a hiking trail in the Puget Sound region. Basic membership is $35 a year.

Kayaking

Puget Sound is prime kayaking territory, though only the quietest bays (such as Shilshole) are for beginners. Popular Seattle-area paddles include a run over to Blake Island, which has a walk-in campground, and north along Discovery Park, past Shilshole to Golden Gardens. Quartermaster Harbor, on Vashon Island, offers a protected inlet paddle with plenty of wildlife to see. The highest-profile kayaking venue around, though, is Lake Union, where fans of the sport take their lunch hour paddling amid the yachts and seaplanes, and are often photographed with the downtown skyline in the background. Several outfitters offer rentals and lessons: **MOSS BAY ROWING & KAYAK CENTER** (682-2031) and **NORTHWEST OUTDOOR CENTER** (281-9694, www.nwoc.com). **AGUA VERDE CAFÉ & PADDLE CLUB** not only has kayaks and canoes to rent, it has some of the best Mexican food in Seattle (545-8570, www.aguaverde.com). The **SEATTLE CANOE & KAYAK CLUB** (684-4074, www.scn.org/rec/sckc) is the umbrella organization for the sport and maintains a facility at Green Lake. At the University of Washington the Waterfront Activities Center rents canoes and kayaks from the lakeshore behind Husky Stadium (543-9433, depts.washington.edu/ima/IMA_wac.php).

Running

Puget Sound is known as a haven for runners, who can practice their sport year-round, rarely facing extremes of heat or cold. The key, much of the year, is a good hat to keep the rain off and reflective gear to establish visibility in low light. The same trails that serve bikers are excellent for runners too, as are trails in the many parks throughout the region. A fairly complete list of Western Washington running events is maintained at www.ontherun.com. Major races include:

BLOOMSDAY RUN: Timed to coincide with the lilac bloom in Spokane in May, the Bloomsday Run is one of the largest recreational races in North America, drawing more than 50,000 participants to a 12K course with two significant climbs along the way. www.bloomsdayrun.org.

SEATTLE MARATHON: The November Seattle Marathon is the major such race in the Northwest and includes a half-marathon as well. The course crosses Lake Washington to Mercer Island and back (the I-90 floating bridge is partly closed for the event), and begins and ends downtown. www.seattlemarathon.org.

SOUND-TO-NARROWS: Tacoma's major annual race, a 12K in June, follows a hilly, scenic course largely within Point Defiance Park and is distinguished by a *steep* quarter-mile hill near the finish. www.soundtonarrows.com.

ST. PATRICK'S DAY DASH: The slogan for this mid-March Seattle institution says it all: "Run, Walk, Jog, Crawl." Serious runners do not participate in the stop-at-a-dozen-bars tradition; the roughly 10K course is largely downhill, for all those, um, fellow travelers, who total about 12,000. www.stpatsdash.com.

Sailboarding

Though the premier windsurfing area in the Northwest (and perhaps the world) is three hours south in the Columbia Gorge, local adherents find great action on Lake Washington—usually using pocket parks along Lake Washington Drive in Kirkland as a launching point. Heartier sorts also essay runs on Puget Sound, where the wakes from cargo ships and tankers offer a reasonable facsimile of ocean surf or the famous windborn standing waves of the Gorge. The leading board shop is **URBAN SURF** (2100 N Northlake Wy, 545-9463). For lessons on the lake try the **MOUNT BAKER ROWING & SAILING CENTER** (3800 Lake Washington Blvd, 386-1913).

But there is no question that the place to go is the Gorge, which is such a desirable boarding area that zealots move to **HOOD RIVER, OREGON,** to live (www.hoodriver.org).

Sailing

The Seattle area sports one of the highest per-capita boat ownership rates in the country, along with San Diego and Miami. Numerous marinas and yacht clubs offer berths for owners up and down Puget Sound and on major local lakes.

The **CENTER FOR WOODEN BOATS** (382-2628, www.cwb.org) on Lake Union is a marvelous institution with a museum, several lovely boats to visit, and rentals and lessons for beginning sailors. Its annual Wooden Boat Festival (see Chapter 8, "That's Entertainment," page 239) in July is a wonderful event.

The annual **SEATTLE BOAT SHOW** (www.seattleboatshow.com) at Qwest Field in January is a glitzy, mind-boggling occasion that requires either very deep pockets or a steady remembrance of the oft-heard saying that a boat is a hole in the water into which you throw money.

Shellfishing

When Ivar Haglund wrote "Acres of Clams" (see Chapter 1, "Seattle Neighborhoods," page 20) there were, indeed, just that up and down Puget Sound. Not any more: Overharvesting, pollution, and shoreline development have erased or contaminated many shellfish beds. However, there remain numerous places to go to gather clams, oysters, mussels, and other more exotic edibles, and anyone with a boat can set a crab pot. A day spent in spring or fall (the best seasons) on a beach at low tide, savoring the salt air and returning with a full bucket of clams for chowder or a full jar of oysters for stew, is a quintessential Seattle activity. Whidbey Island, Kitsap Peninsula, Hood Canal, and south Puget Sound all offer viable shellfish-gathering locales. Most beaches in Seattle, alas, are polluted and their clams, mussels, and oysters are unsafe. Though there are many public beaches along the Sound, a fair number are accessible only by boat. The state maintains a map of beaches on its Web site: wdfw.wa.gov/fish/shellfish/beachreg.

The native bivalves—butter clams, horse clams, and Pacific oysters—are in many places now outnumbered by nonnative imports such as steamer clams and Japanese oysters. All have their virtues, though; horse clams, for instance, which some folks disdain, are excellent for chowder (it only takes a few). Permits are needed for shellfishing, and limits and seasons apply. Some seasons, such as razor-clam digging on the Pacific Coast, are sometimes announced suddenly and closed just as suddenly; see wdfw.wa.gov.

Before harvesting any shellfish, it is imperative that you call the **SHELLFISH ("RED TIDE") HOTLINE** *to learn whether clams, mussels, and other bivalves are safe to eat.* PSP—paralytic shellfish poisoning—is a rare but highly undesirable toxin found in most bivalves. It's also misnamed, as it's not caused by red algae. Cooking does not neutralize it, and all parts of the animal are dangerous; the only way to avoid it is not to eat the affected shellfish. Protect yourself by calling the hotline before you set out to dig: 800-562-5632. The recorded information covers all of Puget Sound and is updated weekly or more often when circumstances warrant.

Skiing (Downhill) and Snowboarding

All those mountains, all that snow—the world-record snowfall buried Mount Baker back in the late '90s—isn't Seattle a world skiing capital? Well, there is one tiny catch: The snow is wet; it packs into a dense surface (hence its nickname "Seattle cement"); and you're likely, even in the dead of winter, to find yourself skiing in the rain. Nonetheless, many thousands of Seattleites adapt to these challenges and ski regularly and enthusiastically. There are half a dozen excellent downhill areas within day-trip distance. Just don't let anyone tell you that the snow is no different from inland areas.

CRYSTAL MOUNTAIN: This resort is widely regarded as the best skiing close to Seattle, with its high base (4,400 feet and a 3,100-foot vertical), huge annual snowfall, and slightly drier exposure on the back, northeast flank of Rainier. Crystal is the closest thing to a major resort in the Washington Cascades, and clear mornings after a major snowfall are exquisite. It's about three hours from downtown Seattle. 888-754-6199, www.skicrystal.com.

MOUNT BAKER: This is where the world-record single-season snowfall was registered: 1,140 inches back in the late '90s. That's impressive, but let's face it: It wasn't dry powder. Baker is particularly popular with boarders; it's about a four-hour drive north and east from downtown Seattle. 360-671-0211, www.mtbakerskiarea.com.

SNOQUALMIE PASS: The slopes at Snoqualmie Pass aren't going to win any prizes compared with other world-class ski destinations in the West. But they certainly are convenient—it's less than two hours from your downtown office (if your skis are stashed in the back of the Subaru) to the slopes, via I-90. The first significant autumn snowfall at Snoqualmie is an event Seattleites escape seeing with difficulty, as all the local TV stations mount reporter-cam expeditions to the Pass and broadcast live from the base. Technically, there are four separate areas here. 236-7277, www.summitatsnoqualmie.com.

Check Road Conditions

CASCADE SKI REPORT: 634-0200

WASHINGTON DOT MOUNTAIN PASS REPORT:
888-SNO-INFO

WASHINGTON ONLINE WEATHER: 877-969-4786,
www.wowweather.com

Avalanche Awareness

Avalanches have killed nearly 200 people in Washington since 1910, and according to the Washington Military Department Emergency Management Division, this exceeds deaths from any other natural cause. Avoid becoming a statistic and learn to read the snow conditions by taking an avalanche awareness class. They're offered in various forms by area outdoor retailers, such as Bellevue's Marmot Mountain Works, REI outlets, and outdoors clubs. Always call for the avalanche forecast before you head out: 526-6677

STEVENS PASS: Higher than Snoqualmie by more than 1,000 feet, Stevens is not as subject to drenching rain and cement snow. It's a compact, family-friendly area, about two-and-a-half hours from downtown Seattle on Highway 2. 812-4510, www.stevenspass.com.

Skiing (Cross-Country and Skate)

There are thousands of miles of groomed and ungroomed cross-country trails in the mountains east and west of Seattle. Many of the downhill resorts also have groomed trails for track skiers: The **NORDIC CENTER AT SNOQUALMIE PASS** (425-434-6708, www.summitatsnoqualmie.com) has 46 km of groomed trails over varying terrain, for example, and **STEVENS PASS** has 28 km of groomed trails. There are also several area clubs devoted to classic and skate skiing, such as the **WASHINGTON SKI TOURING CLUB** (525-4451, www.wstc.org), which organizes group day trips and multiday excursions around the Northwest.

Hands down, one of the most popular Nordic destinations in Washington is the **METHOW VALLEY:** Tucked up against the east side of North Cascades National Park, this high desert valley enjoys dry snow, lots of it, and a community of small, friendly resorts devoted to cross-country skiers, with lots of ski-in, ski-out accommodations. Alas, it's a five-hour trek from Seattle in winter—but worth it (www.winthropwashington.com). Aside from a large selection of small inns and B&Bs, the Northwest's premier Nordic ski resort is here, **SUN MOUNTAIN LODGE** (800-572-0493, www.sunmountainlodge.com).

Soccer and Other League Sports

Seattle is one of the recreational soccer capitals of the country. There are also leagues for baseball, slow- and fast-pitch softball, field and ice hockey, lacrosse, and rugby. Numerous leagues offer indoor and outdoor schedules, with categories for every possible age and skill level; see www.seattlesportsleagues.com.

Swimming

The City of Seattle has eight indoor pools and two outdoor ones. Of the latter, Colman Pool at Lincoln Park is unique, a heated saltwater pool that draws throngs on sunny summer days. The other pools are distributed widely throughout the city and can get quite crowded on weekends; 684-4075, www.cityofseattle.net/parks/Aquatics/index.htm.

Pools are operated by numerous other jurisdictions in the Seattle area; check the Web sites for individual cities. The King County Aquatic Center in Federal Way is a world-class swimming facility; see Chapter 3, "Nearby Burgs," page 120.

The best freshwater swimming in the area is at Seward, Magnuson, Matthews Beach, Juanita Bay (Kirkland), Luther Burbank (Mercer Island), and Gene Coulon (Renton) Parks on Lake Washington and at Lake Sammamish State Park. The best saltwater swimming is at Carkeek Park in Seattle, Quartermaster Harbor on Vashon Island, and in protected inlets on the Kitsap Peninsula, such as at Penrose Point State Park.

Other Pursuits

BLADING: Green Lake, Myrtle-Edwards, and of course the Burke-Gilman offer the best local routes for bladers. First-timers can rent equipment and receive cursory instruction at The Prime Skate & Snow Shop in the U-District. 1406 NE 50th St, 528-3773, www.theprime.com.

CAMPING: There are virtually no noncommercial campgrounds within an hour of Seattle, save the RV facility at Marymoor Park. But farther out are a bevy of fine state parks and the vast recreational expanses of the Cascades and Olympics. Popular camping parks include Deception Pass on Whidbey Island, Dash Point in Federal Way, and Belfair, Penrose Point, and Scenic Beach over on the Kitsap Peninsula. Camping reservations are imperative at these parks; visit www.parks.wa.gov. The majority of the federal campgrounds near Seattle are in Mount Baker–Snoqualmie National Forest. The **OUT-DOOR RECREATION INFORMATION CENTER** at the downtown REI store (222 Yale Ave N, 470-4060, www.fs.fed.us/r6/mbs) provides information for camping in national and state parks, and national forests.

CANOEING: Fans of open-boat paddling can rent canoes on Lake Union for a spin through the lily-clad coves at the southeastern end of the Montlake Cut; the **PADDLE TRAILS CANOE CLUB** is the local umbrella organization, www.paddletrails.org. Or, rent canoes from the university's **WATERFRONT ACTIVITIES CENTER** (3900 Montlake Blvd and Pacific Ave NE, 543-9433). Up in British Columbia, several of the best and most famous wilderness canoe circuits on earth (including one that's on a saltwater inlet) beckon: the Powell River, Bowron Lake, and Murtle Lake routes. For more info, contact Tourism BC, 800-HELLO-BC, www.hellobc.com.

ROWING: It's not just for university students anymore—youth and adult programs thrive here, where there's plenty of water to skim across. A few places offering equipment and/or lessons: Lake Union Crew (11 E Allison St, 860-4199, www.lakeunioncrew.com); Green Lake Small Craft Center (5900 W Green Lake Wy N, 684-4074); Lake Washington Rowing Club (910 N. Northlake Wy, 547-1583, lakewashingtonrowing.com); and the Mount Baker Rowing & Sailing Center (3800 Lake Washington Blvd S, 386-1913).

SEATTLE-AREA PARKS

Itching to stretch your legs after a long commute? Thankfully, in Seattle you're never far from a park or green space. Here is a list of local favorites. (For additional information on regional parks, see descriptions by neighborhood in Chapters 1–3.)

BRIDLE TRAILS: Long trails through fir forest for fillies and their mounts, in Bellevue. NE 53rd & 116th NE, 360-902-8844, www.parks.wa.gov.

CARKEEK: Another Sound-front park whose adherents believe has the best beach in Seattle. The narrow roads winding along wooded hillsides are great for biking. 684-4075, www.cityofseattle.net/parks.

COUGAR MOUNTAIN: Steep uphill trails, high plateaus, dense forests, hidden glades—Cougar is the premier hiking draw in the immediate Seattle area. It would take a month for a dedicated hiker to encompass it all. www.issaquahalps.org.

DASH POINT STATE PARK: The nearest state camping area to Seattle, plus lots of low-tide sand beach to wander, in Federal Way. www.parks.wa.gov.

DISCOVERY: Seattle's biggest city park is a magnificent 534-acre expanse of bluff-top field and forest, and cliffside beach in the Magnolia neighborhood. More than 11 miles of trails beckon people and dogs, and there are innumerable picnic spots, some remarkably secluded if you poke around a bit. Several pairs of bald eagles nest here. 684-4075, www.cityofseattle.net/parks.

GOLDEN GARDENS: Beach bonfires were almost a thing of the past at this Ballard park under an ill-considered plan to quell the tendency toward keggers. Watching the sun set over the Olympics here is a Seattle tradition—please help maintain the family-friendly atmosphere. There's also a dandy little wetland area. 684-4075, www.cityofseattle.net/parks.

GREEN LAKE/WOODLAND PARK ZOO: The zoo is one of the world leaders in creating more natural habitats for its denizens, and it regularly sees births among rare animals. Green Lake may be the most crowded recreational path in any city park anywhere; algae problems plague the lake itself. All in all, it's a lovely example of what virtues an urban park can offer—and the problems that can result. 684-4075, www.cityofseattle.net/parks.

LAKE SAMMAMISH STATE PARK: The best swimming beaches on Lake Sammamish are here, along with grassy meadows set amid cottonwood groves and the outlet for Issaquah Creek and its salmon runs. 1700 NW Sammamish Rd, www.parks.wa.gov.

LINCOLN: Aside from its beautiful location atop a bluff overlooking the Sound from West Seattle, the Olympics, and the north end of Vashon Island, Lincoln Park has a sensationally popular (heated) saltwater swimming pool. 684-4075, www.cityofseattle.net/parks.

LUTHER BURBANK PARK: At 77 acres, Mercer Island's biggest and best park has beaches, gardens, a playfield, and a forest. 2040 84th Ave SE, 296-4232, www.ci.mercer-island.wa.us.

MAGNUSON: This Laurelhurst green space used to be known by its geographic moniker, Sand Point Park, but was officially renamed after the long-term senator, Warren G. Magnuson. It's one of the city's biggest, noted for its large leash-free dog area. 684-4075, www.cityofseattle.net/parks.

MARYMOOR: With Lake Sammamish, miles of open fields, playfields of every type, a velodrome for cycling speedsters, and wonderful gardens around the old Clise Mansion, Marymoor is the Eastside's finest park; located in Redmond. 6046 W Lake Sammamish Pkwy NE, 205-3661, www.metrokc.gov/parks.

MYRTLE-EDWARDS: This waterfront strip, from the north end of Alaskan Way north to Interbay, has picnic tables, grassy lawns for sun-napping, a trail that ultimately wends its way through Magnolia to Ballard, and a semihidden pocket beach. 684-4075, www.cityofseattle.net/parks.

SAINT EDWARD STATE PARK: Overlooking Lake Washington in Kirkland with clifftop trails and ample solitude. 14445 Juanita Dr NE, 425-823-2992, www.parks.wa.gov.

SALTWATER STATE PARK: One of the longest stretches of flat sand beach along the Sound, in Burien. www.parks.wa.gov.

SEWARD: Lake Washington beaches, forest trails, and hydros during Seafair; near Columbia City. 684-4075, www.cityofseattle.net/parks.

WASHINGTON PARK ARBORETUM: This beloved Madison Park institution has hundreds of different trees, long strolling paths, and coves for canoeing. depts.washington.edu/wpa.

VOLUNTEER: The water tower here, with its steep stairway to the top, affords splendid views of Seattle from Capitol Hill. There is also a conservatory. Despite numerous campaigns to quell gay-cruising and drug using, it's no place to be after dark. 684-4075, www.cityofseattle.net/parks.

INDOOR RECREATION

Climbing

The most conspicuous and most popular climbing wall is at the **MAIN REI STORE** downtown (222 Yale Ave N, 223-1944, www.rei.com). It's also one of the tallest in the world. There are **VERTICAL WORLD** gyms in Seattle, Redmond, and Kitsap (283-4497, www.verticalworld.com), and **STONE GARDENS** in Ballard has both indoor and outdoor climbing (781-9828).

There's an outdoor wall in Marymoor Park as well; see www.metrokc.gov/parks.

Fitness

While Seattle seems to have as many outposts of the major fitness chains—Bally's, Gold's, and so on—as most major cities do, there is also a large community of locally owned clubs that can be more economical and offer a better atmosphere.

WASHINGTON ATHLETIC CLUB (WAC): The WAC is the granddaddy of them all, a club whose social cachet pretty much equals its heart-of-downtown exercise facilities. 622-7900, www.wac.net.

SEATTLE ATHLETIC CLUB: This is the newer, hipper, younger answer to the WAC, located near Pike Place Market. 443-1111, www.sacdt.com.

BELLEVUE CLUB: The counterpart to WAC on the Eastside, the Bellevue Club even has one of the top-rated boutique hotels in Western Washington, should you tire yourself out too much to get home. 425-688-3150, www.bellevueclub.com.

Other locally owned clubs include Ballard Health Club, Columbia Athletic Clubs, Magnolia Health Club, Olympic Athletic Club, Sound Mind & Body, University Fitness, and West Seattle Gym.

Skating

Puget Sound's climate makes outdoor ice rinks a near impossibility, but there are indoor rinks in Shoreline (**HIGHLAND ICE ARENA,** the area's major facility; 546-2431, www.highlandice.com), Lynnwood (**LYNNWOOD ICE CENTER,** 425-640-9999, www.lynnwoodicecenter.com), and Kent (**KENT VALLEY ICE CENTER,** 253-850-2400, www.familynightout.com).

Those who like to skate on wheels head to Bellevue's **SKATE KING,** which has a large well-maintained floor, schedules sessions for all skill levels, and enforces civil behavior. 2301 140th Ave NE, 425-458-4707.

CHAPTER 10

By the People, For the People

Process. Process, process, process. Whenever there's a decision to be made in the Seattle metro area, there's usually a committee or citizen's group somewhere trying to slow it down, speed it up, or make sure that it's culturally, politically, environmentally, ethnically, demographically, and socially sensitive—and as inclusive as possible. As a result, local officials have to find a way to maintain a delicate balance between responding to the needs of the community as a whole and to the desires of a seemingly inexhaustible array of interest groups within the community. If they do not, they run the risk of initiative petitions or lawsuits that can render government action invalid at worst, or tardy at best.

Ongoing **BATTLES OVER PUBLIC TRANSIT** are a prime example. Years after voters approved a Seattle monorail and a regional light rail system, the options remain bogged down in battles that have included initiative efforts to derail them both. Specific routes and configurations are subject to attack and review; go-ahead decisions have often failed to result in actual ability to proceed. As a result, Seattle—often considered the most progressive of cities—is the only major metro area on the West Coast to lack light rail.

Whether you see this as a detriment (much-needed public improvements go undone) or an advantage (everyone has their say), it's a fact of life in an area that is in perpetual political ferment. One one hand, **LIGHT RAIL** may not be running until well after 2010; on the other hand, **CITIZEN ACTIVISM** is what saved Pike Place Market from urban "renewal" in the late '60s.

The other political fact of life in the Seattle area is a decided liberal lean that, coupled with the metro area's sheer number of voters, dominates state politics. Though the rest of Washington state is far more conservative than Puget Sound, the state's two senators and governor are usually Democrats or at least moderate Republicans. Across Lake Washington politics veers right a bit—radio programmers have found enough interest to support two conservative radio stations—and across the Cascades the rightward shift is pronounced.

However, a more evident strain in local politics is a defiant independence that confounds strategists and party activists. Despite the local liberal bent, Tim Eyman (see sidebar, page 285) won overwhelming support for his first few antitax initiatives. And state voters were hugely displeased when the courts threw out the open primary system in which voters could enter the booth and pick any political party they chose.

It's useful to remember that process fervor to understand why the open primary was scotched. Voters loved it, but party activists complained that it subverted the purpose of a two-party system. (Democrats could, and did, vote for Republicans and vice versa.) So the two parties found common ground and sued.

Regardless of which way they lean, Seattle-area residents have numerous ways to participate in the political system at the neighborhood, municipal, county, regional, and statewide level. All they need to know is where to go, who to talk to, and what to do. This chapter describes those venues.

POLL POSITION

The best way to get involved in the political process is at the polls, and the best way to do that is to register to vote by contacting the **KING COUNTY SUPERINTENDENT OF ELECTIONS** at 296-VOTE (8683), www.metrokc.gov/elections. This office also provides information on the precinct you live in and the location of your polling place.

Voting is open to legal residents of Washington who are 18 years old and registered. Registration must take place by mail 30 days before an election or in person 15 days beforehand. Polling places are usually open 7am–7pm election days; many voters take advantage of the system's friendliness to absentee voting and send their ballots in by mail. The elections Web site has information on how to sign up for absentee voting.

EMERALD CITY HALL

The Mayor

Elected every four years in a nonpartisan race, Seattle's top executive oversees the day-to-day operations of the city, prepares a budget for distribution to the council in September, appoints department heads (subject to city council approval), gives a State of the City address every June, and has the power to veto legislation approved by the council. That doesn't mean the mayor always has the final word, though. The council can override the veto with a two-thirds vote.

The mayoral election is held the same year as federal midterm elections (in 2006, 2010, and so on).

The mayor's office is on City Hall's seventh floor, but you'll have to go through a phalanx of staffers to meet with him or her. It's best to start with someone on the mayor's staff. 600 4th Ave, 7th Fl, 684-4000, www.cityofseattle.net/mayor.

Seattle City Council

In addition to reviewing and approving the city's annual budget, the council meets in its chambers, on the second floor of City Hall, every Monday at 2pm to discuss policies and pass ordinances covering everything from housing and zoning codes

I'm Just a Bill . . .

If you've ever thought, "There ought to be a law . . . ," you can take an active role in making it happen. As long as you can find a council member to sponsor it, that is. It's best to start with a member of the committee that has jurisdiction over your particular issue. For information on committee assignments or to set an appointment, call 684-8888. Be prepared to discuss the proposal with committee members or to explain your idea at a public hearing if there's enough citizen interest. An additional public hearing could follow if the committee recommends that the council approve the ordinance.

If you want to propose an ordinance for King County, start with the council member representing your district or the district affected by the issue. If it's a countywide concern, seek out a member of the committee that has the proper jurisdiction.

to crime and traffic. Candidates for four-year terms in nine at-large districts run in nonpartisan elections on an at-large basis. Terms are staggered to keep the entire council from having to run at the same time. 684-8888, www.cityofseattle.net/council.

Council Committees

Typically, most decisions are made in committee meetings so that once the proposal reaches the council all that's required is a yes or no vote. The council's 11 committees are as follows:

- *Budget*: 2:30pm on the first Monday of the month
- *Energy & Environmental Policy*: 9:30am, second and fourth Wednesdays
- *Finance & Budget*: 9:30am, first and third Wednesdays
- *Government Affairs & Labor*: 9:30am, first and third Thursdays
- *Housing, Human Services & Health*: 9:30am, first and third Tuesdays
- *Monorail*: no regularly scheduled meetings
- *Parks, Neighborhoods & Education*: 2pm, first and third Wednesdays
- *Public Safety, Civil Rights & Arts*: 2pm, first and third Tuesdays
- *Transportation*: 9:30am, second and fourth Tuesdays
- *Urban Development & Planning*: 2pm, second and fourth Wednesdays
- *Utilities & Technology*: 2pm, second and fourth Tuesdays

SEATTLE SCHOOL BOARD

Seattle's schools are governed and managed independently of city government. See Chapter 7, "School Daze," page 205, for more information.

OTHER JURISDICTIONS

Auburn: 253-931-3000, www.ci.auburn.wa.us

Bellevue: 425-452-6800, www.cityofbellevue.org

Black Diamond: 360-886-2560, www.cityofblackdiamond.com

Bothell: 425-486-3256, www.ci.bothell.wa.us

Burien: 206-241-4647, www.ci.burien.wa.us

Des Moines: 206-870-4595, www.desmoineswa.gov

Duvall: 425-788-1185, www.cityofduvall.com

Enumclaw: 360-825-3591, www.cityofenumclaw.net

Federal Way: 253-835-7000, www.cityoffederalway.com

Issaquah: 425-837-3000, www.ci.issaquah.wa.us

Kenmore: 425-398-8900, www.cityofkenmore.com

Kent: 253-856-5700, www.ci.kent.wa.us

Kirkland: 425-828-1100, www.ci.kirkland.wa.us

Lake Forest Park: 206-368-5440, www.cityoflfp.com

Lynnwood: 425-775-1971, www.ci.lynnwood.wa.us

Maple Valley: 425-413-8800, www.ci.maple-valley.wa.us

Mercer Island: 206-236-5300, www.ci.mercer-island.wa.us

Newcastle: 425-649-4444, www.ci.newcastle.wa.us

Normandy Park: 206-248-7603, www.ci.normandy-park.wa.us

North Bend: 425-888-1211, www.ci.north-bend.wa.us

Pierce County: (no general phone number), www.co.pierce.wa.us

Puyallup: 253-841-4321, www.ci.puyallup.wa.us

Redmond: 425-556-2900, www.redmond.gov

Renton: 425-430-6400, www.ci.renton.wa.us

Sammamish: 425-898-0660, www.ci.sammamish.wa.us

SeaTac: 206-973-4800, www.ci.seatac.wa.us

Shoreline: 206-546-1700, www.cityofshoreline.com

Snohomish County: 425-388-3411 or 800-562-4367, www.co.snohomish.wa.us

Snoqualmie: 425-888-1555, www.cityofsnoqualmie.net

Tacoma: 253-591-5000, www.cityoftacoma.org

Tukwila: 206-433-1800, www.ci.tukwila.wa.us

Woodinville: 425-489-2700, www.ci.woodinville.wa.us

KING COUNTY

The county provides a variety of regional services (elections, health department, and libraries) to many cities and general government services (road work, police, and parks) to unincorporated areas. It also provides transit to the entire county through Metro and sewer service to much of the county, also through Metro.

The County Executive

The holder of King County's highest elective office prepares the budget and oversees the day-to-day operations of the state's largest regional government. The exec serves a four-year term and is elected in odd-numbered years: 2005, 2009, and so on. 701 5th Ave, Suite 3210, 296-4040, www.metrokc.gov/exec.

Metropolitan King County Council

The 13-member council meets Mondays at 1:30pm in the council chambers on the 10th floor of the King County Courthouse. The body passes rules and ordinances, establishes government policies, and has the final say on the county executive's proposed annual budget. All members serve four-year terms representing geographic districts and run for office in odd-numbered years. Elections are staggered with races in even-numbered districts one year and odd-numbered districts two years later. King County Courthouse, 12th Fl, 296-1000, www.metrokc.gov/mkcc.

Committees

As with the city council, members of the county council serve on a variety of committees with assignments changing every year. The committees include the following:

- *Committee of the Whole*: 9:30am, Mondays
- *Budget & Fiscal Management*: 9:30am, first, second, fourth, and if applicable, fifth Wednesdays
- *Growth, Management & Unincorporated Areas*: 9:30am, first and third Tuesdays
- *Employment*: 1:30pm, first and third Tuesdays
- *Law, Justice & Human Services*: 9:30am, first and third Thursdays

- *Labor, Operations & Technology*: 9:30am second and fourth Tuesdays

- *Legislative Steering Committee*: 8am, first, second, and fourth Mondays

- *Natural Resources & Utilities*: 1:30pm, first, second, and third Thursdays

- *Regional Policy*: 3pm, first Wednesday

- *Regional Transit*: 3pm, first Wednesday

- *Regional Water Quality*: 3pm, second Wednesday

- *Transportation*: 1:30pm, second and fourth Wednesdays

PORT OF SEATTLE

In addition to running most of the port facilities on the waterfront—including container terminals, Fishermen's Terminal, Shilshole Marina, the Bell Harbor International Conference Center and cruise ship dock—the organization also operates Sea-Tac International Airport. The Port's impact on life and the economy in the Seattle area is vast: Its long and fervent recruitment of cruise ship visits to Elliott Bay is the main reason these massive vessels, packed with (supposedly) free-spending tourists, come to Seattle. Its decision to build a third runway at Sea-Tac, rather than build an entirely new airport somewhere else, set the fate of air travel to Western Washington for decades to come.

The five-member Port Commission meets at 1pm on the second and fourth Tuesdays of the month. The first meeting of the month is held at the Port's office on Pier 69, and the second is at the International Auditorium at Sea-Tac Airport.

The five members serve four-year terms and are elected on a staggered basis every two years. 2711 Alaskan Wy, Pier 69, 728-3000, www.portseattle.org.

STATE GOVERNMENT

The Governor

As chief executive of Washington, the Olympia-based governor's duties include overseeing state operations, planning the budget, delivering an annual State of the State message, and approving or vetoing proposed laws. The term lasts four years and comes up for reelection the same year as the president of the United States. Because of the Seattle area's political heft, the governor has almost always come from Puget Sound and has been liberal or moderate. 360-902-4111, www.governor.wa.gov.

The Legislature

Washington's legislature operates on a biennial schedule, meeting for 105 consecutive days during the first year of the cycle in order to pass a budget and for 60 consecutive days the second year. Sessions start on the second Monday of January, and both houses typically review 5,000 proposed bills and pass about 600. The governor can call the body back into a special 30-day session if legislators fail to finish all their work before the regular session adjourns—and budget wrangles have recently required that to happen almost every time.

The Senate has 49 members who serve four-year terms with half up for reelection every two years. The 98 members of the House of Representatives have two-year terms. The responsibilities of both houses are essentially the same, with senators and representatives enacting legislation and approving the annual budget. The senate can veto gubernatorial appointments. Senate: 360-786-7550, www.leg.wa.gov/senate; House of Representatives: 360-786-7750, www.leg.wa.gov/house; general legislative information: 800-562-6000.

FEDERAL GOVERNMENT

Washington has two senators and nine representatives. The number of representatives may fluctuate depending on population trends throughout the country. Senators serve six-year terms and are elected on a staggered basis with a third of the body up for election every two years. Representatives serve two-year terms.

To find out who your senators and representatives are and how to contact them, call the **FEDERAL INFORMATION CENTER**, 800-688-9889, or visit www.info.gov.

How to Complain

Regardless of whether you're calling to complain about noisy floatplanes, litter in county parks, or questionable insurance-company practices, there are offices you can call at all levels of government within Washington State to air your displeasure and ask for help.

In Seattle the **CITIZENS SERVICE BUREAU** is where residents start their search for redress. The bureau also takes complaints about the police department, but does not investigate the claims. 684-CITY (2489), www.seattle.gov/citizenservice.

In King County the **COUNTY OMBUDSMAN** looks into complaints on issues ranging from building permits to prisoner rights at regional correctional facilities. The office has no jurisdiction in complaints about court-related issues, however. 296-3452, www.metrokc.gov/ombuds.

Call **WASHINGTON STATE INFORMATION** to find the complaint line for the state agency your problem concerns. 800-321-2808.

Two particular state offices are of great use to citizens. The Washington Attorney General has an active **CONSUMER PROTECTION DIVISION** that responds to all sorts of complaints about commercial fraud, telemarketing, business scams, vehicle sales, and so on; it's one of the national leaders in consumer protection. 464-6684, www.atg.wa.gov/consumer.

The **INSURANCE COMMISSIONER'S OFFICE** fields complaints about insurance of all kinds—health, auto, home, life—and the sales and claims processes associated with each type. 800-562-6900, www.insurance.wa.gov.

BUILDING & ZONING ISSUES

Your neighbor is building a pink castle with a 70-foot observation tower that looks directly into your bedroom. Want to find out if that's legal? (Probably not.) Contact the Seattle Department of Planning and Development. Seattle Municipal Tower, 700 5th Ave, 684-8600 (24-hour info), www.cityofseattle.net/dclu.

Taking the Initiative

If your concern is an issue that would require passage of a law or ordinance and you can't find someone to take up your cause, an initiative petition may be the answer. City, county, and state requirements vary slightly, but all provide citizens a way to either put the particular proposal before a legislative body or take it directly to the electorate. All it takes is filing the proposal with the secretary of state's office at the state level or the city or county clerk at the local level and getting the required number of signatures from registered voters by a preset deadline. State initiatives must be signed by the equivalent of 8 percent of the votes cast in the last gubernatorial election. City and county initiatives require the equivalent of 10 percent of the votes cast in the last executive or mayoral election.

To find out more, contact the municipal or county offices where you live; for statewide issues contact the Washington Secretary of State's office. 360-902-4151, www.secstate.wa.gov.

HERE COMES THE JUDGE

Everyone deserves their day in court. All they have to do is figure out which one to go to.

KING COUNTY DISTRICT COURT: The court's jurisdiction covers civil cases, traffic cases, and small claims. King County Courthouse, Third Ave & James St; 205-9200, www.metrokc.gov/kcdc.

KING COUNTY SUPERIOR COURT: Jurisdiction includes juvenile, civil, and criminal cases throughout King County. King County Courthouse, 3rd Ave & James St, 296-9300, www.metrokc.gov/kcsc.

MUNICIPAL COURT OF SEATTLE: The court's jurisdiction covers small civil disputes involving less than $10,000 and misdemeanor crimes where fines are less than $5,000 and sentences less than one year in jail, including domestic violence, theft, and driving under the influence. Public Safety Building, 610 3rd Ave, 684-5600, www.ci.seattle.wa.us/courts.

The Antitax King

While some politicians are famed for their ability to use pork-barrel politics to bring home the bacon to their districts, in his heyday **TIM EYMAN** excelled at taking it all away.

The king of the antitax initiative petition drive initially came to prominence for his efforts to capitalize on voter anger over high motor-vehicle excise taxes. His 1999 initiative, I-695, called for a reduction of tab fees to $30 and required that voters approve any tax or fee increases by state and local governments. The ballot measure passed, but the state Supreme Court overturned it because the measure violated the requirement that initiatives only deal with one subject. Despite the court's finding, the legislature agreed to keep the lower tab fees, taking a large bite out of state and local revenues.

Eyman and his political committee, Permanent Offense, followed up with a series of tax-cutting initiatives that covered everything from capping property tax increases to 2 percent to requiring that 90 percent of all state transportation money be used for road-building projects.

His fall from grace began in 2002 after the public learned Eyman had used $50,000 in Permanent Offense funds to pay himself for his campaigning efforts, even though he had claimed to be volunteering. His first initiative effort after the funding flap succeeded, but subsequent efforts to get initiatives on the ballot had less success.

Eyman himself became the subject of an initiative when local computer programmer David Goldstein gathered signatures to have voters declare the controversial activist a "horse's ass." A challenge by the attorney general's office kept the initiative off the ballot, but Eyman's legacy persists in the form of cash-strapped schools and local governments.

STATE COURT OF APPEALS: Reviews decisions in civil and criminal cases from the Superior Court. 600 University Ave, 464-7750, www.courts.wa.gov/appellate_trial_courts.

U.S. BANKRUPTCY COURT: Handles bankruptcy cases. 700 Stewart St, 370-5200, www.wawb.uscourts.gov.

U.S. DISTRICT COURT: Jurisdiction covers federal criminal felonies and civil cases. 700 Stewart St, 370-8400, www.wawd.uscourts.gov/wawd.

GONE BUT NOT FORGOTTEN

Scoop & Maggie

There was a time when pork-barrel politics wasn't considered a bad thing, and few senators were better at it than Washington's Henry Jackson and Warren G. Magnuson—"Scoop" and "Maggie," respectively. Each spent more than four decades on Capitol Hill, and their dual power matched that of senators from more famously weighty states such as Texas.

A University of Washington Law School graduate, Magnuson (1905–1989) quickly rose from his position as director of the Seattle Municipal League in 1929 to influential politician, serving two years in the state legislature, eight years in the U.S. House of Representatives, and 36 in the Senate, ending with his loss to Republican Slade Gorton in 1980. At each step along the way, Maggie made sure Washington got its share of federal funds for projects, including eight hydroelectric dams, research grants at the University of Washington, two World's Fairs, Metro Transit in Seattle, and more than a million dollars in disaster relief assistance following the eruption of Mount St. Helens.

At the same time, Jackson, a five-term congressman and five-term senator, was instrumental in helping Washington state employers such as the Boeing Company secure federal contracts and getting the Pentagon to open a submarine base on Hood Canal. As chairman of the powerful Energy & Natural Resources Committee, he wrote the National Environmental Policy Act and was responsible for protecting much of the current wilderness in Washington state.

Their influence wasn't just limited to the Evergreen State. Both men had a major impact on domestic and foreign policy. Magnuson was instrumental in pushing through legislation covering civil rights, consumer protection, and the environment; shepherding the Marine Mammals Protection Act; and banning supertankers from Puget Sound. In addition to actively supporting environmental legislation, Jackson was concerned with the military and international affairs, and helped pass the Jackson-Vanik Act limiting trade with countries that had restrictive emigration policies, thus freeing Soviet Jews in the 1970s.

Few states have ever enjoyed such a pair of powerful voices in DC.

CHAPTER 11

A Picture of Health

Seattle is one of the nation's leading centers for the improvement of body, mind, and soul—a pathfinder in health care, mental health, social services, cultural diversity, and volunteer activism. If you are in need of a helping hand, a world-class medical expert, or a veteran holistic medicine practitioner, you're in the right spot. Oh, and by the way, we are quite a healthy bunch: In 2004 *Self* magazine rated Seattle the fittest city in the country (based on the fact that supposedly 9 of 10 Seattleites exercise regularly).

That doesn't mean everything is dandy, of course. There are as many homeless individuals on our streets as in any other city, partly because the relatively benign Puget Sound climate draws them from elsewhere. Several studies, such as the 2004 HealthGrades study of hospital care, have called into question the overall quality of local health care, and a billing scandal swept the University of Washington medical school in 2003. The high-tech economic collapse that drove our unemployment rate near 8 percent in the first few years of the century also ended health-care coverage for thousands of families. While the state does have a basic coverage plan for needy citizens, the waiting list is dishearteningly long.

When it comes to other aspects of healthy communities, however, the city's cultural diversity is a definite bright spot. With literally

One-Stop Resource Center

The **SEATTLE COMMUNITY NETWORK** at www.scn.org is an outgrowth of a Web site created by computer professionals in the mid-'90s. It demonstrates the Internet's profound utility to human life, maintaining page after page of listings for community groups and agencies of all sorts, from activism to volunteering. The nonprofit site operates by donations and the efforts of its own volunteers. It's an incomparable community resource for anyone living in Seattle and King County.

dozens and dozens of separate ethnic groups, and numerous organizations devoted to them, Seattle and the Puget Sound region comprise one of the most diverse areas in the United States, a match for larger metro areas such as San Francisco and New York.

HEALTH CARE

Seattle has two of the country's top medical research institutions: UW Medical Center and Fred Hutchinson Cancer Research Center. The city is home to one of the oldest, biggest, and most dynamic HMOs in the nation: Group Health. Our hospitals include such national care leaders as Harborview, one of America's top trauma centers, and Virginia Mason, a leading general-care hospital. We are a leader in alternative care, too; Bastyr University offers courses in everything from acupuncture to Watsu, a kind of aquatic massage. In other words, in addition to our overall fondness for fitness, Seattle's medical services make it one of the best places to live a long life of well-being. All you have to do is participate.

How to Find a Provider

DENTISTS: The Washington State Dental Association (www.wsda.org) offers consumer tips for finding a dentist. Seattle–King County Dental Society includes its members in a dentist referral service at www.dentistdirectory.com.

PHYSICIANS: All the major hospitals and insurance services operate find-a-doc services by location and specialty. The King County Medical Society (621-9393, www.kcmsociety.org) operates an umbrella referral service. *Seattle Magazine* publishes an annual survey of the best doctors in the metro area.

Due Diligence

Offered by the Washington State Department of Health, the **HEALTH PROFESSIONS QUALITY ASSURANCE** Web site provides information concerning health-care professionals' credential status and any record of restrictions or disciplinary action. Should you wish to file a complaint, the Web site also has the required forms and instructions. 360-236-4700, www.doh.wa.gov/.

Hospitals/Medical Research

There is a point to checking out the virtues of various hospitals, aside from location. As in almost everything these days, hospitals specialize, and even facilities for common services such as obstetrics vary—birthing rooms, for instance. The **WASHINGTON STATE HOSPITALS ASSOCIATION** operates a Web site (www.wsha.org) that describes its various members.

CHILDREN'S HOSPITAL: This Laurelhurst facility is the tertiary pediatric-care center for children in Washington, Alaska, Montana, and Idaho, with clinics in Bellevue, Everett, Federal Way, and Olympia. The hospital celebrates its centennial in 2007. 987-2000, www.chmc.org.

FRED HUTCHINSON CANCER RESEARCH CENTER: One of the top four cancer research institutions in the United States perches beside Lake Union and attracts Nobel Prize–winning talent from around the world. Among other things, this is the world's leading center for bone-marrow transplants, which were pioneered here. The Hutch, as it's called, is a partner with Children's Hospital and UW in the Seattle Cancer Care Alliance, a consortium that offers a level of expertise matching the other three major cancer centers in the country. The center's Cancer Information Service can answer any and all questions about cancer, as well as provide written information on risk, diagnosis, and treatment. 667-5000, www.fhcrc.org.

GROUP HEALTH COOPERATIVE (GHC): Group Health's services emphasize preventive and rehabilitative care. It's a national leader in attempting to address endemic problems such as smoking and high blood pressure. Its main clinic is on Capitol Hill, with 26 other facilities in Western Washington and contracted providers throughout the region. Founded as a cooperative in 1947, GHC remains a consumer-governed organization (though few members actually vote) that offers health care to more than 540,000 subscribers in Washington and Idaho. 888-901-4636 or 800-542-6312, www.ghc.org.

HARBORVIEW MEDICAL CENTER: Harborview is one of the leading trauma-care centers in the United States. An arm of the UW Medical system (see listing, below), it is also a leader in community psychiatric and acute substance-abuse services. 731-3000, www.uwmedicine.org/facilities/harborview.

HIGHLINE COMMUNITY HOSPITAL: Serving South King County from its Burien base, this nonprofit subscribes to the "Planetree" health-care philosophy, which seeks to embed medicine within a nurturing, holistic environment. 244-9970, www.hchnet.org.

OVERLAKE: The Eastside's leading hospital plans a satellite in Issaquah. Its strengths are family and cardiac care. 425-688-5000, www.overlakehospital.org.

SWEDISH MEDICAL CENTER: Dating back to 1910, Swedish is Seattle's oldest and biggest mainstream hospital—many native Seattleites have its name on their birth certificates. Its three main facilities are on First Hill, Capitol Hill (the former Providence Medical Center), and Ballard. It also operates a network of 11 primary care clinics. 386-6000, www.swedish.org.

UNIVERSITY OF WASHINGTON PHYSICIANS AND MEDICAL CENTER: Association with UW means this institution has some of the leading experts in their fields in the United States, and the organization's stand-alone clinics provide classic family medicine. 800-852-8546, www.uwmedicine.org.

VALLEY MEDICAL CENTER: South King County's major health-care center (located in south Renton) is a leader in family-care services such as birthing and postnatal care. It was one of the first hospitals in the nation to actively market its services (it's a for-profit operation). 425-228-3450, www.valleymedical.org.

VIRGINIA MASON MEDICAL CENTER: Its Capitol Hill facility is one of the best-rated hospitals in the country for quality of care. VM also operates clinics in Bellevue, Federal Way, Issaquah, Kirkland, Lynnwood, Port Angeles, Sand Point, and Winslow. 223-6600, www.vmmc.org.

ALTERNATIVE MEDICINE

Alternative medicine isn't quite so alternative anymore, especially in Seattle. Home to dozens of leading complementary and alternative medicine researchers, teachers, and care providers, Seattle boasts a healthy community of naturopathic physicians, acupuncturists, massage therapists, nutritionists, Chinese medicine herbalists, and other nontraditional healers. Unlike most other states, Washington licenses naturopaths and requires insurance companies to cover at least some alternative health care. Puget Sound doctors are also getting hip to alternative medicine and in many clinics collaborate to help patients get the best of both worlds. If you're looking for a new practitioner, it's always a good idea to get a referral from a trusted friend or physician, but if you have to start fresh, here are a few good places to begin your search.

ACUPUNCTURE & ORIENTAL MEDICINE ASSOCIATION OF WASHINGTON: Most, though not all, acupuncture specialists belong to this professional organization. 329-9094, www.acupuncturewashington.org.

BASTYR CENTER FOR NATURAL HEALTH: Using health-care teams that include advanced students under the supervision of Bastyr University's clinical faculty, the center offers naturopathic medicine, homeopathy, acupuncture, Chinese herbal medicine, counseling, nutrition, and physical medicine. Community outreach projects include services for homeless youth, retirees, and people living with HIV/AIDS. 834-4100, www.bastyrcenter.org.

BRENNEKE SCHOOL OF MASSAGE: This long-established and highly regarded school offers low-cost massage through its outreach clinic. 282-1233 or 866-BRENNEKE, www.brennekeschool.com.

BRIAN UTTING SCHOOL OF MASSAGE: A school with a similar service as Brenneke. 292-8055 or 800-842-8731, www.busm.edu.

MIDWIFERY: Seattle is a national leader in natural childbirth—the movement even led local hospitals to add more appealing birthing centers, and some readily embrace midwifing services within the traditional birth wards. For those who wish to give birth at home, first consult your physician; then ask for references to midwives and doulas (birthing aides) they may have worked with. Or contact the Washington Association of Midwives, which maintains an extensive online catalog and information resource; 860-4120, www.washingtonmidwives.org. Seattle is also home to one of the leading midwifery schools in the country; 322-8834, seattlemidwifery.org.

NATURAL CHOICE DIRECTORY OF PUGET SOUND: Available in hard copy and online, the directory lists Puget Sound–area holistic health, fitness, and bodywork practitioners; natural food and remedy resources; and other health and spiritual services. 425-373-1987 or 800-465-0595, www.naturalchoice.net.

SEATTLE INSTITUTE OF ORIENTAL MEDICINE: This school offers low-cost acupuncture sessions performed by supervised student interns or teaching faculty with student assistants. 517-4541, www.siom.com.

WASHINGTON ASSOCIATION OF NATUROPATHIC PHYSICIANS: The group's Web site allows you to search for naturopaths by zip code, county, town, name, type of practice, or specialty. 547-2130, www.wanp.org.

WASHINGTON OSTEOPATHIC MEDICAL ASSOCIATION: Lists osteopaths by city and specialty. 937-5358, www.woma.org.

WASHINGTON STATE CHIROPRACTIC ASSOCIATION: Its Web site allows you to search its membership by city or name. 800-824-4918, www.chirohealth.org.

HIV/AIDS AND STD RESOURCES

King County has been at the forefront of the AIDS battle for two decades and remains so even as the epidemic shifts into a new phase. Though no longer quite as deadly, infection rates spiked in the late '90s and early 2000s, and new populations encountered significant incursions of the disease. The early part of the new millennium saw roughly 300 new cases, and 100 deaths, per year. The incidence among heterosexuals and women was growing. Overall, the public health department reports about 6,000 King County residents are living with HIV/AIDS, and the cumulative death total is 4,000.

Affected men still outnumber women 10 to 1, and whites outnumber nonwhites 5 to 1. Thus there has been a renewed emphasis on preventing the spread of the disease, accompanied by numerous controversies within the gay and public health communities on the best ways to do so. The battle is covered regularly in *The Stranger*.

AIDS CARE TEAM PROGRAM: A nonprofit organization that provides one-to-one emotional support, affordable low-income housing, and community reconciliation services for people living with HIV/AIDS. 324-1520, www.multifaith.org.

AIDS WALK: A yearly autumn fund-raiser sponsored by the Lifelong AIDS Alliance. 328-8979, www.llaa.org.

COUNTRY DOCTOR COMMUNITY CLINIC: This is a health organization that provides medical care, case management, and mental health and nutrition services for men, women, and children living with AIDS. It is a community organization that honors most insurance plans and will not turn someone away based on an inability to pay. 299-1600, www.wacmhc.org.

PLANNED PARENTHOOD (PP): An international organization with 10 health centers for women, men, and teenagers in King County. PP provides confidential and/or anonymous HIV/AIDS and STD testing, by appointment, for a fee ranging from $38 to $60. Also offers counseling and treatment. 328-7700 or 800-230-7626, www.ppww.org.

SEATTLE GAY CLINIC: Provides confidential and/or anonymous HIV/AIDS testing, counseling, and treatment. The clinic is open to everyone and the fee is an individual donation, but nobody will be turned away. 299-1623, www.seattlegayclinic.org.

STDS: King County Public Health is the prime provider for help with sexually transmitted diseases, including HIV/AIDS. Clinics provide confidential and/or anonymous testing by appointment and walk-in, if there is availability. Cost ranges from free to $46, depending on need and income status. 731-3590; STD hotline 205-7837; herpes 726-4478; www.metrokc.gov/health/apu/std.

Flame Out

According to the Public Health Department, 19 percent of adults in King County smoke, down from 25 percent in 1992. Telephone-based tobacco cessation programs are common these days, and for good reason—they work. The basic offering is phone counseling and support; the quit lines also arm their clients with "quit kits," information packets that help educate and motivate a smoker to quit.

The Washington State Department of Health sponsors the **TOBACCO QUIT LINE** (877-270-STOP, www.quitline.com) with funding from the settlement of a lawsuit against tobacco companies and from cigarette taxes. It is a free service available to all residents of Washington State. The state believes calling the Quit Line improves the success of quitters by almost 20 percent. Group Health Cooperative also operates a smoking quit line, **FREE & CLEAR,** at 800-292-2336, www.freeandclear.org.

King County's Tobacco Prevention Program works hard to encourage area restaurants to ban smoking, and it's working: About 70 percent are now smoke-free.

INSURANCE

The **WASHINGTON STATE INSURANCE COMMISSIONER'S** office is one of the nation's most vigorous consumer-advocacy regulators in its industry. Its progressive outlook was aptly represented by the commissioner's 2002 ruling that state health insurers must cover prescription contraceptives for women. In addition, Washington has stringent regulations on the preexisting condition bugaboo that so troubles consumers in other states: If you do not allow a gap of more than 63 days in coverage, nothing can be excluded. Even if there are coverage gaps beyond that, the maximum exclusion is nine months. The office's Web site has reams of information to help consumers navigate the insurance maze, and phone help lines offer easy access to experts. 360-725-7080 or 800-562-6900, www.insurance.wa.gov.

The state's insurance complaint hotline and health coverage help line are both reached through 800-562-6900.

Insurance Providers

DELTA DENTAL SERVICE/WASHINGTON DENTAL SERVICES: Provides coverage for dental care, usually provided through employers or other carriers such as Group Health; almost 2 million subscribers in Washington. 522-1300, www.deltadentalwa.com.

GROUP HEALTH COOPERATIVE (GHC): Group Health is both a health care and health insurance provider, and does offer individual policies (which have high deductibles and amount to stop-loss coverage). Coverage is offered by many employers, and GHC operates more than two dozen clinics in Western Washington, as well as covering numerous independent service providers. 888-901-4636 or 800-542-6312, www.ghc.org.

PREMERA BLUE CROSS: With more than 1 million subscribers, this is one of the major coverage providers in Washington (and Alaska). Premera offers classic health insurance with numerous refinement options, as well as preferred-provider coverage. The organization is a nonprofit but has been attempting to convert to a for-profit company; it is affiliated with 100 hospitals and 18,000 service providers in the state. Individual health plans are available. 800-722-2103, www.premera.com.

> ### Nothing's Certain But . . .
>
> Seattle area residents head for the pearly gates at slightly fewer than 2,000 per year, a rate that has grown apace with the population, but not faster than. Most people die of accidental or natural causes; the murder rate has been declining, with firearms deaths dropping even faster; and suicides and traffic deaths have remained constant (but are dropping as a percentage).
>
> If you want to bury yourself even deeper in mortality statistics, check out the King County Medical Examiners annual report at www.metrokc.gov/health/med_ex. The county is well ahead of the nation on infant mortality—4.5 deaths per 1,000 births, compared with 7 nationally. However, African Americans and Native American infants are twice as likely to suffer infant mortality as the rest of the county's population.

REGENCE BLUE SHIELD: This classic health insurance provider covers 22 counties in Washington, including all of Puget Sound. Individual health, dental, and vision coverage packages are available. 464-3600 or 888-344-8234, www.wa.regence.com.

WASHINGTON BASIC HEALTH PLAN: The state subsidizes health coverage for needy families meeting income qualification criteria, but there is a long waiting list. 800-826-2444, www.basichealth.hca.wa.gov.

WASHINGTON STATE HEALTH INSURANCE POOL: State regulation also requires that most people rejected for individual coverage be accepted into the state Health Insurance Pool, which provides basic health insurance. 800-877-5187, www.wship.org.

SUBSTANCE ABUSE

Having been forced to address several substance abuse crises—cocaine addiction in the '80s, heroin addiction in the '90s, and an ongoing community of alcoholics who flock to Seattle for the mild climate and forgiving social environment—Seattle has a well-developed community of care and treatment providers in the area of substance abuse. This tradition is nothing new: The Fremont group of Alcoholics Anonymous is one of the oldest and best known in the United States, and Milam Recovery Center has been a leader in residential drug and alcohol treatment for half a century.

For those who can't pay, Medicaid Programs and the Alcohol, Drug Abuse Treatment & Support Act (ADATSA) may cover treatment. To apply for these contact your local DSHS Community Service Office (see "Social & Community Services," page 299).

ADATSA: Provides assessment, screening, referral, and case-monitoring services for chemically dependent persons who have applied for assistance. 296-7604, www.metrokc.gov/dchs/mhd/adatsa/htm.

ALCOHOLICS ANONYMOUS (AA): The oldest, most successful self-help group of all, with millions of members living in recovery worldwide. 587-2838, seattleaa.org.

COMMUNITY PSYCHIATRIC CLINIC: 461-3614, www.cpcwa.org.

DUTCH SHISLER SOBERING CENTER: Provides transportation, sobering, and intensive case-management services to homeless chronic substance abusers. 205-1080, www.metrokc.gov/dchs/mhd/sobering.htm.

EMERGENCY SERVICES PATROL: Provides screening for publicly inebriated persons in the downtown Seattle area and transportation to appropriate service agencies. 205-1076, www.metrokc.gov/dchs/mhd/sobering.htm.

KING COUNTY MENTAL HEALTH, CHEMICAL ABUSE & DEPENDENCY SERVICES DIVISION: The overall umbrella agency within the county for mental health and substance abuse services. 296-5213, www.metrokc.gov/dchs/mhd.

LAKESIDE-MILAM RECOVERY CENTERS: One of the nation's oldest and most progressive drug and alcohol treatment centers, Milam focuses on nutrition and overall health as well as treating the disease of addiction. The residential adult program center is in Kirkland, the adolescent center is in Burien, and Lakeside Milam operates outpatient clinics in Auburn, Everett, Federal Way, Issaquah, Kirkland, North Seattle, Puyallup, downtown Seattle, South Seattle, and Tacoma. Waiting lists are often long for residential admission. 425-823-3116 or 800-231-4303, www.lakesidemilam.com.

NARCOTICS ANONYMOUS: Patterned after AA, but focused on nonalcohol drugs such as heroin, speed, and cocaine. 790-8888, www.seattlena.org.

OVEREATERS ANONYMOUS: Self-help for the obese. 264-5045, www.seattleoa.org.

RECOVERY CENTERS OF KING COUNTY: Umbrella organization for substance abuse treatment and detox centers. 322-2970; detox, 325-5000; www.rckc.org.

Several agencies will help clients through the process of obtaining drug/alcohol treatment, starting with public funding:

PEOPLE OF COLOR AGAINST AIDS NETWORK (POCAAN): 322-7061, www.pocaan.org.

SEATTLE INDIAN HEALTH BOARD: 324-9360, www.sihb.org.

STREET OUTREACH SERVICES: 625-0854, www.metrokc.gov/health/apu/resources.

Emergencies

Emergency help for substance abusers and their friends and family is available from the **ALCOHOL AND DRUG 24-HOUR HELPLINE** (722-3700 or 800-562-1240, www.adhl.org). For general, nonemergency problems or questions related to treatment services, call the **KING COUNTY CHEMICAL DEPENDENCY COORDINATOR** at 205-1312. **SEATTLE CRISIS CLINIC** (461-3222, www.crisisclinic.org) is the central resource for mental health emergencies, including substance abuse.

Involuntary Treatment

Involuntary treatment for substance abuse has been available since 1972, but it is neither emotionally nor legally simple or easy. Families resort to this extreme step only after private intervention and ordinary treatment have been to no avail. Over the years the rules have changed, most recently by limiting the criteria for those eligible for commitment. Even with the new, more stringent criteria (gravely disabled or posing the potential for harm to self, others, or property), the wait for treatment beds is long. King County competes with the other 38 counties in Washington for the few beds at Pioneer Center North. The involuntary commitment process takes three to four weeks. After that, the wait period for a bed can be quite lengthy, up to 90 days in some cases; call 296-7615.

The **MENTAL HEALTH COURT** (684-5600, www.cityofseattle.net/courts) offers specialized judicial services for patients, including provision of liaison professionals who help shepherd individuals through both court and treatment.

MENTAL HEALTH

Washington State's current public mental-health-care system took shape in 1995. What we have now is a state-funded, county-run, managed-care system in which the state gives money to the county for rendering Medicaid services. People without Medicaid either have to pay for treatment or in many cases go without.

There are 17 mental-health agencies in the King County system, many of which work with specific populations. To get help for yourself or someone close to you, contact your physician, the **CRISIS CLINIC** at 461-3222, or the **KING COUNTY MENTAL HEALTH PLAN (MHP)** at 800-790-8049. If you need care and have been told you are not eligible, you may call the MHP Client Services Coordinator at 800-790-8049 for help.

Service providers include:

COMMUNITY PSYCHIATRIC CLINIC: 461-3614, www.cpcwa.org

HARBORVIEW MENTAL HEALTH SERVICES: 731-3438, www.washington.edu/medical/hmc/services

HIGHLINE–WEST SEATTLE MENTAL HEALTH CENTER: 933-7000, www.highlinementalhealth.org

KING COUNTY MENTAL HEALTH, CHEMICAL ABUSE AND DEPENDENCY SERVICES DIVISION (see "Substance Abuse," above.)

SEATTLE COUNSELING SERVICE: 323-1768, www.seattlecounseling.org

SEATTLE CRISIS CLINIC: 461-3210 (crisis 461-3222), www.crisisclinic.org

SEATTLE MENTAL HEALTH: 302-2200, www.smh.org

STARS ALTERNATIVES: (Mental Health Ombudsman Service of King County), 205-5329, www.metrokc.gov/dchs/mhd/ombuds.htm.

VALLEY CITIES COUNSELING & CONSULTATION: Kent & Auburn, 253-833-7444, www.valleycities.com

SOCIAL & COMMUNITY SERVICES

As a progressive city that believes in people's well-being, the Seattle area has innumerable agencies, groups, and programs devoted to assisting its residents with life's problems. That's the good news. The challenge is navigating the huge landscape of service providers—the numbers are daunting, the various parameters and philosophies seemingly limitless, and the criteria sometimes remarkably arcane.

The best place to start is with the state government, which has taken seriously its responsibility to offer open access to everyone. The other major player is King County, which operates and supports numerous public and nonprofit programs. Rest assured that if you need help, you can find it—if you're willing to make a few phone calls or visit a few Web sites.

Department of Social & Health Services

The key provider of social services in the Seattle area is the state, through the Department of Social and Health Services. DSHS offers literally hundreds of types of aid, everything from adoption counseling to victim advocacy. The main contact location for the department is 800-737-0617 or www1.dshs.wa.gov. A comprehensive list of all available services—there are dozens of main headings—can be found at www1.dshs.wa.gov/basicneeds.

Community-service offices in King County are as follows:
Auburn: 253-804-5357
Ballard: 206-341-7424
Belltown: 206-341-7427
Capitol Hill: 206-341-7431
Eastside: 206-341-7404 or 800-662-6715
Federal Way: 206-341-7426
Rainier Valley: 206-341-7429
Renton: 206-341-7434
South King County: (Kent) 206-341-7428 or 800-422-7912
White Center: 206-341-7430

Other key DSHS contacts are:
Aging and disability services: 800-422-3263
Alcohol & substance abuse: 877-301-4557
Child and adult abuse hotline: 866-363-4276

Foster parent/adoptive services: 888-794-1794
Medical assistance: 800-562-3022
Mental health: 888-713-6010

> ## Numbers to Know
>
> The City of Seattle maintains a **COMMUNITY INFORMATION LINE** at 461-3200, and has links to dozens of resources at www.crisisclinic.org.
>
> **ACCESS WASHINGTON** is a comprehensive guide to state services for individuals. 877-265-6553, access.wa.gov.

Sexual Assault

King County has been a national leader in deterring sexual assault, helping its victims, and prosecuting offenders. Several local agencies have long experience and compassionate staffers to aid victims under these most traumatic circumstances. The central resource is the **KING COUNTY SEXUAL ASSAULT RESOURCE CENTER**, which maintains a hotline for aiding victims at 800-825-7273, and will otherwise offer advice, counseling, advocacy, and medical care assistance. 425-226-7273, www.kcsarc.org.

The **WASHINGTON STATE DOMESTIC ABUSE HOTLINE** is 800-562-6025; and the **DOMESTIC ABUSE WOMEN'S NETWORK** offers help with domestic assault, housing, and other needs through their crisis line at 425-656-7867. Lesbians, bisexuals, and transgendered individuals can find help at 568-7777. **HARBORVIEW HOSPITAL** operates one of the nation's leading sexual assault medical clinics. This is the place to go if you have been raped; you will receive medical care and counseling, and evidence will be taken for legal purposes. 521-1800, depts.washington.edu/hcsats.

PUBLIC HEALTH CLINICS

There are 16 King County clinics operated by the county's Department of Public Health, four in Seattle. Clinics are generally open 8am–5pm Monday to Friday, and offer services ranging from family planning to childhood immunizations to dental care (not all services are available at all clinics). Fees are based on ability to pay. 296-4600, www.metrokc.gov/health.

COUNSELING & OTHER SERVICES

ACLU (AMERICAN CIVIL LIBERTIES UNION): The prime organization for people with legal troubles of all sorts who don't qualify for public-defender assistance. 624-2180, www.aclu-wa.org.

DAWN (DOMESTIC ABUSE WOMEN'S NETWORK): This is the key umbrella organization for women in abusive situations, offering counseling, emergency aid, and referrals to shelters. 622-1881 or 425-656-4305; statewide domestic violence hotline 800-562-6025, www.dawnonline.org.

LUTHERAN COMMUNITY SERVICES (LCS): One of the largest faith-based assistance organizations in the Northwest, LCS offers adoption counseling, crisis intervention, transitional housing, multicultural outreach, and violence prevention, among other services. 694-5700, www.lcsnw.org.

YMCA: General housing, counseling, and other assistance for at-risk individuals. 382-5340, www.seattleymca.org.

YWCA: Counseling, assistance, and health education for 55,000 women and families a year. It focuses particularly on housing, work training, and violence prevention. 461-4888, www.ywcaworks.org.

CHARITABLE GIVING

COMMUNITY SERVICES FOR THE BLIND & PARTIALLY SIGHTED: This enterprising agency provides an estimable service for everyone, no matter what your vision is, because it will send a truck to your house to pick up donation items (usable, clean stuff only, please, such as small furniture, clothing, recreational equipment). It inaugurated an innovation worthy of a high-tech capital in 2004 with an online scheduling option for pickup: www.donatecsbps.org. To schedule by phone, 767-2177, www.csbps.com.

FOOD LIFELINE: Distributes food to food banks and meal programs. Volunteers and donations welcome. 1702 NE 150th St, 545-6600.

A Worldly City

Seattle residents born outside the U.S.: 104,000 (18%)
Seattle households in which a language other than English is spoken: 108,000 households (21%)
(Source: SEHC)

NORTHWEST HARVEST: This food-distribution program was developed in the 1970s and now operates statewide, serving 16 million pounds of food a year through community hunger programs and relief missions. Most-needed items include baby food (jars and formula), milk, canned fruits and vegetables, canned meat, pasta, and prepackaged meals and soups. 625-0755, www.northwestharvest.org.

THE SEATTLE FOUNDATION (TSF): This foundation administers philanthropic funds for families and individuals (and has its own hefty endowment). You can set up the John and Jane Doe Family Fund to benefit Northwest leash-free dog run projects; TSF will administer it for you and distribute annual grants to worthy parks agencies. Overall, the foundation administers 1,300 funds with assets totaling $350 million; at 2 percent its administrative costs are remarkably low, much more so than any individual foundation is likely to achieve. 622-2294, www.seattlefoundation.org.

UNITED WAY: King County's United Way raises more than $90 million, which it distributes to agencies of all descriptions throughout the county. It is also the prime volunteer-coordination agency, helping place more than 20,000 volunteers a year. Its particular focus is on helping homeless families and improving education. 461-3700, www.uwkc.org.

ETHNIC DIVERSITY

It's worth remembering that the original inhabitants of Puget Sound, Coast Salish Indians, belonged to one of the oldest and most advanced Native societies in North America. Relying on salmon and cedar as the foundations of their lives, they created economically and culturally prosperous societies whose rich traditions of storytelling, dance, and song remain vital and relevant today.

The many succeeding waves of immigrants—American and European trappers, loggers, and farmers; Chinese labor-

Nickeled and Dimed

Seattle is a national panhandling capital, despite the fact that a city ordinance bars aggressive solicitation. (Panhandlers cannot block your way, or approach you, or push their desires on you in any way.) Our mild climate draws transients, as does the city's relatively lax attitude on begging and alcohol abuse. (Until the late '90s chronic alcoholics were entitled to support checks from city coffers.) Enough visitors and residents hand over their quarters to keep the trade thriving. The city actively discourages it, as do most experienced downtown workers and visitors.

---

ers; Japanese and Hispanic workers; Southeast Asian, Russian, and East European refugees—have all added their own considerable flavors to the Seattle metro cultural ferment. The **SEATTLE ETHNIC HERITAGE COUNCIL** (443-1410, www.ethnicheritagecouncil.org) tracks more than 100 separate ethnic groups and estimates there are more than 1,000 organizations and associations around Puget Sound devoted to their cultures and needs. It publishes a comprehensive directory covering all such organizations.

ASIAN COUNSELING AND REFERRAL SERVICE: Guidance for those of Asian heritage in gaining legal, medical, social services, and other assistance. 695-7600, www.acrs.org.

EL CENTRO DE LA RAZA: The prime cultural and social services organization for Hispanics and Latinos in the Seattle area. 329-9442, www.elcentrodelaraza.com.

NAACP: Seattle's chapter of the country's largest civil rights group dates back to 1913. 324-6600, www.scn.org/naacp.

NORDIC HERITAGE MUSEUM: See Chapter 1, "Seattle Neighborhoods," page 5.

SEATTLE CELTIC HERITAGE SOCIETY: Umbrella organization for people of Celtic descent. www.auldk.addr.com/schf.

UNITED INDIANS OF ALL TRIBES: The umbrella group for Native Americans in Seattle is based at the Daybreak Star Cultural Center in Discovery Park. It serves more than 25,000 Indians in the Seattle area. 285-4425, www.unitedindians.com.

URBAN LEAGUE: Seattle's chapter focuses on promoting self-sufficiency for inner-city peoples. 461-3792, www.urbanleague.org.

WASHINGTON STATE DIVERSITY NETWORK: Focused on promoting workforce diversity, this group links big and small businesses, ethnic organizations, government agencies, and community groups of all types. www.scn.org/civic/diversity.

WING LUKE ASIAN MUSEUM: See Chapter 1, "Seattle Neighborhoods," page 59.

CHAPTER 12

Weather Wise

Seattle weather is, in a word, legendary. It's not only much-discussed and distinctive—it's also subject to myths.

Myth No. 1: It rains all the time. Hardly: On average there are 154 days a year with measurable precipitation. That's a lot, but it's not even half.

Myth No. 2: It's rainy all year. In fact, the summer months are as dry as almost anywhere in the United States—some years, less than an inch of rain falls in June, July, and August.

Myth No. 3: It gets no snow. True, there is on average less than a foot of snow a year, and most of that is usually washed away soon by rain. But an occasional heavy snow does tie the city in knots, and even the threat of snow causes a fascinating cultural phenomenon: "storm watch" hysteria on local TV and preparations so extreme that school is sometimes canceled on the basis of a forecast.

Myth No. 4: It's a mild climate. That depends on your definition of mild. The Seattle area is not generally subject to wild extremes of heat, cold, rain, or wind—but "mild" is not the word that comes to mind when you're trudging First Avenue on a late November day, head burrowed into your collar, your umbrella blown apart, sideways rain stinging your nose, the temperature a sharp 39 degrees.

Technically, the term most often applied to the Seattle climate is maritime, a distinction it shares with coastal British Columbia (BC), Britain, and parts of northern Europe, plus some of North Pacific Asia.

Though Seattle is farther north (47 degrees latitude) than Fargo, North Dakota, we don't share the cold winters, hot summers, or flat topography of that city. The Puget Sound area has more in common with coastal Northern California or Southern Alaska than it does with neighboring Eastern Washington. The key weather determinants are the Pacific Ocean, which sends storms our way; Puget Sound, which moderates temperatures; the Cascade and Olympic Mountains, which hold clouds within the Puget Sound basin; and the Cascades and interior ranges up in BC, which block the arctic air masses that bring wintry weather into the rest of the United States far south of Seattle's latitude.

Weather Axioms

- Summer in Seattle begins July 5.
- If there's a cap on Mount Rainier, rain is coming.
- Buttermilk clouds mean rain is imminent.
- Fog will close Sea-Tac airport sometime during the Christmas/New Year holiday.

For those who don't mind rain and clouds, Seattle weather is nearly perfect. Our summers are sunny and dry but relatively mild, moderated by breezes from the Puget Sound and the Pacific Ocean, and the temperature rarely surpasses 90 degrees. Between October and March the area is cloudy and cool without being too cold—it rarely drops below 28 or so. (That's why you can grow palm trees in protected locations.)

So in comparison to Fargo and Boston and even Forks, Washington, we have a mild climate. Best to keep in mind that it's also temperamental, though. Seattle weather is often assertive, and that's what gives the weather around here character.

MILD-MANNERED AND PLEASANT

Seattle's first entry in the U.S. Weather Bureau log read, "May 1, 1893: Cloudy but pleasant with light to fresh southerly winds." That could apply to many local forecasts since then. Winds average around 8 mph, enough to be felt, yet without being a nuisance. We can go many days without clouds in the summer, or without sun in the winter, but otherwise Seattle weather runs along fairly predictable lines: some variant of "partly cloudy" with moderately cold to moderately warm temperatures.

Yet, paradoxically, the exact weather can be surprisingly difficult to predict. Forecasters in Western Washington have a harder time of it than their brethren in other parts of the country. The lack of weather stations in the Pacific Ocean makes it difficult to get details about incoming formations (although we are able to fill in the gaps with data from ships, buoys, and satellites). To add to the confusion, anything coming in to Seattle from the ocean has to go around or over the Olympics and the Sound—both of which can influence the weather in some way. It takes considerable savvy to interpret the satellite images and computer forecasts. That's why the forecasts rendered by experienced local meteorologists, such as the veterans at Seattle's three major TV stations, are usually better than those offered by distant entities such as Internet sites and New York–based network forecasters.

JUST THE FACTS

Statistics don't tell the whole story about anything. But the charts below depict Seattle's climate in cold, hard (maybe we should say "mild, wet") numbers.

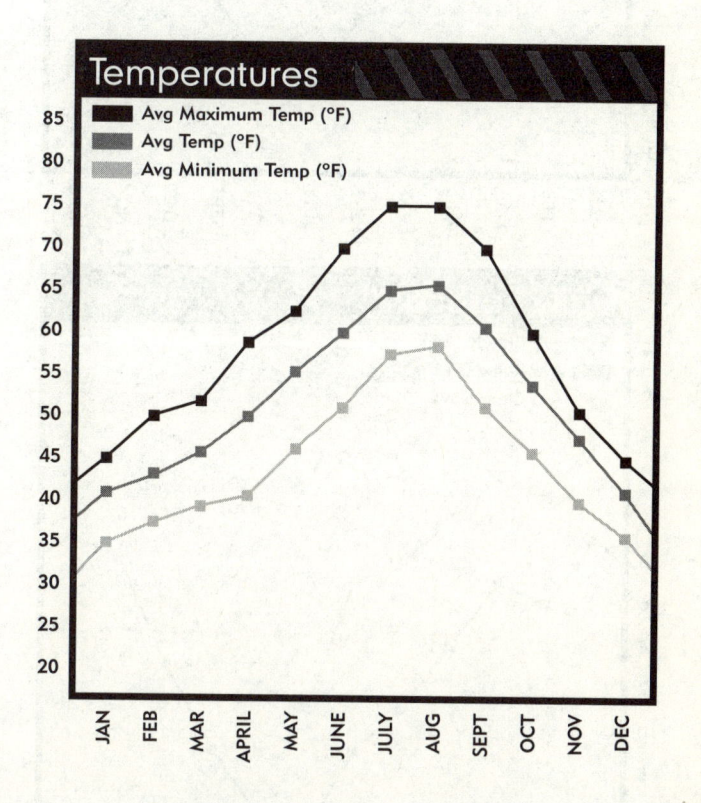

Temperatures

- Avg Maximum Temp (°F)
- Avg Temp (°F)
- Avg Minimum Temp (°F)

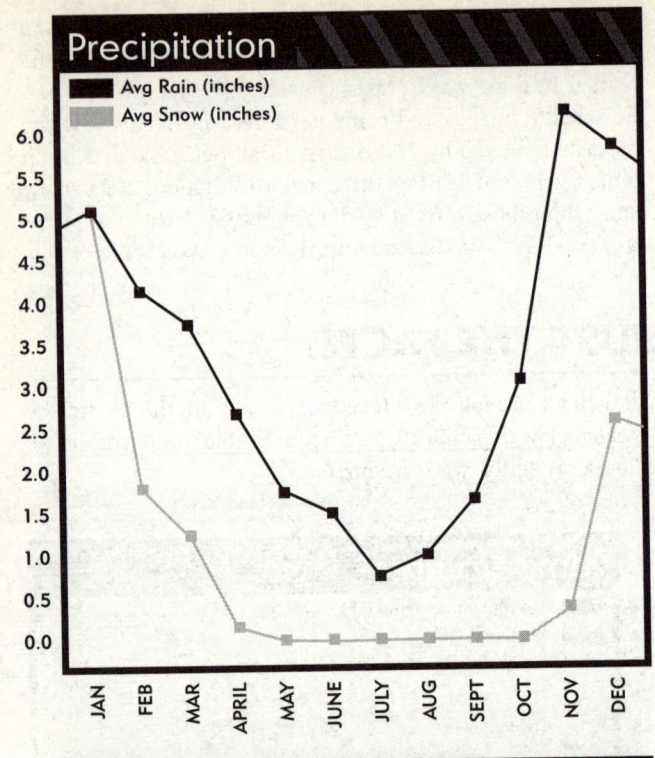

Precipitation

- Avg Rain (inches)
- Avg Snow (inches)

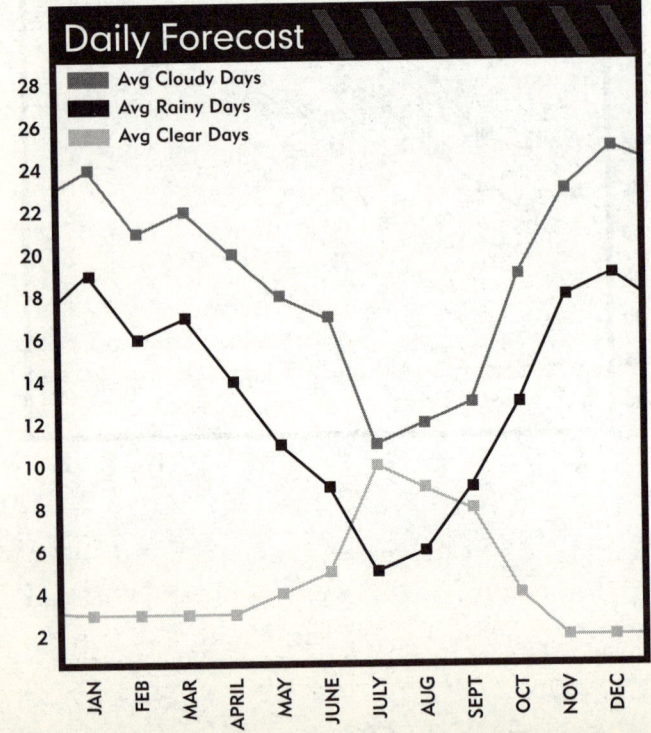

Daily Forecast

- Avg Cloudy Days
- Avg Rainy Days
- Avg Clear Days

308 | Seattle Survival Guide | Chapter 12

PUGET SOUND CONVERGENCE ZONE

You've seen those cartoons where a character in a bad mood grows his own personal thunderhead, a dark cloud that rains only on him? The Puget Sound convergence zone is the metro area's version of that. Incoming fronts off the Pacific Ocean collide with the Olympic Mountains and are deflected to the north and south. The air currents meet again in the Puget Sound basin, where the unstable convergence forms clouds and rain. The result is a strip of bad weather about 10 or 15 miles wide, with calmer, drier weather on either side. The convergence zone is difficult to predict, but it most often forms between Seattle and Everett. That's why you can leave Seattle on a fine day with fair skies, head north on I-5, drive into rain at Lynnwood, and drive back into clear weather once you're past Marysville. The phenomenon occurs 10 to 25 times per year.

THE MARINE PUSH

During the late spring, summer, and early fall, Seattle days often begin with a low blanket of clouds, which the sun burns off by afternoon. This is caused by a movement of cool marine air from high-pressure areas offshore toward warmer, low-pressure areas on land (Eastern Washington or Seattle itself). The marine air arrives from the coast late at night, bringing clouds and fog with it. Sometimes the marine air arrives after dawn, providing the odd circumstance of a sunny sunrise followed by a foggy morning followed by a sunny afternoon with temperatures climbing to the 70s or even 80s. Sometimes there are entire days with cloud cover, drizzle, and temperatures in the 50s and 60s. The same phenomenon causes San Francisco's famously foggy summers—marine air is sucked through the Golden Gate by the low pressure in the hot Central Valley.

MOUNTAINS OF RAIN

When moving air hits a hill or mountain and rises, its temperature drops and water vapor precipitates out in the form of clouds and rain. This can create a "rain shadow" effect on the opposite side of the hill or mountain where the air warms

Shades Yes, 'Shoots No

It's against the code to use an umbrella if you are a real Seattleite. It's also not very practical—rain is usually accompanied by gusty south winds that can make short work of the average brolly. (Thus the sculpture of the blown-apart bumbershoot on Western Avenue at the south end of Pike Place Market.) If there's even a glimmer of solar light on the horizon, put on your shades, dude, it's bright out. It's long been rumored that Seattle leads the nation in sunglasses sales—an odd fact for a city with just 58 clear days a year!

---

as it descends, releasing little or no precipitation. Locally, our most spectacular rain shadow is created by the Olympic Mountains: West- and south-facing portions of the Olympic Peninsula receive close to 200 inches of rain per year, yet the city of Sequim on the northeast side of the mountains averages about 16. There aren't any contrasts that striking within the city itself, but our hills do cause some neighborhood variation in rainfall. And the same phenomenon occurs as you approach the Cascades: The Snoqualmie Valley gets more rain than Seattle, and by the time you get out to North Bend, it's temperate rainforest, with almost 90 inches of rain a year.

TEMPERATURE TEMPERANCE

While Puget Sound moderates the temperature of the whole city, its influence is particularly strong on the neighborhoods nearest to it. This can mean the difference between rain in Ballard and snow on Capitol Hill, or a cool summer breeze in Alki versus hot, still air in the U-District. Also, all the concrete in downtown Seattle tends to retain heat, making it consistently warmer than more residential areas by 1 to 3 degrees.

Still, the city's seasons are quite moderate; the average summer temperature is only about 25 degrees higher than the average winter temperature. Seattle's coldest day, on January 31, 1950, was 0 degrees; its hottest, on July 20, 1994, was 100 degrees—hardly impressive to those from more extreme climes. Even San Francisco has been hotter, at 101. A more typical continental range is posed by Spokane, with records of 108 and minus 30. And with average first and last frosts of November 11 and March 24, respectively, the growing season is longer than most places this far north.

If the climate is really so mild in the Puget Sound area, why do Seattleites complain about heat in the summer and cold in the winter? Everything's relative, isn't it: If the average you're used to is 70 degrees (95 days a year), then when it hits 90 (two days a year, on average) it seems suffocating by comparison.

RAIN CITY

The truth about our legendary rain is that there isn't an excessive amount of it. Seattle receives about 38 inches of precipitation a year, which is a good amount, but less than New York City (42 inches) or Miami (56 inches). Perhaps our reputation is based on the frequency of rainfall? More likely: The city averages 154 days with precipitation a year, though often that "rain" is in the form of a short, soft drizzle. If anything, we should be known for our overcast skies. They are cloudy or partly cloudy more than 300 days of the year.

Most of the remaining 58 clear days are concentrated in the "dog days" of summer between July and August. The term refers to a period of four to six weeks when Sirius, the Dog Star, rises with the sun. Ancient astronomers believed this event heralded a time of madness, plagues, and drought. They got at least one of those right: In July the month's rainfall usually averages less than an inch. In July 2003 it was less than one-tenth of an inch! The last week of July and the first week of August traditionally make up the driest part of the year, which makes this a popular time for outdoor events. The average chance of rain those two weeks is less than 10 percent. By

For the Record

Coldest day: 0 degrees, Jan 31, 1950

Hottest day: 100 degrees, July 20, 1994

Highest wind: 64 mph, Jan 7, 1993

Worst fog: 13 days (at Sea-Tac airport), Dec 16–28, 1985

Greatest single-day rain: 5.02 inches, Oct 20, 2003

Longest drought: 51 days, summer of 1951

(Source: National Weather Service)

contrast, the long-term rainiest day is November 19, with a 60 percent chance of rain.

Seattle summers overall are dry—in June, July, and August the average rainfall is just over 3 inches, and two recent summers, 1987 and 2003, brought less than an inch of rain from June 1 to August 31. (Oddly enough, the Fourth of July is a notable exception; that holiday has been cursed with rain 32 times in the past 110 years.)

Excesses of rain can be hazardous, too. Landslides are a common problem in the Puget Sound area, usually happening between Thanksgiving and Valentine's Day. They're commonly triggered by heavy, persistent rain falling on ground that's already saturated with moisture from the winter. The last serious landslides in the city occurred early in 1997, after near-record Christmas snowfall, followed by an ice storm, followed by rain. Seattle experienced more than 100 landslides that year, many of them in West Seattle and Magnolia. The landslides caused millions of dollars in property damage, derailed a freight train, and killed a Bainbridge Island family whose house washed into the Sound.

Although Seattle's rainiest season is November to February, the single-day greatest rainfall was October 20, 2003, with 5.02 inches.

Learn the Lingo

BLACK ICE: A thin, hard-to-see layer of frozen rain or frost on asphalt.

CAP CLOUD: A mushroom cap–shaped cirrus cloud that forms atop Mount Rainier. It often signifies moisture in the upper-level jet stream, and that signifies an approaching Pacific weather front.

MARINE LAYER: A thin layer of clouds caused by air from the Pacific that drifts into the Puget Sound basin overnight. It often extends no more than a few thousand feet, leading to the odd fact that the weather is nicer on Mount Rainier than in Seattle.

PINEAPPLE EXPRESS: A flow of moisture from the Hawaiian Islands to the Northwest that brings heavy rains.

> **GONE BUT NOT FORGOTTEN**
>
> ## Galloping Gertie
>
> In a 1940 windstorm the Tacoma Narrows Bridge, instantly nicknamed "Galloping Gertie," shimmied and stretched like a rubber band for some 30 minutes before its center section finally fell into the Sound, an event captured on film that has been replayed countless times. The problem was the span design, which was just the right length and shape to be set vibrating like a clarinet reed. It was rebuilt in a different configuration.
>
> Western Washington bridges have not fared well in windstorms. A 1979 tempest destroyed the Hood Canal floating bridge. And a 1995 storm sank the I-90 floating bridge over Lake Washington. Both were rebuilt, supposedly more stormproof.

THE WINTER BLUES

Around mid-January, when it seems like it's been 20 days or so since the sun last showed its face (and often enough, it has been—November and December average just two clear days each, and January only three), people get bummed out. Some are tired of not being able to do much outdoors; some are just fed up with seeing gray every time they look up. Some, however, suffer from a fairly common biopsychological affliction known as **SEASONAL AFFECTIVE DISORDER (SAD)**.

SAD is a form of depression that begins in fall or winter and remits in spring or summer. Its incidence varies with latitude. University of Washington professor Dr. David Avery estimates that 10 percent of the population of Seattle suffers from SAD, with another 20 percent having a milder form he calls the "winter blues." Symptoms of SAD include the usual symptoms of depression—lethargy, hopelessness, social withdrawal, and so forth—but with an emphasis on weight gain, oversleeping, and, strangely, carbohydrate craving. (Apparently, carbohydrate consumption increases the release of serotonin, a neurotransmitter that is vital for regulating a person's mood.)

Since lack of light is a key factor in the onset of SAD (there are just 8.5 hours of daylight per day in mid-December), treatments for the disorder generally revolve around exposing the

The Wappler Dynasty

Newly arrived from Chicago to escape ragweed pollen, Harry Wappler took up weathercasting for KIRO television in 1970. Except for a short stint in New York from 1972 to 1975 ("I thought KIRO was a zoo until I went to New York,"), he held sway as the dean of Seattle weather forecasters until his May 2002 retirement. Wappler was noted for his genial personality and accurate forecasts.

His son, Andy Wappler, succeeded him as KIRO's chief meteorologist in September 2002. Andy Wappler is known for the same sunny disposition before the camera that characterized his dad. And you thought dynasties were limited to royalty and privately held companies.

---

patient to more light—usually a much stronger source than ordinary household light. The National Organization for Seasonal Affective Disorder recommends spending time in front of a specially designed light box, or waking up with a "dawn simulator," which gradually increases the light in peoples' rooms as they sleep. Daily exposure to as much sunlight as possible is also helpful.

STORMY WEATHER

You know those movies set in Seattle that feature booming thunder and sheets of rain? Ah, Hollywood. Thunderstorms are an atypical weather phenomenon here: We only get about seven per year, in contrast to thunderstruck places like Colorado Springs (56) or the national champion, Cimarron, New Mexico (110). The only major city with fewer thunderstorms a year is San Francisco, with just two. The clash of cold and warm air needed for thunderstorms just doesn't happen here, primarily because of the Pacific Ocean's moderating influence. Tornadoes are rare for the same reason. We don't even get hurricanes; they require ocean temperatures in the upper 70s, and the northern Pacific usually falls about 20 degrees shy of that.

This doesn't mean we escape roaring tempests, however. Every now and then we get cyclonic windstorms that rival hurricanes for sheer force. The most famous of these was the 1962 Columbus Day storm, which caused property damage all along the West Coast, leveled billions of board feet of timber, killed 46 people, and hit the Seattle area with sustained wind speeds of 85 mph. That storm was actually the remnant of a western Pacific hurricane, Freda, that crossed the entire ocean and roared back onshore in Oregon and Washington. More recently, the Inauguration Day storm of 1993 destroyed 79 homes and knocked out power to hundreds of thousands more, with wind gusts up to 74 mph.

DREAMING OF A WET CHRISTMAS

The winter temperature in Seattle tends to hover between 40 degrees and the freezing point rather than drop below it, and this is a mixed blessing. On the one hand, snow and ice are rare. On the other hand, the shifts between freezing and melting can make black ice a problem. Black ice is a transparent film of frozen water that takes on the color of the material on which it forms. Typically, moisture freezes on a roadway, melts, and freezes again. Unbeknownst to a traveler, the road then becomes treacherously slick—and the ice is practically invisible, as it transmits the color of the pavement beneath.

Anyone who dreams of spending Christmas surrounded by blankets of soft, fluffy snow will be disappointed here. Seattle gets less snow—an average of only 11 to 12 inches per

Weather Resources

If you have further questions about weather, the local TV stations are great places to start. KOMO's "Ask Steve" features explain a number of our more mysterious local phenomena (KOMO TV: www.komotv.com/weather), and Andy Wappler's weather quizzes on the KIRO site are great (KIRO-TV: www.kirotv.com/weather).

For a detailed, easily digestible source of data on Seattle's weather patterns over the past five years, see BeautifulSeattle.com: www.beautifulseattle.com/clisea.htm.

For an archive of the Pacific Northwest's major storms over the last hundred years, see the Storm King at oregonstate.edu/~readw/index.html. Entertaining, informative, and scary.

But Who's Counting?

Average annual number of days with rain: 154

Average annual number of cloudy days: 226

Average annual number of clear days: 58

Average annual snowfall, in inches: 11.7

---

year—than any city eastward on the continent with the same latitude. And when we do get it, it's relatively warm, contains more than the usual amount of moisture, and often doesn't stick. It compacts easily, which makes it ideal for snowballs but tough for skiing.

Seattle also has "graupel," which looks like a cross between snow and hail, but is really a bunch of crumbly snow pellets ranging in size from buckshot to small peas.

Snowstorms aren't usually a problem around here, but the occasional doozy can wreak havoc. During the "Big Snow" of 1880, still regarded by many as Seattle's greatest snowstorm, some 40 inches covered the city—and because the snow we get is wet and heavy, a lot of roofs collapsed. More recently, in December 1996 a three-day snowstorm closed bridges and highways, disrupted air traffic and garbage service, and severed power lines. When a heavy rain came down on top of the snow days later, the accumulated weight of water and snow damaged roofs, collapsed garages and marinas, sank some 270 boats in Edmonds, and contributed to landslides and flooding less than a week later.

Not surprisingly, a year after that storm, the city increased its available snowplows from 11 to 18 and began using de-icing products on roads. However, preparing for snowstorms is still a difficult task in Seattle; it's hard to practice dealing with something that doesn't often happen. (Compare the snow-laden city of Minneapolis, for instance, which has up to 100 snowplows available for emergencies.) The Seattle Emergency Management Office recommends being "prepared to take care of [your] emergency needs for two or more days while the City and other agencies work to provide assistance." We'd like to add this advice for drivers: Slow down and be prepared to stop. It seems obvious, but remember that you'll be sharing the road with people who probably don't have much practice driving on snow and ice.

CHAPTER 13

Mother Nature

Few, if any, U.S. cities enjoy the splendid natural environment that Seattle does. Sure, other cities have mountain backdrops. Others lie beside sparkling ocean waters and are brushed by fresh breezes. Still others have mild, bountiful climates. But no other city has all that, along with bookend snow-draped volcanic cones, vast clean lakes fed by mountain waters, burbling rivers, and a landscape so green our nickname is the "Emerald City."

Seattle residents are the only U.S. urban denizens with a chance to watch some of the world's most charismatic wild creatures—eagles and orcas—go by. No other residents of a major metropolitan area can make day trips to three of the best known, largest, and most impressive national parks. Salmon still run our rivers, though woefully diminished, and a few of the fish sold in local markets still come from nearby waters. Seattle gardens thrive—12 months a year, for those who make the effort—with everything from subtropical to alpine species.

But it would be a mistake to say all is well. The keys to it all, Puget Sound and the Olympic and Cascade ranges, have been severely depleted by human activity. The water we draw from our taps—the cleanest in the country—is so overdrawn in drought years that rationing is needed. The magnificent forests that sheltered, clothed, and fed the original inhabitants are for all practical purposes gone, and Seattle residents have to drive many miles to see large remnants. The salmon runs that once thronged local inlets so thick that pioneers claimed they could walk across on the backs of fish—gone.

More than almost any other city, Seattleites revere and embrace the natural environment we inhabit. And perhaps more than any other city, too, we are our home's own worst enemies. "Man did not weave the web of life," Chief Seatlh supposedly warned. "He is merely a strand in it. Whatever he does to the web he does to himself." No matter who said it, the wind still echoes the words in the fronds of cedar and fir.

PUGET SOUND

The centerpiece of the Puget Sound region is one of the largest inland seas on earth, an ecological marvel as vital and delicate as Chesapeake Bay. The entire basin (the Sound and its watersheds) encompasses 10,000 square miles; the Sound itself has a surface area of 786 square nautical miles, framed by 2,000 miles of shoreline.

The deepest point is 930 feet, at Point Jefferson just north of Seattle; the average depth is 205 feet. The volume of water is so huge in the Sound that, despite the fact it receives 140 billion cubic feet of freshwater a year, it is not noticeably less saline than the ocean itself. Tidal flux provides constant mixing; the average daily range is 11.3 feet, and the maximum is more than 15 feet. That helps ensure the water temperature stays in a narrow range: in most places between 48 and 56 degrees.

The Sound is an uncommonly rich and diverse inland sea. Its inhabitants range from tiny ghost shrimp to the world's largest octopus and the world's largest mammals, whales. It contains a wealth of fish and shellfish, and there are hundreds of miles of beaches to roam.

And . . . it's in trouble.

It's not as beleaguered by human activity as San Francisco Bay, but it could be a half-century from now. A few facts, from People for Puget Sound:

- More than 90,000 acres of the Sound's seafloor are contaminated by toxic chemicals.

- Millions of gallons of sewage still pour into the Sound every time it rains.

- Salmon, pollock, rockfish, and cod have all declined from historical abundance to levels approaching extinction in some areas.

- PCB contamination is nine times higher in Puget Sound than in San Francisco Bay and has reached dangerous levels in salmon in Elliott Bay.

- The Sound's resident native orcas, about 100 animals in three pods, have declined 20 percent since the mid-'90s. PCBs, loss of salmon runs, and disturbance by boat traffic (particularly whale-watching) are suspected as causes.

Simple Ways to Save the Sound

1. Don't use lawn and garden pesticides and chemical fertilizers. They wind up in the Sound.

2. Compost yard and garden waste.

3. Water your lawn sparingly, if at all. The grass will not die (it goes dormant in summer), and most Puget Sound city water comes from salmon-spawning streams.

4. Turn off the lights and turn down the heat. Air-conditioning is ridiculous in Northwest homes; we live in one of the mildest climates on earth.

5. Pave as little as possible. Every new square foot of impermeable surface washes urban runoff into the Sound.

6. Discard all chemical waste and garbage—motor oil, paint, turpentine, batteries—at city or county hazardous waste facilities; www.govlink.org/hazwaste/.

7. Use energy-efficient appliances. Both the city and county have programs supporting their purchase; www.pse.com/yourhome/rebates/index.html.

8. Do your whale-watching from shore.

9. Visit a beach and pick up trash, especially plastic.

10. Vote for new waste-treatment facilities and sewer expansions.

11. Reduce, reuse, recycle: Resource use consumes trees, water (for electricity), and other natural elements.

12. Walk, bike, carpool, take the bus: Reducing vehicle use reduces contamination of the Sound.

Washington State and Canada have asked for federal protection for them, but the other Washington has said no.

The Sound is the focus of a large, dynamic, and thoughtful citizen advocacy organization, which lobbies for its protection, conducts volunteer conservation activities such as beach cleanups, and offers environmental and natural history education events. Its cruises and beachwalks are both fun and eye-opening. People for Puget Sound, 382-7007, www.pugetsound.org.

Oil Spills

Though most people think of the open ocean as the province of oil tankers, both petroleum ships and fuel barges ply Puget Sound every day. Furthermore, large ships of all sorts use bunker fuel to fire their engines—and periodically, some of this escapes confinement. The consequences can be severe: A 1,000-gallon oil spill in 2004 fouled 21 miles of beach in South Puget Sound, mostly along Vashon Island. That spill was first reported by area residents who noticed the contamination and performed a good deed for all of us. The sooner a spill is reported (as in that case, the miscreants are unlikely to do it) the more likely the damage can be contained; the state's oil spill hotline is 800-424-8802.

A worthy organization called **PUGET SOUNDKEEPER ALLIANCE** actively monitors water quality and pollution sources in our area. (Companies and individuals still do dump waste and toxic chemicals in the Sound.) In addition to regular patrols, the group also trains citizens to report polluters and participate in cleanup days. 800-42PUGET or 297-7002, www.pugetsoundkeeper.org.

GO AHEAD, BREATHE THE AIR

Puget Sound air quality has been improving steadily since the early '80s, and now has reached the point that there were only two days of unhealthy air in 2003, and none in the "very unhealthy" range since 1986. Carbon monoxide, the most troublesome (and unhealthiest) pollutant, has decreased to the point that it is the leading problem less than one week a year, compared to 35 weeks in 1980.

It would be nice for our community to claim credit for this improvement (and vehicle inspections have helped), but scientists say the greatest benefit has been gained by national standards regulating new car emissions. Today the most significant problems are ozone buildups during hot, stagnant summer days, and particulates (smoke and dust) in wintertime temperature inversions. More information is available from the **PUGET SOUND CLEAN AIR AGENCY (PSCAA)**, 343-8800 or 800-552-3565, www.pscleanair.org.

Burn Bans

Thus the most significant aspect of clean air maintenance in Puget Sound: burn bans. There are two facets:

OUTDOOR BURNING is prohibited in urban and exurban areas. You can't burn garbage, yard waste, brush, and all other detritus. Period. This regulation scotched the old Western Washington habit of piling up excess shrubbery, greens, and such and incinerating it, a spring tradition that was interrupted by a mid-'80s federal study showing the famous Puget Sound haze was not humidity but smoke. If you must burn outdoors, you have to 1) live in the country, and 2) get a burn permit from the local fire department.

INDOOR BURNING is subject to burn bans whenever air quality trouble demands it. There are two stages: Stage 1, residents may not use uncertified woodstoves and fireplaces unless that is their only source of heat; Stage 2, no woodstoves may be used at all, unless it is the only source of heat. Burn bans are widely reported on radio and TV outlets; any time the weather is still and cold, one is likely. You can check on ban status at 800-595-4341.

Most people observe burn bans. Those who don't can be reported, in writing, using forms available from PSCAA. Other polluters—industrial and commercial—can be reported to the agency, which will investigate immediately; 343-8800 or 800-552-3565.

Numerous local agencies offer assistance, including financial, in converting fireplaces and woodstoves to natural gas. If you still want to burn wood, modern certified woodstoves are fairly clean, and are all that can be sold in Western Washington. They are also far more fuel efficient, if heating is your goal. The warmth and comfort of a flickering fire is undeniably appealing—but clean air is not only appealing, it's essential.

CASCADES & OLYMPICS

The two mountain ranges that flank Seattle and Puget Sound are visual, geographic, and climatic daily presences even when you can't see them, which is often, because they hold in cloud banks. Both ranges were once clothed, toe to timberline, in almost unbroken old-growth forests of Douglas fir, western red cedar, and western hemlock, with bigleaf maple, red alder, madrona, and willows the deciduous trees found along riverways, in burn zones, and other disturbed areas. Timberline is at 6,000 feet or so, glaciers abound (25 on Mount Rainier alone), and the melting snow that pours down the west slope of the Cascades is, among other things, the source of much of Western Washington's water supply.

Nearly all the lowland old-growth forest was logged long ago; much of the private land between the Sound and mountains is managed as timberland, with trees (mostly Doug fir) grown for a half-century or so and then harvested. Ironically, one of the biggest threats to timber growth is not logging but urban development.

Much of the Cascade and Olympic high country is national forest, and a fair portion of that is wilderness (thank former Senators Henry Jackson and Warren Magnuson for that). The centerpieces are three of the country's finest national parks, each accessible by day trip (OK, *long* day trip) from Seattle.

MOUNT RAINIER NATIONAL PARK: Roughly two hours southeast of Seattle, this is the highest volcano in the Lower 48 and the fifth-highest peak overall, at 14,410 feet. Rainier has cathedral-like old-growth forests, alpine meadows strewn with flowers, glistening sapphire lakes, and glaciers and ice fields looming above. Most people first visit Longmire and Paradise on the southwest side, but Sunrise, on the southeast flank, is often rated the best spot. The two lodges (Paradise is open only in summer) are historic landmarks. 360-569-2211, www.nps.gov/mora.

OLYMPIC NATIONAL PARK: This huge park encompasses most of the heart of the Olympic Peninsula, and most of that is wilderness—some of the longest wilderness hikes possible in the Lower 48 are treks up one of the park's river valleys, across an alpine pass, and down into yet another long river valley. The park is famed for its west-side rain forests—particularly the Hoh and Quinault River Valleys—but there are about a dozen other roads penetrating partway into the forest fastness, plus two alpine drives. Hurricane Ridge is the best known of the latter; from on top the views north across the Strait of Juan de Fuca and south into the mountains are sensational. 360-565-3131, www.nps.gov/olym.

Cascades Volcano Observatory

U.S. Geological Survey's current reports about volcano hazards and instructions on what to do during ashfall can be found at vulcan.wr.usgs.gov/.

GONE BUT NOT FORGOTTEN

Mount St. Helens

Until May 18, 1980, this Cascade volcano south of Seattle topped out at 9,677 feet. That morning, a months long series of rumblings, swellings, steam vents, and earthquakes culminated in an explosion that blew the upper cone off, leaving the mountain at 8,363 feet. The eruption devastated 250 square miles, blew down 4 billion board feet of timber, and spread an ash cloud 150 miles. Loss of life was relatively small (57), but anyone in Washington or Northern Oregon that day remembers the pillar of ash and steam climbing skyward.

The area is now a National Volcanic Monument, with a highway winding up into the blast zone, several visitors centers, and an unearthly landscape that seems extraterrestrial. From the air (pilots almost always point St. Helens out on West Coast flights) the blast zone is quite visible; the region's heightened volcanic consciousness has led to the realization that most of the Cascade volcanoes are quiescent—a term that means, in essence, likely to erupt sometime in the next few millennia—not dormant. Mount St. Helens reminded everyone of this fact when it renewed steaming and building a lava dome in 2004.

The park is an eminently worthwhile long day trip from Seattle. 360-449-7800, www.fs.fed.us/gpnf/mshnvm.

NORTH CASCADES NATIONAL PARK: This impossibly scenic park northeast of Seattle along Highway 20 is almost three times the size of Mount Rainier National Park (634,000 acres to 235,000 acres) and gets one-third the visitors. If you lust for wilderness, this park is for you; in fact, 93 percent is designated wilderness. But that doesn't mean you have to be hard-core to have fun here: There are endless hiking trails with jaw-dropping views of jagged peaks—home to 700 glaciers—and glistening ribbons of waterfalls, great backcountry camping, fishing and boating on Ross Lake, mountain climbing, wildlife and bird viewing, and more. 360-856-5700, www.nps.gov/noca.

OLD-GROWTH FOREST 101

Many people have the notion that true old-growth forest consists of unbroken stands of towering Douglas firs and western red cedars with massive trunks and shafts of sunlight reaching to open forest floor. There are some spots where it is just like that, but the reality is more complex.

An established old-growth grove is not usually as homogeneous as the classic image; some trees will have toppled, opening areas to undergrowth such as salmonberries, huckleberries, and the notorious devil's club (thorny and aptly named). Many trees will have tops snapped by storms—old cedars, in particular, are almost always broken-topped, sometimes leading to a sprouting of secondary branches called a "candelabra."

"Virgin" forest and "climax" forest are terms not used by foresters much any more, because they convey the mistaken impression that an old-growth forest is static. In fact, change—from storms, floods, landslides, fires, and other natural events—is constant.

Unfortunately, the most widespread change over the past 150 years has been clear-cutting. There are virtually no extensive lowland old-growth groves left. The best to visit include **SCHMITZ PARK** in West Seattle; **SEWARD PARK** on Lake Washington; **FEDERATION STATE FOREST**, east of Enumclaw on State Route 410; and **POINT DEFIANCE PARK** in Tacoma (look for the really big trees on the north end of the peninsula).

HOW DOES YOUR GARDEN GROW?

Seattle is one of the most abundant and adaptable areas in the United States for horticulture. A simple glance around town reveals that—everything from palm trees and hardy bananas to rhododendrons and high-altitude firs grows here. That's because our temperature ranges are moderate, winter rains abundant, and severe weather rare. The official home-garden growing season—last frost in the spring to first frost in the fall—is a long 230 days or so, and both vegetables and flowers can be grown well before and after those dates. Year-round, in fact. Some years there is not even a hard freeze in low-lying areas, especially along the water; petunias, geraniums, calendulas, nasturtiums, and other semihardy plants will overwinter and bloom again. Even pole beans—normally an annual—can overwinter!

Furthermore, pest problems are few—no squash bugs, no Japanese beetles. What few bugs there are can almost always be dealt with naturally: Ladybugs, for instance, will defeat your aphids. *Please do not use pesticides*—they poison the Sound and are unnecessary. For information on sustainable gardening, contact the Center for Urban Horticulture (see "Essential Gardening Resources," below).

The full list of what can be grown here would take pages. Some of the classic landscape plants noted for their suitability to Puget Sound are as follows:

TREES: Natives such as cedar, fir, madrona, maple; imports such as sycamore, beeches, birches, Asian maples, oaks; flowering trees such as Japanese cherries, catalpas, horse chestnut, crabapple, plums, dogwoods.

FRUITS: Apples, pears, plums, cherries, figs, nuts, and every kind of berry: blueberry, raspberry, blackberry, loganberry, marionberry, strawberry.

SHRUBS: Almost all rhododendrons and azaleas (there are thousands), roses, mock orange, bamboo, viburnum.

FLOWERS: This is one of the best climates anywhere for dahlias and lilies; also fuchsias, daisies, gladiolus, iris, and spring bulbs like tulips and daffodils.

There are just a few things that don't do well. Dyed-in-the-wool heat-loving vegetables such as eggplant, bell peppers, and melons are marginal, though some gardeners devote all-out efforts to these hot-weather fussbudgets. Okra? Forget it. Some fruits that bloom early, such as peaches and apricots, are chancy.

Tips for Gardening Success

VARIETIES COUNT: This is one of the toughest lessons for transplants (people, not flora) to learn. The big bruiser ears of corn you may have known in the Midwest won't grow here. Slicing tomatoes as big as plates—nah. Juicy watermelons—nope. Even fruits, berries, and shrubs must be suited to a cool, damp climate; some apples are so susceptible to fungus and blight that they fail here, while others do fine.

KNOW YOUR MICROCLIMATES: The back of your neighbor's yard may have a different horticultural regime than your front yard. Hard to believe, but it's true: Exposure (to cold north winds or warm southern sun) makes a huge difference. Areas near the water rarely freeze but lack summer heat to ripen tomatoes and peppers easily. Fuchsias may freeze to the ground in Enumclaw, but there's plenty of warmth in the summer for corn.

MULCH AND COMPOST: Most of our soils are glacial debris and not very rich. And (the other hard lesson for transplants) summer drought causes water stress; mulching helps ease the need for water.

Peas in the Urban Pod

P-patch gardens are public plots in which nearby residents grow vegetables and flowers, from artichokes to zucchini. There are more than two dozen around Seattle, including such high-density locales as Belltown; each P-patch has up to 20 individual plots, plots range from 100 to 400 square feet, and annual fees are $30 to $60. You can grow a heck of a lot of good food in 400 square feet! That's the good news. Bad news: Lots of people want to do exactly that, and waiting lists for plots range from moderate to very long at different locations. The city supplies the ground and water source; you do the digging, planting, and seed-buying. P-patchers are also required to contribute time to annual maintenance of the whole garden. 684-0264, www.seattle.gov/neighborhoods/ppatch.

Essential Gardening Resources

In addition to the five public resources that begin this list, the commercial suppliers offer splendid advice on what to grow and how to do it. The Territorial and Raintree catalogs are, by themselves, remarkable how-to manuals.

CENTER FOR URBAN HORTICULTURE: A most worthwhile adjunct of the University of Washington, the center promotes sustainable food production for city gardeners and is the best source for information on organic gardening in Puget Sound. 897-5268 (206-UW-PLANT), www.depts.washington.edu/urbhort.

KING COUNTY MASTER GARDENERS: A program run by the Cooperative Extension that enlists veteran gardeners as volunteers to dispense advice. This is the best resource for highly specific questions: What are the best dahlias for partial-shade beds? What's the best corn variety for the Enumclaw Plateau? and so on. 296-3440.

PLANTAMNESTY: This group's mission is to "end the senseless torture and mutilation of trees and shrubs." Classes and workshops encourage proper pruning techniques. 783-9813, www.plantamnesty.org.

Helpful Books

Northwest Gardeners' Resource Directory: Debra Prinzing's catalog, published by Sasquatch Books, is an indispensable compendium of hundreds of suppliers, information resources, and places to visit; www.sasquatchbooks.com. *Sunset Western Garden Book:* Published by *Sunset* magazine, it explains Western Washington horticulture in far more exacting terms than the USDA's rather broad categories and offers encyclopedic advice on almost everything that can be grown here.

SEATTLE TILTH: A hotbed of organic gardening classes and resources, including soil building and composting, recycling, and community-supported agriculture. Holds a popular Edible Plant Sale in May and Organic Harvest Fair in September. 4649 Sunnyside Ave N, 633-0451, www.seattletilth.org.

WASHINGTON STATE COOPERATIVE EXTENSION/KING COUNTY: Mainstream advice from agronomic professionals familiar with Puget Sound growing conditions. 205-3100, www.metrokc.gov/dchs/csd/wsu-ce.

ABUNDANT LIFE SEED FOUNDATION: Though a fire destroyed this Port Townsend organization, Territorial Seeds (see listing, below) has taken over its catalog and continues its work, preserving and distributing rare heritage vegetable and flower varieties. www.abundantlifeseed.com.

BAMBOO GARDENS OF WASHINGTON: The Puget Sound area is one of the world's best climates for bamboo landscaping, and these commercial gardens near Redmond demonstrate why. 425-868-5166, www.bamboogardenswa.com.

HERONSWOOD GARDENS: One of North America's leading propagators and purveyors of exotic plants from around the world. Hours are limited, but a visit to this 7.5-acre retreat on Bainbridge Island is an adventure into the flora of distant locales. 360-297-4172, www.heronswood.com.

MOLBAK'S: This massive Woodinville garden center is a day trip in itself, with literally thousands of plants to buy. In December it becomes a rainbow of poinsettias. 425-483-5000, www.molbaks.com.

RAINTREE NURSERY: Located in Morton, east of Chehalis in the Cascade foothills, Raintree is the leading Northwest mail-

Planting Dates

Late February (Washington's birthday): Plant peas, mustard

Mid-March: Plant other spring crops—onions, leeks, broccoli, lettuce

Early April: Start summer vegetables such as basil and tomatoes indoors

Late April: Plant beans, potatoes

Early May: Plant corn, pumpkins, zucchini

End of May: Set out tomatoes, basil, peppers

End of June: Plant fall/winter crops such as broccoli, cabbage, kale

October: Plant garlic, overwintered onions, spring bulbs

November–February: Plant bare-root shrubs, perennials, and trees

---

order supplier of trees, shrubs, and perennials. The catalog is particularly good for rare apples and fruit varieties that do well west of the Cascades. 360-496-6400, www.raintreenursery.com.

SWANSON'S NURSERY: One of Seattle's oldest (1924), Swanson's has 5 acres of plants and garden materials for sale; the September fall sale draws crowds. In Crown Hill. 782-2543, www.swansonsnursery.com.

TERRITORIAL SEEDS: This Oregon-based company specializes in seeds bred to grow in cool-climate areas, with lots of vegetable varieties (corn, tomatoes, peppers, squash) that succeed in Puget Sound where others don't. It offers catalogs for both spring/summer and fall/winter gardening. 541-942-9547, www.territorialseed.com.

FRESH FOOD OPTIONS

Farmers Markets

Pike Place Market was founded in 1907 to offer Puget Sound food producers a clean, sheltered central location where they could offer produce to city residents. Pretty good idea: It's been going strong for almost a century and survived demolition threats in the '60s to see dozens of neighborhood farmers markets spring up as consumers began to embrace fresh, locally produced foods.

Today there are dozens of farmers markets in the area, usually open just one day a week (Pike Place Market is open seven days). The vast majority operate May through late autumn; some have limited winter schedules. There are also markets in numerous cities in Pierce and Snohomish counties. Most limit stand operators to growers, family members, and their representatives, and many have rules requiring that vendors make or grow what they sell.

Markets are so popular that much of the best stuff is sold out in the first two hours; market managers report that it's sometimes more difficult to find producers, and space for them, than customers. Aside from the unparalleled quality of the produce, foods, and crafts, customers particularly like being able to talk to growers who can explain the virtues of particular varieties. And it's a good feeling to know your dollars are supporting farm families, not distribution and packaging corporations.

Many of the Seattle area markets are managed by one organization, **SEATTLE FARM MARKETS,** www.seattlefarmersmarkets.org. A comprehensive listing of all the Western Washington markets, as well as U-pick farms and specialty growers open to the public, is maintained by **PUGET SOUND FRESH,** www.pugetsoundfresh.org. A comprehensive list of all farmers markets in the state is at www.wafarmersmarkets.com.

For specific locations and dates of neighborhood farmers markets, see listings in Chapters 1–3.

U-Pick Farms

There is literally nothing better than spending a half day in a strawberry patch in the Snoqualmie Valley, filling flats with fresh berries; or on a ladder in cherry or apple trees near Puyallup, filling a bucket with pie makings; or in a pumpkin patch with your 3-year-old, picking out the Halloween jack-o-lantern for your front porch. When you visit a U-pick farm, keep in mind the tradition that you pay for what goes in the bucket, but on-site sampling is free; and it's not just good food, it's good fun. There are more than a dozen U-pick farms in the Seattle area, some offering just a few crops, such as strawberries or blueberries, some with a wide range of comestibles. The range of items available is huge, including apples, cherries, peaches, pears, blueberries, raspberries, strawberries, blackberries, pumpkins, and fresh vegetables. Puget Sound Fresh is the umbrella agency for locally grown fresh produce, and lists almost all the U-pick farms; www.pugetsoundfresh.org.

The two leading U-pick farms, with literally dozens of crops throughout the year, are **REMLINGER FARMS** near Carnation (425-333-4135, www.remlingerfarms.com) and **BIRINGER FARM** outside Everett (425-259-0255, www.biringerfarm.com).

Subscription Farming

Subscription farms practice what's known as community-supported agriculture—area residents subscribe to regular delivery of fresh produce. When you sign up, you receive once or twice a week a box on your doorstep of whatever's fresh from the farm then, ranging from beets in midwinter to tomatoes in September. You also are supporting a local independent farm family. For a list of area subscription farms, visit www.pugetsoundfresh.org, or call the **KING COUNTY "FARMBUDSMAN"** at 296-7824.

WILDLIFE

Bald eagles nest in Discovery Park. Coyotes roam the greenbelts. Raccoons are omnipresent. Bears and cougars are occasional visitors to Eastside backyards—and cougar tracks have even been spotted in Seattle city parks. Deer are so common that gardeners outside the urban core must protect their gardens from them.

Hummingbirds, finches, jays, chickadees, and many other birds will come readily to feeders; butterflies are drawn by many flowering shrubs, including the aptly named butterfly bush. Many homeowners manage to lure Anna's hummingbirds into setting up year-round residence—a cheery sight at feeders in January. For information on attracting birds and beneficial insects to your garden, consult Washington State Cooperative Extension/King County (see "Essential Gardening Resources," page 326).

Seattle's master birders, as elsewhere across the U.S., are found in the **AUDUBON SOCIETY**. These are the folks to contact for local field trips, education, birding trail maps, and all things avian; www.seattleaudubon.org.

Orcas: More Than a Fluke

There are three pods of orca whales in Puget Sound, creatively labeled J, K, and L. They travel a 200-mile range north and south, and J and K are likely to pass through Seattle area waters approximately once a month—an occurrence that never fails to delight ferry commuters and lucky tourists. The best time and place to see them with any amount of predictability is the summer months (June and July) in the San Juan Islands. Perch yourself on a rock at Limekiln State Park on San Juan Island and keep your eyes peeled. To report whale sightings or strandings, call the **WHALE HOTLINE** at 800-562-8832.

Predatory Nature

Cute or charismatic as they are, it's necessary to remember that some of the larger animals found in the Puget Sound area can be dangerous. There have been no fatalities so far, as there have in California's exurban areas. But conflicts are increasing. The state offers common-sense information on living with wild animals: www.wdfw.wa.gov/viewing/wildview.htm. If a predator is consistently lurking in your vicinity and you are worried about it, call the **KING COUNTY SHERIFF** (296-4155) or your municipal police department. For more information about wildlife management issues, contact Washington Department Fish & Wildlife at 360-902-2515.

BEARS: First, we're talking black bears, not grizzlies. They are most common on the Olympic Peninsula and North Cascades, but shrinking habitat means that sightings out the outskirts of the metro area are not uncommon. Keep your garbage secured in bear-proof containers. If you encounter a bear while hiking, back away slowly and speak calmly, avoiding eye contact. If you cannot move away from the bear and the animal doesn't move, try clapping your hands or shouting to scare it away. If you're camping, be sure to follow park rules for bear-proofing your camp (check at local ranger stations for specifics).

COUGARS: If you live in rural or exurban areas, keep your pets indoors or secured in kennels at night, and don't leave pet food or food scraps outside. Closely watch small pets and small children, especially at dusk when cougars are most active. This also goes for when you're hiking (there is a reason it's called Cougar Mountain, and the same goes for Tiger, Squak, and Mount Si). If you encounter a cougar, stand as tall as you can, pick up small children, and speak loudly. Don't run, don't crouch down, try to hide, or turn your back. Maintain eye contact. According to the Washington Department of Fish and Wildlife, if the animal becomes aggressive, be aggressive back: shout, wave your arms, throw rocks.

COYOTES: Most often encountered in parks and exurbs. Bring pets in at night and don't let small dogs wander while hiking.

RACCOONS: These rapacious animals are not considered cute by homeowners who have ever lost a cat to one, had them invade the house to gorge on dog food, or, worst case, been nipped by one. They will break through screens, pull open unlatched doors, and trash bird feeders and loose garbage. Keep your garbage secured in sturdy containers. Bring pets in at night. Make sure doors are latched. *Do not* feed raccoons—they don't need any extra nourishment (Puget Sound is a smorgasbord to them), and if you have misguided neighbors who do, ask them to stop. If they won't, complain as vociferously as you can.

Canada's Pesky Geese

We love our outdoor spaces—and we're not alone. Neatly trimmed grasses, plentiful access to water, and few predators make Seattle a prime habitat for Canada geese. However, lots of geese can mean lots of poop, which, according to Seattle Parks and Recreation (SPR), makes some parks (Green Lake, for one), athletic fields, and waterfront areas unusable and poses the threat of disease to humans (though no reports of disease or illness have been received).

Since 2003 SPR has been working in partnership with PAWS (Progressive Animal Welfare Society) and the Humane Society to control the goose population through nonlethal methods. Effective deterrents include dogs to chase the geese away and spraying grass with a substance that tastes bad to the waterfowl (but is safe for humans). According to SPR, the multiple methods of control used during the past five years have reduced the goose population by 60 to 65 percent—well within a manageable level.

FISHING FOR KNOWLEDGE

First things first: Geoduck is pronounced *gooey-duck*. And "fresh frozen" is not comparable to fresh, no matter what anyone tells you. Oh, and "king," "chinook" and "spring" salmon are all the same. Sockeye and red are identical; coho and silver, likewise. Same for pinks and humpies, and for chum and dog salmon.

Confusing, eh? Seafood expertise is among the most arcane of culinary niches, but something every Seattleite should embrace. Even if you don't particularly care, you need to sound reasonably knowledgeable when Aunt Ethel breezes in from Keokuk and wants to know what those bizarre shellfish are with the long, saggy protuberance.

Another tip: When you take your guests out to dinner: Dungeness crab is local. Lobster is not. (This is worth repeating, because so many Seattle visitors fly here thousands of miles looking forward to eating lobsters that have themselves flown even farther. There is no Northwest lobster.) Snow crab and king crab are from Alaska, and almost always frozen.

Salmon is King

The linchpin of Puget Sound seafood is **SALMON**, once abundant locally, now mostly brought in from Alaska and British Columbia. Salmon season starts with a bang in May, when the first sockeyes arrive from **ALASKA'S COPPER RIVER**, flown in at stratospheric prices ($20/pound). Wait a few weeks and the price halves, then halves again, and silvers, pinks, and chum salmon appear. By the end of summer you can find fresh salmon at less than $2/pound; most people prefer kings (chinook), while many connoisseurs rate sockeyes and silvers the best. Whatever you're looking for, a fresh fish is firm, well-colored, and not overly fishy-smelling: If the vendor you're visiting won't let you check an individual fish, it's probably not fresh and you should shop elsewhere. When you buy a whole salmon, tell the vendor to leave it whole, or it's likely to be fileted before you realize it.

Salmon season peters out in late fall; by December, most of the fish for sale is farm-raised. These Atlantic salmon grown in pens have come under much attack, as their culture pollutes the oceans, they have unhealthy levels of contaminants, and they make it harder for commercial fishermen to make a living. Many chefs will not serve farm salmon.

Beyond Salmon

Other West Coast fish worth trying are rockfish (sometimes, inaccurately and illegally, called snapper), which has a light texture and medium-bodied flavor; various kinds of tuna, a hearty, firm fish with strong flavor; sturgeon, a dense white fish; lingcod, another heavy, full-flavored fish; and other forms of cod, which are best baked.

Oysters

Oysters are fresh year-round (worries about summer spawning have been erased by breeding) and raised locally, as are clams. Geoducks, scallops, and occasionally shrimp are from Alaska and sometimes Washington or BC; unless they are called "spot prawns," they are probably tropical shrimp from Texas, Florida, or Thailand.

Geoducks

Yes, it's spelled wrong. (Or pronounced oddly, depending on your perspective.) "Gooey-ducks" are large native clams found throughout Puget Sound that are particular favorites of experienced shellfish gatherers. They can range up to 2 pounds, though most people discard the part within the shell and eat the foot, which usually happens to be about a foot long; once it's skinned, it yields a large segment of meaty, firm flesh that sautés nicely.

The trick is getting them. Geoducks inhabit deep sand beds at or below the zero-tide line; it's pretty simple to find them by scouting for the tip of the foot protruding from the sand during a deep low tide. But the shell itself is 18 inches or more deep, and excavating it from its subsurface fastness is a major project. Many believe the clams move down quickly, but that's not the case (the foot does, but the animal stays put) and it's not the problem. The challenge is digging quickly and expertly enough to keep the hole from collapsing before you can get the shovel beneath the shell.

Veteran clam-diggers all have their own tricks, none of which will be revealed here. Find some Seattle natives and ask their secret—if they'll tell you.

Fresh or Frozen?

Can frozen fish—"flash-frozen," it's often called, or the Orwellian "fresh-frozen"—ever be as good as fresh? Hardcore seafood fanciers doubt it. With a year-round supply of fresh seafood available, it's also a moot point. No other area in the United States has as much good-quality seafood at hand, so dive in.

INDEX

A

Access Washington, 300
Ace Hotel & Cyclops, 19
ACLU, 301
ACT (A Contemporary Theatre), 233
Acupuncture, 291
Adams & Associates, Inc., 187
African American Academy at Magnolia Elementary School, 212
AIDS, 292–93
Air quality, 320–21
Airport. *See* Sea-Tac Airport
A&J Meats, 62
Alaska Airlines, 194–95
Alcoholism, 296
Alderwood Mall, 122–23
Alki Beach, 84
Alki Lighthouse, 85
Allen, Paul, 193, 196, 198
Alternative medicine, 291–93
Alternative schools, 203, 212–15
Amazon, 195
American Society of Home Inspectors, 140
Amgen, 199
Amtrak, 167–68
Annie Wright School, 210
Animals
  pets, 150–51
  wildlife, 330–32
Antioch University Seattle, 215
Aqua Verde Café & Paddle Club, 265
Aquariums, 237
AquaSox, 118
Archie McPhee's, 4
Argosy Cruises, 97
Argosy University Seattle, 215
Armadillo Barbecue, 108
Art, 180, 237
Art Institute of Seattle, 218
Art museums, 235–37
Asarco Smelter, 129
Asian Counseling and Referral Service, 303
Athletics, 203, 252–58
Attorneyfind, 141
Attorney General, 283
Auburn, 111–13, 207
Available Personnel Services, 187
Avalanches, 269

B

Bai Tong, 127
Bailey/Coy Books, 241
Bainbridge Gardens, 114
Bainbridge Island, 113–15
Bainbridge Island Vineyards & Winery, 114
Ballard
  attractions and institutions in, 4–6
  description of, 3–4
  history of, 3
  map of, **xiv**, 5
  neighborhood service centers for, 2
Ballard Avenue, 3
Ballard Locks, 3–5
Ballard Market, 5, 63
Ballet, 231
Bank of America Tower, 19–20
Bankruptcy, 285
Barking Frog, 108–09
Baseball, 171–72, 252–53, 257–58
Basketball, 172, 257–58

Page numbers in **boldface** denote maps

Bastyr University, 215
Bathhouse, 233
Beacon Hill
    attractions and institutions in, 9
    description of, 6–8
    facts about, 9
    history of, 8
    map of, **xiv**, 7
Beacon Hill Old Indian Cemetery, 9
Bears, 331
Beaux Arts Rialto Theater, 129
Beaver Lake, 104
Beecher's Cheese, 24
Be'Er Sheva Park, 67
Bellevue, **86**, 87–89, **110**, 207
Bellevue Art Museum, 89
Bellevue Botanical Garden, 89
Bellevue Club, 274
Bellevue Community College, 218
Bellevue Philharmonic, 224
Bellevue Square, 88, 90
Belltown, 17–18
Benaroya Hall, 224
Bertschi School, 210
Beyond the Closet, 241
Bicycle & Pedestrian Safety Program, 169
Bicycle Alliance of Washington, 169
Bicycling, 154
    commuting, 168–69
    recreational, 260–61
Biringer Farms, 118
Bistro Pleasant Beach, 114
Bite of Seattle, 238
Blackbird Bakery, 113
Black ice, 312
Blading, 270
Blob, The, 64
Bloedel Reserve, 114

Blue Moon Tavern, 78
Blue Mouse Theatre, 243
Boat licensing, 165
Boating, 266
Boehm's Candy Factory, 93–94
Boeing, x–xi, 125, 192, 195, 196
Boeing Everett Plant, 117–18
Boeing Field, 161
Boeing Space Center, 121
Book-It, 233
Bookstores, 12, 79, 241–42
Bothell
    description of, 91–92
    map of, **86**
    University of Washington campus, 217
Bothell Landing, 92
Bradner Gardens, 52, 54–55
Bridges, 162, 164
Bridle Trails State Park, 90, 271
Broadmoor Golf Club, 43
Buckaroo Tavern, 32
Bud's Jazz Records, 58
Building complaints, 283
Bumbershoot, 238
Burien, 115
Burke Museum of Natural History & Culture, 78, 234–35
Burke-Gilman Trail, 3, 39, 260
Burn bans, 320–21
Buses, 165–67, 177–78
Bush School, The, 210–11
Business
    economy effects on, 191–93
    local companies, 199
    public companies, 194–98
    self-employment, 188, 199–200
    start-up, 188, 199–200
Business license, 200

C

Cable television, 246
Café Flora, 45
Campagne, 22
Camping, 270–71
Canlis, 22, 62
Canoeing, 271
Cap cloud, 312
Capitol Hill
   attractions and institutions in, 13–14
   description of, 10–11
   facts about, 12
   map of, 11
   neighborhood service centers for, 2
Car(s)
   emissions tests for, 165
   parking of, 170–73
   registration of, 163–65
   ticketing of, 172–73
   See also Driving
Car theft, 154
Career counselors, 184
Carkeek Park, 37, 271
Carlson, Linda, 184
Carpool lanes, 156
Cascade Bicycle Club, 169, 260
Cascades, 321–23
Cascades Volcano Observatory, 322
Cascadia, 22
Celtic Bayou, 102
Center for Wooden Boats, 28, 235, 266
Central Community College, 11, 219
Central District
   attractions and institutions in, 16–17
   facts about, 16
   history of, 14–16
   map of, **xiv**, **15**
   neighborhood service centers for, 2
Central Tavern, 58
Century Ballroom, 228
Chapel of St. Ignatius, 13
Charitable giving, 301–02
Charles Wright Academy, 211
Chateau Ste. Michelle, 108–09, 227
Chicago Title, 141
Chief Sealth, xiii
Chihuly, Dale, 27, 130
Child care, 220–21
Child Care resources, 220
Children's Hospital, 289
Children's Regional Hospital and Medical Center, 39–40
Chilly Hilly, 261
Chiropractic, 292
Choir music, 225
Cinerama, 243
Citizens Service Bureau, 283
City People's Mercantile, 41
Classical music, 224–26
Climate, 305–16
Climbing, 273–74
Clubs, 228–30
Cobain, Kurt, 182, 229
College(s), 11–12, 216, 218–20
   See also Universities; Vocational Schools; specific college
College sports, 258–59
Colman Park, 55
Colors NW, 245
Columbia City
   attractions and institutions in, 74–75
   description of, 72–73
   facts about, 73–74
   map of, **xiv**, **73**

Columbia City Cinema, 74
Comcast, 246
Commencement Bay, 128
Community colleges, 218–20
Community Information Line, 300
Community learning centers, 204
Community services, 299–300
Commuting, 153, 155–57
Complaints, 283
Comprehensive Child Care Program, 221
Concerts at the Pier, 227
Condominiums, 133
Conservation, 319
Continuing education, 222
Cook's World, 71
Cornish College of the Arts, 11–12, 216
Costco, 195–96
Cougar Mountain, 271–72
Cougar Mountain Zoo, 94, 237
Cougars, 331
Counseling, 301
Country Doctor Community Clinic, 292
Country Village, 92
County Ombudsman, 283
Courts, 284–85
Coyotes, 332
Cray, 199
Crepe de Paris, 226
Crest, The, 243
Crocodile Cafe, 228
Cross-country skiing, 269
Crossroads Shopping Center, 90
Crystal Mountain, 268

D

Dahlia Lounge, 22
Dance, 231
Dash Point State Park, 119–20, 272
Dating, 249
Day care, 204, 220–21
Dead Horse Canyon, 67
Death rates, 295
Decatur Elementary, 212
Delaurenti, 24
Delridge, 2
Dental insurance, 294
Dentists, 288
Department of Planning and Development, 143–44
Department of Social and Health Services, 299–300
Dick's Drive-In, 81
Dilettante Chocolates, 13
Dimitriou's Jazz Alley, 230
Disability resources, 190–91
Discover U, 222
Discovery Park, 47–48, 272
District courts, 284–85
Domestic abuse, 300–301
Dot-coms, 181–82
Downtown
  attractions and institutions in, 19–25
  description of, 17–18
  facts about, 18–19
  housing in, 133–34
  map of, **xiv**, 19
  neighborhood service centers for, 2
  Pike Place Market, 18, 21, 24–25
Dress codes, 182

Driver's licenses, 163
Driving
　facts about, 153–54
　highways to avoid, 157
　navigation tips, 158–59
　shortcuts for, 159–60
　speed limit for, 161
　telephone numbers, 155
　See also Car(s)
Drugstore.com, 199
Duck Island, 37
Dusty Strings, 32

E

Eagle Harbor Books, 113
Early Music Guild, 224
Earthquakes, 141–42
Eastide Preparatory School, 211
Eastlake
　attractions and institutions in, 28
　facts about, 27
　history of, 25–27
　map of, xiv, 26
Economy, 181, 191–93
Eddie Bauer, 199
Edmonds, 207
Education, 222
　See also Colleges; Universities; Schools
El Centro De La Raza, 7–8
El Gaucho, 22
El Mercado Latino, 24
Elliott Bay Book Company, 58, 239, 241–42
Elliott Bay Water Taxi, 174
Emerald City Hall, 277–78
Emerald Downs, 112
Emerald Queen Casino, 228
Emergencies, 297

Emissions tests, 165
EMP, 235
Employment. See Job(s); Job-hunting
Energy-efficient homes, 143
Enrollment in schools, 204, 206
Entertainment
　ballet, 231
　bookstores, 241–42
　clubs, 228–30
　dance, 231
　festivals, 238–39
　lectures, 239
　libraries, 240–41
　magazines, 245–46
　museums, 234–36
　music. See Music
　newspapers, 244–45
　overview of, 223
　radio stations, 247–48
　readings, 239
　singles, 249
　television, 246–47
　zoo, 237–38
Enumclaw, 116–17
Erotic Bakery, The, 81
Essential Baking Co., 32, 82
Ethnic diversity, 302–04
Everett, 110, 117–18
Everett Aquasox, 118
Everett Homeport, 118
Evergreen State College, 216
Expedia, 199
Expeditors International, 196
Experience Music Project, 235
Eyman, Tim, 285
Ezell's Fried Chicken & Catfish Corner, 14, 16

F

Farestart, 20
Farmers markets, 328–29
Farrel McWhirter Park, 102
Federal Army & Navy Surplus, 20
Federal government, 282
Federal Way, 119–20, 208
Ferries, 173–75
Festivals, 238–39
Fifth Avenue Theatre, 226, 233
Filson, 58
Fiorini Sports, 41–42
First Hill, 10
Fishermen's Terminal, 48
Fishing, 261–62, 332–34
Fitness, 274
Flexcar, 169
Floating homes, 138
Flooding, 146
Flora & Fauna bookstore, 242
Flying Fish, 22–23
Folklife, 238
Football, 171–72, 255, 258–59
Forests, 323–24
14 Carrot Café, 28
Fred Hutchinson Cancer Research Center, 28, 289
Free & Clear smoking quit line, 293
Freelancing, 188
Fremont
    attractions and institutions in, 32–33
    facts about, 31
    history of, 29–31
    map of, **xiv, 30**
    neighborhood service centers for, 2
Fremont Outdoor Cinema, 243
Fremont Public Association, 30
Fresh foods, 328–30
Frink Park, 55
Frisko Freeze, 129
Frye Art Museum, 13, 235

G

Galloping Gertie, 313
Garden of Everyday Miracles, The, 33
Gardens, 324–28
Gas Works Park, 82
Gates, Bill, xi, 193, 198
    See also Microsoft
Gays and lesbians, 241, 292–93
Geoducks, 334
Getty Images, 199
Gilman Village, 94
Glamorama, 33
Golden Gardens Park, 5, 272
Golf, 262
Gorge Amphitheater, The, 228
Government, 281–82
Governor, 281–82
Grand Central Bakery, 58
Great Wall Mall, 122
Greater Duwamish, 2
Green Lake
    attractions and institutions in, 37–39
    description of, 34–36
    facts about, 36–37
    map of, **xiv, 35**
Green Lake Library, 36
Green Lake Park, 272
Green River, 120
Greenwood
    attractions and institutions in, 37–39
    description of, 34–36
    facts about, 36–37
    map of, **35**
    neighborhood service centers for, 2

Greenwood Market, 63
Gregg's Greenlake Cycle, 37–38
Griffey, Jr., Ken, 253
Group Health Cooperative, 289, 294

H

Half-Price Books, 242
Harborview Medical Center, 289
Health insurance, 294–95
Health services, 287–304
Hendrix, Jimi, 126, 229
Henry Art Gallery, 78
Herbfarm, 23, 108–09
Heronswood Nursery, 114–15
High schools. *See* Alternative schools; Seattle Public Schools
Highland Ice Arena, 274
Highline, 208
Highline Community College, 218–19
Highline Community Hospital, 289–90
Hiking, 262–64
Hillclimb (Queen Anne), 61
History of Seattle, ix–xi
History House, 31
HIV/AIDS resources, 292–93
Hockey, 258
Home(s)
  buying of, 134–38
  earthquake risks, 141–42
  energy-efficient, 143
  fixing of, 145
  floating, 138
  inspections, 139
  median sales prices of, 133
  permits for, 143–44
  property taxes for, 136–37
  property titles, 140–41
  renting of, 147–49
  views, 137–38
  zoning regulations for, 144–45
Home builders, 194
Home inspections, 139–40
Home Owners Club, 137
Hood Canal Bridge, 164
Hospitals, 289–90
Hovhaness, Alan, 232
Hugo House, 239
Humane Society, 151
Huskies. *See* University of Washington

I

I-90 Bike Trail, 99
I-90 floating bridge, 164
Ice skating, 274
Icons, x–xi
IKEA, 126
Immigrant services, 302–04
Immunizations, 204
Infant mortality rates, 295
Initiatives, 284
Insurance
  earthquake, 142
  health and dental, 294–95
Insurance Commissioner, 283
Interlaken Park, 50
International District
  attractions and institutions in, 58–59
  description of, 55–57
  facts about, 57
  map of, **xiv, 56**
International Fountain at Seattle Center, The, 62–63

Internet-based job hunting, 181, 185–86
Intiman, 233
Issaquah, **86**, 92–95, 208
Issaquah Alps, 94
Issaquah Skyport, 96
Ivar's, 20

J

Jack's Fish Spot, 24
Jackson, Henry, 286
Jazz, 230–31
Jefferson Park, 8
Jewish Transcript, The, 245
Job(s)
  career counselors for, 184
  dress codes, 182
  economy effects on, 181
  temporary, 186–89
Job fairs, 185
Job-hunting
  description of, 181–82
  Internet for, 181, 185–86
  by networking, 184
  in newspapers, 183
  resources for, 183–84
  web searches, 185–86
John L. Scott Real Estate, 135
John Marshall High School, 212–13
Johnston, Tex, 196
Jose Rizal Park, 9
Julia's, 82
Jurisdictions, 279

K

Katterman's Sand Point Pharmacy, 42
Kayaking, 265
Kelsey Creek Park, 90–91
Kent, **86**, 120–22, 208–09
Kent Valley Ice Center, 274
Kerry Park, 61, 63–64
KEXP 90.3, 248
Kimball Elementary, 213
King County
  courts in, 284
  government of, 280–81
King County Animal Control, 151
King County Fair, 117
King County Journal, 245
King County Library, 240–41
King County Superintendent of Elections, 276
Kingdome, 256
Kingfish Café, 23
Kingsmen, 230
Kirkland, **86**, 95–98
Kirkland Performance Center, 97–98, 227
Klondike Gold Rush Museum, 235
Kubota Gardens, 67–68

L

Lake City, 2
Lake Sammamish, 103
Lake Sammamish State Park, 93, 95, 272
Lake Union, 2
Lake View Cemetery, 13
Lake Washington, 209
Lake Washington Ship Canal, 26
Lakeside School, 211
Landlord-Tenant Act, 149
Landmark Library, 46
Landmark Theatres, 243–44

Langston Hughes Cultural
  Center, 16–17
Larry's Markets, 63
Laurelhurst
  attractions and institutions
    in, 41–42
  description of, 39–40
  facts about, 41
  map of, **xiv, 40**
Laurelhurst Beach Club, 42
Law firms, 194
Law making, 277
Lawrence, Jacob, 232
Lease, 148–49
Lectures, 239
Left Bank Books, 242
Legislature, 282
Lenin Square, 31–32
Lesbians and gays, 241,
  292–93
Leschi, 52–55, **53**
Leschi Park, 55
Libraries, 240–41
License(s)
  business, 200
  driver's, 163
Licensing
  boat, 165
  child care, 220
  pets, 150
  vehicle, 163–65
Limousines, 175, 178
Lincoln Park, 83, 85, 272
Local companies, 199
Lottie Mott's, 74
"Louie, Louie", 230
Lutefisk, 3
Luther Burbank Park, 100, 272
Lynnwood, 122–23
Lynnwood Ice Center, 274

M

Macrina Bakery & Cafe, 20
Macy's, 20–21
Madison Park
  attractions and institutions
    in, 45
  description of, 42–43
  facts about, 43
  map of, **xiv, 44**
Mae's Phinney Ridge Café, 38
Magazines, 245–46
Magic Shop, 24–25
Magnolia
  attractions and institutions
    in, 47–49
  facts about, 46
  history of, 45–46
  map of, **xiv, 47**
  neighborhood service centers for, 2
Magnolia Elementary School,
  212
Magnolia Park, 48
Magnuson Park, 42, 272–73
Magnuson, Warren G., 286
Manning, Harvey, 95
Manpower, 187
Map store, 242
Marathon running, 265
Marina Park, 96, 98
Marine layer, 312
Mariners. *See* Seattle Mariners
Market Spice, 25
Marymoor Park, 102, 228, 273
Massage schools, 291
McCaw Hall, 224–25
Meany Theater, 227
Mecca Café, 64
Medina, 90
Meeker Mansion, 124–25
Mental disability, 190–91

Mental health, 298
Mercer Island, 98–100, 162, 209
Methow Valley, 269
Metro Transit, 165–67
Metro Vanpool, 156
Metropolitan Grill, 23
Metropolitan Markets, 63
Metsker Maps, 242
Microbreweries, 30
Microsoft
　description of, 102, 196
　millionaires at, 193
　temporary employment with, 188–89
Middle College High School, 213
Midwifery, 291
Mildew, 140
MOG. *See* Museum of Glass
MOHAI, 48–50, 235
Molbak's, 109
Mold, 140
Molly Brown Temps, Inc., 187
Montlake
　attractions and institutions in, 50–51
　description of, 48–49
　facts about, 49–50
　map of, **xiv, 51**
Montlake Bridge, 49
Montlake Park, 50
Moore Theater, 227
Moss Bay Rowing & Kayak Center, 265
Mount Baker, 268
　attractions and institutions in, 54–55
　description of, 52–54
　facts about, 54
　map of, **xiv, 53**
Mount Baker Community Clubhouse, 55
Mount Baker Park, 55

Mount Baker Rowing & Sailing Center, 266
Mount Pleasant Cemetery, 64
Mount Rainier National Park, 322
Mount Si, 106, 263
Mount St. Helens, 323
Mount Zion Baptist Church, 14
Mountaineers, The, 95, 259, 264
Movie theaters, 243–44
Mt. Baker–Snoqualmie National Forest, 110
Muckleshoot Casino, 112
Mudslides, 139, 146
Municipal Court of Seattle, 284
Municipal Spay and Neuter Clinic, 150
Museum(s), 234–36
Museum of Flight, 235–36
Museum of Glass, 129–30
Museum of History and Industry. *See* MOHAI
Music
　choir, 225
　classical, 224–26
　clubs, 228–30
　jazz, 230–31
　opera, 225–26
　orchestra, 225
　pop, 227–28
　rock, 227–28
　symphony, 226
Musical theater, 226–27
Mutual Fish, 68
Myrtle-Edwards Park, 273

N

National parks, 321–23
Native Americans, resources for, 303
Nature, 317–34

Neighborhood(s)
  Ballard, 3–6
  Beacon Hill, 6–9
  Bellevue, 87–91
  Belltown. See Downtown
  Bothell, 91–92
  Capitol Hill, 10–14
  Central District, 14–17
  Columbia City. See Seward Park/Columbia City
  Downtown, 17–25
  Eastlake, 25–28
  Fremont, 29–33
  Green Lake/Greenwood, Phinney Ridge, 34–39
  International District. See Pioneer Square/International District
  Issaquah, 92–95
  Kirkland, 95–98
  Laurelhurst, 39–42
  Madison Park, 42–45
  Magnolia, 45–48
  Mercer Island, 98–100
  Montlake, 48–51
  Mount Baker/Leschi, 52–55
  Phinney Ridge. See Green Lake/Greenwood/Phinney Ridge
  Pioneer Square/International District, 55–59
  Queen Anne, 59–64
  Rainier Beach/Rainier Valley, 64–68
  Ravenna, 68–72
  Redmond, 100–03
  Sammamish, 103–04
  Seward Park/Columbia City, 72–75
  Snoqualmie Valley, 104–07
  University District, 75–79
  Wallingford, 79–82
  West Seattle, 82–85
  Woodinville, 107–09
Neighborhood service centers, 1–2
Networking, 184
Newspapers
  for job-hunting, 183
  for reading, 244–45
Nordic Center at Snoqualmie Pass, 269
Nordic Heritage Museum, 5, 236
Nordstrom, 21, 197
North Cascades National Park, 323
North Seattle Community College, 219, 221
North Shore School District, 209
Northwest Chamber Orchestra, 225
Northwest Gardeners' Resource Directory, 327
Northwest Harvest, 302
Northwest Multiple Listing Service, 135
Northwest Outdoor Center, 265
Nova school, 213
NW Sinfonietta, 225

O

Oberto Sausage, 122
Occidental Park, 58
Odyssey Maritime Discovery Center, 236
Office Team, 187
Olympic National Park, 322
On the Boards, 231
Opera, 225–26
Orca (school), 213
Orca (wildlife), 330–31

Orchestral music, 225
Oriental Food Mart, 25
Oriental medicine, 290–91
Outdoor recreation, 259–71
Outdoor Recreation Information Center, 263–64, 271
Over the Rainbow Balloon Rides, 109
Overlake Hospital, 290
Oysters, 333–34

P

Paccar, 197
Pace Staffing Network, 188
Pacific Crest Trail, 263
Pacific Lutheran University, 130–31
Pacific Northwest Ballet, 231
Pacific Northwest Seismograph Network, 141–42
Pacific Northwest Title, 141
Pacific Place Shopping Center, 21
Pacific Science Center, 236
Paddle Trails Canoe Club, 271
Paderewski, The, 70
Panhandling, 303
Paramount Theater, 227, 233
Parentmap, 221
Parents
  child care for, 220–21
  public school involvement by, 205
Park(s), 271–73
  See also specific park
Park & ride lots, 156–57
Parker Services, Inc., 188
Parking, 170–73
  at Pike Place Market, 171
  at Mariners/Seahawks games, 171–72
  at Seattle Center events, 172
  at Sea-Tac Airport, 178–79
  National Forest Service parking pass, 263
  Neighborhood Parking Zones, 171
  Sno-Park Pass, 263
Pathfinder, 214
Patrick's Fly Shop, 28
Paul Revere and the Raiders, 230
Peach-O-Rama, 63
Pedestrians, 169–70
Peet, Alfred, 200
PEPS, 221
Permatemps, 189
Permits, 143–44
Pests, 151–52
Pets, 150–51
Piniella, Lou, 253
Phinney Ridge, 34–39
Phinney Ridge Community Center, 34
Physical disability, 190–91
Physicians, 288
Pierce County Transit, 167
Pike & Western Wine, 25
Pike Place Fish, 25
Pike Place Market, 18, 21, 24–25, 171
Pine Lake, 104
Pioneer Square
  attractions and institutions in, 58–59
  description of, 55–57
  facts about, 57
  map of, 56
Planned Parenthood, 293
Planting dates, 328
Plum Creek Timber, 199
Point Defiance Park, 130
Point Defiance Zoo, 130, 237

Point Robinson Lighthouse, 132
Pontow, Regina, 184
Pop music, 227–28
Population, ix
Port of Seattle, 281
Potholes, 146
Precipitation, 308–12
Predators (urban wildlife), 331–32
Premera Blue Cross, 294
Pritchard Island Beach, 64–65, 68
Private schools, 210–12
Professional sports, 252–58
Progressive Animal Welfare Society, 151
Project Impact, 142
Property taxes, 136–37
Property titles, 140–41
Prost Tavern, 38
Proyecto Saber, 214
Public companies, 194–98
Public health clinics, 300
Public libraries, 17–18, 240–41
Public schools. *See* Seattle Public Schools
Puget Consumers' Co-op, 29, 63
Puget Sound, 309, 318–20
Puget Sound Business Journal, 194
Puget Sound Energy, 143, 197
Puyallup, 123–25
Puyallup Fair, 124

Q

Queen Anne
   attractions and institutions in, 62–64
   description of, 59–61
   facts about, 62
   map of, **xiv, 61**
   neighborhood service centers for, 2
Queen Mary Tearoom, 71
Qwest Field, 59, 256

R

Raccoons, 332
Radio stations, 247–48
Rainfall, 308–12
Rainier Beach
   attractions and institutions in, 67–68
   description of, 64–66
   facts about, 67
   map of, **xiv, 66**
Rainier Brewery, 162
Rainier Club, 195
Rainier Valley
   attractions and institutions in, 67–68
   description of, 64–66
   facts about, 67
   map of, **66**
Rats, 152
Rattlesnake Ledge, 263
Ravenna
   attractions and institutions in, 71–72
   description of, 68–70
   facts about, 70–71
   map of, **xiv, 69**
Ravenna Park, 70–71
Ray's Boathouse, 6, 23
Readings, 239
Real Change, 245
Real estate agents, 134–35
Real estate attorneys, 141
Real Networks, 199
Re-Bar, 228–29

Recruiters, 186–88
Recycling, 146–47
Red Mill Burgers, 38
Red Robin, 28
Redhook Brewery, 108–09
Redmond, **86**, 100–103, **110**
Redmond Town Center, 102
Regence Blue Shield, 294–95
REI, 199, 263–64, 273
Remlinger Farms, 106
Remo Borracchini's Bakery, 68
Renters, 149
Renting a home, 147–49
Renton, **86**, 125–26, 209–10
Renton Technical College, 219
Restaurants. *See also* neighborhood listings
   local favorites, 22–23
Résumés, 182–83, 187
Rhododendron Species Botanical Garden, 120
Riverbend Golf Complex, 122
Road conditions, 268
Road Maintenance Office, 146
Roanoke Inn Tavern, 100
Roberto's Pizza and Pasta, 100
Robinson Newspapers, 245
Rock music, 227–28
Rocket, The, 32
Rodents, 152
Roller skating, 274
Roosevelt, Theodore, 70
Rot, 140
Rotary clubs, 195
Rover's, 23
Rowing, 259, 271
Running, 265–66
Rush hour traffic, 153, 156
Ryan, Robin, 184

S

Safeco, 197
Safeco Field, 253
Sahalee Country Club, 104
Sail Sand Point, 42
Sailboarding, 266
Sailing, 266
Salish Lodge & Spa, 106
Salmon, 333
Salmon Bay, 214
Saltwater State Park, 273
Salty's, 85
Sammamish, **86**, 103–04
Sammamish Slough Trail, 260
Scalping tickets, 254
Scarecrow Video, 78
Schmitz Park, 324
School(s)
   alternative, 203, 212–15
   continuing education, 222
   private, 210–12
   public. *See* Seattle Public Schools
   selection of, 206–07
   vocational, 218–20
   See also Colleges; Universities
School districts, 207–10
Science Fiction Museum & Hall of Fame, 235
Scottish Highland Games, 117
S-curves, 163
Seafair, 238–39
Seahawks. *See* Seattle Seahawks
Seahurst Park, 115
Seasonal affective disorder, 313–14
Seastar, 23
SeaTac (town), 126-127

Sea-Tac Airport
  description of, 176–77
  parking at, 178–79
  tips for, 179–80
  transportation, 177–78
Seatlh, Chief, x, xiii
Seattle Academy, 211
Seattle Animal Shelter, 151
Seattle Aquarium, 237
Seattle Art Museum, 236
Seattle Arts & Lectures, 222, 239
Seattle Asian Art Museum, 14, 236–37
Seattle Athletic Club, 274
Seattle Baroque Orchestra, 225
Seattle Bike Club, 260–61
Seattle Boat Show, 266
Seattle Canoe & Kayak Club, 265
Seattle Center Monorail, 23–24
Seattle Central Community College, 11, 219
Seattle Children's Theatre, 233
Seattle City Council, 277–78
Seattle Community Network, 287
Seattle Emergency Management, 142
Seattle Foundation, The, 302
Seattle Gay Clinic, 293
Seattle Homes&Lifestyle, 246
Seattle International Film Festival, 244
Seattle Magazine, 246
Seattle Mariners, 171–72, 252–53
Seattle Men's Chorus, 225
Seattle Opera, 225–26
Seattle Pacific University, 216
Seattle Post-Intelligencer, 183, 244
Seattle Public Library, 17, 18, 240

Seattle Public Schools
  after-school programs, 203
  alternative schools, 203
  athletics at, 203
  community learning centers, 204
  crime at, 206
  day care, 204
  description of, 201–03
  districts, 207–10
  enrollment in, 204, 206
  facts about, 203
  immunizations, 204
  lunch programs, 204–05
  parental involvement in, 205
  school board, 205–06, 278
  security at, 206
  test scores in, 202
Seattle Rentals, 147
Seattle Rep, 233
Seattle Seahawks, 171–72, 255
Seattle Shakespeare Company, 233
Seattle Sounders, 257
Seattle Storm, 257
Seattle SuperSonics, 172, 257
Seattle Symphony Orchestra, 226
Seattle Tennis Club, 43
Seattle Thunderbirds, 258
Seattle Times, 183, 199, 244
Seattle Tixx, 234
Seattle to Portland Bicycle Classic, 261
Seattle University, 11, 216–17
Seattle Vocational Institute, 219
Seattle Weekly, 244–45
Seattle Yacht Club, 48, 50
Seattle–King County Association of Realtors, 136, 141
Seattle's Child, 221
Seattle-Tacoma International Airport. *See* Sea-Tac Airport

Second Ascent, 6
Self-employment, 188, 199–200
Serafina, 28
Services Group of America, 199
74th Street Alehouse, 38
Seward Park, 72–75, 273, 324
Sexual assault, 300
Sexually transmitted disease resources, 293
Shellfishing, 267
Shoreline Community College, 219–20
Showbox, 228
Shuttles, 178
Simpson Investment, 199
Singles, 249
Skate King, 274
Skating, 274
Skiing, 267–69
Smith Tower, 21, 23
Smoking, 293
Snelling Personnel Services, 188
Snohomish County, 167
Snoqualmie Falls, 106
Snoqualmie Pass, 268
Snoqualmie Valley, 104–07
Snoqualmie Valley Trail, 106–07
Snowboarding, 267–68
Snowstorms, 316
Soccer, 270
Social services, 299–300
SODO, 255–56
Softball, 258
Sonic Boom Records, 32
Sorrento Hotel, 13
Souk, The, 25
Sound Food, 132
South Hill Mall, 123
South Lake High School, 214
South Seattle Community College, 220

Southcenter Mall, 126
Spar Tavern, The, 130
Spectrum Dance Theater, 231
Speed limit, 161
Speed traps, 161
Sports
 college, 258–59
 high school, 203
 professional, 252–58
Spring, Ira, 95
Spud Fish and Chips, 38
St. Demetrios Greek Orthodox Church, 48
St. Edwards State Park, 98, 273
St. James Cathedral, 11
S&T Onsite, 188
Stanford, John, 205
Starbucks, 192, 197, 200
Start-up business, 188, 199–200
State government, 281–82
Statue of Liberty, 85
Stevens Pass, 269
Stewart Title, 141
Stone Gardens, 273
Stranger, The, 245
Streamliner Diner, 113
Streetcars, 168
Subscription farming, 330
Substance abuse, 295–97
Summer, 306, 312
Summit K-12, 214
Sunglasses, 310
Sunset Hill Community Club, 6
Sunset Hill Park, 6
Sunset Park, 3
Sunset Western Garden Book, 327
Supermall of the Great Northwest, 113
Supermarkets, 63
Swedish Medical Center, 290
Swimming, 270
Symphony, 226

T

Tacoma
   history of, 127–28
   map of, 110
   museums in, 237
   school district, 210
   University of Washington campus, 217
Tacoma Art Museum, 130
Tacoma Dome, 130
Tacoma Narrows Bridge, 164, 313
Tacoma Rainiers, 130, 257–58
Tall Grass Bakery, 6
Taproot Theatre, 234
Taxes, 285
Tax registration number, 200
Taxis, 175–76, 178
Teatro Zinzanni, 227
Television stations, 246–47
Temp agencies, 187–88
Temperature, 307, 310–11
Temporarily Yours, 188
Temporary jobs, 186–89
Tenants Union, 149
The Option Program at Seward, 214–15
Theater
   dance, 231
   film, 243–44
   movies, 243–44
   musical, 226–27
   performing arts, 233–34
Theno's Dairy, 102
Third Floor Fish Café, 98
Third Place Books, 242
Ticket(s)
   entertainment, 234
   parking, 172–73
   sports, 254
Ticket scalping, 254
Ticketmaster, 234
Ticket/Ticket, 226, 234

Ticketweb, 234
Today's Careers, 183
Tobacco Quit Line, 293
TOPS, 214–15
Totem Lake, 97
Town & Country Markets, 63
Town Hall, 239
Toxic materials, 147
Tractor Tavern, 228
Traffic, 153–61
   highway stretches to avoid, 157–58
   jargon, 161–62
   navigation, 158
   shortcuts, 159
Trails, 3, 39, 50–51, 106–07, 260, 263–64
Trains, 167–68
Transportation
   alternative methods of, 165–69
   bicycling, 168–69
   buses, 165–67, 177–78
   ferries, 173–75
   to stadiums, 255
   limousines, 175, 178
   options for, 156–57
   Sea-Tac, 177–78
   streetcars, 168
   taxis, 175–76, 178
   trains, 167–68
   vehicle registration and licensing, 163–65
   walking, 169–70
Trees
   city arborist, 146
   growing, 325
   old-growth forests, 323
   Ravenna's toppled giants, 70
Trek Tri-Island, 261
Triple Door, 231
Troll, The, 33
Tula's, 231
Tully's, 199

Tutta Bella Neapolitan Pizzeria, 75
Twice Sold Tales, 242

U

Unemployment, 181, 188–90
Unified Business Identifier, 200
United Way, 302
Universities
 Antioch University Seattle, 215
 Argosy University Seattle, 215
 Bastyr University, 215
 Pacific Lutheran University, 130–31
 Seattle Pacific University, 216
 Seattle University, 11, 216–17
 University of Puget Sound, 131, 217
 University of Washington. *See* University of Washington
 Washington State University, 218
 Western Washington University, 218
 See also Colleges
University Bookstore, 242
University District
 attractions and institutions in, 78
 facts about, 77
 history of, 75–77
 map of, **xiv, 76**
 neighborhood service centers for, 2
University of Washington
 description of, 78, 217, 241
 library at, 241
 Physicians and Medical Center at, 290
 sports at, 258–59
University Prep, 212
University Village, 72, 79
U-pick farms, 239
Uptown-Queen Anne, 60
Urban Surf, 266
UW World Dance Series, 231
Uwajimaya Village, 59

V

Valley Medical Center, 290
Vashon Island, 131–32
Vehicle(s). *See* Car(s)
Velocity Dance Center, 231
Victor's Celtic Coffee Co, 102
Viewland-Hoffman Electrical Substation, 38
Village Theater, 234
Virginia Mason Medical Center, 290
Vocational schools, 218–20
Volt Services Group, 188
Volunteer Park, 13–14, 273
Vulcan, 199

W

Wade's Eastside Guns & Indoor Range, 91
Waiting for the Interurban, 33
Walking, 169–70
Wallingford, **xiv,** 79–82
Wallingford Center, 80, 82
Wappler, Andy 314
Wappler, Harry, 314
Washington, Tom, 184
Washington Alliance of Technology Workers, 189

Washington Assessment of Student Learning, 201–02
Washington Athletic Club, 274
Washington Center for the Book, 241
Washington CEO, 246
Washington Mutual, 197
Washington Park Arboretum, 43, 45, 50–51, 273
Washington Ski Touring Club, 269
Washington State Cougars, 259
Washington State Department of Health, 288
Washington State History Museum, 129
Washington State Hospitals Association, 289
Washington State University, 218, 259
Washington Trails Association, 264
Waterfront Activities Center, 51
Waterfront Trail, 50–51
Weather, 305–16
West Seattle
  attractions and institutions in, 84–85
  description of, 82–83
  facts about, 83
  map of, xiv, **84**
  neighborhood service centers for, 2
West Seattle Golf Course, 85
Western Washington Fair, 124
Western Washington University, 218
Westfarm Foods, 199
Westlake Park, 17
Westlake Park & Center, 23–24
Weyerhaeuser, 120, 128, 192, 198
Weyerhaeuser King County Aquatic Center, 120
Whales, 330–31
White River Amphitheater, 228
Wild Ginger, 23
Wild Waves State Park, 120
Wildlife, 330–32
Willows Lodge, 108–09
Willows Run, 102–03
Windermere Place, 39
Windermere Real Estate, 42, 135, 194
Wing Luke Asian Museum, 59
Winter, 313–15
Wonderland Trail, 263
Wooden Boat Festival, 239
Woodinville, 107–09
Woodland Park, 34
Woodland Park Zoo, 38–39, 228, 238, 272
Worker's compensation, 191
Working Connections Childcare, 221
Worksource Washington, 183
World Spice Market, 25
World Wide Books & Maps, 242

X

XXX Drive-In, 95

Z

Zoning, 144–45, 283
Zoo(s), 38–39, 94, 130, 228, 237, 238, 272
Zoo Tavern, The, 28

ABOUT THE AUTHOR

Long-time writer and editor Eric Lucas moved to Seattle in August 1986—on the first day of the longest drought the city has ever experienced. After learning that it does occasionally rain in Seattle, he has gone on to write about Puget Sound and the Northwest for numerous publications. He is a widely published freelance writer, and has authored and co-authored several guidebooks to the Pacific Northwest and British Columbia. Over the last 20 years, Lucas has lived in Kirkland, Federal Way, Tacoma, Vashon Island, and Ballard, and has worked in Seattle, Kent, and Everett. He lives in the Sunset Hill neighborhood with two Washington natives: his wife Leslie and stepdaughter Kirsten.